# Essays in New Testament Interpretation

### C. F. D. MOULE
*Emeritus Lady Margaret's Professor of*
*Divinity in the University of Cambridge*

CAMBRIDGE UNIVERSITY PRESS

Cambridge

London   New York   New Rochelle

Melbourne   Sydney

Published by the Press Syndicate of the University of Cambridge
The Pitt Building, Trumpington Street, Cambridge CB2 1RP
32 East 57th Street, New York, NY 10022, USA
296 Beaconsfield Parade, Middle Park, Melbourne 3206, Australia

First published 1982

Printed in Great Britain at the University Press, Cambridge

Library of Congress catalogue card number: 81-10144

*British Library Cataloguing in Publication Data*
Moule, C. F. D.
Essays in New Testament interpretation.
1. Bible. N.T. – Hermeneutics –
Addresses, essays, lectures
I. Title
225.6   BS2331
ISBN 0 521 23783 1

# Contents

# Contents

# Foreword

The suggestion that a selection of my published essays be collected into a single volume came from a friend, who must remain anonymous, for he must not be implicated in their imperfections; but I offer him my thanks for his encouraging estimate of them. It was on his initiative that the Cambridge University Press, to whom also I owe thanks, approached me with the proposal – a proposal too flattering to be easily resisted. The choice of papers for the collection is largely that of the same friend. A writer is in a bad position to judge of the respective merits of his own pieces so I have accepted his guidance. At the Press, I owe special thanks to my friend Dr R. L. Williams for devoting much precious time to checking references and supervising the preparation of materials for printing, and to Mrs A. W. Field, to whom fell the exacting task of bringing some sort of consistency into articles printed in a wide diversity of styles.

Especially in New Testament scholarship work moves fast and fashions change still faster. Is it desirable to reprint studies related to the debates of former years? Ought they not at least to be revised and redirected? That is a fair question. Indeed, I have recently been struggling to revise and rewrite an old book with just such an end in view; and, in the present collection, I have added a few notes at several points and modified a paragraph in one essay where a friend convinces me that the evidence at that point would not bear the weight I was laying on it, although I believe that the thesis as a whole still stands without it.

But although if I were writing the essays today I should of course have to take issue with much work that has appeared since they were written, I venture to think that, in the main, their arguments still hold. And although I have admitted to being flattered by the Press's proposal, there are, I hope, more worthy reasons to justify their republication.

Some of the essays concern principles that are basic to New Testament research. Some touch on matters of interpretation that are perennially important. Above all, I dare to hope that among them will be found examples, on however small a scale, of the kind of exegesis that J. D. Smart desiderates in his book *The Past, Present and Future of Biblical Theology* (Philadelphia, 1979). Analysing the causes of the widespread failure of biblical scholarship to speak effectively to contemporary needs, he finds at the heart of them an evasion of the problem 'caused by the presence in Scripture of historical phenomena which are comprehensible and meaningful only on the basis of an interacting of God and man in history' (pp. 93 ff.). The longer I study Christian origins the more I am convinced that what may be called the ordinary, rational, 'secular' study of the documents is the right starting point. They ought to be analysed critically like any other works of antiquity. But, if so, the student is quickly led to a point - namely, the genesis of the conviction that Jesus had gone through death to eternal life - at which he is nonplussed as an ordinary, rational, 'secular' student of history. Within the terms of his discipline he is unable to give a convincing account of this juncture. It is true that many historians refuse to admit this. But I can only say that their rationalizing does seem to me to fail to offer a convincing account. Here is a historical phenomenon - the coming of the disciples of Jesus to this strange belief - which, in Smart's phrase, is 'comprehensible and meaningful' only on the assumption that there is more in this event than the ordinary canons of historical research can embrace - the assumption, in this case, that the aliveness of Jesus corresponded to reality and was a divine revelation.

If the assumption is sound, then there will begin to be some two-way traffic. On returning within the limits of his discipline, the historian will find that, in the last analysis, no part of history is satisfactorily described except as an interacting of God and man. All history turns out to be, in a measure, woven of a lateral warp and a vertical weft, and to be incomplete until the 'vertical' dimension is recognized. This means - and this is part of J. D. Smart's thesis - that no biblical exegesis is satisfactory which does not link theological meaning with the purely historical findings. Human events turn out to be adequately describable only in terms of the biblical conviction that the living God reveals himself to men. It is the task of the interpreter of Scripture to hold the two together. Some of the following essays are only peripheral to this central task. But that the task is central is the conviction within which all of them were written, and some of them directly exemplify the linking of the purely historical with the theological.

## Foreword

In any case, I do not wish to withdraw the main contention of any of them. I believe that a study of 'fulfilment words' (essay 1) is a clue to far-reaching conclusions about the relation of the New to the Old Testament - indeed about the Person of Christ. I am more than ever convinced (essays 12 and 13) that the themes of St Paul's epistles are largely conditioned by the particular battle he is fighting in each of them, and that it is a mistake to imagine that, for example, Galatians must have been written at more or less the same period as Romans merely because their themes are similar. I still believe that the proposals in essay 5 about the character of St Matthew's Gospel are plausible, and (essay 7) that the Johannine eschatology is in part to be explained by the individualism of the Gospel.

In spite of influential books by F. M. Young and R. J. Daly,[1] I am still prepared (essay 21) to argue that, in the Christian dispensation, sacrifice is replaced by sacrament, and that there is no essential element in the Christian Gospel that necessitates the language of sacrifice in the strict, cultic sense. Of course sacrifice is a metaphor used in the New Testament and hallowed by long usage in the Christian Church, and of course it is one way of expressing the cost which is at the heart of atonement. But I still ask whether there is any distinctive and essential part of the Christian good news of salvation that cannot be expressed without this strictly cultic term. Similarly (essays 16 and 17) I find myself still calling in question the idea of retribution in any fully Christian account of reconciliation.

I remain convinced (essays 2 and 3) that there is no evidence that St Paul was not interested in the deeds and words of the historical Jesus. This widespread assumption can hardly be challenged too often, and Christological judgements of great importance are involved. I still believe (essay 6) that that tell-tale definite article in '*the* Son of Man' has not been given its proper weight in hundreds of pages published on the phrase, and that attempts to refute my arguments have missed the point.

I have yet to see any evidence that in II Cor. v. 3 (essay 14), εἴ γε καί, as contrasted with simple εἴ γε, can mean 'assuming that' (in a tone of affirmation) rather than 'if indeed' (an expression of doubt). Oddly enough, in the theological interpretation of that entire context, much depends on this and on the enigmatic κατεργασάμενος of verse 5 in the same passage.

1 F. M. Young, *Sacrifice and the Death of Christ* (London, 1975). R. J. Daly, *The Origins of the Christian Doctrine of Sacrifice* (London, 1978).

These and other matters, all of which, however small in themselves, concern decisions of real importance in Christology, soteriology, or ethics, I am glad to be allowed to present again, more accessibly, perhaps, than before. Whatever the inadequacies of the essays, the questions behind them are as urgent as ever, and if there are readers who will actively respond, whether with refutation or with support, then progress will be made.

*July 1980*                                         C. F. D. Moule

# Acknowledgements

The author and publisher are grateful to the following for permission to reproduce essays first published by them.

The Oxford University Press for 'The Use of Parables and Sayings as Illustrative Material in Early Christian Catechesis', *The Journal of Theological Studies* n.s. 3 (1952), 75ff.; 'The Influence of Circumstances on the Use of Christological Terms', *The Journal of Theological Studies* n.s. 10 (1959), 247ff.; 'The Influence of Circumstances on the Use of Eschatological Terms', *The Journal of Theological Studies* n.s. 15 (1964), 1ff.; '"... As we forgive ...": a Note on the Distinction between Deserts and Capacity in the Understanding of Forgiveness', E. Bammel, C. K. Barrett, W. D. Davies, edd., *Donum Gentilicium*, Festschrift for D. Daube (Oxford: Clarendon Press, 1978), pp. 68ff. © Oxford University Press 1952, 1959, 1964, 1978.

The John Rylands Library for 'The Problem of the Pastoral Epistles: A Reappraisal', *The Bulletin of the John Rylands Library* 47 (1965), 430ff. © The John Rylands Library 1965.

T. and T. Clark (Publishers), Edinburgh for 'The Ascension – Acts 1:9', *The Expository Times* 68 (1956/7), 205ff. © T. & T. Clark (Publishers) 1956.

Theologischer Verlag Rolf Brockhaus, Wuppertal for 'Jesus in New Testament Kerygma', O. Bocher und K. Haacker Hrsgg., *Verborum Veritas*, Festschrift for G. Stählin (Wuppertal: Brockhaus 1970), pp. 15ff. © Theologischer Verlag Rolf Brockhaus 1970.

Akademie-Verlag GmbH, Berlin for 'St Matthew: Some Neglected Features', *Studia Evangelica II = Texte und Untersuchungen* 87 (1964), 91ff. © Akademie-Verlag GmbH 1964.

Verlag Herder KG, Freiburg im Breisgau for 'Neglected Features in the Problem of "The Son of Man"', J. Gnilka Hrsg., *Neues Testament und Kirche*, Festschrift for R. Schnackenburg (Freiburg/Basel/Wien: Herder 1974), pp. 413ff. © Verlag Herder KG 1974.

## Acknowledgements

Theologischer Verlag, Zürich for '2 Corinthians 3:18b, καθάπερ ἀπὸ κυρίου πνεύματος', H. Baltensweiler und B. Reicke Hrsgg., *Neues Testament und Geschichte*, Festschrift for O. Cullmann (Zürich: Theologischer Verlag/Tübingen: Mohr 1972), pp. 231ff. © Theologischer Verlag 1972.

Editions J. Duculot SA for 'Death "to Sin", "to Law", and "to the World": A Note on Certain Datives', A. Descamps et A. de Halleux dir., *Mélanges Bibliques*, Festschrift B. Rigaux (Gembloux: Duculot 1970), pp. 367ff. © Editions J. Duculot SA 1970.

E. J. Brill, Leiden for 'Peculiarities in the Language of 2 Corinthians', D. A. Brownell, W. C. Weinrich, J. Brownell edd., Festschrift for B. Reicke (Leiden: Brill forthcoming) and 'The Individualism of the Fourth Gospel', *Novum Testamentum* 5 (1962), 171ff. © E. J. Brill 1962.

C. W. K. Gleerup, Lund & Munksgaard for 'Punishment and Retribution: An Attempt to Delimit their Scope in New Testament Thought', *Svensk Exegetisk Årsbok* 30 (1965), 21ff. © C. W. K. Gleerup, Lund & Munksgaard 1965.

'The Theology of Forgiveness' first appeared in N. Autton ed., *From Fear to Faith* (London: SPCK, 1971), pp. 61ff; and 'The Sacrifice of the People of God' in D. M. Paton ed., *The Parish Communion Today* (London: SPCK, 1962), pp. 78ff. © C. F. D. Moule 1971, 1962. 'Fulfilment Words in the New Testament: Use and Abuse' first appeared in *New Testament Studies* 14 (1967/8), 293ff.; 'The Nature and Purpose of I Peter' in *New Testament Studies* 3 (1956), 1ff.; 'St Paul and "Dualism": The Pauline Conception of Resurrection' in *New Testament Studies* 12 (1965/6), 106ff.; 'A Reconsideration of the Context of Maranatha' in *New Testament Studies* 6 (1959), 307ff.; and 'Obligation in the Ethic of Paul' in W. R. Farmer, C. F. D. Moule, R. R. Niebuhr edd., *Christian History and Interpretation*, Festschrift for John Knox (Cambridge: University Press, 1967), pp. 389ff. © Cambridge University Press 1967, 1956, 1965, 1959, 1967.

# Abbreviations

| | |
|---|---|
| *Acta Sem. Neot. Upsal.* | *Acta seminarii neotestamentici Upsaliensis* |
| *Amer. J. Arch.* | *American Journal of Archaeology* |
| *Bibl. Theol. Lovan.* | *Bibliotheca Ephemeridum Theologicarum Lovaniensium* |
| *B.J.R.L.* | *Bulletin of the John Rylands Library* |
| *C.B.Q.* | *The Catholic Biblical Quarterly* |
| *C.I.G.* | *Corpus inscriptionum graecarum* |
| *Class. Philol.* | *Classical Philology* |
| E.T. | English translation |
| *Exp. T.* | *The Expository Times* |
| *F.R.L.A.N.T.* | *Forschungen zur Religion und Literatur des Alten und Neuen Testaments* |
| *H.T.R.* | *The Harvard Theological Review* |
| *I.C.C.* | *International Critical Commentary* |
| *J.B.L.* | *Journal of Biblical Literature* |
| *J.J.S.* | *Journal of Jewish Studies* |
| *J.T.S.* | *Journal of Theological Studies* |
| L. and S. | Liddell and Scott, *Greek–English Lexicon* |
| M.T. | Masoretic text |
| *Nov. Test.* | *Novum Testamentum* |
| *N.T.D.* | *Das Neue Testament Deutsch* |
| *N.T.S.* | *New Testament Studies* |
| *P.G.* | *Patrologiae cursus completus, series graeca*, edited by J. P. Migne |
| *R.B.* | *Revue biblique* |
| *R.H.P.R.* | *Revue d'Histoire et de Philosophie religieuses* |
| *S.-B.* | *Kommentar zum Neuen Testament aus* |

| | |
|---|---|
| | *Talmud und Midrasch*, edited by H. L. Strack and P. Billerbeck (5 volumes) |
| *S.J.T.* | *Scottish Journal of Theology* |
| *S.N.T.S.* | *Studiorum Novi Testamenti Societas* |
| *Th.Bl.* | *Theologische Blätter* |
| *T.L.Z.* | *Theologische Literatur-Zeitung* |
| *T.U.* | *Texte und Untersuchungen zur Geschichte der altchristlichen Literatur* |
| *T.W.N.T.* | *Theologisches Wörterbuch zum Neuen Testament*, edited by G. Kittel and G. Friedrich |
| *V.C.* | *Vigiliae Christianae* |
| *Vetus Test.* | *Vetus Testamentum* |
| *W.M.A.N.T.* | *Wissenschaftliche Monographien zum Alten und Neuen Testament* |
| *Z.K.G.* | *Zeitschrift für Kirchengeschichte* |
| *Z.N.T.W.* | *Zeitschrift für die neutestamentliche Wissenschaft* |
| *Z.T.K.* | *Zeitschrift für Theologie und Kirche* |

Jesus in Early Christian Interpretation

# 1

## Fulfilment-words in the New Testament: Use and Abuse*

'Promise and fulfilment', 'Verheissung und Erfüllung', is a familiar phrase in New Testament theology. It has furnished the title for at least one notable book,[1] and occupies considerable sections of other works in the New Testament field. It is a well-known fact, too, that, in some senses at least, it belongs also to the Old Testament scene. It is possible, as an article by W. Zimmerli illustrates,[2] to tell the Old Testament story under the same title.

But its very merits as an epitome of biblical eschatology have made it such a cliché that it is easy to accept it as a matter of course, without examining either its distinctiveness or its exact incidence. The purpose of this paper, accordingly, is to bring the implications of the correlatives, promise and fulfilment, into sharper focus, to ask what, more precisely, it is that gives them their special appropriateness in the area of the New Testament, and to initiate (it cannot attempt to do more) an inquiry into their incidence in ancient literature generally.

Among the causes of imprecision in the use of the phrase is the fact that both words, 'promise' and 'fulfilment', and the equivalents in Hebrew and Greek of at least fulfilment (מלא and πληροῦν), are often used inexactly - not least by the biblical writers themselves - where precision would require some defining phrase, or even where some different word would be more appropriate. Thus, it is possible at once, without

---

* Presidential Address to *S.N.T.S.* delivered at the General Meeting in Gwat, Switzerland, 28 August 1967.
1 By W. G. Kümmel (Zürich,[3] 1956; E.T., London, 1957), though here it is used in a different and special sense, of the anticipatory fulfilment, in Jesus, of the final, eschatological promise.
2 Originally published in *Evangelische Theologie* 12, 1/2 (1952), 6 ff.; reprinted in *Probleme alttestamentlicher Hermeneutik*, ed. C. Westermann (München, 1960), E.T. *Essays on Old Testament Interpretation* (London, 1963), pp. 89 ff. A *Festschrift* for S. H. Hooke bears the same title, *Promise and Fulfilment*, ed. F. F. Bruce (Edinburgh, 1963).

3

going into more elaborate detail, to name at least three sets of correlatives which, carefully defined, are distinguishable, but which could all be included, and sometimes are, both in the Bible and outside it, under the single umbrella of a loosely-defined 'promise and fulfilment'. The sets of correlatives which I have in mind are these. First, there is simply a prediction over against verification. Today this stands, for a thoughtful person, at the bottom of the scale of religious values, though the ancient world thought otherwise.[3] Secondly, one may group together words such as beginning or project, undertaking or obligation, promise (but not with the content I shall define in a moment) or threat, and set these over against words denoting termination, completion or achievement, discharge, confirmation or realization. That is a second set of correlatives. And only then, thirdly, comes what I suggest should be called covenant-promise over against fulfilment proper or consummation in its strictest sense. It is for the apodosis in that final pair of correlatives that I suggest we would do well, when we are aiming at a measure of precision in our use of the phrase in New Testament theology, to reserve the term fulfilment, Erfüllung, מלא, πληροῦν, because only in such a context does its content of finality and insurpassability come into its own. The protasis in this pair as I am defining it is no mere prediction, nor a mere beginning, nor even a promise or threat in general, but God's covenant-promise in particular; and by this is meant not any single, limited promise, but all the promise and hope attaching to all that is epitomized in the Bible by God's covenant with his people. It means his plan for achieving a truly personal relationship between himself and his people – all that we associate with his kingship and his fatherhood – and his design for accomplishing it. As soon as 'promise' is filled out with such a content, it is clear that its correlative cannot be mere verification – no mere 'coming to pass' or 'coming true' is sufficient; nor yet the mere completion or termination of a project; nor even the mere discharge of some obligation as such. All these may contribute to the realization of a relationship, but are not as comprehensive as the fully achieved relationship itself. The proper correlative to covenant-promise is the perfecting and realization of the entire relationship which is its goal; and there is a special appropriateness in the application of the terms מלא, πληροῦν, which properly denote filling to capacity, to any symbol of such a relationship. It is worthy of note, at

3 'Weissagung und Erfüllung', as the title of a well-known article by Bultmann (*Z.T.K.* 47 (1950), 360 ff.), was chosen with a special purpose. In the English version in *Essays on Old Testament Interpretation* (as n. 2 p. 3), it appears as 'Prophecy and Fulfilment'.

this point, that just as the neutral and undefined 'promise' in my second pair of correlatives has been augmented to 'covenant-promise' in the third, so an alternative protasis in the second, namely, 'obligation', can be filled out into 'covenant-obligation' and thus find a place in the protasis of the third set.

And to speak of 'fulfilling' Torah (covenant-obligation) is, thus, a parallel way of expressing the total realization of a right relationship, comparable to the phrase 'to fulfil covenant-promise': the moral and volitional is obviously a very important factor in relationship. The combination under the single, comprehensive apodosis, 'fulfilment', of a protasis consisting of both 'covenant-promise' and 'covenant-law' is characteristic of *Heilsgeschichte* precisely because it is characteristic of incarnation.[4]

In thus attempting some preliminary clarification of the meaning of 'promise and fulfilment' as the phrase is commonly used by biblical theologians, I realize, of course, that I have done what the Bible does not do explicitly, and that I have had recourse to some non-biblical terms such as 'personal relationship'. But it is not only usual but legitimate to use such convenient epitomes of what the Bible – more concretely but also more diffusely – does present. For that matter, the actual combination, 'promise and fulfilment', as we shall remind ourselves shortly, is extremely rare in the Bible.

So much, then, for the setting of the stage. What I offer by way of reflexion on the subject will fall into three sections. First, an attempt to locate that in the faith of the New Testament which gives unique and distinctive appropriateness to the use of promise and fulfilment to describe the 'Christ-event' in its relation to the entire design of God. Secondly, some consideration of correlatives in which מלא/πληροῦν is not used, and some indication of their incidence in ancient literature. And thirdly, a closer examination of the incidence and use of מלא and πληροῦν, with some reflexions on the phenomena.

I

The article I have just referred to, by W. Zimmerli, expressly calls attention to ways in which the New Testament transcends the Old in respect

---

4 It is noteworthy, if not immediately relevant, that Isa. xl. 3 is used in 1QS viii. 13–16 as an injunction or authorization, whereas in the Gospels it is treated as a prediction. (But see a rather different formulation by J. A. Fitzmyer, 'The Use of Explicit Old Testament Quotations in Qumran Literature and in the New Testament', *N.T.S.* 7 (1961), 297 ff. (318), F. F. Bruce, *Biblical Exegesis in the Qumran Texts* (Grand Rapids, Michigan, 1959; London, 1960), p. 28.)

of fulfilment. Similarly (if I may make a passing allusion to one other recent example of the same insight) R. N. Longenecker couches his estimate of the newness of Paul's Christian experience in contrast to his former Judaism in terms of promise and fulfilment.[5] Talking of the dual message of judgement and mercy, death and life, in the Old Testament,[6] Zimmerli observes: '*The* Yahweh-event, which would unite the elements of death and life proclaimed by the prophet in a conclusive fulfilment, has not yet [i.e. in the Old Testament] come to pass' (E.T. p. 105). And again, commenting (p. 112) on the הַכֹּל בָּא of Joshua xxi. 45, he says that, although here the movement from promise to fulfilment might appear to have reached its goal and come to a standstill, it transpires that, in fact, there is more – much more – yet to come. And when Zimmerli comes to the New Testament (p. 113) he says that its message of fulfilment stands over against the situation in the Old Testament. 'In Jesus Christ the Apostles attest the Word of God which has become wholly event, and the event that is the Word of God, wholly and completely.' This formulation, you will observe, while connecting the New Testament closely with the Old, acknowledges a difference in the New Testament, and describes that difference in terms of wholeness and completeness. This is the Christian claim that has now to be in some measure spelt out; and, for a start, a foil is provided by the much more jejune conception of mere prediction and verification (the first and, to us, the least religiously important of my pairs of correlatives).

It serves the better as a foil precisely because, in the ancient world, it was highly valued. I suppose it would be true to say that most, if not all, ancient religions regarded prediction and verification as of high importance. To them it meant that God was wise and was in control of things. He was as good as his word: 'Hath he said, and shall he not do it?' Things happen as God has devised them, not by chance nor according to any other pattern than the one he lays down. A god who can see the end from the beginning is obviously a competent god and a living god, unlike the dumb idols (cf. Deutero-Isaiah, e.g. Isa. xli. 21 ff., and Wisd. vii. 18). And his true prophet enjoys a correspondingly high esteem. One of the deuteronomic tests of a true prophet is the verification of his predictions (Deut. xviii. 22). Of Samuel it was said (I Sam. ix. 6): '. . . he is a man that is held in honour; all that he says comes true.' Daniel enjoys high prestige as one who knows 'a God in heaven

5 *Paul, Apostle of Liberty* (New York, etc., 1964); see p. 84.
6 Cf. C. H. Dodd, *According to the Scriptures* (London, 1952), pp. 108 ff.

who reveals mysteries' (Dan. ii. 28 f.).[7] And then, again, for the ancient world, the central figure concerned with the verification was also marked out as in some way important, even if not necessarily good or heroic. If Oedipus is unconsciously instrumental in verifying a terrible prediction, he may be the most miserable - even the most execrable - of men on earth, but he is significant, he is a figure of importance. If Judas is the one who was to lift up his heel against his familiar friend, he is marked as the archetypal traitor - but, as such, he is a figure of sinister importance in the working out of the divine will.[8] But more often the central figure of a prediction which has come to pass is good as well as important.

A convenient illustration of many of the features of the ancient attitude to prediction-verification is afforded by the nightmare story in I Kings xiii, with its sequel in II Kings xxiii. 15-18, about the prophet from Judah who predicted the destruction of Jeroboam's altar at Bethel by Josiah. The prophet inveighs against the altar and predicts its fate circumstantially, including the actual name of Josiah (*v.* 2); according to the text as it now stands, he also gives interim, authenticating signs[9] - the altar is, there and then, miraculously split and the ashes poured out (*vv.* 3 and 5 - though this may well originally have been a reference to the subsequent events under Josiah), and Jeroboam's hand, stretched out against the prophet, is paralysed. The prophet's prediction comes true in Josiah's reform, as explicitly recorded in II Kings xxiii. 15-18. But meanwhile, in I Kings xiii itself, there is a further example of prediction and verification, when another prophet, living at Bethel, sends a lying message to recall the Judaean prophet who is returning home in obedience to Yahweh's instructions; and then, having recalled him by telling an arrant lie, he predicts that, because of the disobedience into which he has himself enticed him, his body will not come to the tomb of his fathers. And, sure enough, on his return journey the Judaean prophet is killed by a lion - a discriminating animal, who demonstrates his own obedience to the very letter of his commission by sparing the poor prophet's donkey. *Cadavera* (it must have said to itself) *non sunt multiplicanda praeter necessitatem.* The wicked old liar of a prophet then makes what reparation he can by giving the Judaean prophet

---

7 Cf. Isa. xliv. 26a: 'who confirms the word of his servant, and performs the counsel of his messengers.'
8 Cf. Gen. l. 20; Acts iii. 17 f.; xiii. 27; and Justin, *Dial.* xcvi. 1.
9 Cf. I Sam. ii. 34 (Hophni and Phinehas); x. 1 ff. (signs for Saul); II Kings xx. 8 ff. (sign for Hezekiah).

honourable burial, and asking to be buried, when he dies, in the same grave, and confirming that his prediction against the Bethel altar will come true. So, here is prediction in detail by men who know because God has told them; and the hero or victim of the prediction, as the case may be, is given prominence as an important person.

If one once accepts this view, that the competence and truthfulness of God himself is exhibited in foreseeing the future – or, to put it otherwise, in the ability to carry through his predetermined plan – then prediction-verification does acquire a religious importance, even if only derivatively and in the context of this outlook. It is taken as confirmation that things do not happen by chance: there is a God who is in charge;[10] and that there are important people who are let into God's counsels; and that there are others, again, who, whether they like it or not, have to play leading roles in God's drama. And, on this showing, it is not only not necessary that predictions should have any intrinsic ethical importance: it is a positive advantage when they concern such arbitrary and peripheral details that their realization presents evidence which is the more convincing in proportion as it is the less likely to be coincidental. Best and most cunning of all is when God sets a sort of conundrum or crossword puzzle – a רז, which has to be subtly decoded by someone with the gift of פשר.[11] For the early Christians with this outlook, the climax of all previous demonstrations of God's control was reached when it could be proved that Jesus was Messiah by his performance of some obscure detail deemed to be a prediction about the Messiah.[12] This is the mentality behind most of the Matthaean 'formula-quotations' (*Reflexionszitate*);[13] and it comes to a riot of proliferation

10 So G. Delling, *s.v.* πληρόω, *T.W.N.T.* vi, 295, 5 f. Cf. 'The prophecies prove that the historical events happened according to the will of God', N. A. Dahl, 'The Story of Abraham in Luke-Acts', *Studies in Luke-Acts* (Festschrift for Paul Schubert, edd. Leander E. Keck and J. Louis Martyn, Nashville and New York, 1966), pp. 139 ff. (p. 153).

11 So Rom. xvi. 25 f. Cf. Bruce, *Biblical Exegesis*, p. 8. 1QpHab vii. 5 speaks of כּוֹל רָזֵי דִּבְרֵי עֲבָדָיו הַנְּבִאִים (E. Lohse, *Die Texte aus Qumran* (München, 1964), p. 234); and ii. 8 seems to refer to the gift of פשר as given to a Priest (who is the Right Teacher). I wish I had lived in the age of פשר. I would have shown how II Kings vi. 5 f. is an account of St Paul's conversion in code: the lost axe-head was שאול; what rescued it was עץ!

12 Acts xvii. 3, xviii. 28 are references to this occupation in the course of the early Church's evangelism. See Paul S. Minear, 'Luke's Use of the Birth-Stories', in Keck and Martyn, *Luke-Acts*, pp. 118 ff.; and Dahl, 'Story of Abraham', p. 152.

13 Cf. R. Hummel, *Die Auseinandersetzung zwischen Kirche und Judentum im Mattäusevangelium* (München, 1963), p. 130 and n. 12 (following Goppelt). A. Suhl, *Die Funktion der alttestamentlichen Zitate und Anspiel-*

in Justin's *Dialogue*. It is a conspicuous motif also in Jewish–Christian apocalyptic.

Now, if this mere prediction-fulfilment leaves the modern religious consciousness stone cold, that is largely because, in spite of the high value set upon it by the biblical writers (not least the writer of St Matthew's Gospel, who uses πληροῦν to describe it, in the way I am inviting you to avoid), they bear witness, despite themselves, to a principle which, for religion, has proved to be incomparably more important.

These writers do not themselves say so; they do not seem consciously to rank this principle above prediction-verification; and yet, if we, in our day, have learnt to despise mere prediction-verification as a phenomenon which (even if and when established) is religiously neutral, it is from these very writers, and the experience they mediate, that we have learnt our lesson. That incomparably more important principle to which, only half-consciously, they bear witness exercises a decisive influence on the whole shape of their gospel, and, as I shall suggest, may even have left traces of itself in the frequency of their use or abuse of πληροῦν. The principle to which I refer is, in essence, what is summed up in the term *Heilsgeschichte*. I know that this is a controverted term; but, in the present context, I take it as a symbol for the recognition that God's personal relations with man assume, for those who are sensitive to personal values,[14] a recognizable pattern. Those who are sensitive can recognize God's pattern of relationship as it shapes itself out of the different materials of successive generations, particularly in God's covenant-relation with Israel, and they can see that the pattern has a purpose and is developing 'teleologically' towards a goal.

And so, if Christians found in the pattern shown in the story of Jesus of Nazareth a unique finality or 'fulness', this was not really because a uniquely large number of predictions seemed to be verified in it, but because they found uniquely reflected in Jesus a perfect filial

*ungen im Markusevangelium* (Gütersloh, 1965), denies this mentality to Mark. But see the critical review by E. Grässer, *T.L.Z.* 91 (1966), 668[a, b], 669[a]. See, further, a brief discussion of this matter by Ellen Flessemann-van Leer, 'Die Interpretation der Passionsgeschichte von Alten Testament aus' in *Zur Bedeutung des Todes Jesu: exegetische Beiträge*, H. Conzelmann, E. Flessemann-van Leer, E. Haenchen, E. Käsemann, E. Lohse (Gütersloh, 1967), pp. 79 ff.

14 I use this qualifying phrase advisedly. We are not to assume that Old Testament history, without some such interpreting agency, of itself presents a clear pattern. There have, for instance, been warnings enough in the past against the assumption that there is a clearly defined 'doctrine of the remnant' in the Old Testament. See, e.g. E. W. Heaton 'The Root שאר and the Doctrine of the Remnant', *J.T.S.* n.s. 3 (1952), 27 ff.

relationship with God.[15] They had come to estimate Jesus, in his ministry, his crucifixion, and his resurrection to life, as the climax, the coping-stone, of an entire edifice of relationship. He was the inaugurator of a new and decisive covenant. The word τελειωτής, applied to Jesus in Heb. xii. 2, is found only in Christian literature,[16] and it epitomizes this estimate - an estimate of Jesus as the climax of an eschatological and teleological process. Even more important, among single words in this connexion, is τύπος, which L. Goppelt has examined so exhaustively.[17] There is a distinctively Christian conception of typology which bears witness to the recognition of covenant-promise and fulfilment in its stricter sense. Harnack credited Paul with being the originator of typological exegesis.[18] and, although this judgement has been modified by E. E. Ellis,[19] there is, at any rate in the New Testament as a whole, a distinctive attitude to what may be called the pattern of God's dealings.[20]

Now, out of a large number of symptoms which give evidence of this estimate of Jesus as the climax and fulfilment, not of mere prediction, but of a pattern of personal relationship, I choose for the present occasion what is perhaps the most impressive and the most inclusive. I mean the fact that upon the single figure of Jesus there have converged, in Christian thought, an unprecedented and unsurpassed number of dif-

15 So G. Delling, *s.v.* πληρόω in *T.W.N.T.* vi, 295, 15: 'Der nt.liche Gedanke der Erfüllung ist zusammengefasst in der Person Jesu'; and L. Goppelt, *s.v.* τύπος in *T.W.N.T.* viii, 251, 24 f.: 'Dabei ist die Entsprechung nicht nur in äusseren Ähnlichkeiten der Vorgäange, sondern vor allem in der Wesensgleichheit von Gottes Handeln zu suchen'; and Bruce, *Biblical Exegesis*, p. 77; and J. Barr, *Old and New in Interpretation* (London, 1966), p. 138.

16 *T.W.N.T.* viii, 87, 10. Cf. Heb. vii. 11, 19, denying τελείωσις to the Levitical System; and note the theme of τελειοῦν throughout the Epistle. See further below, p. 29.

17 *Tupos: Die typologische Deutung des Alten Testament im Neuen* (Gütersloh, 1938; reprinted 1966); and *T.W.N.T.* viii, 246 ff.

18 See Fitzmyer, *N.T.S.* 7 (1961), 297 ff. (332); and cf. Goppelt, *T.W.N.T.* viii, 252, claiming that in I Cor. x. 6, 11 the words τύπος and τυπικῶς are used for the first time in the technical sense in which they are often used in early Christian literature subsequently. See also G. W. H. Lampe and K. J. Woollcombe, *Essays on Typology* (London, 1957).

19 *Paul's Use of the Old Testament* (Edinburgh, 1957), pp. 129 and 90 ff., cited by Fitzmyer, *N.T.S.* 7 (1961).

20 See further L. Goppelt, 'Paulus und die Heilsgeschichte: Schlussfolgerungen aus Röm. iv und 1. Kor. x. 1–13', and G. Klein, 'Heil und Geschichte nach Römer iv', *N.T.S.* 13 (1966), 31 ff. and 43 ff.

ferent images and titles from pre-Christian Judaism.[21] That many of them are Israel-terms, that is, terms for a collective relationship, is itself a Christological phenomenon of importance.

The convergence of an exceptional number of images on the single figure of Jesus is illustrated with almost ludicrous volubility in Justin's *Dial.* cxxvi. 1: τίς δ' ἐστὶν οὗτος, ὃς καὶ ἄγγελος μεγάλης βουλῆς ποτέ, καὶ ἀνὴρ διὰ Ἰεζεκιήλ, καὶ ὡς υἱὸς ἀνθρώπου διὰ Δανιήλ, καὶ παιδίον διὰ Ἡσαΐου, καὶ Χριστὸς καὶ Θεὸς προσκυνητὸς διὰ Δαβίδ, καὶ Χριστὸς καὶ λίθος διὰ πολλῶν, καὶ σοφία διὰ Σολομῶνος, καὶ Ἰωσὴφ καὶ Ἰούδας καὶ ἄστρον διὰ Μωσέως, καὶ ἀνατολὴ διὰ Ζαχαρίου, καὶ παθητὸς καὶ Ἰακὼβ καὶ Ἰσραὴλ πάλιν διὰ Ἡσαΐου καὶ ῥάβδος καὶ ἄνθος καὶ λίθος ἀκρογωνιαῖος κέκληται καὶ υἱὸς θεοῦ . . . ; (cf. lxxxvii). But even so sweeping a claim as this is already implied when Paul says (II Cor. i. 20) that Christ is the confirmation (τὸ Ναί and τὸ Ἀμήν) of all the promises (ἐπαγγελίαι) of God; for by God's promises, in this kind of context, is meant what I am calling God's covenant-promise – his promise of a developing personal relationship between himself and his people, rooted in his own character and in their ethical response, and symbolized by such Israel-figures as appear in a list like Justin's. And within the New Testament itself, as we know well, there converges on Jesus a very remarkable number of images and titles, which, in Hebrew-Jewish writings, had been unrelated and scattered. That a Jewish leader should win the titles of divinely appointed royalty is not particularly surprising: Messiah, Chosen, Only, Beloved, Son of God in a messianic sense – such titles would not be too difficult to account for in any outstanding leader in Israel. Non-Christian explanations have been offered also for the application to Jesus of such quasi-divine titles as κύριος and σωτήρ (though the latter is, as a matter of fact, rare in the New Testament). But it is when, in addition to reverential and adorative individual titles such as these, there occurs a great convergence of Israel-titles and other collectives (and even God-titles) that the phenomenon assumes unique proportions. Servant of Yahweh, Son of Man, Zechariah martyr, rejected-but-vindicated stone, cornerstone, foundation stone, stumbling-stone, temple, Melchizedek-priest, Emmanuel, Adam, Word, Wisdom, bridegroom, even θεός – here is a convergence which, together with the titles of reverence and adoration, constitutes, taking the New Testament as a whole, a symptom of an estimate of Jesus as incomparably more than the mere verifier of predictions. This marks him as,

21 Cf. Zimmerli, in *Essays on Old Testament Interpretation*, p. 121; Bruce, *Biblical Exegesis*, p. 77.

in the estimate of Christians, the climax of the pattern of true covenant-relationship. Perhaps the most significant Old Testament passage, judged from the Christian angle, is the great promise in II Sam. vii. 14;[22] and the most significant Christian development is the new insight into the meaning of the Father–Son relationship brought by Christ. Already an Israel-figure and perhaps a messianic title, the term 'son' is given a completely new depth in the Christian tradition by Christ's own interpretation of sonship in terms of his own life of self-dedication even to death. It is summed up in Christ's new use of Abba,[23] and in his implicit interpretation of (to put it in terms of Phil. ii) τὰ ἴσα τῷ θεῷ as κένωσις, not ἁρπαγμός; and it is taken up in the Pauline epistles and in Hebrews, with its emphasis on filial obedience as well as filial status.

Naturally, one looks, by way of comparison, to see what happened in the case of the Right Teacher of the Sectarians. The contrast is striking. In H. Braun's close study,[24] good evidence is adduced to show that the Servant figure applies, in the Qumran use, not to the Teacher but to the community collectively.[25] It appears, again, that, if the Teacher was regarded as Messiah at all (which is by no means established (pp. 64 f.)), this was far from characteristic of the community's thought. I need not here pursue other points made by Braun in the comparison (for instance, in regard to the claim that the Teacher is crucified, and that his death has atoning efficacy, and that he is raised or will come again), for these are not relevant to the present inquiry. The immediate point is simply that the Right Teacher provides no parallel to the extraordinary wealth of figures converging upon Jesus. Nor, for that matter, do the Messiahs of Qumran expectation.[26]

Even the more modest claim, made by some scholars, that the two Messiahs of 1QS were, in the thinking of the sectarians, ultimately fused into one inclusive figure is shown by Braun[27] to be very precarious. (CD vi. 1, ii. 12 – both of doubtful meaning – are, at best, abnormal.) One is reminded, at this point, of the well-known fact that traces of the pre-Christian convergence of a plurality of Israel-figures have been discerned outside the Qumran literature also. Upon a single figure (actual or hypothetical) groups of titles such as Wisdom and

22 Cf. O. Betz, *Was wissen wir von Jesus?* (Stuttgart–Berlin, 1965), *passim*.
23 Cf. J. Jeremias, *Abba: Studien zur neutestamentlichen Theologie und Zeitgeschichte* (Göttingen, 1966); *The Prayers of Jesus* (London, 1967).
24 *Qumran und das neue Testament*, II (Tübingen, 1966), pp. 54 ff.
25 1QH ix. 6–8, 11–12, 23–7.
26 Braun, *Qumran*, II, p. 80.
27 *Qumran*, II, p. 79.

Messiah, or Servant, Son, and Son of Man are believed to have converged in certain areas of pre-Christian literature outside the Dead Sea scrolls.[28] But here, too, the extent is incomparably smaller than we find in the case of Jesus.

Thus, to a unique degree, Jesus is seen as the goal, the convergence-point, of God's plan for Israel, his covenant-promise. Even while the New Testament writers are ostensibly claiming what I have classified as the much more superficial prediction-verifications, what shouts louder than their expressed claims is their portrayal of Jesus as the coping-stone of God's edifice. By implication, they are really talking about the fulfilment of covenant-promise, even when explicitly they are only illustrating what they believe to be prediction-verification. Their understanding of the person of Jesus, indicated by the titles they attach to him and the role he plays, is far deeper than is suggested by most of their express citations of scripture. The implication of what they show us is a finality, completeness, and fulfilment involving an essentially personal and relational interpretation of God's design. The bare claim, 'God is as good as his word', has developed into, 'God has now achieved, completely and without remainder, in the person of his Son, a relationship and a communication which he had been partially expressing hitherto in other ways' (Heb. i. 1).

It has to be added that this finality and completeness, just because it is essentially personal and also greater than individual, is not of a negatively terminal quality. If Christ is τέλος νόμου in a great, fulfilling sense, he is more than the mere terminator of the Law.[29] If he is πλήρωμα in the sense indicated, it is so that the Christian Church may, in him, go on to contribute to God's πλήρωμα.[30] If anything is superseded, it is

28 J. Jeremias, παῖς θεοῦ, *T.W.N.T.* v, 685 ff.; E.T., W. Zimmerli and J. Jeremias, *The Servant of God* (London, 1957), pp. 50 ff. Cf. H. Windisch, 'Die göttliche Weisheit der Juden und die paulinische Christologie' in *Neutestamentliche Studien*, Festschrift für G. Heinrici (Leipzig, 1914), pp. 220 ff.; and E. Lövestam, *Son and Saviour, a Study of Acts 13, 32–37* (*Coniectanea Neotestamentica* 18, Lund, 1961), pp. 88 ff. (appendix on ' "Son of God" in the Synoptic Gospels').

29 See the discussions (to name only two recent ones) by C. E. B. Cranfield, 'St Paul and the Law', *S.J.T.* 17 (1964), 43 ff., and E. Bammel 'Νόμος Χριστοῦ', *Studia Evangelica*, 3 (ed. F. L. Cross, *T.U.* 88, Berlin, 1964), 120 ff.

30 See M. Bouttier, 'Remarques sur la conscience Apostolique de St Paul', in *Oikonomia: Heilsgeschichte als Thema der Theologie*, Festschrift für O. Cullmann, ed. Felix Christ (Hamburg, 1967), pp. 100 ff.

not Torah as such but a temporary covenant;[31] and thus the finality, paradoxically, is the beginning of a new era.

Another way of bringing the same phenomenon into focus is to go back to the other end - to the protasis, the promise-clause - and to observe that it is not the form but the content of the protasis that makes it a strictly appropriate correlative to fulfilment in its biggest sense. What I am calling 'covenant-promise' is more than a mere promise or prediction. It is a plurality of promises and predictions related to that pattern of personal relationship between God and his people which Christians recognize as culminating in the relation between the Father and his unique Son, Jesus Christ. There is no essential difference in structure between the two sentences, 'He shall be called a Nazarene' and 'He shall be to me a son'; or between 'I will open my mouth in parables' and 'on him shall the gentiles set their hopes'; but whereas the second in each pair is closely concerned with relationship and personal function, the first in each pair is trivial and incidental, as well as being, as we know, false to the original intention of the passage in question. (This holds good, fairly certainly, wherever 'he shall be called a Nazarene' may have come from, or whatever it represents or misrepresents.) In other words, the decisive pattern and the significant direction are shown in what we associate with *Heilsgeschichte* and with the teaching of the great prophets of Israel - the proclamation of God as moral and personal, as the God who enters into a covenant with his people with the intention of bringing them into a fully personal relationship with him. It is because prediction-verification was thought to authenticate the divine foreknowledge and overruling of the plan and the centrality of Jesus in the covenant-pattern that it came to occupy a position of importance in the Christian Gospel; but, as I have already said, it is precisely because of the infinitely greater moral and religious importance of the covenant-relation and its culmination in Jesus that mere prediction-verification was destined ultimately to lose its value in the eyes of thoughtful Christians. Hence arise both the imprecision of the usage of the New Testament, and the greater discrimination which, in our day, we are able and bound to exercise. From the witness of the New Testament we have learnt what its writers had not, by that time, consciously formulated.

31 This is the theme of the Epistle to the Hebrews; see below, p. 29. Contrast Justin's more uncompromising position (e.g. *Dial.* xi. 2 and 4, xliii. 1) that Law is superseded and the Church ousts Israel. Hummel, *Matthäusevangelium*, pp. 156 f., judges that this is *not* what Matthew is saying.

## II

I turn, now, to a consideration of the incidence in ancient Hebrew and Greek literature of certain formulae related, if only by contrast, to our theme. This is, of course, very far indeed from an exhaustive examination. It would be a major undertaking to cover that literature so as to get anything like a sound statistical picture. And, incidentally, one would need to ask where the vast problem of foreknowledge and predestination fits into the theme. But I suspect that an exhaustive examination would confirm what is certainly my impression, that (quite apart from the fact the Hebrew possesses no single word for 'promise') the literal equivalents even of 'promise and implementation' – let alone 'promise and fulfilment' – are not common; and that the Greek words used in the apodosis of such a phrase belong far more often to the τελεῖν-group than to the πληροῦν-group, while of the various Hebrew words employed, מלא is among the least frequent.

The purpose of this section is no more than to bring to mind, by the use of an arbitrary selection, the variety of expressions that occur in the general area of thought under examination, and to provide a foil to the more specialized uses to which the third and last section is devoted. But even a highly selective survey is difficult to organize. In the interests of clarity, I reserve for the last section of this paper all clauses containing words of the מלא and πληροῦν groups, even when they express something less than the strictly defined 'covenant-promise and fulfilment' motif. Conversely, I include here, in this second section, clauses which come close to the full 'covenant-promise and fulfilment' meaning, if they, in fact, use some other word than מלא or πληροῦν. This second section contains, therefore, simply a few illustrations (other than those containing מלא or πληροῦν) of various protases and apodoses falling mostly but not quite exclusively within those first two categories of meaning which I defined earlier, namely: (1) *protasis*, prediction, with *apodosis*, verification; (2) *protasis*, any promise (with or without the full 'covenant'-content, as defined) or threat, undertaking, or obligation, with *apodosis*, discharge, confirmation, realization, or completion. And, before these, I prefix some phrases which combine protasis and apodosis by implication in a single expression of the type 'as it was said (or written)'. This type of expression can, of course, be used with an explicitly apodotic phrase such as 'so it came to pass'; but the reason for classifying it in a separate, prefixed category (labelled 'combination') is that it can, if necessary, stand alone and does not positively need an explicit apodotic clause: it is possible simply to make a statement constituting the confirmation of a prediction - for instance, 'Oedipus killed his father' - alluding obliquely to the prediction with nothing more than an 'as it was said (or written)' clause.

Under each of these three categories, 'combination phrase', (1), and (2), I offer merely such material as has come to hand, and present it in the order (when available) of: (A) Old Testament and Apocrypha; (B) Qumran; (C) other Jewish writings; (D) secular literature; (E) New Testament; (F) other Christian literature. In my illustrations drawn from Qumran, I am greatly indebted to J. A. Fitmyer's important article, 'The Use of Explicit Old Testament Quotations in Qumran Literature and in the New Testament'.[32] It was, in fact, certain observations in this article about the absence of fulfilment phrases from Qumran that first set me thinking along these lines.[33] For some of the classical references, in addition to those provided by word-books, I am indebted to Mr Philip Scholfield of the Department of Linguistics in the University College of North Wales, Bangor.

## Phrases without *ml'/plēroun*

### 'Combination phrase'

(A) *Old Testament.* I Kings xiii. 5: according to the sign (כַּמּוֹפֵת, κατὰ τὸ τέρας) which the man of God gave by the word of Y″ (בִּדְבַר יְהֹוָה, ἐν λόγῳ κυρίου); I Kings xiii. 26: according to the word of Y″... (כִּדְבַר יְהֹוָה, LXX otherwise); II Kings* xiv. 25, xxiii. 16, similarly (כִּדְבַר יְהֹוָה, κατὰ τὸ ῥῆμα κυρίου); Ezra i. 1 (LXX II Esdras i. 1): ...so as to accomplish (לִכְלוֹת, τοῦ τελεσθῆναι) the word of Y″ from the lips of Jeremiah, Y″ stirred up the spirit of Cyrus...

(B) *Qumran.* CD iv. 13 f.: Belial shall be unleashed ... as God spoke (כַּאֲשֶׁר דִּבֶּר אֵל) by Isaiah the prophet ... saying (לֵאמוֹר); vii. 14: ...

---

32 *N.T.S.* 7 (1961), 297 ff. Cf. also his 'Jewish Christianity in Acts in Light of the Qumran Scrolls', in Keck and Martyn, *Luke-Acts*, pp. 233 ff. (see pp. 251–4).

33 In my *The Birth of the New Testament* (London, 1962), p. 57, n. 1, I called attention to this. In an extremely generous anonymous review in *The Times Literary Supplement* (1963), p. 220, this conclusion was challenged: 'It is at least arguable', wrote the reviewer, '...that though the object of applied prophecy in the New Testament is more specific than in the Qumran literature, the application of prophecy itself is in the latter just as much concerned with fulfilment'; and it was partly in a desire to examine the force of this challenge that I was led to offer this paper.

[*Add: ix. 26.]

escaped to the land of the North, as he said (אמר כאשר) ... (Amos v.
26 f. follows) (so vii. 16); 1QM xi. 5 f.: Our strength and the power of
our hand accomplish no mighty deeds except by thy power ... as thou
hast declared (כאשר הגדת) to us from of old, saying (לאמור) ... (Num.
xxiv. 17 ff. follows).
(D) Hdt. i. 86: κατὰ τὸ χρηστήριον (of Croesus' oracle).
(E) *New Testament*. Mk i. 2 ff.; Rom. i. 17; ii. 24 (all καθὼς γέγραπται); ix. 29 (καθὼς προείρηκεν); xv. 3 (καθὼς γέγραπται); I Cor. xv.
3 f. (κατὰ τὰς γραφάς).

## (1) *Prediction/verification*

As soon as one tries to illustrate this category, it becomes evident that
the border-line between it and category (2) - promise, threat, etc. - is
often very indistinct. I have tried to reserve (1) for passages where the
main importance attaches to the sheer verification rather than to the
content of the prediction. But obviously it is impossible ultimately to
segregate the two.

(A) *Old Testament*. Deut. xviii. 22 (negative): ... which the prophet
speaks (יְדַבֵּר, λαλήσῃ) in the name of Yʺ and the word (הַדָּבָר, τὸ ῥῆμα)
does not happen (יִהְיֶה, γένηται) and does not come (יָבוֹא, συμβῇ)...; I
Kings xii. 15:... in order that (לְמַעַן, ὅπως) Yʺ might confirm (הָקִים,
στήσῃ) his word (דְּבָרוֹ, τὸ ῥῆμα αὐτοῦ) which he spoke (דִּבֶּר, ἐλάλησεν)
by Ahijah...; II Kings xxiii. 17:... and he uttered (וַיִּקְרָא, καὶ ἐπικα-
λεσάμενος) these words (דְּבָרִים, λόγους) which you have accomplished
(עָשִׂיתָ, LXX otherwise (ἐπεκαλέσατο)) against the altar...; Isa. xliv.
26: who confirms the word of his servant (מֵקִים דְּבַר עַבְדּוֹ, ἱστῶν
ῥήματα παιδὸς αὐτοῦ), and performs the counsel of his messengers
(וַעֲצַת מַלְאָכָיו יַשְׁלִים, καὶ τὴν βουλὴν τῶν ἀγγέλων αὐτοῦ ἀληθεύων);
Isa. xlvi. 10a: declaring (מַגִּיד, ἀναγγέλλων) the end (אַחֲרִית, τὰ ἔσχατα)
from the beginning (מֵרֵאשִׁית, πρότερον), and from ancient times (וּמִקֶּדֶם)
things not yet done (אֲשֶׁר לֹא־נַעֲשׂוּ) (LXX πρὶν αὐτὰ γενέσθαι, καὶ ἅμα
συνετελέσθη).

(B) *Qumran*. CD i. 13: This was the time (היא העת) of which it was
written (אשר היה כתוב)...(Hos. iv. 16 follows); CD iv. 19 f.: 'Zaw' (צו)
is a preacher (הוא מטיף), of whom he said (אשר אמר)...(a reference
follows to ?Mic. ii. 6); CD vii. 15b ff.: here is a series of 'identifications'
from Amos v. 26, with such formulae as 'The books of the Law are the
tabernacle...' (ספרי התורה הם סוכת), or 'The star is the Interpreter of
the Law who shall come to Damascus; as it is written...' (...והכוכב הוא
כאשר כתוב); 1 QpHab ii. 7-10 contains the famous reference to the

gift of 'pesher' given by God to the Priest ('. . . that he might interpret all the words of his servants the prophets . . .'); 1QpHab vii. 13 f. states the principle: '. . . all the ages of God reach their appointed end as he determines for them the mysteries of his wisdom', (כול קיצי אל יבואו לתכונם כאשר חקק לה[ם] ברזי ערמתו). Most of the examples of 'pesher' also illustrate this category.

(C) *Other Jewish writings.* Philo, *de Iosepho* 164: when [Joseph's] brothers received confirmation of his dreams (τῶν ὀνειράτων αὐτοῦ λαμβανόντων βεβαίωσιν); *vit. Mos.* ii. 275: (with reference to Moses' prediction of the fate of Cora, Dathan, and Abiram) . . . an oracle . . . fulfilled not long years afterwards but immediately, when it was being uttered ( . . . λόγιον . . . τελειωθὲν οὐ μακροῖς χρόνοις ὕστερον, ἀλλ' εὐθὺς ὅτ' ἐχρησμῳδεῖτο).

(D) *Secular literature.* Hom. *Od.* xiii. 178: ὡς ἀγόρευ' ὁ γέρων τὰ δὲ δὴ νῦν πάντα τελεῖται. Hdt. i. 13: τούτου τοῦ ἔπεος (the Pythian oracle's) Λυδοί τε καὶ οἱ βασιλέες αὐτῶν λόγον οὐδένα ἐποιεῦντο, πρὶν δὴ ἐπετελέσθη.* Soph. *O.T.* 1329 f.:

> Ἀπόλλων τάδ' ἦν, Ἀπόλλων, φίλοι,
> ὁ κακὰ κακὰ τελῶν ἐμὰ τάδ' ἐμὰ πάθεα.

(E) *New Testament.* Lk. i. 45: ἔσται τελείωσις τοῖς λελαλημένοις; xviii. 31: τελεσθήσεται πάντα τὰ γεγραμμένα; xxii. 37:† τὸ περὶ ἐμοῦ τέλος ἔχει; Jo. xix. 38: ἵνα τελειωθῇ ἡ γραφή; Acts iv. 28: ποιῆσαι ὅσα ἡ χείρ σου καὶ ἡ βουλὴ προώρισεν γενέσθαι; xiii. 29: ὡς δὲ ἐτέλεσαν πάντα τὰ περὶ αὐτοῦ γεγραμμένα . . . ; II Pet. iii. 2: μνησθῆναι τῶν προειρημένων ῥημάτων ὑπὸ τῶν ἁγίων προφητῶν.

(F) *Other Christian Literature.* Justin, *Dial.* xxxv. 2: ἃ γὰρ προλαβὼν μέλλειν γίνεσθαι . . . ἔφη, ταῦτα ὄψει καὶ ἐνεργείᾳ ὁρῶμεν τελούμενα; cxxxix. 1: ἄλλο μυστήριον . . . προεφητεύθη τελούμενον . . .

### (2) *Promise or threat, undertaking or obligation/discharge, confirmation, realization, or completion*

(A) *Old Testament and Apocrypha.* Deut. viii. 18: . . . in order that (לְמַעַן, ἵνα) he might confirm (הָקִים, στήσῃ) his covenant which he swore, as has taken place today (כַּיּוֹם הַזֶּה, ὡς σήμερον) (Deut. ix. 5 similarly); Josh. xxi. 45: nothing has failed (לֹא־נָפַל דָּבָר, οὐ διέπεσεν) of all the good that Y″ promised (הַדָּבָר הַטּוֹב אֲשֶׁר־דִּבֶּר יְהוָה, τῶν

[* Add: Aesch. *Agam.* 68: τελεῖται δ'ἐς τὸ πεπρωμένον.
† Add: τοῦτο τὸ γεγραμμένον δεῖ τελεσθῆναι ἐν ἐμοί . . . ]

ῥημάτων τῶν καλῶν ὧν ἐλάλησεν κύριος); xxiii. 14: for nothing has
failed (similar to xxi. 45). . . all has come for you (בָּאוּ לָכֶם, LXX
otherwise), not one thing has failed (לֹא נָפַל, οὐ διεφώνησεν) from it; I
Kings ii. 4: that Y″ may confirm (יָקִים, στήσῃ) his word which he
spoke concerning me, saying, If. . ., then. . .; viii. 20: and Y″ has
confirmed (וַיָּקֶם, καὶ ἀνέστησεν) his word (דְּבָרוֹ, τὸ ῥῆμα αὐτοῦ). . . as
Y″ promised (כַּאֲשֶׁר דִּבֶּר יְהוָה, καθὼς ἐλάλησεν κύριος); II Kings x.
10: there shall fall to the earth nothing of what Y″ spoke (מִדְּבַר יְהוָה
אֲשֶׁר דִּבֶּר. . . , ἀπὸ τοῦ ῥήματος κυρίου. . . οὗ ἐλάλησεν). . . for Y″ has
done (עָשָׂה, ἐποίησεν) what he spoke by his servant Elijah; xv. 12: this
was the promise of Y″ which he made (דְּבַר־יְהוָה אֲשֶׁר דִּבֶּר, ὁ λόγος
κυρίου ὃν ἐλάλησεν). . . and so it came to pass (וַיְהִי־כֵן, καὶ ἐγένετο
οὕτως); xxiv. 2 f.:. . .according to what Y″ had said (כִּדְבַר יְהוָה אֲשֶׁר
דִּבֶּר, κατὰ τὸν λόγον κυρίου ὃν ἐλάλησεν) by his prophets; surely this
came upon Judah (הָיְתָה בִּיהוּדָה, ἦν ἐν τῷ Ιουδα) at the command of
Y″. . .; Isa* xlvi. 10b: my counsel shall stand (עֲצָתִי תָקוּם, πᾶσά μου ἡ
βουλὴ στήσεται), and I will accomplish (אֶעֱשֶׂה, ποιήσω) all my purpose
(כָּל־חֶפְצִי, ὅσα βεβούλευμαι; Jer. xxxiv. 18 (LXX xli. 18):. . . the men
who . . . did not keep (לֹא־הֵקִימוּ, μὴ στήσαντας) the terms of the
covenant (אֶת־דִּבְרֵי הַבְּרִית, τὴν διαθήκην μου). . .; Dan. iv. 30 (LXX
33): immediately the [divine] word (מִלְּתָא, πάντα (ο′), λόγος (θ)) was
performed (סָפַת, τελεσθήσεται (ο′), συνετελέσθη (θ)) on Nebuchadnes-
sar. . .; ix. 12: he has confirmed his words ((sic) אֶת־דְּבָרֹיו, καὶ
ἔστησεν. . . τὰ προστάγματα αὐτοῦ (ο′), τοὺς λόγους αὐτοῦ (θ)). . . by
bringing (לְהָבִיא, ἐπαγαγεῖν) upon us great evil; xii 7: I heard him swear
. . . that . . . all these things would be accomplished (תִּכְלֶינָה, συντελεσθήσεται (ο′), otherwise (θ));† Neh. v. 13 (LXX II Esdras xv. 13):. . .
every man. . . who does not perform (לֹא־יָקִים, οὐ στήσει) this promise
(אֶת־הַדָּבָר הַזֶּה, τὸν λόγον τοῦτον). . .; Thr. ii. 17: Y″ has done (עָשָׂה,
ἐποίησεν) what he purposed (זָמָם, ἐνεθυμήθη), has carried out (בִּצַּע,
συνετέλεσεν) his threat (אֶמְרָתוֹ, ῥήματα αὐτοῦ), as he ordained (אֲשֶׁר
צִוָּה, ἃ ἐνετείλατο) long ago; III Macc. vi. 15: as thou hast promised
(καθὼς εἶπας). . .so accomplish it (οὕτως ἐπιτέλεσον); Judith vi. 9:
I have spoken (ἐλάλησα), and none of my words shall fail (οὐδὲν
διαπεσεῖται τῶν ῥημάτων μου); Tobit xiv. 4 (S): . . . because I believe
the word of God against Nineve, and all that the prophets of Israel spoke
(ἐλάλησαν) whom God sent, everything will come to pass (ἀπαντήσει)

[* Add: xl. 2: she has fulfilled her term of bondage (מָלְאָה צְבָאָהּ, ἐπληρώθη
ἡ ταπείνωσις αὐτῆς.]
† Add: Esra i. 1 (LXX II Esdras i. 1): . . . that the word of Y″ might be
accomplished (לִכְלוֹת דְּבַר־יְהוָה, τοῦ τελεσθῆναι λόγον κυρίου.)]

and nothing at all will be missing (ἐλαττονωθῇ) from all the words (ῥημάτων), and everything will happen (συμβήσεται) at its proper time . . . ; therefore I know and believe that everything that God said (εἶπεν) shall be accomplished (συντελεσθήσεται) and shall happen (ἔσται), and not a word (ῥῆμα) shall fail (διαπέσῃ) from the words (λόγων). . .

(B) *Qumran.* CD vii. 10 f. offers a good example of a threat/confirmation phrase: '. . . when the saying shall come to pass (בבוא הדבר) which is written (אשר כתוב) in the words of Isaiah. . .' (there follows a phrase from Isa. vii. 17).

Examples of the performance of obligation or of paraenetic exhortations to its performance (chiefly with reference to the Sectarians' observance of Torah) are frequent; and many of the same formulae as are used in combination-phrases or in prediction/fulfilment, etc., are used also for this. There is no need here to do more than record this fact. (See Fitzmyer, *N.T.S.* 7 (1961), 300 ff., where, among the paraenetic uses with various formulae, are quotations from 1QS v. 15, 17; CD v. 1; vi. 13; vii. 8; viii. 14; ix. 2, 5; xi. 18, 20; xvi. 6, 15; xix. 26 f.; 1QM x. 1.)

(C) *Other Jewish writers.* Philo, *leg. alleg.* iii. 204: (on God's oath, Gen. xxii) ὃ ἐὰν εἴπῃ γίνεται . . . πάντες οἱ τοῦ θεοῦ λόγοι εἰσὶν ὅρκοι βεβαιούμενοι ἔργων ἀποτελέσμασι; *vit. Mos.* i. 283: [God] φθέγξεται τὸ παράπαν οὐδέν, ὃ μὴ τελειωθήσεται βεβαίως, ἐπεὶ ὁ λόγος ἔργον ἐστὶν αὐτῷ; *q.r.d.h.* 96: τοῦτ' (promise in Gen. xv. 7) οὐχ ὑπόσχεσιν μόνον, ἀλλὰ καὶ παλαιᾶς ὑποσχέσεως βεβαίωσιν ἐμφαίνει; *opif. mund.* 99: τὴν δ᾽ ὑπόσχεσιν ἀποδείξει βεβαιωτέον; *spec. leg.* i. 267: ἤδη δ᾽ ἀναγκαῖον καὶ τὴν ὑπόσχεσιν ἀποδοῦναι. . .Josephus, *Ant.* xi. 315: τὰς 315: τὰς ὑποσχέσεις τελέσειν.

(D) *Secular literature.* Hom. *Il.* ix. 244 f.: μή οἱ ἀπειλὰς | ἐκτελέσωσι θεοί; *Od.* xiii. 40: ἤδη γὰρ τετέλεσται ἅ μοι φίλος ἤθελε θυμός; xv. 111 f.: Τηλέμαχ᾽, ἢ τοι νόστον, ὅπως φρεσὶ σῇσι μενοινᾷς, | ὥς τοι Ζεὺς τελέσειεν, ἐρίγδουπος πόσις Ἥρης; 203: ὅππως οἱ κατὰ μοῖραν ὑποσχόμενος τελέσειεν. Thuc. i. 138. 4: . . . ἀδύνατον νομίσαντα εἶναι ἐπιτελέσαι βασιλεῖ ἃ ὑπέσχετο. Plut. *Numa* 14: ἐπιτελείωσις τῆς εὐχῆς.

(E) *New Testament.* Matt. x. 23: οὐ μὴ τελέσητε τὰς πόλεις τοῦ Ἰσραήλ (but most relevant if the reference is not to 'cities of refuge' but to evangelization); xi. 1, xiii. 53, xix. 1, xxvi. 1 (all ἐτέλεσεν, of Jesus finishing a task); Mk xiii. 4: ὅταν μέλλῃ ταῦτα συντελεῖσθαι πάντα; Lk. ii. 39: ὡς ἐτέλεσαν πάντα τὰ κατὰ τὸν νόμον κυρίου; 43: τελειωσάντων τὰς ἡμέρας (cf. ix. 51; Acts ii. 1; xxi. 27); iv. 2: συντελεσθεισῶν (τῶν ἡμερῶν); 13: συντελέσας πάντα πειρασμόν; xii. 50: ἕως ὅτου τελεσθῇ (βάπτισμα); xiv. 10: ἤρξατο οἰκοδομεῖν καὶ οὐκ ἴσχυσεν ἐκτελέσαι; Jo. iv. 34: ἵνα... τελειώσω αὐτοῦ τὸ ἔργον (cf. v. 36; xvii. 4; xix. 30 (τετέλεσται)); Acts xx. 24: ὡς τελειώσω τὸν δρόμον μου καὶ τὴν διακονίαν... ; Rom. ii. 27: ἠ... ἀκροβυστία τὸν νόμον τελοῦσα; xiii. 6: φόρους τελεῖτε: xv. 8: εἰς τὸ βεβαιῶσαι τὰς ἐπαγγελίας (cf. II Cor. i. 20); Phil. i. 6: ὁ ἐναρξάμενος ἐν ὑμῖν ἔργον ἀγαθὸν ἐπιτελέσει... ; II Tim. iv. 7: τὸν δρόμον τετέλεκα; Heb vii. 11: εἰ μὲν οὖν τελείωσις διὰ τῆς Λευιτικῆς ἱερωσύνης ἦν... (cf. ii. 10; v. 9; vii. 19, 28; ix. 9, 14; xi. 40; xii. 23); viii. 8: συντελέσω... διαθήκην καινήν; Jas ii. 8: νόμον τελεῖτε βασιλικόν; Rev. x. 7: ἐτελέσθη τὸ μυστήριον; xi. 7: ὅταν τελέσωσιν τὴν μαρτυρίαν αὐτῶν; xv. 1: ἐν αὐταῖς ἐτελέσθη ὁ θυμὸς τοῦ θεοῦ; 8: ἄχρι τελεσθῶσιν αἱ ἑπτὰ πληγαί; xvii. 17: ἄχρι τελεσθήσονται οἱ λόγοι τοῦ θεοῦ; xx. 3, 5, 7 (τελεῖν of fixed periods of time).

(F) *Other Christian Literature.* I Clem. xiii. 5: τελειωθήσεται τὸ βούλημα αὐτοῦ... ; xxvii. 5: οὐδὲν μὴ παρέλθῃ τῶν δεδογματισμένων ὑπ' αὐτοῦ.

## III

We come, thirdly and lastly, to a closer examination of the incidence and use of the מלא/πληροῦν group of words, and to some reflexions on the phenomena they constitute. And the first and most striking fact that meets us is simply the comparative infrequency of this word outside the New Testament, in the kind of usage with which we are concerned, in contrast with the considerable efflorescence of πληροῦν within certain areas of the New Testament.

(A) In the Old Testament the only occurrences of מלא,[34] in the kind of protasis-and-apodosis complex with which we are concerned, are the following: I Kings ii. 27: so Solomon expelled Abiathar... thus fulfilling the word of Y″ which he had spoken (לְמַלֵּא אֶת־דְּבַר־יְהוָה אֲשֶׁר דִּבֶּר, πληρωθῆναι τὸ ῥῆμα κυρίου, ὃ ἐλάλησεν); viii. 15: Y″... who with his hand has fulfilled what he promised with his mouth... saying (וּבְיָדוֹ מִלֵּא לֵאמֹר... אֲשֶׁר דִּבֶּר בְּפִיו... יְהוָה, ὃς ἐλάλησεν ἐν τῷ στόματι αὐτοῦ... καὶ ἐν ταῖς χερσὶν αὐτοῦ ἐπλήρωσεν λέγων...); 24 (similarly); II Chron. vi. 4 (similarly); 15 (similarly); xxxvi. 21 f.: to fulfil the word of Y″ by the mouth of Jeremiah (לְמַלֹּאות דְּבַר־יְהוָה בְּפִי יִרְמְיָהוּ, τοῦ πληρωθῆναι λόγον κυρίου διὰ στόματος Ιερεμιου)... that the word of Y″ by the mouth of Jeremiah might be accomplished

34 In the protasis, 'promise'-words are lacking from Hebrew, though of course there are periphrases for them. In the Greek books, ἐπαγγελία and ὑπισχ- occur occasionally, though not, as it happens, in any of the πληροῦν- phrases which follow in this list.

(לְכְלוֹת דְּבַר־יְהוָה בְּפִי יִרְמְיָהוּ), μετὰ τὸ πληρωθῆναι ῥῆμα κυρίου διὰ στόματος Ιερεμιου); Ps. xx (LXX xix). 5b: may Y″ fulfil all your petitions (וְכָל־עֲצָתְךָ יְמַלֵּא, καὶ πᾶσαν τὴν βουλήν σου πληρώσαι; cf. 6b); LXX cxxvi. 5: (μακάριος ἄνθρωπος, ὃς πληρώσει τὴν ἐπιθυμίαν...; M.T. cxxvii. 5: אַשְׁפָּתוֹ (!)); LXX Isa. xiii. 3: (πληρῶσαι τὸν θυμόν μου, M.T. ? לְאַפִּי); Jer. xliv (LXX li). 25: you and your wives have declared with your mouths, and have fulfilled it with your hands (וַתְּדַבֵּרְנָה בְּפִיכֶם וּבִידֵיכֶם מִלֵּאתֶם, τῷ στόματι ὑμῶν ἐλαλήσατε καὶ ταῖς χερσὶν ὑμῶν ἐπληρώσατε).

(B) Next, turning to Qumran, we may remind ourselves of J. A. Fitzmyer's article, which has already been cited, and of his observation[35] that, in its specific quotations from the Old Testament, the Qumran literature lacks both the fulfilment formulae found in Matthew and also the 'pattern' in the use of the Old Testament which C. H. Dodd finds (*According to the Scriptures*) in the New Testament. And, to the best of my knowledge, the Qumran literature (thus far) offers, even beyond the limits of explicit quotation, scarcely any examples of the use of מלא in a phrase referring to the confirmation or completion of God's promises or plan. In K. G. Kuhn's *Konkordanz*,[36] the only at all relevant use of מלא that I can find is in 1QS iii. 15b, 16a, where it is related, though not to Scripture, at least indirectly to the fulfilling of God's plan:

מֵאֵל הַדֵּעוֹת כּוֹל הֹוֶה וְנִהְיֶה (וְנִהְיָה=) ¹ וְלִפְנֵי הֱיוֹתָם הֵכִין כּוֹל מַחֲשַׁבְתָּם¹

(16) וּבִהְיוֹתָם לִתְעוּדוֹתָם כְּמַחֲשֶׁבֶת כְּבוֹדוֹ יְמַלְאוּ פְּעוּלָתָם ...

(pointing from Lohse, *Die Texte*). 'From the God of knowledge comes all that is and shall be. Before ever they existed He established their whole design, and when, as ordained for them, they come into being, it is in accord with His glorious design that they fulfil their work' (translation from G. Vermés).[37] But even here, the immediate sense of מלא is no more than that of discharging a function, and it is only from the context, if at all, that it gains any relevance to the fulfilment of God's designs. In all the other passages in which מלא occurs,[38] it relates either

35 Pp. 303 f., 331. Cf. also the findings of B. M. Metzger, 'The Formulas Introducing Quotations of Scripture in the NT and the Mishnah', *J.B.L.* 70 (1951), 297 ff., cited by Fitzmyer, *N.T.S.* 7 (1961), 301, n. 1. Metzger's conclusion regarding the New Testament in relation to the Mishnah is similar (see pp. 306 f., and especially the first note on p. 307).

36 K. G. Kuhn (*et al.*), *Konkordanz zu den Qumrantexten* (Göttingen, 1960).

37 *The Dead Sea Scrolls in English* (Harmondsworth, 1962), p. 75.

38 And add to K. G. Kuhn's list 4QpNah i. 6 (Lohse, *Die Texte*, p. 262).

to literal filling (including the phrase 'to fill the hand' = 'to consecrate', 1QSb v. 17, apparently (text defective)) or to the completion of a stated period of time or of a process (the latter in 1QM xvii. 9: עַד יָמִין יָדוֹ [וּ]מִלֵּא מַצְרְפָיו, Lohse, p. 218).

Whatever the reason for the non-use of מלא, it is not because the Sectarians did not believe themselves to be living in the eschatologically final period. Indeed they were expressly thinking, as we know well, in terms of a New Covenant (CD vii. 21; xix. 33; xx. 12; 1QpHab ii. 3 – see Braun, *Qumran und das Neue Testament*, I, pp. 198; and, at length, II, pp. 266 ff.); and their use of testimonies suggests the same (CD vii. 18-21 – Balaam's star and sceptre come true for the Damascus figures; 4Qtest. 9-13; 4Qflor i. 11-13;[39] and n.b. 1QpHab vii. 7 ff.). But I chose 'covenant-promise' as the best short phrase I could find to define collectively the promises of God which converge on the perfect relationship between himself and his people which Christians find fulfilled in Jesus Christ. And despite the Sectarians' emphasis on the covenant (which, indeed, has won them the title of 'Covenanters'), there is lacking from their literature this pregnant understanding of its meaning. And even if there is, in their covenant references, an implication of finality, at any rate it is scarcely at all brought to explicit statement by the מלא-theme, as it is in the New Testament – where it is further reinforced by all the τελ- phrases which, for the purposes of analysis, we have temporarily segregated; and the contrast between Qumran and the New Testament, as formulated by Fitzmyer for explicit citations, seems therefore to hold good also outside the area of explicit quotation.

L. Goppelt, in the same vein, sums up the relevant part of his article with the observation:[40] 'Die Sekte stellt sich als die Fortsetzung des stets vorhandenen hl [heiligen] Restes unter die Schrift, aber sie versteht sich nicht als Erbin einer neuen Erwählung.'

In the light of this, it may be questioned whether H. Braun's use of 'Erfüllung' is entirely justified when, emphasizing the common ground between the Sectarians and the New Testament in their treatment of scripture, he writes: '. . . als eschatologischer Erfüllung versteht sich auch die Qumrangemeinde, so wie die neutestamentliche Gemeindetradition Jesus als eschatologische Phänomen und als Erfüllung des Alten

---

39 See Fitzmyer, *N.T.S.* 7 (1961), 314, 331 and Keck and Martyn, *Luke-Acts*, pp. 251–4; Bruce, *Biblical Exegesis*, pp. 9, 20; G. Delling (*s.v.* τέλος), *T.W.N.T.* viii, 54.

40 *T.W.N.T.* viii, 256, 3–5. G. Delling (*s.v.* τέλος), *T.W.N.T.* viii, 54, calls attention to the (apparent) application of Ps. ii. 1 f. to בְּחִרֵי יִשְׂרָאֵל בְּאַחֲרִית הַיָּמִים in 4Qflor i. 19 (pointing from Lohse, *Die Texte*, p. 258); but this is obscure.

Testaments auslegt.'[41] Braun is at pains to deny (II, 70) that the expectation of the *eschaton* in the case of the Right Teacher should be contrasted with the teaching of Jesus, as though, for Jesus, its presence was complete, since, with Jesus no less than with the Teacher, there is still an expectation of a near future. This is true; but it does not therefore follow that there is no difference between the two in respect of completeness. As Braun (following Schubert) allows (p. 72), for Qumran the End is more important than its representative, whereas for the Early Church Jesus is the central figure; and for Qumran the Messiahs are still expected, whereas for the Early Church the Messiah has already come (p. 145; see also p. 280). This, I suspect, is the most important factor in the difference; and Fitzmyer sums it up when he says: 'At Qumran many of the Old Testament texts were applied to events in the recent history of the sect; in this respect there is some similarity to the backward glance of the New Testament writers. But the messianic hope at Qumran shifted the emphasis much more to a *coming fulfilment* of the Old Testament scriptures' (p. 331). And again: '... Christian writers were often looking back at the central event in which salvation had been accomplished rather than forward to a deliverance by Yahweh, which seems to characterize the Qumran literature' (p. 329). Here it

41 *Qumran*, II, p. 88. So on p. 172 he uses the phrase '[neben] der eschatologischen Schrifterfüllung...' in reference to Qumran and Paul alike. In his section on eschatology he says, of the Qumran outlook, 'Das Alte Testament erfüllte sich im jetzt' (p. 267), and, 'Kurz, man darf Qumran eine Schriftauslegung im Sinne der eschatologischen Erfüllung nicht absprechen...' (*ibid.*). Again, '... die Dauer der Endzeiten [which, Braun fully recognizes, is reflected in the impatience and anxiety of the Sect] gibt nicht die Berechtigung, die qumranische Enderwartung ihres Erfüllungsbewusstseins zu berauben...' ( p. 268).

   Similarly, to take at random another example of the use of 'fulfilment' without an equivalent word in the original, M. Black, in a note entitled 'The "Fulfilment" in the Kingdom of God', *Exp. T.* 57 (1945), 25 f., wrote: 'The idea of a "fulfilment" or a "consummation" by the coming of the Messianic Kingdom is a familiar one in contemporary Judaism. In the Syriac Apocalypse of Baruch it is made clear that the coming of the Messianic Age was expressly known and referred to as "the fulfilment" or "the consummation" (30³).' Again (p. 29): 'In I Enoch the "consummation" (16¹ τελείωσις) is the Great Judgment.' Here Black was, of course, using 'fulfilment', perfectly legitimately, in its wider, looser sense. But it is relevant to our attempt to delimit its meaning to note not only that the word in I Enoch (as he himself quotes it) is not πληροῦν, but that the Syr. Apoc. Bar., in the passage cited, similarly uses not the root מלא but the root שׁלם. (See R. Graffin, *Patrologia Syriaca*, Pars 1, Tom. II (Paris, 1907), *in loc.*)

may be repeated that, in assessing the contrast with the New Testamemt, it is legitimate to bring back the whole τελ-group of words - which, for our purpose, have been relegated to a separate section - for these add to the New Testament's greater sense of completeness as compared with the Qumran literature.

(C) *Other Jewish literature*. In Philo there is practically no relevant use of πληροῦν-words (if H. Leisegang's index[42] serves), although, as we have already seen, he has a good number of clauses relevant to our investigation with τελεῖν- or τελειοῦν-words. Perhaps the only phrases from Philo to be included here are πλήρωμα χρηστῶν ἐλπίδων, *de Abrahamo* 268 (of Abraham's faith in God); and πληρῶσαι τοὺς λόγους ἔργοις ἐπαινετοῖς, *praem. poen.* 83. Josephus sometimes uses πληροῦν of a kind of 'fulfilment', as, for example, to denote the realization of a longing (ἐπιθυμία, *Ant.* v. 145), or of a divinely promised time (καιρός, *Ant.* vi. 49), or the performance of a (human) promise (τὰς ὑποσχέσεις ἐπλήρωσε (Herod), *Ant.* xiv. 486). Perhaps the most distinctly relevant phrase from Jewish Hellenistic writings is in Test. Naphth. 7. 1, δεῖ ταῦτα πληρωθῆναι. But, so far as I have been able to test, there are not many relevant uses of πληροῦν in this area.

(D) *Secular literature*. In secular literature, τελ-words seem to be commoner than πληροῦν in the sort of clause we are considering. But here are some miscellaneous specimens presented more or less in chronological order. The classes into which they fall are obvious enough.

v B.C. Hdt. viii. 144: ἡ χάρις (debt of gratitude) ἐκπεπλήρωται (has been discharged).

iv B.C. Plato *Gorg.* 63 p. 507E: ταύτας [ἐπιθυμίας] ἐπιχειροῦντα πληροῦν.

iii B.C. Herodian 2. 7. 6: τὰς ὑποσχέσεις οὐκ ἐπλήρου τῶν χρημάτων (i.e. promises of money).

ii. B.C. Polybius 1. 67. 1: μὴ οἷον τὰς ἐλπίδας καί τὰς ἐπαγγελίας ἐκπληροῦν.

i/ii A.D. Epictet. 2. 9. 3: ὅταν τὴν ἐπαγγελίαν πληρωσῇ; 2. 9. 8: οὐκ ἐπλήρωσας τὴν ἐπαγγελίαν.

i/ii A.D. Plut. *Cic.* 17.5: πεπληρωκέναι τὸ χρεών (fulfilled the requirement. This is in a reference to Cornelius Lentius' false hopes, based on fictitious Sibylline oracles about the 'third Cornelius'. Two before him (Cinna and Sulla) had already fulfilled the oracles' requirement.)

ii A.D. Polyaenus 1. 18: τοῦ λογίου πεπληρωμένου (i.e. an oracle

---

42 *Philonis opera*, vii (Berlin, 1926).

25

which said - ὁ θεὸς ἔχρησε - that the Athenians would conquer the Peloponnesians if the Athenians' king was killed by a Peloponnesian. Codrus, disguised as a woodcutter, was killed by an unwitting Peloponnesian. The Athenians raised a paean - because the logion was fulfilled). ii/iii A.D. Alexander Aphrodisiensis *fat.* 31, 11. 2 p. 202, 21: ὅπως πληρωθῇ τὸ τῆς εἱμαρμένης δρᾶμα. vi A.D. Procopius of Gaza *ep.* 68: πληρῶσαι. . . ἐλπίδας. ? *Vita Thuc.* 1. 8: ἐπλήρωσε τὰ μεμαντευμένα.

(E) When we come to the New Testament, the most obvious fact is that the Gospels, taken together, present a comparatively high number of πληροῦν-phrases belonging to the various types with which we are concerned. But beyond that easily stated observation, matters become more complicated. By far the greatest number of significant πληροῦν-phrases are in Matthew. Next in order of frequency comes John. Then Luke-Acts; and, finally, Mark, with two. The full list for the New Testament (including compounds ἀνα-, συν-) is as follows.* Matt. i. 22; ii. 15; iv. 14; xii. 17; xxi. 4: ἵνα πληρωθῇ τὸ ῥηθέν. . . ; ii. 23; viii. 17; xiii. 35: ὅπως πληρωθῇ τὸ ῥηθέν. . . ; ii. 17; xxvii. 9: τότε ἐπληρώθη τὸ ῥηθέν. . . ; iii. 15: πληρῶσαι πᾶσαν δικαιοσύνην; v. 17: οὐκ ἦλθον κατα-λῦσαι ἀλλὰ πληρῶσαι; xiii. 14: ἀναπληροῦται αὐτοῖς ἡ προφητεία Ἡσαΐου. . . ; xxvi. 54: πῶς οὖν πληρωθῶσιν αἱ γραφαί; 56: ἵνα πληρωθῶσιν αἱ γραφαὶ τῶν προφητῶν; xxiii. 32: πληρώσατε τὸ μέτρον τῶν πατέρων ὑμῶν. One less relevant occurrence: xiii. 48.

Mk i. 15: πεπλήρωται ὁ καιρός; xiv. 49: ἀλλ' ἵνα πληρωθῶσιν αἱ γραφαί; xv. 28: καὶ ἐπληρώθη ἡ γραφὴ ἡ λέγουσα (but *falsa lectio*).†

Lk. i. 20: οἵτινες (λόγοι) πληρωθήσονται. . . ; iv. 21: σήμερον πεπ-λήρωται ἡ γραφὴ αὕτη. . . ; ix. 31: ἣν (ἔξοδον) ἤμελλεν πληροῦν ἐν Ἰερουσαλήμ; xxi.§ 24: ἄχρι οὗ πληρωθῶσιν καιροὶ ἐθνῶν; xxii. 16: ἕως ὅτου πληρωθῇ (τὸ πάσχα) ἐν τῇ βασιλείᾳ τοῦ θεοῦ; xxiv. 44: δεῖ πληρωθῆναι πάντα τὰ γεγραμμένα. Other, less relevant, occurrences: ii. 40; iii. 5; vii. 1; viii. 23; ix. 51.

Jo. vii. 8: ὁ ἐμὸς καιρὸς οὔπω πεπλήρωται; xii. 38, ἵνα ὁ λόγος Ἡσαΐου τοῦ προφήτου πληρωθῇ; xiii. 18; xvii. 12; xix. 24, 36: ἵνα ἡ

[* There should be added πίμπλημι, which, unimportant in Matt. (xxii. 10, xxvii. 48), occurs in Luke-Acts, significantly at Lk. i. 23, 57, ii. 6, 21, 22, xxi. 22. Of these, all except xxi. 22 are of completion of periods. Other occurrences are not significant.

† Add the 'Freer *logion*' (at xvi. 14), with πεπλήρωται ὁ ὅρος τῶν ἐτῶν τῆς ἐξουσίας τοῦ σατανᾶ.

§ Add: 22: τοῦ πλησθῆναι πάντα τὰ γεγραμμένα.]

## Fulfilment-words in New Testament kerygma

γραφὴ πληρωθῇ; xv. 25: ἵνα πληρωθῇ ὁ λόγος ὁ ἐν τῷ νόμῳ αὐτῶν γεγραμμένος...; xviii. 9: ἵνα πληρωθῇ ὁ λόγος ὃν εἶπεν (ὁ Ἰησοῦς). Other, less relevant, occurrences: xii. 3; xvi. 6; (with χαρά) xv. 11; xvi. 24; xvii. 13.

Acts i. 16: ἔδει πληρωθῆναι τὴν γραφήν...; iii. 18: ὁ δὲ θεὸς ἃ προκατήγγειλεν ... ἐπλήρωσεν οὕτως; xii. 25: πληρώσαντες τὴν δια-κονίαν; xiii. 25: ὡς δὲ ἐπλήρου Ἰωάννης τὸν δρόμον; 27: ...τοῦτον ἀγνοήσαντες καὶ τὰς φωνὰς τῶν προφητῶν ... κρίναντες ἐπλήρωσαν; 32 f.: τὴν πρὸς τοὺς πατέρας ἐπαγγελίαν γενομένην ... ταύτην ὁ θεὸς ἐκπεπλήρωκεν...; xiv. 26: τὸ ἔργον ὃ ἐπλήρωσαν; xix. 21: ὡς δὲ ἐπληρώθη ταῦτα. Other, less relevant, occurrences: ii. 1, 2, 28; v. 3, 28; vii. 23, 30; ix. 23; xiii. 52; xxiv. 27.

Rom. viii. 4: ἵνα τὸ δικαίωμα τοῦ νόμου πληρωθῇ; xiii. 8: ὁ γὰρ ἀγαπῶν τὸν ἕτερον νόμον πεπλήρωκεν; 10: πλήρωμα οὖν νόμου ἡ ἀγάπη. Gal. v. 14: ὁ γὰρ πᾶς νόμος ἐν ἑνὶ λόγῳ πεπλήρωται...; vi. 2: οὕτως ἀναπληρώσετε τὸν νόμον τοῦ Χριστοῦ. Col. iv. 17: βλέπε τὴν διακονίαν ... ἵνα αὐτὴν πληροῖς. I Thess. ii. 16: εἰς τὸ ἀναπληρῶσαι αὐτῶν τὰς ἁμαρτίας. II Thess. i. 11: ἵνα ... πληρώσῃ πᾶσαν εὐδοκίαν ... Jas ii. 23: ἐπληρώθη ἡ γραφή. Other, less relevant, occurrences (not including πλήρωμα): Rom. i. 29; xv. 13, 14, 19; I Cor. xiv. 16; II Cor. vii. 4; x. 6; Eph. i. 23; iii. 19; iv. 10; v. 18; Phil. i. 11; (χαρά) ii. 2, 30; iv. 18 f.; Col. i. 9, 25; ii. 10; II Tim. i. 4; (χαρά) I Jo. i. 4; (χαρά) II Jo. 12; (ἔργα) Rev. iii. 2; (σύνδουλοι) vi. 11.

Out of all these there is only one instance of the actual correlatives 'promise and fulfilment' together, and that is in Acts xiii. 32 f.:[43] καὶ ἡμεῖς ὑμᾶς εὐαγγελιζόμεθα τὴν πρὸς τοὺς πατέρας ἐπαγγελίαν γενο-μένην, ὅτι ταύτην ὁ θεὸς ἐκπεπλήρωκεν τοῖς τέκνοις ἡμῶν ἀναστήσας Ἰησοῦς, ὡς καὶ ἐν τῷ ψαλμῷ γέγραπται τῷ δευτέρῳ...

Outside the Gospels and Acts, there is in the New Testament only one other instance of πληροῦν applied to any sort of scripture-fulfilment, and that is the very curious passage in Jas ii. 23, to· which we must return later. But fulfilment as applied to Law, which, as has already

43 It has been said that 'promise-fulfilment', does not actually occur in the New Testament, but this verse (using ἐκπληροῦν) is the one exception. See Franz Hesse, *Das Alte Testament als Buch der Kirche* (Gütersloh, 1966), p. 69; and cf. N. A. Dahl in Keck and Martyn, *Luke-Acts*, p. 142. It is implied, though not fully expressed, in the προεπηγγείλατο of Rom. i. 2. In the Old Testament there is, of course, no one word exactly corresponding to promise. In Hatch and Redpath's LXX Concordance, the only Hebrew equivalent of ἐπαγγέλλειν is אָמַר; of ἐπαγγελία, אֲגֻדָּה, סְפֹרָה (!), פָּרָשָׁה. Ὑπόσχεσις and ὑπισχνεῖσθαι occur only in the Greek books.

27

been stated, is not irrelevant to our theme, occurs outside the Gospels in Paul. And it is in the Pauline corpus also that πληροῦν is applied in a subtle way to the apostolic mission.[44] Other uses, both literal and metaphorical, of πληροῦν-words in the New Testament hardly, if at all, belong to our present concern; but perhaps I may be allowed to ask a question in passing: Why is πληροῦν used with χαρά* as its object in both John, I and II John, and Phil. ii. 2, whereas with ἀγάπη the verb is always τελεῖν?[45] That, however, is by the way.

But before going further it is time to turn to what is perhaps the most significant single passage, for our theme, in the whole New Testament, namely, Matt. v. 17, μὴ νομίσητε ὅτι ἦλθον καταλῦσαι τὸν νόμον ἢ τοὺς προφήτας· οὐκ ἦλθον καταλῦσαι ἀλλὰ πληρῶσαι. The story of this much-debated verse is perhaps nowhere told with more meticulous thoroughness (to his own date, at least) than by Henrik Ljungman in his book *Das Gesetz Erfüllen, Matt. 5, 17 ff. und 3, 15 untersucht* (Lund, 1954).[46] His particular importance for the present discussion is that he challenges the view which had become almost an axiom ever since the time of Dalman, that the Semitic equivalent of πληρῶσαι in this saying would be a part of the verb קום. We are familiar enough with the use of הקים, represented by ἱστάναι or βεβαιῶσαι, to mean 'confirm', and some of my illustrations in section II have included examples of this. And there is certainly something in common between the confirming or establishing signified by קום and the idea of fulfilment; so much so, indeed, that the מלא of the Old Testament is rendered in the Targums by a form of קיים (Ljungman, pp. 28, 32), the one clearly standing as a synonym for the other. But Ljungman's painstaking examination of the facts shows that we have no right to assume, merely on the basis of the Targumic usage, that Matthew's πληρῶσαι (supposing there were a Semitic original behind it) would represent קום rather than מלא.[47] In the LXX there is, as a rule, a perfectly clear distinction between the two roots: קום is generally represented by ἱστάναι (*T.W.N.T.* vi, 292) or βεβαιοῦν, never by πληροῦν, and מלא by some one of the

44 See Bouttier, 'Remarques'.
45 Cf. I Clem. l. 3. Is the answer, conceivably, because love can, by definition, never be *fulfilled* (cf. Rom. xiii. 8), although it can be mature?†
46 For his conclusions, see especially pp. 33–6.
47 See especially pp. 27 f.
[* So ἔργα in Rev. iii. 2.]
[† The Johannine rule is maintained even to the adjective: ἡ τελεία ἀγάπη, I Jo. iv. 18.]

## Fulfilment-words in New Testament kerygma

πληρ-group (and not once by ἱστάναι - Ljungman, p. 31).[48] Further, Ljungman appeals to the element of *completeness* that attaches, strictly speaking, to πληροῦν.[49] He maintains, accordingly, that when in Matt. v. 17, πληρῶσαι (over against καταλῦσαι) is applied to Law, it ought to mean more than merely 'carry out the dictates of the Law', or 'discharge its obligations' (over against 'breaking' it); more, also, I think one may add, than 'confirm the validity of the Law', for which Paul uses ἱστάνομεν in Rom. iii. 31, over against the opposite, καταργεῖν. It means, rather, 'bring to its final conclusion all that the Law stood for'.

Of course, there is no denying that πληροῦν and τελεῖν are sometimes used synonymously, and some of the quotations offered in section II illustrate the fact. Part of the overlap is due to the fact that the sense 'terminate', proper to τελ- words, can easily be represented also by πληροῦν as meaning 'complete'. There may sometimes even be a purely stylistic factor at work in the selection of these two words, as was asserted by A. Descamps when he wrote, of the use of πληροῦν as applied to Law, 'le mot reste un sémitisme. Le thème s'exprime mieux par les verbes plus grecs: τελεῖν et τελειοῦν.'[50] The usage of the Epistle to the Hebrews, to which I have alluded already, is, perhaps, an example of this. On the other hand, the degree of synonymity must not be exaggerated, and it is worthy of note that this Epistle is particularly concerned with the *incompleteness* of the Jewish Law, and it may be this theme, rather than mere stylistic factors, that has determined the use of τελεῖν, τελειοῦν, 'to finish'. At any rate, most striking of all is the parallel use of the two roots in John. Not only is there the curious phenomenon, already noted, of πληροῦν χαράν in contrast to τελεῖν ἀγάπην, but also ἵνα (ἡ γραφή) πληρωθῇ and ἵνα τελειωθῇ ἡ γραφή side by side, xix. 24, 28. This is in keeping with a well-known tendency of the

48 In Hatch and Redpath, the equivalents, taking into account all forms of מלא, verbal and nominal, and including Ecclus (to the date of Hatch and Redpath's appendix), are: ἅλων, ἅλως, ἀναπληροῦν, ἀναπλήρωσις, ἀφαίρεμα, γέμειν, γέν(ν)ημα, ἐμπιπλᾶν, ἐμπιπλάναι, ἐμπλήθειν, ἐπακολουθεῖν, ἐπισυνάγειν, καταριθμεῖν, κατασκεύασμα, κυοφορεῖν, λαμβάνειν, πιμπλάναι, πληθύνειν, πλήρης, πληροῦν, πληροφορεῖσθαι, πλήρωμα, πλήρωσις, συμπληροῦν, συμπλήρωσις, συντελεῖν, τελειοῦν, τελείωσις. Some of these, as will be immediately recognized, are freaks. Τελειοῦν represents only מלא את ידו (='consecrate'); τελείωσις = מִלֻּאִים only; συντελεῖν occurs only twice (Gen. xxix. 27; Dan. x. 3).
49 Cf. Longenecker, *Paul*, pp. 139 f.
50 *Les Justes et la Justice dans les Evangiles et la Christianisme primitif hormis la doctrine proprement paulinienne* (Louvain, 1950), p. 116 (cited by Ljungman, *Das Gesetz Erfüllen*, p. 25).

Fourth Evangelist to use synonyms, apparently simply for the sake of variety; but to this we must return again later, to consider whether there is not more than that to the Johannine phenomena.

It is because of this occasional synonymity of πληροῦν with some other word that Bauer is able to group, under a single section of his analysis of πληροῦν, a series of meanings which cover all my previous categories: 'durch die Tat *erfüllen* eine Voraussage, eine Verpflichtung, ein Versprechen, ein Gesetz, eine Bitte, einen Willen, ein Verlangen, eine Hoffnung, eine Obliegenheit, ein Verhängnis, ein Schicksal u ä...' It would seem that one could scarcely have a more comprehensive word. But Bauer's definition, perfectly correct though it is, must not deceive us into thinking that the two roots are used with equal frequency for all these senses. The incidence of πληροῦν, as we are now witnessing, is far more limited. Accordingly, Ljungman's thesis that – other things being equal – we ought to give full weight to the distinctive completeness that properly inheres in the meaning of πληροῦν, is worthy of serious consideration. G. Delling, in his articles πληρόω and τελέω in *T.W.N.T.*, seems to register agreement with this opinion. Referring back to the earlier article (πληρόω), he writes, on τελέω (viii, 60, Anm. 6): 'Zu dem in der Anwendung par[allelen], der Herkunft u[nd] deshalb dem speziellen Wortgehalt nach nicht synon[ymen] πληρόω→ [siehe] vi. 296, 2 ff.' (Cf. also *ibid.* p. 292.) That is the point. Words that strictly are not synonymous are often used loosely as though synonymous, when no particular issue hangs on the choice; but that does not prevent the choice of one word rather than another being significant, when there is reason to believe that the choice was a considered and deliberate one. And incidental support seems to be given to the view that, where it is used deliberately and strictly, πληροῦν emphasizes filling to capacity or accomplishing without remainder by the fact that the Hebrew idiom מִלֵּא אַחֲרֵי evidently means 'to follow *wholeheartedly*, with *undivided* loyalty'.[51] A comparable use in Greek is that of Rev. iii. 2, οὐ γὰρ εὕρηκά σου ἔργα πεπληρωμένα ἐνώπιον τοῦ θεοῦ

---

51 Num. xiv. 24; xxxii. 11 f.; Deut. i. 36; Josh. xiv. 8, 9, 14; I Kings xi. 6, paraphrased by LXX (except in I Kings xi. 6, where it is lacking) by some phrase of 'following' (ἐπηκολούθησέν μοι, etc.). That in I Kings xi. 6 the phrase is evidently parallel to לֵב שָׁלֵם, καρδία τελεία (v. 5, LXX 4) is only another example of the 'loose' synonymity already referred to. In I Kings i. 14, where וּמִלֵּאתִי אֶת־דְּבָרָיִךְ is sometimes taken to mean 'I will confirm your story', it might mean, rather, 'I will ... tell the whole story'; LXX renders literally, πληρώσω τοὺς λόγους σου.

μου.[52] Again, in II Kings ix. 24, מָלְאָה יָדוֹ בַקֶּשֶׁת (LXX ἐπλήρωσεν . . . τὴν χεῖρα αὐτοῦ ἐν τῷ τόξῳ) means 'drew the bow *at full stretch*'. It is, perhaps, ironical that Paul uses the phrase πεπληρωκέναι τὸ εὐαγγέλιον τοῦ Χριστοῦ in Rom. xv. 19 in a context where it is widely recognized that he cannot mean that he has fully evangelized all the areas he specifies. But it seems, nevertheless, that, even if he is thinking of key centres only, he does mean that, within these terms, he has *finished* the task and discharged it *completely*.

Now, in the case of Matt. v. 17, the use of πληρῶσαι in a single phrase relating to both Law and Prophets in the context of the Sermon on the Mount compels us to take notice of its sense. It is perfectly true, of course that the object of the verb is, in the case of πληροῦν-clauses, the decisive factor; and that πληροῦν can, when governing inferior objects, be debased to an inferior meaning. It is perfectly true that Luke can use the same verb (Lk. xxiv. 44) and apply it to Law, Prophets, and Psalms – in other words the whole Scriptures – in a context which practically compels us to interpret it in the shallower sense of prediction-fulfilment (as in Matthew's formula-citations). But in the context of Matt. v. 17, we are compelled to ask ourselves whether something special is not meant by a claim to be 'fulfilling' law and prophets, made in the same breath as the claim, 'It was said to them of old, but I say to you. . .' Are we not driven by the context to say that πληρῶσαι here implies something far deeper than mere prediction-verification? Does not fulfilling the Law in a way which is evidently far deeper than the merely legal imply also fulfilling the Prophets in a way far deeper than merely predictional? 'Insofar as the Law bears witness to the will of God as an ideal yet to be achieved, and the Prophets hold out hope of a time coming when it shall be fulfilled, one who perfectly fulfils the will of God confirms also the predictions of prophecy.'[53] Jesus is the one who brings to its perfect expression the ideal relationship between God and man expressed in the covenant-theme of the Torah and in the ideals of the great Prophets of Israel, and, in doing so, even through death to resurrection, fulfils all that the Law stood for.[54] Ljungman, accordingly, interprets the fulfilling of the Law in Matt v. 17 along the same

---

52 For a religious–philosophical use in a strictly comprehensive sense, see Philo, *leg. alleg.* i. 23.
53 From my article 'Fulfil' in *The Interpreter's Dictionary of the Bible*, edd. G. A. Buttrick *et al.* (Nashville, 1962), pp. 327 ff. (328b).
54 For the idea of bringing words to expression, cf. Philo's phrase, πληρῶσαι τοὺς λόγους ἔργοις ἐπαινετοῖς *praem. poen.* 83 (cited in *T.W.N.T.* vii, 286 and noted under (C), p. 25, above).

lines as St Paul when, in Gal. v. 14, he says ὁ γὰρ πᾶς νόμος ἐν ἑνὶ λόγῳ πεπλήρωται, ἐν τῷ Ἀγαπήσεις τὸν πλησίον σου ὡς σεαυτόν (cf. Rom. xiii. 9 f., ... πλήρωμα οὖν νόμου ἡ ἀγάπη). And similarly Siegfried Schulz, more recently, writes: ' "Erfüllung" kann hier [i.e. in Matt. v. 17] also nur "verwirklichen" bedeuten. Der irdische Jesus verwirklicht eschatologisch das ganze Gesetz, das will heissen: den grundsätzlichen und allein wesentlichen Gotteswillen, wie er in den zehn Geboten als den fundamentalen Geboten der Gottes- und Nächstenliebe und den Antithesen unverrückbar und bleibend zum Ausdruck gebracht ist.'[55] Schulz believes that Matthew radically Christianizes the Old Testament and Jewish notions of Law.

It would take us too long if we now followed Ljungman in his examination of that other crucial Matthaean passage, namely, iii. 15, with its difficult πληρῶσαι πᾶσαν δικαιοσύνην. The main point is, I hope, sufficiently clear - namely, that, within the ambit of the type of phrase under examination, מלא/πληροῦν seem, strictly and properly used, to signify a completeness and finality which are germane, even though they are not by any means always so used, to more than prediction-verification, and which belong, rather, to the completion and full realization of a personal relationship, involving an ethical and moral 'fulfilment' of God's will. If Lk. xxiv. 44 uses it (as has already been remarked) in a prediction-fulfilment context, it comes into its own in Acts xiii. 16 ff., because of the choice there of the pregnant theme of II Sam. vii as the main prediction. (Is this, it may be asked in passing, a reflexion of the greater depth of Paul's own mind?) And, again, if one of Mark's few examples (i. 15) referes only to καιρός, yet it may imply a significantly complete and final coming of the eschatological epoch.

But, if there is anything in the suggestion that πληροῦν properly implies more than mere implementation or discharge, why is it that the New Testament so often uses it in contexts of mere prediction-verification? Matthew and John, who between them account for most of its significant uses, are particularly prone to this shallow usage. Conversely, does not the profound and theologically significant use of τελεῖν and τελειοῦν in Hebrews (and here and there also in John) give the lie to the notion that there is any special meaning in πληροῦν?

In reply to these questions, certain observations may be made. First, as I have already suggested (p. 29 above) the use of τελεῖν and τελειοῦν in Hebrews may be explained by the fact that the special concern of this writer is the termination (and supersession) of the old covenant by

55 *Die Stunde der Botschaft* (Hamburg, 1967), p. 182.

the new. For this theme, a termination-word is more appropriate than a completion-word. To the Johannine usage I will return in a moment. About the Matthaean use of πληροῦν the most obvious fact is that by far the greater number of occurrences is accounted for by the 'formula-quotations': and, since these are largely homogeneous and stylized, one need only postulate the selection of πληροῦν (by the evangelist or his source) in a single, initial instance, and the rest would naturally follow. Yes: but why that initial selection? Is mere chance a sufficient explanation? My 'non-πληροῦν' tables offer us a wide range of alternative forms of expression. The formula for Matthew's testimonia might easily, instead of employing πληροῦν, have taken any of the following shapes : (1) τοῦτο δὲ ὅλον γέγονεν ἵνα (a) βεβαιωθῇ, or (b) σταθῇ, or (c) συμβῇ, or (d) τελειωθῇ. . .; (2) τοῦτο δὲ ὅλον ἐστὶν (ἐκεῖνο) ὃ ἐλάλησεν. . . And there are other variations which tables (1) and (2) above (pp. 17 ff.) might suggest. That the comparatively rare πληροῦν was nevertheless, chosen thus still calls for some explanation, even if the multiplication of the formula, once chosen, is not statistically significant.

The very tentative suggestion that, with acknowledgements to R. N. Longenecker, I offer – simply for consideration – is that the use of מלא in its deeper, stricter sense, may, just possibly, have been characteristic of the language of Jesus himself; and, if so, that this fastened the word in the Christian vocabulary, wherever there were Semitic forms of the traditions and a Semitic context. Its most obvious equivalent, πληροῦν, came correspondingly into the Greek forms of the tradition. And Christians, not themselves always grasping its full significance, used the word with less discrimination. I have already argued that the fuller, deeper meaning is unconsciously pointed to by the Christology of the New Testament generally, despite a failure to recognize the inferior value of mere prediction-verification.[56] It would be in keeping with this if the evangelists found the word in their traditions and gave it a wider, less discriminating currency.

This idea that it came in via actual words of Jesus is suggested by R. N. Longenecker in the book already cited. He quotes[57] S.-B. and J. Jocz, *The Jewish People and Jesus Christ* (London, 1949), p. 26, for the usual view that πληρῶσαι in Matt. v. 17 represents קיים, and asks (like Ljungman) whether this is so assured; and then goes on to ask whether it may not have been, rather, that Jesus himself used מלא. Without pursuing the matter, he simply adds the following references, where alleged λόγια Ἰησοῦ contain the word: Lk. iv. 21; Mk i. 15

56 The New Testament writers would have endorsed Philo's aphorism οὐδὲν . . . λεχθὲν παρέργως εὑρήσεις *leg. alleg.* iii. 147.     57 *Paul*, pp. 139 f.

33

(καιρός); Lk. xxiv. 44; Matt. xxvi. 54; Mk xiv. 49; Matt. iii. 15; v. 17. Of these, Lk. xxiv. 44 (in the post-resurrection setting) is, as we have seen, a disappointingly shallow use; but the others - mostly general - could well bear out the idea. And there is one other alleged saying of Jesus which is worthy of remembrance, which is not in Dr Longenecker's list only because it does not expressly concern the fulfilment of Scripture. This is Lk. xxii. 16: ... οὐκέτι οὐ μὴ φάγω αὐτὸ [τὸ πάσχα] ἕως ὅτου πληρωθῇ ἐν τῇ βασιλείᾳ τοῦ θεοῦ. The Passover gathers up into itself a large number of various strands of covenant-promise: to speak of its 'full realization' is to use the root we are considering in a highly significant manner. But of course we know that Luke himself can use the verb in this pregnant way: Lk. ix. 31, ... τὴν ἔξοδον αὐτοῦ, ἣν ἤμελλεν πληροῦν ... Be this as it may, I believe that it is worthy of consideration - I cannot say more - whether Jesus himself did not inject the intensification of the מלא /πληροῦν group into the Christian vocabulary. If there is anything in this suggestion, then we must simply acknowledge that John sometimes uses τελειοῦν as exactly parallel to πληροῦν for the sake, simply, of variety. There appears to be absolutely no difference in sense between ἵνα ἡ γραφὴ πληρωθῇ (xix. 24) and ἵνα τελειωθῇ ἡ γραφή (xix. 28). This would be in keeping with his acknowledged habit of rendering traditional *pericopae* in his own vocabulary. On the other hand, there is no need to assume that the famous τετέλεσται of Jo. xix. 30 is the same as πεπλήρωται. What is the implied object of τελεῖν in this case? The Johannine thought as a whole suggests the answer; the task which God has given to his Son to complete (not τελεῖν but τελειοῦν is used in all the specific references to this - iv. 34; v. 36; xvii. 4 - but the change is hardly significant). And, if so, then τελεῖν, 'to complete', 'to terminate', is eminently suitable, and does not encroach upon the special meanings of πληροῦν.[58]

(F) An examination of the Apostolic Fathers[59] shows that the use of πληροῦν in the relevant senses, though not frequent, tends simply to follow the New Testament, but more often in reference to *Torah* than to prophecy. The same - but with an even further diminution in frequency - applies to the early Apologists.[60]

---

58 The usage of the Peshitta is interesting; τελεῖν (xix. 28, 30) and τελειοῦν (iv. 34; v. 36; xvii. 4) is rendered by ܐ ; τελειοῦν in xvii. 23 (of the disciples, τετελειωμένοι εἰς ἕν) by ܐ , and in xix. 28 (of ἡ γραφή) by ܐ : i.e. the only use in relation to scripture is rendered by מלא ; for the completing of the task, שלם is used.

59 In E. J. Goodspeed's *Index Patristicus* (Leipzig, 1907).

60 E. J. Goodspeed, *Index Apologeticus* (Leipzig, 1912).

Ign., *Trall*. xiii. 3: πιστὸς ὁ πατὴρ ἐν Ἰησοῦ Χριστῷ πληρῶσαί μου τὴν αἴτησιν καὶ ὑμῶν; *Smyrn*. i. 1: ἵνα πληρωθῇ πᾶσα δικαιοσύνη (=Matt. iii. 15). Polycarp, *Phil*. iii. 3: πεπλήρωκεν ἐντολὴν δικαιοσύνης. *Mart. Polyc*. xii. 3: ἔδει γὰρ τὸ τῆς ὀπτασίας πληρωθῆναι; xiv. 2: καθὼς προητοίμασας καὶ προεφανέρωσας καὶ ἐπλήρωσας. *Diogn*. ix. 2: ἐπεὶ δὲ πεπλήρωτο μὲν ἡ ἡμετέρα ἀδικία... Barn. xxi. 8: ἀναπληροῦτε πᾶσαν ἐντολήν. I Clem. xxv. 2. 5 (of Phoenix's time). Hermas, *Vis*. iii. 3. 2: αἱ γὰρ ἀποκαλύψεις αὗται τέλος ἔχουσιν, πεπληρωμέναι γάρ εἰσιν. Justin, *Dial*. xii. 3: πεπληρωκέναι τὸ θέλημα τοῦ θεοῦ φατέ; xlv. 1; l. 3 (= discharge, complete); xciii. 2: ἐν δυσὶν ἐντολαῖς πᾶσαν δικαιοσύνην καὶ εὐσέβειαν πληροῦσθαι.

Finally, and bearing in mind the suggestion that the word in the New Testament came into prominence because of a specially significant use but then came to be used less precisely and more generally, we return to that strange usage in Jas ii. 22 f. Arguing against 'faith without works', the writer appeals to the instance of Abraham, and first says that his faith was *completed* by his deeds (ἐκ τῶν ἔργων ἡ πίστις ἐτελειώθη), and then that the scripture which says that Abraham believed God and it was reckoned to him for righteousness was *fulfilled* (ἐπληρώθη ἡ γραφὴ ἡ λέγουσα Ἐπίστευσεν κ.τ.λ.). But the scripture in question is itself a retrospective description of this very action and attitude of Abraham: it is neither *Torah* nor prediction nor promise but narrative concerning precisely what James says was its fulfilment. It would seem that its writer is using πληροῦν quite thoughtlessly, as though he had pulled it out of his vocabulary merely because the word γραφή (with which, by now, it was perhaps habitually associated) 'triggered it off'. If so, it is conceivably a scrap of further evidence for a Christian standing usage, when the context is Semitic or quasi-Semitic, and adds urgency to the question, How did this usage come into existence?

The latter part of what I have laid before you is extremely speculative, and I present it more as a series of unanswered questions than as a solution of a problem. It concerns itself chiefly with the reason for the concentration of πληροῦν-phrases in the New Testament, and especially in the Gospels. But my main point is, I believe, a secure one. Promise and fulfilment is a wide and loosely-used phrase that requires definition. If one attempts to define it so as to give it the distinctiveness which belongs to its strictly Christian application, it must be along the lines of an achievement, by God himself in Jesus Christ, of the covenant-promise

35

in terms of a fully personal relationship - which, through its long history, has been struggling towards such a fulfilment. It is not merely that the time of Jesus is ἡ ἐσχάτη ὥρα; much more significantly, Jesus is himself ὁ ἔσχατος Ἀδάμ. This personal achievement, in Jesus Christ, is a collective and corporate fulfilment, as well as an individual one; and it sets in motion a new train of relationships inherited by the Christian Church, to whose corporate achievement the words can then be applied in a new way. The actual use of the מלא /πληροῦν group in such contexts is limited in extent; but it is also fluid and imprecise in application; it is other Christological indications that help us, today, towards a more precise and discriminating use of its equivalents. As so often happens, the distinctive insights of the New Testament need, in our day, to be reformulated, often with the help of words that are not in the New Testament vocabulary (e.g. personality, personal values, sonship).

# 2

## Jesus in New Testament Kerygma
### for G. Stählin

The main purpose of this paper is (1) to re-examine and call in question an assertion that has frequently been made over the past century – that Paul was not interested in the historical Jesus.[1] But, since the discussion of this question involves asking what the Pauline epistles were for and in what category they should be classified in contrast to other Christian writings,[2] a further inquiry springs quite naturally from it by way of contrast, namely, an inquiry (2) into the purpose and category of the Synoptic Gospels. And the comparative study of the purpose and category of the Gospels and the Pauline epistles respectively involves, finally (3), a brief reassessment of the structure and contents of Christian evangelism or 'initial preaching'. A question-mark is thus placed (or replaced, for it has been done again and again before)[3] against several assumptions which are characteristic of much current New Testament scholarship. Whether or not this is acceptable (many of my German colleagues, whose friendship I greatly value, will, I am afraid, view it only as a typically English tilting at windmills), it is at any rate offered, with high regard and friendship, to a scholar who has always had the courage to pursue truth without deference to prevailing fashions.

1 For authoritative accounts of the debate, see W. G. Kümmel, 'Jesus und Paulus', *Heilsgeschehen und Geschichte: Gesammelte Aufsätze 1933–1964* (Marburg, 1965), pp. 81 ff. and 439 ff.; and V. P. Furnish, 'The Jesus–Paul Debate: from Baur to Bultmann', *B.J.R.L.* 47 (1964-5), 342 ff.

2 On the differences in 'perspective' between them, see a fresh and interesting study by D. T. Rowlingson, *The Gospel-Perspective on Jesus Christ* (Philadelphia, 1968).

3 Not to mention earlier writers, a considerable list could be made of contemporary writers. Among these, note, in England (though published in U.S.A.) J. J. Vincent, *Secular Christ* (Nashville and New York, 1968), especially pp. 153 f.; in Germany, W. G. Kümmel, *passim*, but especially 'Jesus and Paulus' (= *N.T.S.* 10 (1963-4), 163 ff.); and G. Ebeling, *Theologie und Verkündigung: Ein Gespräch mit Rudolf Bultmann* (Tübingen,[2] 1963), 19 ff. (57 ff.).

I

It is a common practice to declare that Paul, and, indeed, the early Church generally, was not interested in the story or the personality of Jesus. Paul, it is alleged, did not know Christ 'after the flesh', neither did he care about this kind of information. One or two examples, arbitrarily chosen, will illustrate the attitude. Bultmann, in his celebrated essay, 'Die Bedeutung des geschichtlichen Jesus für die Theologie des Paulus',[4] wrote:

> *Jede 'Würdigung' der 'Persönlichkeit' Jesu fehlt* und muß fehlen, da sie nur ein γινώσκειν κατὰ σάρκα wäre, in Doppelsinn, daß solches γινώσκειν den Christus nur als einen Christus κατὰ σάρκα, d. h. als ein vorfindliches Weltphänomen sehen würde, und daß es eben deshalb ein γινώσκειν κατὰ σάρκα, ein fleischliches Verstehen, ein bloßes Rechnen mit Weltlich-Vorfindlichem wäre...
> (pp. 206 f.).

Again:

> Man darf also nicht hinter das Kerygma zurückgehen, es als 'Quelle' benutzend, um einen 'historischen Jesus' mit seinem 'Messiasbewußtsein', seiner 'Innerlichkeit' oder seinem 'Heroismus' zu rekonstruieren. Das wäre gerade der Χριστὸς κατὰ σάρκα, der vergangen ist. Nicht der historische Jesus, sondern Jesus Christus, der Gepredigte, ist der Herr (p. 208).

And again:

> Wenn also Paulus sagt, daß *die entscheidende Heilstat Christi* ὑπακοή *und* ἀγάπη ist, so sind damit nicht die Charaktereigenschaften des historischen Jesus gemeint (Phil 2, 6 ff.; 2 Kor 8, 9; Röm 5, 18 f.; 15, 1 f.), die ja als ὑπακοή und ἀγάπη gar nicht anschaulich sind. Die betreffenden Stellen reden vielmehr vom Präexistenten . . . (p. 213).

In the same vein, E. Käsemann could write:

> Vor allem muß auffallen, daß nur die Evangelien die Christusbotschaft im Rahmen der Geschichte des irdischen Lebens Jesu darbieten. Mögen die andern Schriften gelegentlich darauf verweisen, daß sie nicht ohne Kunde von diesem Leben geblieben

---

4 *Th. Bl.* 8 (1929), 137 ff. (= *Glauben und Verstehen* I (Tübingen, 1933), 188 ff.).

sind, Wichtigkeit besitzt für sie im Grunde doch nur das Geschehen von Kreuz und Auferstehung. Die Historie Jesu ist bei ihnen also in erstaunlichem Maße zusammengeschrumpft. Man kann sogar sagen, sie sei überhaupt nur noch als Schatten vorhanden. Denn Kreuz und Auferstehung werden ja nicht mehr unter dem Aspekt des Historikers betrachtet, sondern nach ihrer Heilsbedeutung entfaltet. Von da aus gesehen, will es geradezu seltsam erscheinen, daß wir im NT so etwas wie Evangelien vorfinden, die sich mit dem irdischen Leben Jesu befassen.[5]

Now, on examination, it appears that the allegation that Paul and the rest were not concerned with the story or personality of Jesus but only with the plain fact of his existence – the mere 'daß'[6] – rests on four pillars. (1) First, there is this much-quoted phrase from II Cor. v. 16 with κατὰ σάρκα, which we have just met in the quotations from Bultmann. (2) Secondly, there is what might be called Paul's 'declaration of independence' in Gal. i. 11 f. (3) Thirdly, there is the fact that, in the entire Pauline *corpus*, very little reference is made to the story of Jesus. (4) Fourthly, there is the fear that attention to the story and personality of Jesus may distort a true, transcendental faith, in the direction of a rationalistic, Liberal Protestant exemplarism. But if we look at these four pillars in turn, we shall see what a rickety support they are for the massive structure that is set upon them.

(1) Regarding II Cor. v. 16, there are excellent reasons for believing that the crucial phrase, κατὰ σάρκα, has nothing whatever to do with the question of historicity. Long ago, none other than F. C. Baur wrote: 'κατὰ σάρκα erkannte er Christus, solange er nur die nationaljüdische Vorstellung vom Messias hatte, und das Wesentliche dieser Vorstellung war, daß der Messias keines solchen Todes sterben sollte, wie der Tod Jesu war'.[7]

Baur was right in recognizing that κατὰ σάρκα does not refer adjectivally to Χριστός, but adverbially to the verbs of knowing (though he was probably wrong in thinking that the manner of knowing in question was a nationalistic, messianic manner, and still further astray in driving

5 'Das Problem des historischen Jesus', *Z.T.K.* 51 (1954), 125 ff. (= *Exegetische Versuche und Besinnungen* I (Göttingen, 1960), 187 ff., 192 f.). Cf. U. Wilckens, 'Tradition de Jésus et Kérygme du Christ', *R.H.P.R.* 47 (Strasbourg, 1957), 1 ff.; *idem* 'Hellenistisch-christliche Missionsüberlieferung und Jesustradition', *T.L.Z.* 89 (1964), 518 ff.

6 See W. Schmithals' summary of the view in: *Die Theologie Rudolf Bultmanns* (Tübingen, 1966), pp. 200 f.

7 *Vorlesungen über neutestamentliche Theologie* (Leipzig, 1864), p. 131.

his notorious wedge between Paul and the early Jerusalem community: but that is a long story). Similarly, J. Weiss saw[8] that κατὰ σάρκα went with the verb, not with the noun (though he, too, interpreted it implausibly, in terms of knowing Jesus in his human, earthly nature). But it was F. C. Porter[9] who presented a thorough statement of the case for κατὰ σάρκα (again, taken adverbially with the verbs of knowing) meaning 'from the point of view of selfish interests'. That this interpretation does justice to the parallelism between the two halves of the verse is a decisive point in its favour; for one is almost compelled to find a sense of 'knowing κατὰ σάρκα' which will make sense both with οὐδένα and with Χριστόν as its object, and the apostle could hardly have been saying that henceforth he had no knowledge of anybody as an historical person. But if he was saying that his mode of knowing (and that of others also, if they were Christians) has been changed, under the constraint of Christ's love (*v.* 14), from a self-interested mode to a mode characterized by ἀγάπη, this makes good sense, both with Christ and with others as object. Much more recently, and with more specific reference to Paul's Gnostic opponents, J. L. Martyn has argued[10] that Paul was contrasting γινώσκειν κατὰ σάρκα with what (by implication) he understood as γινώσκειν κατὰ σταυρόν – knowing in the way in which one knows 'at the painful and glorious juncture of the ages'. If Porter's exegesis, or Martyn's more sophisticated variant, is accepted, or even allowed to be plausible, then we must agree with W. G. Kümmel when he says:[11] 'Über die Frage der Bedeutung des geschichtlichen Jesus für Paulus, gibt [2 Kor] 5[16] . . . Keinerlei Auskunft'; and 'pillar number one' collapses.

8 *Paulus und Jesus* (1909). (The German original was not available to me. In the English translation, *Paul and Jesus*, trans. H. J. Chaytor (London, 1909), it is on pp. 43 f.). Also *Das Urchristentum*, posthumously edited by R. Knopf (Göttingen, 1917), pp. 137 ff., pp. 347 ff.

9 'Does Paul claim to have known the Historical Jesus? A Study of 2 Corinthians 5[16]', *J.B.L.* 47 (1928), 257 ff. Porter points out that his interpretation had already been recognized as possible (though not decisively adopted) by W. M. L. de Wette, in his *Kurzgefasstes exegetisches Handbuch zum NT* (Leipzig, 1836), *in loc.* Subsequently, T. W. Manson confirmed it in: 'St Paul in Ephesus: (4) The Corinthian Correspondence', *B.J.R.L.* 26 (1941–2), pp. 327 ff. (341) (= 'The Corinthian Correspondence (2)' in: *Studies in the Gospels and Epistles*, ed. M. Black (Manchester, 1962), pp. 210 ff. (224).

10 'Epistemology at the Turn of the Ages: 2 Corinthians 5, 16' in *Christian History and Interpretation: Studies Presented to John Knox*, W. R. Farmer, C. F. D. Moule, and R. R. Niebuhr edd. (Cambridge, 1967), pp. 269 ff. (285).

11 Lietzmann's *Kommentar* (4. ergänzte Aufl. Tübingen, 1949), p. 205.

(2) The second pillar consists of appeal to the heated assertions which Paul makes in Gal. i. about his independence of the Jerusalem apostles, especially in *vv.* 11 f. But it is at least as plausible to interpret this of his divine commissioning to preach the gospel to the Gentiles as of the content of the message. In any case, Paul is explicit in Gal. ii. 2 about his checking his message by the Jerusalem tradition. Thus, at the very least it must be said that Galatians provides no secure support for the theory that Paul neither knew nor cared about the historical traditions. Rather the contrary.

(3) What of the third pillar, the argument from silence? Some arguments from silence are legitimate. This one is demonstrably unreliable, and it is amazing that it has been allowed such a long run in scholarly fields. It is demonstrably unreliable, simply because there is no reason why Paul should have shown interest in the story of Jesus (however much he felt it) in letters written, for highly specialized purposes, to persons who were already Christians. For this reason, to argue that, because there are few allusions in the epistles to the Jesus-traditions, therefore the writer was not concerned with them, is a major blunder in classification. If the epistles represented Paul's evangelistic gospel and the substance of his primary proclamation, then of course we should be justified in deducing that the story of Jesus did not interest him. But they simply do not represent anything of the sort. All the prolegomena are assumed in them, because he is addressing Christian congregations.[12]

12 The point was tersely made by the late J. Munck of Aarhus, when he wrote. 'It is important at the outset to realize that though we have none of Paul's sermons, they must have differed in form at least from his letters', *The Acts of the Apostles*, Anchor Bible (New York, 1967), p. 127. See also so recent a work as O. Merk, *Handeln aus Glauben* (Marburg, 1968), p. 19; also, C. W. F. Smith, *The Paradox of Jesus in the Gospels* (Philadelphia, 1969), p. 184. But as long ago as 1858 it was stated at length by Heinrich Paret, in an article (referred to by Furnish, *B.J.R.L.* 47 (1964–5); p. 343, n. 4), 'Paulus und Jesus: einige Bemerkungen über das Verhältnis des Apostels Paulus und seiner Lehre zu der Person, dem Leben und der Lehre des geschichtlichen Christus', *Jahrbücher für deutsche Theologie* 3 (Stuttgart, 1858), 1 ff. This was a criticism of Baur's general position; and even in those days, he had to apologize for the observation as one 'welche man sehr trivial nennen mag', and to defend it as 'notwendig gegenüber von einer Kritik, welche bei allem Scharfsinn oft gerade das Einfachste und Nächstliegende nicht sieht oder nicht sehen mag' (p. 9). He then points out (pp. 9–11) how inevitable it is that Paul must, especially in Gentile contexts, have characterized and identified the Jesus whom he was preaching, and he sketches the points and the disputes involved in this; and then he continues (p. 11): 'Freilich, diese grundlegenden Auseinandersetzungen

And on the rare occasions when he does refer back to his initial preaching, he begins to use narrative terms. It so happens that even such references are very limited, because, when he does make them it is to remind his readers of only one or another specific matter within the initial preaching: in Gal. iii. 1 and I Cor. ii. 1 f. it is the crucifixion; in I Cor. xv. 1 ff. it is the resurrection. Thus, even here there is no ground for finding an index of his whole gospel. Incidentally, it is possible that certain other words and phrases in the Pauline epistles reflect a greater knowledge of the 'Gospel' traditions than is sometimes allowed.[13] But even if these are altogether discounted, the non-occurrence of such allusions would prove nothing at all as to Paul's interests, or the contents of his initial preaching, simply because the epistles are not the sort of documents that can yield such evidence. Like Paret (see n. 2 on p. 41), I recognize that this is an elementary point, and may even seem trivial; but disregard of it has dramatically warped the judgement of generations of scholars. Even V. P. Furnish, who, in a recent work of his,[14] makes the point I have been labouring, namely, that the epistles are addressed to already established Christian congregations, continues: 'It is, however, both reasonable and necessary to presume that Paul's letters in general reflect the themes and perspectives of his "preaching" as such. One important function of his letters is to remind his congrega-

haben wir in seinen Briefen, welche ja alle an bereits Überzeugte (Gläubige) geschrieben sind, nicht, können sie auch hier nicht erwarten. Die große Masse der geschichtlichen Mittheilungen über Jesum gehörte jedesmal jener Zeit an, wo er, nach seinem eigenen bildlichen Ausdrucke, eine Gemeinde zeugte (I Kor 4, 15), Ammendienste an ihr versah (I Thess 2, 7) und sie mit Milch nährte (I Kor 3, 2).' Baur made a contemptuous reply to Paret in the third edition of *Das Christenthum und die Christliche Kirche der drei ersten Jahrhunderten*, (¹1853). (This edition is not available to me except in an English trans., London, 1878, p. 50, n. 2.) But Baur only dealt with Paret's attempt to find *Jesusüberlieferung* in Paul; like so many of his successors, he ignored the decisive point about the nature and purpose of the epistles.

13 Resch's enthusiasm is rightly suspected (see, e.g. V. P. Furnish, *Theology and Ethics in Paul* (Nashville and New York, 1968), pp. 52, 59); but see C. F. D. Moule, 'The use of Parables and Sayings as Illustrative Material in Early Christian Catechesis', *J.T.S.* n.s. 3 (Oxford, 1952), 75 ff. (pp. 50 ff. below); H. Riesenfeld, 'Le Langage parabolique dans les épîtres de saint Paul', *Recherches bibliques* 5 (1960), 47 ff.; X. Léon-Dufour, *Les Evangiles et l'Histoire de Jésus* (Paris, 1963), pp. 66 ff.; and cf. (though in a different vein) J. P. Brown, 'Synoptic Parallels in the Epistles and Form-History', *N.T.S.* 10 (Cambridge, 1963-4), 27 ff.

14 *Theology and Ethics.*

tions of the gospel he had preached to them and to reaffirm its essential points'. But how does Dr Furnish know this? I whole-heartedly agree with him when (pp. 106 ff.) he refuses to make a sharp distinction between 'kerygma' and 'didache'; but it does not seem to me to follow that therefore the epistles show us all that Paul put into his *initial* kerygma.

The only evidence that might legitimately lead to some estimate of what Paul's initial gospel contained, and of whether or not he and other early evangelists were interested in the portraiture of Jesus, would be evidence outside the epistles relating to the proclamation of the Gospel to unbelievers. For this – if, for the moment, we postpone the discussion of the Gospels – the main evidence is in the Acts. Of course we have no right to assume that this faithfully represents the manner of the early preaching, and there are many who believe that the Acts sermons are late, purely imaginative constructions. But, at the very least, they show how one Christian writer within the New Testament period conceived of the preaching of the gospel. What is the evidence of the sermons and descriptions of preaching in Acts?

The answer is that it is only sketchy. But, as far as it goes, it contains at least some instances of sermons in which the proclamation of the death and resurrection of Christ is supported by narrative material (though in a highly compressed or abbreviated form) similar to what is found in the Gospels.

In Ch. viii, Philip the evangelist is represented (*v.* 12) as 'proclaiming the good news about the Kingdom of God and the name of Jesus Christ' - a hint, at least, of narrative content. In *vv.* 26 ff., preaching to the Ethiopian eunuch, Philip first identifies Jesus as the one who, according to Isa. liii, was denied justice and put to death; and goes on to proclaim the good news which is Jesus (εὐηγγελίσατο αὐτῷ τὸν Ἰησοῦν) - a sufficiently pregnant phrase. Peter's sermon to Cornelius and his friends (Ch. x) contains a notable approximation to 'Gospel' content. First, the story is located; it is set in the whole of Judaea (i.e. Palestine) beginning from Galilee after John the Baptist's mission. And then, it is duly described as concerning Jesus of Nazareth, and how God anointed him (made him Messiah) with the Holy Spirit and power, and how he went about doing good and curing all who were under the tyranny of the devil, because God was with him; and how he was killed, by hanging on a 'tree', and raised by God, and shown, not to all the people, but to chosen witnesses, who ate and drank with him after his resurrection, and who were commissioned by him to proclaim that he is the one appointed by God to be Judge of living and dead. It is to him (so runs the climax of the sermon) that all the prophets bear witness, saying that everyone who believes in him may receive forgiveness of sins through his name.

Then come the Pauline 'sermons'. The one in Ch. xiii, at Pisidian Antioch, starts by putting the story in its setting of Old Testament promise; then it mentions the ministry of the Baptist, and his reverential reference to his successor; and then comes the climax, in the death and resurrection – all according to Scripture – and the promise of a forgiveness in Christ which could not be had from the Mosaic system. This presentation is heavily weighted in the direction of scriptural attestation; but as far as it goes, with its mention of the Baptist as well as of the death and resurrection, it follows the 'Gospel' pattern.

The addresses at Lystra in Ch. xiv, and before the Areopagus in Ch. xvii, are specialized attacks on idolatry, and are scarcely representative 'Gospel'; but the very abbreviated allusion to evangelizing in a Synagogue at Thessalonica in xvii. 2 f., while it represents, once again, arguments from Scripture to prove Jesus to be Messiah, suggests also that Jesus had to be described: ... οὗτός ἐστιν ὁ Χριστός, ὁ Ἰησοῦς, ὃν ἐγὼ καταγγέλλω ὑμῖν. The argument from Scripture is again indicated for Beroea, in xvii. 11. As for Paul's words to the defective 'disciples' at Ephesus (xix. 4 f.), these take up again the witness of the Baptist to Jesus (cf. xiii. 25), like the beginning of a Gospel. But of course their main point is simply the contrast between the Baptist's baptism and Christian baptism, and there is probably no intention here of representing full-scale preaching.

Acts xx. 17 ff. is particularly interesting, as the exact counterpart, in Acts, to the situation implied in the epistles. It is an appeal to those who had already been evangelized. Paul addresses the elders of the Ephesian Church, declaring that he had faithfully discharged his task as an evangelist, and that it is for them now to remain faithful and to beware of the ravages of false teachers. He had no occasion to repeat his initial evangelism; but he briefly alludes to it in terms of announcing all God's purpose (*v.* 27, ἀναγγεῖλαι πᾶσαν τὴν βουλὴν τοῦ θεοῦ), warning and admonishing them (*v.* 31, νουθετῶν), and telling them the story of God's graciousness, which can build them up and give them their share among all God's dedicated people (*v.* 32, ... τῷ λόγῳ τῆς χάριτος αὐτοῦ, τῷ δυναμένῳ οἰκοδομῆσαι καὶ δοῦναι τὴν κληρονομίαν ἐν τοῖς ἡγιασμένοις πᾶσιν). Finally, and significantly, he recalls an otherwise unknown saying of Jesus (*v.* 35, Μακάριόν ἐστιν μᾶλλον διδόναι ἢ λαμβάνειν), which he is evidently deemed to have told them before. All this is exactly in the manner of the epistles, which assume, but also

44

occasionally allude to, initial evangelism, and also - as in I Cor. vii - show a knowledge of the sayings-traditions. The Pauline addresses in Chh. xxii, xxiii, xxiv, xxvi are an *apologia pro vita sua*, and not primarily evangelistic, although the usual appeal to the fulfilment of prophecy does occur. Finally, in xxviii. 23 we are given the content of Paul's discourse with the Jews at Rome: . . . οἷς ἐξετίθετο διαμαρτυρόμενος τὴν βασιλείαν τοῦ θεοῦ, πείθων τε αὐτοὺς περὶ τοῦ Ἰησοῦ ἀπό τε τοῦ νόμου Μωϋσέως καὶ τῶν προφητῶν . . . This, as far as it goes, is reminiscent of the Synoptic Gospels.

Thus, the only evidence outside the epistles and the Gospels themselves, even if it amounts to nothing more objective than what seemed appropriate to a narrator of the ancient world, represents the apostolic message as containing the kind of material that is to be found in the Gospels. And what is there implausible about that? The epistles, by reason of their purpose and character, could not be expected to contain such material; but the Gospels, and the earlier traditions to which they point, bear witness to the existence of such material; common-sense shows that it would be likely to be used in explaining Jesus to hearers who had not known him; and, so far as it goes, the Acts endorses this. Where is the necessity to adopt this strange dogma about Paul's neglect of it? What is there scientific about the dogma? So much for 'pillar number three'.

II

This brings us (deferring number four for the time being) to consider the relation between the Gospels and the Epistles from the other end, asking what is the purpose of the Gospels.[15] Nothing is more fashionable, at the moment, than to say that Mark is a theologian. Indeed, some would say that he is a Pauline theologian.[16] But what is there distinctively Pauline in Mark? And what is there in Mark that is theologically reflective and explanatory at all, in the sense in which the

15 An unpublished Cambridge dissertation by G. N. Stanton* goes into detail over this question, especially with reference to Luke, and I owe much (including some references in this essay) to Dr Stanton. See also my essay, 'The Intention of the Evangelists' in *New Testament Essays: Studies in Memory of T. W. Manson*, ed. A. J. B. Higgings (Manchester, 1959), pp. 165 ff.

16 See e.g. V. Taylor, *The Gospel according to St Mark* (London, 1952), pp. 125 ff.

[* Now published as *Jesus of Nazareth in New Testament Preaching* (Cambridge, 1974).]

Johannine and Pauline writings are? Indeed, what is there in any of the Synoptic Gospels, until their 'post-resurrection' charges, that is comparable even to the summary proclamation of forgiveness in Acts ii. 38, or xiii. 39? Of course, all the implications of the story of Jesus are necessarily theological. That goes without saying. But it is an error in method to assume, without further evidence, that the intention of the Synoptic Evangelists was to do more than provide an account of the character of Jesus' teaching and ministry and the circumstances leading to his death and resurrection. Of course they do this, unavoidably, from the standpoint of a conviction about Jesus as Christ and Son of God. But it is a mistake to start by assuming that a Gospel must have been concerned with the summons to faith and commitment which forms the climax of Christian preaching,[17] or with the elaboration of faith and commitment and guidance for the life of Christian communities such as are the concern of the epistles, and, accordingly, to read these interests into the Gospels, whether or not there is good evidence for their presence. The method of *Formgeschichte* is perfectly right in always asking about the purpose of a *pericope* or a document. Where it so often goes wrong is in its assumption that Christians never opened their mouths or put pen to paper except with a view to eliciting an existential decision or combating opponents. It is every bit as probable, if one is going to make *a priori* assumptions, that they often made statements and told stories about the pre-resurrection ministry of Jesus, with a view to conveying an impression of his person and his message, and explaining how he fell foul of the authorities. Indeed, the burden of this essay is that the proclamation of the Christian message is incomplete and meaningless without this element.

## III

Thus, we have to guard against a 'dogma' about the Gospels which is – though not quite so extreme – the converse of the 'dogma' which I have

---

17 By 'Christian preaching' in this context I mean initial evangelism, not the Gemeindepredigt on which N. A. Dahl's essay, 'Formgeschchtliche Beobachtungen zur Christusverkündigung' in *Neutestamentliche Studien für R. Bultmann*, ed. W. Eltester (Berlin, 1954), pp. 3 ff., throws valuable light. Furnish, *Theology and Ethics*, pp. 109 f., denies this distinction; but it seems to me that, however often the gospel is repeated to the already evangelized, it still remains likely that its initial form will be distinctive, so that this initial form cannot be deduced from subsequent (partial) repetitions alone.

been atta:king about the epistles. To the epistles it is fashionable to deny any interest in the historical Jesus; from the Gospels (except, of course, from the much-belaboured Luke!) it is fashionable to demand, though not narrative, yet the whole range of Christian faith and commitment. Instead of this, common-sense (coupled, one may add, with the evidence of the plain sense of what is before our eyes) suggests that the Synoptic Gospels, and the earlier traditions to which they were the successors, provide an essential part, though only a part, of the total presentation of the Christian message.[18] The evidence we have recalled, and the contents of the Gospels, and, indeed, practical experience of evangelism in our own day all confirm this conclusion: descriptive narrative is an essential part, though only a part, of preaching 'Jesus, crucified and raised according to the Scriptures'. Not only the *dass* but also the *wie* is essential. T. Boman has suggested, in a very interesting study,[19] that, in the early days, there was a class of narrators, whose work supplemented that of the preachers. This is a step in the right direction, in that it recognizes these two activities as complementary; but it is difficult to find direct evidence for his narrators, and, *a priori*, it is difficult to believe that the two activities could be thus separated and given to different functionaries. It is one thing to collect the narrative elements into a separate book, a Gospel, for the benefit of evangelists and catechists. It is another matter to imagine that the actual proclamation of the Christian message could be thus departmentalized. A more plausible form of Boman's idea was put forward in an *obiter dictum* some years earlier by G. J. Paul, when he wrote:[20] 'It may be that Mark was taken on Paul's first missionary journey because his eye-witness reminiscences supplied an element in the Gospel-preaching that neither Paul nor Barnabas could supply. Perhaps Silas, also a Jerusalem man, was taken on the Second Journey for similar reasons.' This would mean, not that evangelists habitually left narration to other functionaries, but that an evangelist who was conscious that he had not the material in as cogent a form as possible might be glad to take with him one who had. He took, as it were, a 'gospel source' with him, in the form of a person acquainted with the facts.

In sum, then, it ought to be possible to read the epistles for what

18 The point is well made by J. H. Reumann, *Jesus in the Church's Gospels* (Philadelphia, 1968), pp. 27 f.

19 *Die Jesus-Überlieferung im Lichte der neueren Volkskunde* (Göttingen, 1967), pp. 42 ff., 45, and *passim.*

20 *St John's Gospel: a Commentary* (Christian Literature Society, for the Senate of Serampore College, 1965), p. 26, n. 1.

they were - pastoral letters, addressed to Christians in whom a knowledge of the gospel is presupposed, designed to meet specific dangers and problems and to elucidate how and why the gospel is effective, and to repulse false substitutes. In this respect, the epistles belong to the reflective, analytical, theological stage, and the level on which the appropriation of salvation and the implementation of its results are prominent concerns. Equally, it should be possible to recognize in the Synoptic Gospels collections of material designed to characterize and explain Jesus and thus to provide an element without which the proclamation of his death and resurrection and the summons to faith in him would be meaningless. The Fourth Gospel is the only New Testament writing which combines in one book the narrative, and the reflective, theological comment, and the summons to faith. This it does, quite explicitly. But it is a major blunder in method to assume that the other documents are meant to perform all these functions, despite the lack of evidence for such intentions, and then to draw conclusions from their one-sidedness, whether about the nature of the Christian message or about the concerns of St Paul. It is quite unthinkable that Paul, or any other evangelist, could have preached the message of the cross without a lively concern for the facts about the crucified. The mere *dass* is not enough: the *wie*, is indispensable; and this must have been provided, from the earliest days, by the sort of material that was ultimately collected in the Gospels. It is time that ungrounded fantasies about the range, respectively, of Gospels and epistles were recognized for what they are, and the wholeness of the Christian gospel reaffirmed. A recent writer, whose words form a fitting summary of the matter, has put it vigorously in a little book that is written for popular use but is not the less scholarly for that. He has been describing the bare, creed-like character of what is ordinarily called the kerygma. He continues:

> But it would be a mistake of the first magnitude to imagine that here, in isolation, we have reached the source or matrix of all the NT writings, still less the ground of its unity . . . The propositions which faith uses to express itself are always provisional, relative to the thought-patterns of the day, never to be identified with the reality itself. Creeds are useful maps, but never to be confused with the territory itself. If anyone doubts this, let him read again the 'kerygma' outlined above, and ask if, on its own, it would ever convert a fly - even a first-century Palestinian fly – let alone one of the twentieth-century European variety.[21]

21 T. G. A. Baker, *What is the New Testament?* (London, 1969), pp. 19 f.

I think that the fourth 'pillar' (which would, had it been necessary, have occupied stage I (4) in the scheme of this essay) has silently toppled by itself, and needs no more attention.[22]

22 As a postscript to Section I of this paper, Dr P. Pokorny of Prague observed to me in conversation that, if we had no Fourth Gospel, some might have surmised that the circle from which the Johannine Epistles emanated had no concern for the sort of material that the Gospel contains. This is a further comment on the mistake of treating an epistle as a full statement of the writer's 'gospel'.

# 3

## The Use of Parables and Sayings as Illustrative Material in Early Christian Catechesis

Archbishop Carrington, Dr Selwyn, and others have made us familiar with the idea of a more or less definable body of teaching for catechumens underlying the New Testament writings; but less attention seems to have been given to the possibility that a body of illustrative material consisting of parables, allegories, and familiar authoritative sayings may also have been current for use in the same connexion, although this is indeed implied by the belief entertained by many scholars that some of the material of this sort in the gospels is to be traced to early catechists and preachers rather than to the Lord himself.

This note, an attempt to ask some questions in relation to this matter, was suggested by the fact that the Lucan story of Martha and Mary (Lk. x. 38–42) provides a curiously apt pictorial illustration of the attitude alluded to by St Paul in I Cor. vii. 35, and is also strikingly close to that verse in vocabulary.[1] St Paul says that his object in urging the single estate is not to cast a snare upon them (is this curious metaphor itself an allusion to some image now lost to us?), but πρὸς τὸ εὔσχημον καὶ εὐπάρεδρον τῷ Κυρίῳ ἀπερισπάστως, 'with a view to their behaving in a decorous way, duly seated by the Lord without distraction'. This precisely describes Mary's condition in the Lucan story: Martha περιεσπᾶτο, 'was distracted', about the task of waiting at table; but Mary παρακαθεσθεῖσα πρὸς τοὺς πόδας τοῦ Κυρίου ἤκουεν τὸν λόγον αὐτοῦ. One cannot help wondering, therefore, whether this story, which St Luke was later to include in his gospel, was not already current, perhaps orally, and whether St Paul was not mentally drawing upon it to illustrate his ethical teaching.[2]

With this clue is it possible, perhaps, to find further echoes of 'Gospel' material, again in a predominantly Lucan form, in the passage

---

1 As was observed long ago by (e.g.) Robertson and Plummer, *I.C.C. in loc.*

2 In I Cor. ix. 13 παρεδρεύοντες τῷ θυσιαστηρίῳ, the verb παρεδρεύω is used in a cultic connexion, and E. B. Allo, *in loc.*, adduces evidence of a similar use from elsewhere. But that does not mean that εὐπάρεδρον is necessarily cultic.

50

about wealth in I Tim. vi? Verses 17-19 contain injunctions for those
who are rich ἐν τῷ νῦν αἰῶνι, 'in the material sense': they are not to be
conceited, ὑψηλοφρονεῖν, nor to pin their hopes on so uncertain a thing
as wealth, but rather to fix them on the generosity of God; they are to
be rich in good deeds, and to be generous, thereby treasuring up for
themselves a good foundation for the future; that is, they are to lay
hold upon life that really is life (cf. also verse 12). But all this is well
illustrated by the Lucan parable of the Unjust Steward, who made plans
for his future by generosity (albeit with stolen wealth), and is held up
(apparently) as a lesson in foresight, with the injunction to use 'Mam-
mon' to make friends who, when riches fail, may receive you into
eternal abodes. In the same context (Lk. xvi. 14, 15) comes the section (peculiar to Luke) about the sneers of the wealth-loving Pharisees,
who are rebuked, in words which include the phrase τὸ ἐν ἀνθρώποις
ὑψηλὸν βδέλυγμα ἐνώπιον τοῦ θεοῦ - suggesting that ὑψηλοφρονεῖν
is precisely the attitude which is condemned. In addition, of course,
the parable of the Rich Fool (Luke xii), with its moral οὕτως ὁ θησαυ-
ρίζων αὐτῷ καὶ μὴ εἰς θεὸν πλουτῶν, forms an apt illustration for the
passage in the Pastoral Epistles, not to mention the even more familiar
saying from the Sermon on the Mount about treasure in heaven. It
seems far from unlikely that the catechetical teaching represented in a
passage like I Tim. vi has been coloured by conscious reminiscences of
the sayings of the Lord, which may sometimes have been quoted in
illustration. In Phil. ii he himself is held up as the supreme example of
not snatching at personal gain. In the Fourth Gospel the double, or
'ambivalent', use of ὑψοῦν makes subtle allusion to the same theme.
One might possibly consider, in the same connexion, the imagery about
wealth, true and false, in the letter to Laodicea of Rev. iii. 17, 18 and
about feminine ornaments in I Pet. iii. 3. Such imagery, even if it does
not link up with any extant dominical sayings, at least indicates that
catechesis was not confined to the bare inculcation of rules for conduct
but was sometimes imaginative and pictorial.

Further parallels between pictorial material in the gospels and the
wording and thought of the other New Testament writings may now be
noted. In II Cor. ix St Paul is writing about the results of generous almsgiving, and in verse 10 what he virtually says is that the principle of
growth holds good for those who part with money for such a purpose
precisely as it holds good for the farmer who commits his seed to the
ground: 'he who supplies "seed for the sower and bread for food" (a
quotation from Isa. lv) shall supply and increase what you sow and give
growth to the produce of your almsgiving (δικαιοσύνης)'. Here, in other

words, is a perfect example of what we are told is the essence of a genuine dominical parable - namely, that it should appeal to one and the same law or principle as operative both in the physical realm and in the spiritual; and St Paul has adapted for his particular purpose the thought which underlies the parables of growth and the Johannine saying about the grain of wheat. It is noteworthy, also, that the figure of 'righteousness' as a 'crop' or 'harvest' yielded by Christian conduct occurs both in Heb. xii. 11 (chastening properly accepted yields the peaceful crop of righteousness) and Jas iii. 18 (righteousness is the crop yielded by the seed of peacemaking); and there is, of course, St Paul's use of the figure in Gal. v. 22 (the crop yielded by the Spirit): and in, Eph. v. 9 the 'harvest of light' consists of all goodness, righteousness, and truth. Again, it may be more than mere coincidence that the metaphor of catching fish or hunting (ζωγρεῖν) appears both in Lk. v. 10 (ἀνθρώπους ἔσῃ ζωγρῶν) and in II Tim. ii. 26 (ἐζωγρημένοι ὑπ' αὐτοῦ εἰς τὸ ἐκείνου θέλημα), although in the latter case it is notoriously ambiguous who is the captor - God or the Devil. Once more, the figure of the thief as applied to the furtive unexpectedness of the Day of the Lord occurs both in the gospels (Matt. xxiv. 43) and in I Thess. v. 2, 4, II Pet. iii. 10, Rev. iii. 3, xvi. 15.[3] Just possibly[4] the metaphor of struggling, as in athletic contest, as applied to prayer and Christian life, may reflect the supreme contest of the Lord in the garden of Gethsemane. Luke xxii. 44 uses ἀγωνία for the latter; and ἀγών, ἀγωνίζομαι are applied in several passages in the Epistles to things spiritual. It is, however, undeniable that Jo. xviii. 36 shows that the metaphor was not confined to spiritual struggles, being here used of the kind of fight which nationalist insurgents might be expected to put up in defence of their leader. With these suggestions in view one might classify New Testament ethical teaching according to the degree and manner of its illustrative material, in some such way as the following:

(1) The completely unadorned injunction. Examples are sufficiently plentiful, and scarcely need quoting. But it is perhaps worth while to note that Rom. xvi. 19, θέλω δὲ ὑμᾶς σοφοὺς εἶναι εἰς τὸ ἀγαθόν, ἀκεραίους δὲ εἰς τὸ κακόν looks like an unadorned version of the picturesque saying in Matt. x. 16 ('φρόνιμοι as serpents, ἀκεραίοι as doves'); and that I Cor. xiv. 20 is the same idea clothed in another metaphor: μὴ παιδία γίνεσθε ταῖς φρεσιν, ἀλλὰ τῇ κακίᾳ νηπιάζετε.

3 I owe this point to Miss M. E. Thrall of Girton College.*
4 A suggestion thrown out in conversation by the Rev. R. C. Walls of Kelham College [now of the Community of the Transfiguration].
[* Now Dr Thrall of the University College of North Wales, Bangor.]

(2) An injunction supported by an Old Testament quotation, e.g. I Cor. ix. 9 (muzzling the ox), I Pet. iii. 9-12 ('he who would see good days . . .'), and the continuation of the adornment passage just alluded to, I Pet. iii. 3 ff. (where the example of Sarah is used), II Pet. ii. 22 ('the dog returned to its vomit').

(3) An injunction supported by a gnomic saying, whether of Jesus or from general proverbial sources, e.g. Acts xx. 36 ('more blessed to give than to receive'), I Cor. ix. 7 (an appeal to the general principle that he who labours, as soldier, vinedresser,[5] or shepherd has a right to the rewards of his work - an appeal then reinforced by the scriptural quotation just alluded to), I Tim. v. 18 (the same Old Testament passage as in I Cor. ix. 9, but with the gospel saying added, 'the labourer is worthy of his hire'[6]), I Thess. v. 21 ('prove all things . . .'), II Pet. ii. 22 (where an apparently proverbial saying, 'the sow to its wallowing . . .', is added to the Old Testament proverb).

(4) Instruction illustrated by a full-length parable, allegory, or anecdote. Such would be any of the gospel parables or allegories which are not genuinely dominical but are creations of the early Church (if such there be), and the passages from which we began, if they were ever so expanded. St Paul's olive-grafting allegory and his appeal to the marriage laws to illustrate his gospel might also be adduced. It should be added that the passage in I Thess. v. 21 just alluded to may well contain an embryonic parable, especially if πάντα δοκιμάζετε is a banking metaphor, as is suggested by the γίνεσθε δόκιμοι τραπεζῖται with which it continues in some patristic quotations. Similarly, it has been suggested that καρπός in Phil. iv. 17 is a monetary metaphor and means 'interest'; in which case it can be classed with the parables of the talents and pounds. If this approach to the catechetical elements in the New Testament is sound, it may serve to bring into clearer light the manner in which not only the Old Testament Scriptures and proverbial wisdom but also the 'floating' units of the traditions about the Lord were applied by Christian pastors. It should be added that most of the gospel material adduced above as parallel to the Epistles is from St Luke, not (as one might have expected) from an undeniably Q source. Whether this is significant or not it is difficult to judge. It may be due to nothing more than the fact that most of the epistolary material of the New Testament is Pauline, and that St Paul was an intimate of St Luke.

5 Cf. Prov. xxvi. 18.
6 Note that, even in I Cor. ix, a dominical saying does also seem to be alluded to, although not quoted: verse 14, οὔτως καὶ ὁ Κύριος διέταξεν . . .

# 4

## The Ascension – Acts i. 9

### THE TEXT

Lk. xxiv. 44 'Then (δέ) he said to them, "These are my words which I spoke to you. . . ." ⁴⁹ "And behold, I send the promise of my Father upon you; but stay in the city, until you are clothed with power from on high." ⁵⁰Then (δέ) he led them out as far as Bethany, and lifting up his hands he blessed them. ⁵¹While he blessed them, he parted from them [and was carried up into heaven].¹ ⁵²And they returned to Jerusalem with great joy, ⁵³and were continually in the temple blessing God.'

Acts i. 2 '. . . until the day when he was taken up,. . . ³To them [the apostles] he presented himself alive . . . appearing to them during forty days, . . . ⁴And while staying [or, eating] with them he charged them not to depart from Jerusalem, but to wait for the promise of the Father. . . . ⁵". . . before many days. . . ." ⁹And when he had said this, as they were looking on, he was lifted up, and a cloud took him out of their sight. ¹⁰And while they were gazing into heaven as he went, behold, two men stood by them in white robes, ¹¹and said, "Men of

---

1 Om ℵ* D it (sy^sin seems to compromise ['while he was blessing them, he was lifted from them'] – see P. Benoit, in *R.B.* 56 (1949), 189). Jeremias (*The Eucharistic Words of Jesus*, E. T. Oxford, 1955, p. 99) holds that the longer text is original, the omission representing a harmonizing attempt to delete a reference to the Ascension on Easter day. A. N. Wilder (in *J.B.L.* 62 (1943)) also prefers the longer text (as does Benoit). J. H. Ropes, on the contrary (in F. J. Foakes Jackson and K. Lake edd., *The Beginnings of Christianity* (London, 1926), iii, pp. 259 f.), suggests that reference to the Ascension was absent originally not only from Lk. xxiv. 51, but also from Acts i. 2. In Acts i. 2 it is not omitted by any Greek ms., though there is variation in word order and though the Old Latin does omit it. In Acts i. 9 D sah have 'he was taken away' instead of 'lifted up' and omit 'as they were looking on'. The omission from Lk. xxiv. 51 (not confined to the 'Western' text) must be taken seriously; but the matter still leaves much scope for guess-work.

Galilee, why do you stand looking into heaven? This Jesus, who was taken up from you into heaven, will come in the same way as you saw him go into heaven." '

## THE PROBLEMS

Few of the Christian festivals are so hard on the preacher as Ascension-tide. Many formidable questions rear their heads. For instance, what, doctrinally speaking, are we to make of a distinction between the resurrection and the ascension, and what is the meaning of the ascension as a separate moment? Is the ascension the vindication of Christ? But that has already been established by the resurrection. Is it (as preachers sometimes say) his 'coronation'? But again – short of some creation-wide acclamation – no kingly crown could shine more brilliantly than that which the resurrection had already placed on the head of Christ. That he was alive meant already that he had conquered. What more, then, is needed? Or again, in what sense, if any, can the ascension be described as historical and what, in particular, are we to make of the forty days' interval between the resurrection and the ascension, alluded to in Acts i. 3 (cf. xiii. 31)? Is this fact or fiction?

## THE FORTY DAYS

This is far from the most important of the questions before us; but, since it is complex, it may as well be taken up at once. Only in Acts i. 3 is there any mention of forty days' interval.[2] All other references in the Gospels or Acts to an ascension or assumption[3] either must, or at least may, be taken as part and parcel of the Easter events.[4] They all point

---

2 Acts xiii. 31 alludes to the appearing of Jesus 'for many' (or, several) 'days'; x. 41 '. . . us. . . who ate and drank with him', specifies no period.

3 'Ascension' (going up) and 'assumption' (being taken up) amount to much the same thing (cf. 'resurrection' and 'being raised'). In I Pet. iii. 22 the verb is simply 'to go'; in Heb. iv. 14 Jesus has 'passed through the heavens'. There is also the verb 'to exalt'. Only at Lk. ix. 51 does a noun (ἀνάλημψις) appear.

4 They are: Lk. xxiv. 51 (in the longer text; and even in the shorter, a *parting* is referred to, apparently as having taken place on Easter day); [Mk] xvi. 19; Acts i. 2 (implying that it had already taken place before the events about to be narrated); i. 9 (supposing this verse were taken without reference to i. 3); ii. 33; Jo. xx. 17 (cf. iii. 13, vi. 62. Jo. xxi, however, describes a subsequent appearance in Galilee). Elsewhere in the New Testament allusions to Christ's ascension, assumption, or going heavenward are

in the direction of making 'resurrection' and 'ascension' interchangeable or identical, rather than of distinguishing them as two separate stages.[5] The terms used (as also the 'heavenly session') mean, broadly, Christ's glorification - the antecedents or accompaniment of the gift of the Spirit.[6] Thus, it will be as well to enquire forthwith whether the 'forty days' element really belongs to the author of the Acts at all. Its authenticity has been challenged from time to time, and among the most recent attempts to excise it is that of Dr P. H. Menoud of Neuchâtel.[7] There is not space here to discuss his arguments.[8] I can only say that I believe that, when examined, his case for interpolation is not a cogent one, at any rate on the literary level.[9] It may be remarked, further, that there are signs elsewhere in Luke-Acts of failure to revise the work;[10] and discrepancies may be easier to account for in this way than by assuming alien interpolation.

found in Eph. i. 20 (by implication), iv. 8 ff., I Tim. iii. 16, Heb. iv. 14 (cf. ix. 24), I Pet. iii. 22 and cf. Rom. x. 6. Incidentally there are striking parallels, as is well known, in Tobit xii. 16–22, where the angel Raphael divulges his identity. This causes alarm, but he says, 'Fear not ... I appeared to you (ὠπτανόμην ὑμῖν) all those days, yet I did not eat or drink but it was a vision you were seeing (cf. Lk. xxiv. 39–43, Acts x. 41). And now praise God, for I am ascending to him who sent me (ἀναβαίνω πρὸς τὸν ἀποστεί-λαντά με)...' And they saw him no more. But they acknowledged the great and marvellous deeds of God.

5 Cf. Barn. 15.9 ... τὴν ὀγδόην ... ἐν ᾗ καὶ ὁ Ἰησοῦς ἀνέστη ἐκ νεκρῶν καὶ φανερωθεὶς ἀνέβη εἰς οὐρανούς; Aristides, Apol. 15: μετὰ δὲ τρεῖς ἡμέρας ἀνεβίω καὶ εἰς οὐρανοὺς ἀνῆλθεν.

6 The chief Old Testament background is Ps. lxviii. 18, whether in its Rabbinic interpretation as quoted in Eph. iv. 8, which speaks of *giving* gifts, or in its Biblical form, alluded to, perhaps, in Acts ii. 33, which has *receiving* instead of giving. In either case, the Psalm was applied by Jewish interpreters to Moses, who ascended the mount to receive the Torah from God and give it to men (see Strack-Billerbeck on Eph. iv. 8 and H. Kretschmar in Z.K.G. 66 (1954–55), 209 ff.): and Christians saw in Christ the new Moses. Ps. cx. 1 '(the session at God's right hand) was also associated in Christian exegesis with the ascension.

7 'Remarques sur les textes de l'ascension dans Luc-Actes', in *Neutestament-liche Studien für Bultmann* (Berlin, 1954), pp. 148 ff.

8 See a discussion in E. Haenchen, *Die Apostelgeschichte* (Göttingen, 1956), pp. 115 ff.

9 Note, in passing, that there is no necessary discrepancy between Bethany (Lk. xxiv. 50) and the Mount of Olives (Acts i. 12): there is reason to believe that Bethany was on the Mount of Olives. See *The Beginnings of Christianity*, v, pp. 475 f.

10 See *Exp. T.* 65. 7 (April 1954), 220.

Perhaps the strongest evidence against the forty days, however, is from outside the New Testament. The early liturgical tendency seems to have been to celebrate the gospel as a whole, not piecemeal. Good Friday and Easter were one. Even Whitsun can only be traced back, as a separate festival, as far as Tertullian's time.[11] There seems to have been no separate festival of the Ascension until the latter part of the fourth century,[12] and then, as it seems, under the influence of the Acts chronology. The Ascension is mentioned as a festival earlier, but as observed on the same day as Pentecost - fifty, not forty, days after Easter.[13] Yet, all said and done, it is questionable whether evidence of liturgical observance necessarily constitutes evidence against the first disciples' actual experience or the narrative traditions. It may be a useful pointer to theological interpretation underlying liturgical practice; indeed, the New Testament itself, as we have seen, may conflate different 'moments' in its theological expressions (sometimes under the influence of Old Testament or Rabbinic concepts, as in the case of Ps. lxviii). But that does not necessarily mean that, in *narrative* form, the 'moments' were not from the first distinguishable. In religious art, all sorts of admittedly different incidents are often brought together in a single, collective scene, without any intention of denying their historical separateness. The only considerable non-Lucan *narrative* evidence which seems to contradict the forty days is [Mk] xvi. 19. But this is widely agreed to be of inferior accuracy, and is presumably more likely to have been theologically conditioned than Luke-Acts - for Luke is, after all, the self-confessed *narrator* of the New Testament (Lk. i. 1 ff.).

Supposing then, that, after all, the forty days are not so easily dismissed, what happens if we try to come to terms with them? We are faced with the old problem of the apparent discrepancy as between Jerusalem and Galilee in the post-Resurrection narratives.[14] Now, the

11 Unless Acts xx. 16 and I Cor. xvi. 8 are allusions to it as a *Christian* festival.
12 Augustine, *Ep.*, liv claims it as likely to have been initiated by the apostles themselves; but in fact, his is perhaps the earliest evidence.
13 Etheria (A.D. 389), *Peregrinatio ad loca sancta*, 43, alludes to a special feast at Bethlehem (for a suggested explanation, see J. G. Davies in *V.C.* 8 (1954), 93 ff.); but (as Kretschmar observes, *Z.K.G.* 66 (1954-55)), she expressly alludes to the Ascension as observed on the afternoon of the same day on which Pentecost was celebrated in the morning.
14 I am well aware of the prevailing fashion for interpreting 'Jerusalem' and 'Galilee' as essentially *theological* symbols, and therefore more or less giving up the search for *historical* tradition behind their use. But I confess that I am profoundly sceptical of such an attitude. At any rate, why not try once more treating them literally?

only circumstantial account of the beginning of the Christian Church among the apostles is St Luke's, who locates it at Jerusalem.[15] If, then, we try, for the moment, assuming that it began not at Passover-time but later, how much later would it be? The next most likely occasion for men of Galilee to be in Jerusalem is, of course, the next festival, namely Pentecost. And Pentecost, about fifty days after Passover, or about forty days after the octave of Passover (the end of the feast of Unleavened Bread), fits the forty days' appearances plus a short period of waiting. Where would the Galileans have been meanwhile? Surely, in Galilee. As soon as a festival was over, these people, who had no home, and indeed found even temporary lodging difficult enough, in Jerusalem or its environs, would naturally return home (cf. Lk. ii. 43, xxiv. 13). Nothing but an express command, or extraordinary circumstances, would hold them in Jerusalem, beyond the week of Unleavened Bread (at the end of which Jo. xx places the last Jerusalem appearance). In both Lk. xxiv. 49 and Acts i. 4 there *is* an express command to stay. But whereas Lk. xxiv. 49 admittedly seems to be in the paschal context, Acts i. 4 puts it shortly before Pentecost. The tradition of a command to stay is exclusively Lucan (assuming, now, the genuineness of the opening verses of Acts); and there seems to be no reason to believe that Luke's second thoughts (Acts i. 4) were not better informed than his first. Is there not some case, then, for believing that there is substance both in the Jerusalemite and in the Galilean traditions of appearances? In the interval between Passover-Unleavened Bread and Weeks (Pentecost), the disciples had naturally gone home to Galilee and had seen Jesus there, just as they had seen him in Jerusalem during the paschal octave; and Mk xvi. 7 προάγει ὑμᾶς εἰς τὴν Γαλιλαίαν (cf. Matt. xxviii. 7) need only mean 'When you return to Galilee (as you naturally will) you will find that he has preceded you.' The fact, moreover, that of all the Jewish festivals, only Passover and Pentecost were taken into the Christian calendar is also perhaps a pointer to Pentecost as a decisive point in the traditions.[16] And it must be noted that there is nothing

---

15 Besides Acts, note also Gal. i. 17. See, however, E. Lohmeyer, *Galiläa und Jerusalem F.R.L.A.N.T.* (Göttingen, 1936), for suggestions about a parallel development of Christianity in Galilee. It is interestingly discussed in F. C. Grant's *The Earliest Gospel* (New York, 1943), ch. 6; but however far one is prepared to go with Lohmeyer (and much of his thesis seems to rest on the slenderest evidence), it is still not wholly relevant to the beginning of the Church of the *Apostles*. For this, such evidence as there is points to Jerusalem, unless Matt. xxviii. 18-20 be pressed to mean the founding of the apostolic community in Galilee (see below).

16 See Kretschmar, *Z.K.G.* 66 (1954–55).

absolutely discrepant with this suggestion except Lk. xxiv. 49 ff., [Mk] xvi. 19 f., and Acts i. 2. Even the Matthaean commission (Matt. xxviii. 18-20) on a mountain in Galilee does not preclude a command to go up to Jerusalem for the forthcoming festival and start to implement the commission there.[17] Even the Johannine 'I am ascending' (Jo. xx. 17), and the account of the bestowal of the Spirit at Easter (xx. 22) do not tie us to a chronology, in view of the Fourth Evangelist's theological emphasis, and in view of the fact that, in any case, there follows the Galilean Ch. xxi (if it is Johannine). Is it not, then, simpler to postulate that Luke did alter his opinion about the chronology[18] when he wrote Acts i. 3 ff., without harmonizing the story, than to assume an interpolator who deliberately interpolates but has not the deliberateness to tidy up? The command to stay in the city, on that showing, was actually part of the events on the eve of Pentecost, though Luke did not find this out until he came to write Acts i. 3 ff., having previously supposed it to be Paschal.

## THE ASCENSION STORY

Would it follow that we must take quite literally the circumstantial account of the Ascension (Acts i. 9-11)? What is the modern mind to make of the upward movement, the intercepting cloud, the straining eyes of the disciples, the apparition of the evidently supernatural figures, and the promise that Christ would come again, exactly as he had gone? Is not such literalism altogether too crude for the integrity of a serious-minded person to-day? In reply, let it be said that it is questionable whether even St Luke himself, for all his known tendency to 'materialize',[19] was so literal-minded as to imagine that Jesus went up vertically and sat down a few miles above the visible sky. But he clearly believed that something significant did 'happen'; and whatever sort of historicity we are prepared to accord to the post-resurrection appearances generally, and (for that matter) to the transfiguration, ought not to be denied *a priori* to the ascension, although it is circumstantially

---

17 Cf. B. W. Bacon's suggestion (*Jesus and Paul* (New York, 1921), p. 113) that the manifestation to more than five hundred (I Cor. xv. 6) might have been just before the company of believers went up to Jerusalem at Pentecost.

18 See Benoit, *R.B.* 62 (1943), 193; and cf. M. S. Enslin, in *J.B.L.* 47 (1928), 61 and n. 2, 64, 72 (he thinks that the forty days is due partly to Pentecost being the term, partly to Biblical and apocryphal analogies).

19 As in the 'bodily form' of the dove at the baptism, and the 'flesh and bones' and the fish of Lk. xxiv. 39-42.

attested only in Luke-Acts and has peculiarities of its own. It is described as a decisive and deliberate withdrawal from sight, to be distinguished from the mere 'disappearance' in the Emmaus story (ἄφαντος ἐγένετο ἀπ' αὐτῶν). May we not accept it as such? It is a vision (if we choose to use that question-begging word) of the closing of a chapter. It is like an acted declaration of finality. Or (for this is equally true), it is an acted declaration of the opening of a new chapter; it is a matter of finality only within a certain period, for it is expressly linked with the hope of Christ's return. In short, there seems to be no intrinsic reason for not accepting the ascension as something (of course we cannot define precisely what) which vividly and ocularly conveyed these convictions to the disciples.[20]

## ST PAUL AND THE ASCENSION OF BELIEVERS

But if so, why does not St Paul endorse it? That he ignores the idea of the ascension as setting a term to the appearances, and (in I Cor. xv. 8) reckons the Damascus road encounter as another appearance of the Risen Christ in the same series as the others, is a well-known fact. It may, however, perhaps be explained along the following lines. 'Decisive withdrawal' obviously had meaning only to the disciples who had first known Jesus from the 'earthly' side, during his ministry. They had seen him risen, and they now had to learn that a term must be set to this type of intercourse. They must learn that Christ's risen body was not of this world only, but transcended it. St Paul, by contrast, began, as it were, at the opposite end. For him, 'the Lord from heaven' was the manner of his first experience of Jesus; and he naturally therefore ranked the Damascus road experience, for that reason, side by side with the encounters which, for the Eleven and their companions, were the beginning of their knowledge of the Risen Lord. Never having known the Lord before the crucifixion,[21] St Paul has no need to learn his heavenly, transcendental nature by a decisive withdrawal: the Lord was manifestly already 'in heaven'.[22]

20 Luke and Matthew are interestingly conflated in Chatterton Dix's hymn, 'Alleluia! sing to Jesus!', in the lines:

> Though the cloud from sight received Him,
>   When the forty days were o'er,
> Shall our hearts forget His promise,
>   'I am with you evermore'?

21 Not, at any rate, as a disciple knows him.

22 What is striking is that (as Professor J. Knox shows, in *Chapters in a Life of Paul* (New York, 1930), pp. 121 ff.) St Paul seems to distinguish the

Moreover, on the positive side, St Paul's teaching throws some light on a matter of great importance, namely, the relation between the ascension of Jesus and the hope for 'those who are in Christ'. For it seems to be true to say that ascension, no less than resurrection, is part of the Christian hope for all believers, and that here St Paul's teaching is relevant to our theme. The Pharisaic doctrine of bodily resurrection tended to link resurrection closely with this world-order; and Christian expectation was no doubt coloured with the same brush. Besides, Christ's own resurrection was, in some sense, realized 'on earth': his risen self became visible in time and space. But Christian thought, at its most authentic, was not earthbound or materialistic. Christ had himself rebuked the Sadducees for assuming a crass materialism as the only conditions for the Pharisaic hopes which they were mocking (Mk xii. 25); and Christian hope looked on to new heavens and a new earth. And the 'symbol' for the transition from the one to the other, as well as for the organic linking together of the two, was 'ascension', or 'assumption'. First the conquest of death, then transition; first resurrection, then ascension: this seems to have been the expected succession of events. It is part of the logic of the resurrection of the body – indeed, of the incarnation.

For Christ himself,[23] the pattern was first the acceptance of death, and so the conquest of it; and then the 'ascent' to a fuller sphere of life. And equally Christians hoped that they too would, in Christ, be brought from this life to the other. I Thess. iv. 17 expresses this hope of transition, both for 'the dead in Christ' and for those who were to survive to the *parousia.* And Rev. xi. 12, after describing the death and resurrection (*v.* 11) of the two witnesses, describes their upward summons and their ascension 'in the cloud' (though cf. iv. 1).

The objection which a large section of Christendom feels to the Roman dogma of the assumption of the Virgin is not that the New Testament does not contemplate the *ultimate* ascension of any besides Christ himself. Rather, it is, first, that there is no shred of reliable evidence for the assumption of the Virgin; and, secondly, that to find this unique *anticipation* of the Christian hope in this one instance besides that of the Saviour himself is manifestly one more step in Roman theology towards the assimilating of the Virgin with Christ as Co-redemptrix.

Damascus road encounter from his subsequent 'trances' or 'visions'. It was not only the beginning but also the end of that particular sort of encounter. In its own way it was as final and decisive as was the ascension for the others.

23 As, perhaps, for the 'Human figure' of Dan. vii (?).

The New Testament hope is for the *ultimate* ascension of all alike who are in Christ; but only because of Christ's conquest of death and his pioneer ascension. He is the 'first fruits'. The New Testament knows of no favoured mortal of the Christian era who has already anticipated this hope.[24] It is part of the hope of the consummation – one of 'the last things'; and it is to be interpreted, like the rest of the symbolism of eschatology, in terms of the corporate fellowship of the redeemed with one another in the Risen Body of Christ. It is one more element in the total reality of our gathering together in the heavenly realm. The resurrection and ascension of Christ are two moments in the anticipation of the ultimate home-gathering of the whole people of God.

## CONCLUSIONS

Thus, just as the *parousia* may be thought of as linking heaven to earth, so the ascension (of Christ and then of believers) links earth with heaven; it completes the 'saving history' in which God redeems his creation and brings his Church into complete fellowship with himself in Jesus. Christ's ascension 'means the taking into heaven of the humanity which the Son had assumed at the moment of the incarnation.'[25] Theologically, therefore, it is by no means an isolated or exclusively Lucan idea. It is a vivid way of expressing an essential Christian truth – that Christ was not somehow 'dematerialized' like a sort of ghost, but that he is fully himself, although no longer limited by 'earthly' existence. This is, presumably, what the fourth of the Thirty-Nine Articles is getting at, although it puts it in a strangely materialistic shape, when it says: 'Christ did truly rise again from death, and took again his body, with flesh, bones, and all things appertaining to the perfection of Man's nature; wherewith he ascended into Heaven, and there sitteth. . . .' Furthermore, if the ascension 'means the taking into heaven of the humanity which the Son had assumed', it means that with it will be taken the humanity which he has redeemed – those who are Christ's,

24 In the Old Testament tradition a very few favoured persons were believed to have made the transition without death: Enoch and Elijah in the canonical, Moses, possibly, in the non-canonical Scriptures. But Moses was *both* buried *and* translated: *i.e.* it is a dualistic idea; the 'soul' is translated. The so-called *Assumption of Isaiah* describes a prophetic trance and a return to the body (cf. Rev. iv). Of course there are passages in the New Testament where resurrection and ascension are described as already belonging to Christians (Eph. ii. 6, Col. iii. 1–3); but this is a matter of proleptic possession in Christ, of what Christ has won.

25 Davies, *V.C.* 8 (1954), 97.

at his coming. It is a powerful expression of the *redemption* of this world, in contrast to mere *escape* from it. Finally, what of the question of historicity? The Person of Christ unifies and brings together to a brilliant focal point all the varied aspects of God's manifold work of redemption. In this sense, all the distinguishable 'moments' - baptism, transfiguration, crucifixion, resurrection, ascension, session at God's right hand, giving of the Spirit, *parousia* - stand for the sure though mysterious good news of the glory of God revealed and communicated in Christ. Sometimes they are seen all conflated together, as the Fourth Gospel tends to show them. Sometimes one or two of them alone are dominant or do duty for the rest - in St Paul, the cross and resurrection, in the Epistle to the Hebrews, the death and ascension. And yet, Christian thought, apparently following eyewitness traditions, did find itself driven at times to analyse and distinguish these 'moments' as successive component parts of a single whole. No language can get far in adumbrating such profundities. But among these component parts the ascension carries its own special significance as the closing of one chapter and the opening of the next, the linking of one world with the other, the seal upon the eternal meaning of the humanity of Christ, and the anticipation, in him, of God's design for the whole Body of Christ. As such, it seems to demand a position 'in history' as truly as the others. If the eternal Word of God became incarnate at a definite time, is it not understandable that at a definite time he should also be seen to have passed on into a wider existence? And although it would be reducing its meaning and behaving childishly with deep mysteries to treat the ascension with a bare and annalistic 'historicism', and although the present writer would be the last to dogmatize about the forty days, yet a better case may be made than is sometimes imagined for 'dating' the event in the manner indicated in the opening verses of the Acts.

# Studies in the Gospels

# 5

## St Matthew's Gospel: Some Neglected Features

It is extremely interesting to watch different books of the New Testament coming successively into the forefront of research. There were the days of the so called 'Marcan hypothesis', when Mark was treated as the most important of all New Testament documents because it was deemed to lead us back, as no other document did, to the original Jesus. Then followed a period when the evangelists were, so to speak, shouldered out of the way in the attempt to see behind them and past them into the oral period before the traditions reached the shape which they assume in the Gospels. But more recently still has come a re-valuation of the work of the evangelists themselves, less for its historical importance than for the religious message they were themselves conveying. And so Mark came back into the foreground, no longer as a chronicler, but rather as a theologian; and there soon followed studies in the distinctive outlook and message of Luke-Acts. And now there are signs of considerable reawakening of interest in Matthew's message and meaning.[1]

In view of this activity over Matthew, it would not be easy to find many, if any, totally neglected features. What I want to do, however, is to call attention to certain features which, although indeed noticed before, seem (to the best of my knowledge) to have been too lightly set aside or forgotten; and then to see whether a plausible account of the Gospel can be offered which will take them all into account.

1 Since G. D. Kilpatrick's intensive study, *The Origins of the Gospel according to St. Matthew* (Oxford, 1946), there have been (to name only some particularly striking examples) K. Stendahl's *The School of St. Matthew* (Uppsala, 1954), P. Nepper-Christensen, *Das Matthäusevangelium: ein juden-christliches Evangelium?* (Aarhus, 1958) (the question in the title is answered in the negative), and W. Trilling, *Das wahre Israel* (Leipzig, 1959), not to mention such studies as those of W. D. Davies (in *Mélanges bibliques en l'honneur A. Robert* (Paris, 1956), pp. 428 ff.), of H. Schürmann (e.g *Biblische Zeitschrift* n. 3 (1959), 82 ff.; 4 (1960), 238 ff.), and of G. Bornkamm, G. Barth, and H.-J. Held, *Überlieferung und Auslegung im Matthäus-Evangelium* (Neukirchen, 1960).

Let me name three main features thus partly, as it would seem, neglected. Later, I shall mention some other, subsidiary ones.

(1) First, there is the narrative of the call of Matthew the tax-collector (Matt. ix. 9), and that tiresome and baffling tradition of Papias (Eusebius, *H.E.* iii. 39. 16). We know how easy it is to shrug off as naive and uncritical any attempt to take the tax-collector story seriously in relation to the contents of the Gospel; and we know the impatience expressed by B. W. Bacon[2] and others with those who glibly talk as though Q were known to be Matthew's Aramaic λόγια (not to mention the exasperation of those who do not believe in any such common Q-tradition at all). But does it not remain a duty for the student of Matthew to see whether he cannot make something of these two traditions – a tax-collector apostle named Matthew (the tradition from the Gospel itself), and the Papias tradition about Matthaean λόγια in a Semitic tongue, giving rise to a number of alternative translations? ('Translation', not 'interpretation' is clearly the meaning of ἑρμηνεύειν in the Papias tradition, for it is in the context of a linguistic description – ἑβραΐδι διαλέκτῳ. If so, no one would be compelled to translate Old Testament *testimonia*, when there were already existing Greek versions of the Scriptures. This, even more than anything that may be said about the inherent meaning of λόγια, clinches the distinctively Christian content of the λόγια in question.)

(2) Secondly, there is a feature of the Gospel which has often been noticed but perhaps not pursued far enough – its anthological character, in the sense that it holds in its single bouquet traditions which seem mutually contradictory, and that it tends to conflate and fuse into one what seems originally to have been multiple. When we consider a little more closely the nature of this conflation, we may agree that it reflects also on the previous observation (1), as likewise on the next, which is –

(3) that, thirdly, there is in Matthew a vigorous anti-Pharisaic strain, together with at least one or two features which it is difficult to ascribe to a Jewish author. In other words, there is the fact, often noticed but not always held before our attention, that Matthew, instead of being styled the Gospel for the Jews, might better be seen as a defence of Christianity against non-Christian Judaism – possibly even as a defence by the true Israel among the Gentiles against false Israel among the Jews. (This kind of approach, though not necessarily in this extreme form, was indeed visible before Nepper-Christensen and Trilling, as is evident from Nepper-Christensen's references[3] to Zahn, Feine-Behm,

2 *Studies in Matthew* (London, 1930), p. xii.
3 *Das Matthäusevangelium*, p. 13, n. 3, 35.

and more recently, J. Schmid. But my impression is that it is still not receiving attention at all widely.) I may say in passing (to illustrate some of the implications of such an approach) that I find it easier to interpret the famous saying, Matt. v. 17-20, which sounds like extreme legalism, as a defence against anti-Christian Pharisaic allegations that Christianity lowered moral standards, than as an attack on antinomianism within the Chruch.

Now, before we go any further beyond the broad statement of these three partly neglected features, let me lay all my cards on the table forthwith, and afterwards attempt to justify my suggestion.

The Gospel in its present form was, I suggest, compiled by a well-educated writer - a scribe in the secular, not the rabbinic, sense. He may or may not have been a Jew himself; but he belonged to a Christian group who lived so close to antagonistic Judaism that they neeeded to be well informed about the credentials of Christianity and about the best way to defend it against non-Christian Jewish attack. In the group there may well have been a preponderance of Jewish Christians; but, to say the least, there is a case to be made for a Gentile - or perhaps a proselyte - element. Either way, the group knew exactly where Judaism attacked, and needed to know how to reply.

Part of their reply lay, of course, in a carefully collected series of Old Testament *testimonia*, duly applied; and behind the group lay a tradition, some years long, of such application of scripture. The tradition contained also a wealth of the sayings of Jesus, and in addition, some anecdotes. To the original body of these traditions belonged Aramaic writings of Matthew himself, the tax-collector turned apostle. But the group, as it grew, had become predominantly Greek-speaking, and its earliest traditions, including these Semitic ones, had latterly come to circulate and be treasured among them in various Greek versions. Latterly, too, if not in its earlier stages, the group had developed a whole-hearted acceptance of the Gentile mission, and an emphasis on the continuing presence of Christ among them, no matter what were the theories of his future παρουσία.

At length had come the time when my well-educated writer of clear, grammatical Greek collected, conflated, and organized the material circulating in his group into a continuous Gospel. He used Mark - probably the only extant Gospel - as his base and guide, but skilfully introduced the extra material at his disposal, especially the traditions peculiar to his own group. Some of these represented comparatively recent adaptations (i. is very difficult, for instance, to believe that Matt. vii. 22 is an original *verbum Domini*, for, although the idea of 'prophecy in the

Lord's name' is actually an Old Testament allusion, prophecy had not re-awoken as a live issue until the Christian era). But others were ancient and authentic, or rested on very early bases – some, as I have said, being actually versions of the Matthaean material.

I have described the whole process as 'some years long', but I do not mean thereby to place the Gospel very late. If Matthew the apostle moved elsewhere or died at an early date, and if the group rapidly grew more Greek and, possibly, also more Gentile, the necessary evolution could take place – especially under the continual stress of attack and defence – in ten or twelve years from the very beginning.

My suggestion, then, is essentially that continuity with Semitic apostolic beginnings, as also rapid change and evolution out beyond them, were secured by the existence of a single and continuous group, living under the stress of attack from Pharisaic Judaism; and that the Gospel is the deposit of this group's traditions, collected and organized by an educated writer of Greek.

Now let me try to relate some of the actual facts and phenomena to this higly speculative story, conflating them gradually with my guesses. There are very few solecisms in Matthew, and it looks as though, left to himself, the evangelist could write good, grammatical Greek. He handled a great deal of material that was Semitic in origin, and which, even if already translated, was in Semitic Greek. Here he generally smoothed away the worst barbarisms and sometimes introduced some of his own vocabulary; but he made it his business as far as possible to retain the variants which were in his tradition and to include all the main material. If variants could be represented by conflation, so much the better: ideally, this scribe aimed at making a harmony, in the Tatian manner. But if conflation was quite impossible, then it had to be simply inclusion of both.

Take some examples. Others have, of course, noted the signs of variant translations of the same basic saying as between Matthew and Luke. C. K. Barrett, for instance,[4] adduces Matt. v. 11, Lk. vi. 22; Matt. v. 12, Lk. vi. 23; Matt. x. 12, Lk. x. 5; Matt. xxiii. 25, Lk. xi. 39; Matt. xxiii. 26, Lk. xi. 41; Matt. xxiii. 31, Lk. xi. 48.[5] And incidentally, H. Schürmann[6] seems to be hot on the trail of the editorial procedures of Matthew and Luke respectively in dealing with a common source. But it has less often been observed that there may be traces even within

---

4 'Q: a reexamination', *Exp. T.* 54 (1943), 320 ff.
5 See J. H. Moulton and W. F. Howard, *A Grammar of N.T. Greek* ii (Edinburgh, 1929), pp. 471 f. C. C. Torrey, *Our Translated Gospels* (London, 1937), *passim.*  6 *Biblische Zeitschrift* 3 (1959); 4 (1960).

St Matthew's Gospel: some neglected features

Matthew of variant versions of the same saying, or variant renderings of the same word or phrase.

Thus:

(a) In Matt. v. 13 f., are γῆ and κόσμος different renderings of the same original (ארעא perhaps, or עלמא? O. Syr. and Pesh. have both)? (b) In *Exp. T.* 50 (1939), 189 f.* I attempted to follow up familiar suggestions about the ῥακά passage (Matt. v. 22), and came to the conclusions that not only was μωρέ a gloss on ῥακά, but also συνέδριον a gloss on κρίσις. If this is correct, then Matthew has conflated (in this case misleadingly) two pairs of equivalents. (c) Again, it is possible to see Matt. xii. 31 f. (the Matthaean version of the saying about the sin against the Spirit) as, if not exactly a conflation, at least a juxtaposition, of two different versions of an original saying, which are more nearly represented in their single forms in Mark and Luke respectively. If a Semitic original ran in some such way as Mark's: 'the sons of men will be forgiven any sin and blasphemy except the blasphemy against the Spirit', then Luke's version (Lk. xii. 10), contrasting blasphemy against the Spirit, as unforgivable, with blasphemy against the Son of man as forgivable, might be a mistaken rendering of this, turning 'the sons of men ' into 'the Son of man'; and Matthew has simply put the two side by side, merely translating 'sons of men' into 'men'. (d) In Matt. xvi. 22,[7] the Hebrew חלילה has been uniquely rendered twice over by two alternative phrases, ἵλεως and οὐ μὴ ἔσται. (e) (an observation I owe to C. H. Dodd) In Matt. xxiii. 8, 10 ῥαββί and καθηγητής look like transliteration and translation respectively. (f) Finally, there is the notorious fact that in the story of Judas returning the money, Matt. xxvii. 3 ff., the alternative readings in Zech. xi. 13, אוצר (𝕿𝕲) and יוצר (M.T.), 'treasury' and 'potter' are both brought in, if only by way of allusion (v. 6 - 'not into the treasury', v. 7 'the potter's field'[8]).

Matthew has not done what might have been expected, and used παρουσία and ἔλευσις (he uses παρουσία alone, while Luke [δ text] and Acts use ἔλευσις only); nor are συναγωγή and ἐκκλησία interchangeable for him: perhaps circumstances made it imperative for him to use ἐκκλησία for the Christian and συναγωγή for the Jewish gathering; and, as G. D. Kilpatrick[9] has suggested, ἔλευσις and παρουσία may also have

[* See, now, *Exp. T.* 81 (1969–70), 10 ff.]

7 As Dr P. Katz has observed, *Kratylos* 5 (1960), 157.

8 But G. D. Kilpatrick's conclusion (*Matthew* 46) is 'that while the story has a complicated history which rests on an early tradition, the evangelist did not derive it from a written source'.

9 'Acts 7, 52, ἔλευσις', *J.T.S.* 46 (1945), 136–45.

71

acquired distinctive associations in the course of time. But enough has perhaps been adduced to make the variant translation theory worthy of consideration.

There can at any rate, be no denying that within this Gospel virtually contradictory traditions are held together. I have come across no interpretation of the Matthaean outlook which does not have to admit that if material 'A' represents the evangelist's own outlook, then material 'B' must have been retained simply because it was there in the traditions, not because it fitted. And I am inclined to believe that such is indeed the explanation. The Matthaean group, as I try to picture it, wholly approved of the Gentile mission, were not Judaizers (see xv. 20), and were more interested in the permanent presence of the Lord with them than in calculations about his return; but they had in their tradition (possibly in their most precious apostolic Aramaic collection) sayings restricting the mission to Jews and expecting a very rapid coming of the Son of man, and sayings going astonishingly far in the direction of a new legalism and of sabbatarianism (n. b. Matt. xxiv. 20); and these the evangelist simply retained – mainly because they were there, though for my part I am inclined to think (as I have said) that the extreme legalistic saying (v. 17 ff.) was actually endorsed by this group in the sense of a hyperbolic affirmation that Christianity did not (as their Pharisaic detractors were saying) reduce their sanctity or devotion and was not minimizing but – on the contrary – maximizing. Also, I am prepared to believe that they not only retained the prohibition against oaths but themselves observed it; for if they were, as I am picturing them, constantly 'up against' opposition from non-Christian Jews living very close to them, it is more than likely that it was as much as their life was worth to get into the power of an opponent by a rash vow. And Jas v. 12, shows that (even if the meaning of ἤτω δὲ ὑμῶν τὸ Ναὶ ναί, καὶ τὸ Οὔ οὔ is not identical with that of the Matthaean saying) there was at least one Christian community which avoided oaths, precisely ἵνα μὴ ὑπὸ κρίσιν πέσητε. The saying about celibacy is much harder to place. Is it dominical; or does it reflect some actual practice of extreme sexual asceticism in some Christian community? Was it a tradition no longer relevant to the evangelist's own group? We cannot say.

Leaving this question, what, now, about the case for Gentiles (or possibly proselytes) within this group? I think it is difficult to sustain the extreme form, as Nepper-Christensen presents it. But at least one or two questions have been noted by commentators, possibly suggesting some inexpertness, somewhere, as to Jewish ways. Thus:

## St Matthew's Gospel: some neglected features

(a) Matt. iii. 7; xvi. 1, 6 ff.: is this combination of Pharisees and Sadducees really plausible?

(b) Matt. xxvii. 62: is it possible that the high-priests and Pharisees went to Pilate on the day after the Preparation – i.e. either Passover day or Sabbath?

And now, can any further substance be given to the attempt to rehabilitate the existence of genuinely apostolic traditions behind the Gospel? Well, whereas, in their present form, some sayings notoriously bear the marks of the post-resurrection Church, there is no difficulty in showing that many others (for instance, many in the sermon on the mount) go convincingly into a Semitic form; and the depth and penetrating quality of their thought again and again suggest that their ultimate origin can only be in the words of the Lord himself. But we have now observed the further fact that, here and there, there may be traces of more than one Greek version of the same saying conflated; and this seems as though it might reflect the Papias tradition about Matthew's sayings being variously translated. Moreover, there are uniquely harsh sayings about Gentiles and tax-collectors (v. 46 f.; vi. 7; xviii. 17; xxi. 31 f.): is it not psychologically plausible to see here the kind of phrase that would be deliberately retained by one who had himself been taunted (as a Jewish tax-officer playing into Gentile hands might be) by that couple of associated words?

And then, what of the famous saying (xiii. 52) about the scribe turned disciple? It has sometimes been called the writer's own signature. But I think that this epigram has usually been interpreted in terms of the rabbinical scribe who was deemed to have compiled the Gospel; and I cannot, myself, see where the Gospel is particularly rabbinic. There are, I know, the applications of scripture, and the numerical observations at the end of the genealogy; but is this exclusively rabbinic? In general, the Gospel presents Jesus as Davidic, not Mosaic, and I am quite unconvinced by the idea that the 'mount' of the sermon is meant to be the new Sinai, or that the structure of the Gospel is deliberately pentateuchal. Why, then, should not this word γραμματεύς be understood in its secular, not rabbinic, sense?

The writer of the Gospel was himself a well-educated literate scribe in this sense. But so must also have been that tax-collector who was called by Jesus to be a disciple. Is it not conceivable that the Lord really did say to that tax-collector Matthew: You have been a 'writer' (as the Navy would put it); you have had plenty to do with the commercial side of just the topics alluded to in the parables – farmer's stock, fields, treasure-trove, fishing revenues; now that you have become a disciple, you can bring all this out again - but with a difference. And is it not conceivable that this was a saying actually recorded in Aramaic by the tax-collector turned disciple? It shows clearer signs of a Semitic base than some other parts of the Gospel. Again is it for nothing that Matthew alone in the New Testament contains the transliterated Latin μίλιον, 'mile', κουστωδία, 'guard', and the words δίδραχμα and στατήρ? Some of these, admittedly, occur in sections which are normally regarded as legendary and non-apostolic (perhaps they belonged to the evangelist-scribe's vocabulary); but μίλιον at least is the kind of Latinism that a Semitic tax-collector might well have used and that might have been retained when his Semitic sayings were translated. And the word μαθητεύειν, three times in Matthew (xiii. 52; xxvii. 57; xxviii. 19) and elsewhere in the New Testament only at Acts xiv. 21, goes straight into a good Semitic word for a disciple-teacher relationship. It seems to me that the assumption that an apostle who was a secular scribe, a writer using primarily a Semitic language, left Aramaic traditions which were translated and ultimately collected, conflated, and arranged, together with other material, by another scribe, a Greek writer, makes quite reasonable sense. One or other of these two scribes seems to have been himself interested in speaking of γραμματεῖς of the other, the rabbinic type; for xxiii. 34, being difficult to regard as an original form of the Lord's words, may be the peculiar form of a scribe-reporter.

This is a tissue of speculation. But if it has any claim to attention, it is that into this tissue it is possible, so far as I can see, to fit, without undue straining, all the well-known features of the Gospel and a number of somewhat neglected features besides.

*Postscript.* I ought to have called attention in this essay to the late E. J. Goodspeed's *Matthew, Apostle and Evangelist* (Philadelphia, 1959), with the strangely conservative conclusions indicated in its title.

# 6

## Neglected Features in the Problem of 'the Son of Man'*

for R. Schrackenburg

This essay, which is dedicated with admiration and regard to one of the most wide-ranging and theologically-minded of New Testament scholars, makes no pretence to being a survey of the present state of studies on 'the Son of Man' to which he himself has contributed substantially. Such is the intensity of this debate and so great the constantly growing volume of literature concerned with it,[1] that it would require a considerable book, as well as more time than most can afford, to give it anything like adequate coverage; and, in any case, surveys are quickly out of date. All that is here attempted is to bring into view certain features of the problem which are widely overlooked. It is well known that British scholarship, as a whole, tends to adopt certain views on the subject which, elsewhere, are regarded as eccentric, and this essay will, incidentally, constitute an attempt to demonstrate that, on the contrary, such views are reasonable. But the writer would not wish to involve his British colleagues in private peculiarities of his own, in addition to what, to Continental and, in part, to American observers, already looks eccentric enough. What follows will, therefore, in the main be a personal statement, although it does owe much to the work of colleagues, of which the notes will, it is hoped, furnish some measure of acknowledgement.[2]

[* See a valuable review of work on 'the Son of Man' by W. G. Kümmel, 'Jesusforschung seit 1965: V. Der personliche Anspruch Jesu', in *Theologische Rundschau* 46 (1980), 40 ff.]

1 Even in English alone, and written within the last thirty years, and for lectures to undergraduates, I found myself naming some thirty specialized articles and monographs on the subject.

2 Among earlier writers special mention may be made of T. W. Manson, 'The Son of Man in Daniel, Enoch, and the Gospels', *B.J.R.L.* 32, 2 (1950), reprinted in M. Black ed., *Studies in the Gospels and Epistles* (Manchester, 1962) and C. H. Dodd, *According to the Scriptures* (London, 1952) and, more recently, M. D. Hooker, *The Son of Man in Mark* (London, 1967).

# I

Let me first outline the interpretation that is here proposed (and it will be evident how much I depend, at certain points, on the work of colleagues), and then amplify and discuss it. The majority of scholars start from the assumption that the term 'the Son of Man' meant, for the Evangelists, and for Jesus (if he used it), a supernatural, apocalyptic figure such as is found in I Enoch 37–71 ('the Similitudes'). They then have to explain how such a figure ever came to be identified with Jesus or associated with his earthly circumstances and suffering; and they conclude either that none of its occurrences is dominical and that it only subsequently became a title applied by Christians to Christ, first in apocalyptic contexts, and then, by extension, in various other contexts; or else that Jesus himself used it but only in certain categories and (according to some schools of thought) not with reference to himself; and they have to explain its use in contexts of suffering by such additional influences as that of Isa. liii. A British school of thought, however, recently joined (partially, and in certain respects) by the Norwegian scholar, R. Leivestad,[3] and by the American scholar, R. Longenecker,[4] has long held that the apocalyptic use, exemplified by the Similitudes of Enoch, is not necessarily a reliable guide to that of the Synoptic Gospels, for which, rather, Dan. vii is the proximate antecedent.[5] What is here proposed, on this basis, is, further, that the 'human figure' of Dan. vii. 13 need not have been understood by Jesus (if he did use it) as even an essentially supernatural figure. In Dan. vii itself, it will be argued, it simply *represents* or *symbolizes* the persecuted loyalists (no doubt, of Maccabaean days) in their ultimate vindication in the court of heaven. Or, if there is anything supernatural about it, it belongs to the vindicated state, only, of what, in origin, is very much on earth. And it is this symbol that Jesus adopted to express his vocation and the voca-

---

3 'Der apokalyptische Menschensohn ein theologisches Phantom', *Annual of the Swedish Theological Institute* 6 (1968), 49 ff. See an English summary by the same author, 'Exit the Apocalyptic Son of Man', *N.T.S.* 18 (1972), 243 ff. See also L. Hartman, 'Scriptural Exegesis in the Gospel of St Matthew and the Problem of Communication', in M. Didier ed., *L'Evangile selon Matthieu* (Bibl. Theol. Lovan. 29) (Gembloux, 1972), pp. 131 ff. (142 f.).

4 *The Christology of Early Jewish Christianity* (London, 1970).

5 That Luke can speak of the *apocalypsis* of the Son of Man (Lk. xvii. 30) is, in itself, no evidence that the Son of Man is, in the technical sense, an 'apocalyptic figure'. It need only mean that the Son of Man will one day be divulged in his true meaning.

tion to which he summoned his followers. It was with reference to
Daniel's 'apparently human figure' that Jesus used the term '*the* Son of
Man' (almost nowhere outside the Christian tradition is the definite
article used); and, having once adopted the phrase, he was able to
apply it alike to his authority, to the exercise of and the challenge to
that authority in his present circumstances and in his impending death,
and to his ultimate vindication. (Hooker has especially emphasized the
theme of authority in this connexion.[6])

Further, it is suggested that, so far as conjecture is permissible on the
sequence and evolution of Son of Man terms, it is important to recol-
lect a broad background of thought about man's function and destiny
in general and Israel's function and destiny in particular, and to see
both Daniel and his successors in the light of this background (cf. the
work of F. H. Borsch[7] and M. D. Hooker[8]). Dan. vii is, in part, an application of 'man'-ideas and 'Israel'-ideas to a crisis of persecution; and
subsequent documents or traditions may be tentatively related to such
antecedents as shown in the diagram on p. 78.[9]

It is in such a situation that the term in the Synoptic and Johannine
traditions needs to be examined; and it is in terms primarily not of an
apocalyptic, supernatural *figure*, but of a *symbol* representing both the
vocation to be true, loyal Israel (and so true Man), and the hope, for
that reason, of ultimate vindication that the phrase, at least in the
Synoptics, may be interpreted.

## II

Now, by way of amplifying and justifying this summary statement,
certain observations need to be made.

(1) First, about the origins of the phrase. The suggestion that we
start, at least, by excluding I Enoch 37-71 ('the Similitudes') and IV
Ezra xiii from consideration when looking for antecedents to the Gospel usage is not unscientific; for, unlike Dan. vii, these works cannot be
proved to be early enough to have been used by the Evangelists, let
alone by Jesus. It is a well known fact that the Similitudes are the only
part of I Enoch so far unrepresented at Qumran. Of course to say that

6 *The Son of Man in Mark.*
7 *The Son of Man in Myth and History* (London, 1967).
8 *The Son of Man in Mark.*
9 Cf. the diagram (quite independently made) by K. M. Fischer in his review
  of F. H. Borsch's *The Christian and the Gnostic Son of Man* (London,
  1970) in *T.L.Z.* 96 (1971), 775 f.

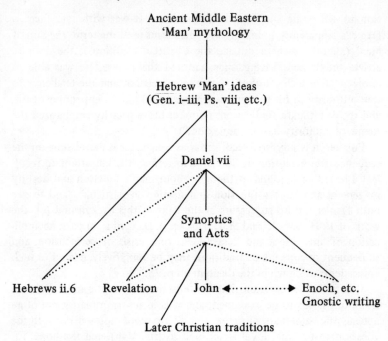

Ancient Middle Eastern
'Man' mythology

Hebrew 'Man' ideas
(Gen. i–iii, Ps. viii, etc.)

Daniel vii

Synoptics
and Acts

Hebrews ii.6      Revelation      John ◄·············► Enoch, etc.
Gnostic writing

Later Christian traditions

(The relative dates of the bottom row are not intended to be prejudged.
Actually, Hebrews may be considerably earlier, and the right hand members considerably later, than the Johannine writings.)

therefore it did not exist so early is an argument from silence, and at any moment evidence may come to light for its existence in the Qumran library; but, unless and until it does, it is unscientific to assume an early date for this, the only section of Enoch that is relevant to 'the Son of Man'. Moreover, J. C. Hindley has argued,[10] from internal evidence, for a date for the Similitudes later than the formation of the Synoptic tradition. At the very best, then, the assumption that the Similitudes constitute a source for the Gospel usage is precarious. As for IV Ezra xiii, this, too, is reasonably excluded from at least preliminary consideration if, as D. S. Russell says,[11] 'it is generally agreed that the contents of these chapters [iii–xiv] come from the latter part of the first century AD'. It is thus a perfectly reasonable suggestion that in the Synoptic tradition, in I Enoch 37–71, and in IV Ezra are to be seen reflexions of

10 'Towards a Date for the Similitudes of Enoch. An Historical Approach', *N.T.S.* 14 (1967–68), 551 ff.
11 *The Method and Message of Jewish Apocalyptic* (London, 1964), p. 62.

parallel and possibly independent developments from Dan. vii, rather than that the Synoptic tradition depends on and is in an evolutionary succession to such developments as are reflected in (say) I Enoch. Dan. vii (which, though it does not contain the phrase 'the Son of Man', contains a phrase from which that phrase could have been derived) is universally agreed to be as early as *c.* 165 B.C., is actually quoted by the Synoptists, and is not unlikely to have been known to Jesus himself. True, it is impossible to be sure how many of the books we know as the *Kethubim* were studied in the kind of education that Jesus received; but it is not unlikely that Dan. vii at least, considering its theme, was prominent in the minds of most loyal Jews of the time. It is therefore a not unreasonable hypothesis that Jesus knew it himself and could allude to it in the confidence that his hearers also would recognize the allusion, and that some, at least, of the references to it in the Synoptic tradition are plausibly dominical.

Some expositors, of course, have proposed Ezekiel as the most probable immediate source of the phrase in the Synoptic tradition; but, although it is true that 'Son of Man!' is a common mode of address to the prophet, it is difficult to see, in this not very colourful vocative use, a more probable source than Dan. vii, for what will shortly be seen to be a highly distinctive phrase in the Gospels.[12] Occurrences of 'son of man' elsewhere in the Old Testament will not be discussed in this article. It need only be said that, as references to man, in his weakness or his glory, they constitute part of the background both of Dan. vii itself and of allusions in the New Testament such as that of Heb. ii. 6 to Ps. viii.

(2) But, next, the actual contents of Dan. vii have to be considered. Nowhere in that chapter does the phrase '*the* son of man' occur. What does occur is an Aramaic phrase, *kbr 'nš*, meaning (apparently) 'something like a human being'. On the view which is here proposed, this 'human figure' is not an apocalyptic, transcendental figure: it simply represents or symbolizes the persecuted loyalists. But that is by no means agreed to by all scholars. There are those who regard this mysterious figure of Daniel's vision as intended to be a permanent, supernatural member of the heavenly court, rather than as simply a symbol or even a mere representative of anything so historical and earthly as

12 It so happens that it is in Ezekiel also that the Almighty is seen in a human shape: in the 'chariot' vision in i. 26, what is seen upon 'something in the shape of a throne' (*dmwt ks'*) is 'a man-like shape' (*dmwt kmr'h 'dm*), LXX ὁμοίωμα ὡς εἶδος ἀνθρώπου. And, for that matter, in Dan. viii. 15 the angel Gabriel looks like a man (*kmr'h gbr*).

the persecuted martyrs. It has been argued that not only did that figure, at an earlier stage in the evolution of Dan. vii, represent a god or a demigod who was ultimately subordinated to the supreme god,[13] but that, even in the present state of the chapter, it is a supernatural figure – a champion, perhaps, of the saints, but not a mere symbol of them. If so, then it is obviously false to *identify* the figure of the vision (as is done in my initial proposal) with the martyrs of the latter part of the chapter. But is the evidence for the independence and transcendence of the figure (in Dan. vii in its final form – which is all that need concern us) compelling? And is it not plausible to suggest that, at least by some ancient interpreters, it could have been seen as a symbol, simply, for the vindication of the saints? After all, the 'beasts' in the vision, and their 'horns', are manifestly symbols for tyrannical empires or princes; why then, should not the 'apparently human figure' be a symbol for the saints? Why should he not symbolize their vindication after and through their suffering?[14] He is given dominion and glory (*v.* 14), and so are the saints (*v.* 27). It is true that he is not, like the saints, explicitly represented as first made war with and prevailed over or worn out (*vv.* 21, 25); but he is given sovereignty and glory and kingship (*vv.* 10-14), and that implies that he did not possess these till then; and why should he not, therefore, symbolize the ultimate vindication of those loyalists after the 'beasts' have done their worst (*vv.* 1-8, 11, 19-27)? If I Enoch 37-71 represents a development of the figure in the direction of making him a supernatural, heavenly *being* (or, if Enoch himself, then Enoch only when lifted to that status),[15] IV Ezra xiii, by contrast, represents a development in the direction of making 'the man' simply a *symbol* for God's people.[16] Why, then, should not the Synoptic tradition represent an interpretation of Dan. vii more like that of IV Ezra xiii (even if independent and earlier) than that of I Enoch 37-71?

It is true that Dan. vii. 21 f., beginning 'As I looked...', is presented as part of a vision rather than, strictly, part of its interpretation; and, if

13 See, for instance, J. A. Emerton, 'The Origin of the Son of Man Imagery', *J.T.S.* n.s. 9 (1958), 225 ff., and literature cited there, and in C. Colpe, ὁ υἱὸς τοῦ ἀνθρώπου, *T.W.N.T.* viii. 423, n. 153.

14 See C. H. Dodd, *According to the Scriptures* (London, 1952), p. 117, n. 2. J. A. T. Robinson also points out to me that in Ps. lxxx. 17 (M.T. 18) the Son of Man is apparently a figure that has suffered.

15 See the note in C. K. Barrett, *The New Testament Background: Selected Documents* (London, 1956), p. 255, on I Enoch 71. 14 (l. 66 in Barrett's selection).

16 I owe this observation to C. C. Rowland of Christ's College, Cambridge, though this is emphatically not to implicate him in my heresies.

so, it might be argued that the conquest of the saints by their persecu-
tors is an additional feature of the vision, *side by side* with the 'apparently human figure' and therefore not to be symbolized by it. But that
would be to press very prosaically and literalistically a piece of writing
whose freedom and looseness, as between vision and interpretation,
scarcely warrant it.

(3) But the question now arises, What actually happens to the
'apparently human figure' in the vision of Dan. vii? It is difficult to
resist the impression that in *vv.* 9 f. a law-court scene is intended:
'thrones were placed and one that was ancient of days took his seat;. . .
the court sat in judgment (*dyn' ytb*), and the books were opened'; and
in *v.* 22 similarly: 'judgment was given for the saints of the Most High'
(*dyn' yhb lqdyšy 'lywnyn*). Although alternative interpretations are not
lacking, the most obvious seems to be that here is a trial in a heavenly
court, where under the presidency of God, the evidence is produced
(from the 'books') and the 'apparently human figure' vindicated against
the 'beasts' who are eliminated, leaving him in possession of an eternal
kingdom (*vv.* 14, 22b, 27 add an enthronement-scene to the law-court
scene). Exactly so, in the latter part of the chapter, the 'saints' are
threatened and hurt by the 'beasts' and the 'horn', but ultimately
vindicated and given dominion.[17] Is it necessary, then, to resist the
suggestion that the 'apparently human figure' *could* be interpreted as a
symbol, simply, for the loyal, martyr people who, after their faithful
endurance on earth, are to be vindicated and given sovereignty in the
heavenly realms, rather than as a heavenly, 'apocalyptic' figure existing
permanently in the heavenly realm and independently of the saints? It
is to be noted that, if this is the meaning of the symbol, it stands,

17 For echoes of the Daniel scene in N.T. sayings other than those containing
'the Son of Man', see Dodd, *According to the Scriptures* (p. 68). The
treatment of themes from Dan. vii in Revelation is interesting. In the two
occurrences of ὅμοιος υἱὸς ἀνθρώπου (a barbarously literal rendering of
*kbr 'nš*), it is applied to Jesus as risen and glorified (i. 13), and as the eschatological vintager (xiv. 14). But the same passage appears to be reflected,
though without this phrase, at xx. 4 ('thrones' and 'judgement') and xx. 12
(the 'books'). In the former of these two references, it looks as though the
saints of the millennium were sitting as judges (they sit on the thrones and
κρίμα ἐδόθη αὐτοῖς, which presumably means, in this context, not that a
verdict was given in their favour but that they were commissioned as judges
– cf. I Cor. vi. 2); in the latter, the scene is the Great Assize, with God
(almost certainly – xx. 11) as Judge. In all these allusions, therefore, the
implications are that the Danielic scene is treated by the Seer as a manifestation of the authority of the crucified and risen One and of his followers,
and so of God's ultimate verdict.

ultimately, also for true man, since Israel fulfilling its destiny is, indeed, representative of man fulfilling his destiny. Hence (though by an indirect route) it becomes the symbol of true humanity.

(4) This brings us, in turn, to linguistic matters. It is not observed as often as it should be that ὁ υἱὸς τοῦ ἀνθρώπου (with the definite article) is an almost exclusively Christian term. In the plural, of course, the phrase with the article is common enough: '*the* sons of men' is no oddity. But in the singular, '*the* son of man' is virtually unknown outside the New Testament until I Enoch and Christian tradition subsequent to the New Testament. In Hebrew, to the best of my knowledge, there is only one instance of '*the* son of man', and that is in the Qumran scrolls, in 1QS xi. 20; and even there, the *h* is an *addition*, written by a scribe over the line.[18] Everywhere in the Old Testament it is anarthrous, and is correspondingly represented in the LXX. In I Enoch, I understand that the Ethiopic terms used (which I cannot myself read) are roughly equivalent to what is found in the Old Syriac as a translation of the Gospel term, ὁ υἱὸς τοῦ ἀνθρώπου, namely, *brh dgbr*'.[19]

In the New Testament, the anarthrous form is used in Jo. v. 27 (where possibly it stands simply for 'humanity': Jesus, because he is a man, is given authority to judge),[20] but otherwise only in Heb. ii. 6, where Ps. viii is directly quoted; and in Rev. i. 13 and xiv. 14, where there is a barbarously literal rendering in Greek of the anarthrous Aramaic phrase of Dan. vii. 13: *kbr 'ns* becomes ὅμοιος υἱὸς ἀνθρώπου. Thus, with almost complete consistency, the New Testament, whenever the phrase is related to Jesus, adheres to a form which is otherwise virtually unexampled. In his new translation of Mark into Hebrew,[21] R. L. Lindsey correctly gives *bn h'dm*. (In parenthesis, it may be observed that, once the υἱός receives the article, it normally follows, by Greek idiom,[22] that the dependent noun in the genitive will have the

18 See Colpe, *T.W.N.T.* viii, 405, ll. 2–5.
19 See F. C. Burkitt's note on this in *Evangelion Da-Mepharreshe* (Cambridge, 1904), II, p. 272. He comments on the strangeness of the phrase, but, ironically, calls it the equivalent of 'Son of Man' (*sic!*), failing apparently, to notice that, on the contrary, it is the equivalent of '*the* Son of Man'.
20 See *Test. Abr.* xii, xiii, cited in this connexion by E. M. Sidebottom, *The Christ of the Fourth Gospel* (London, 1961), p. 94. But, for the great variety of views on this verse, see E. Ruckstuhl, *Die johanneische Menschensohnforschung 1957–1969 = Theologische Berichte* hrsg. von J. Pfamatter und F. Furger (Zürich, 1972), pp. 171–284 (181, 206, 214, 217, 247).
21 *A Hebrew Translation of the Gospel of Mark* (Jerusalem, no date).
22 See the ruling by Apollonius Dyscolus, summarized by T. F. Middleton, *The Doctrine of the Greek Article* (London, 1841), p. 36.

article also: ὁ υἱὸς τοῦ ἀνθρώπου, not ὁ υἱὸς ἀνθρώπου; there is not necessarily, therefore, any special significance in the article before the genitive: the significant phenomenon is that the phrase as a whole is definite, not indefinite.)

Now, it has been urged by G. Vermés[23] that, in the relevant kinds of Palestinian Aramaic at the time of Jesus, there would not have been any significant difference in meaning between the definite and the indefinite forms of such a phrase: br nš and br nš' would be virtually indistinguishable in meaning. J. A. Fitzmyer, however, in a review,[24] points out that the evidence on which Vermés depends is later than the first century and does not come from Palestine, and maintains that the lack of distinction affirmed by Vermés between the definite and the indefinite forms obtains only in that later Aramaic. Incidentally, it has also been alleged[25] that neither nš nor nš' would have been used in the time of Jesus, but only 'nš. But, in any case, it would presumably have been possible, in Aramaic of any period, to represent, if necessary, precisely what is represented by the strange phrase ὁ υἱὸς τοῦ ἀνθρώπου (witness the rendering by the Old Syriac already referred to).*

It appears, therefore, that it is at least conceivable that the very unusual Greek phrase in the Gospels preserves something in the traditions of the sayings of Jesus which is more distinctive than simply an Aramaic phrase meaning 'a man', or 'somebody' or even (by an idiomatic use of the third person for the speaker) 'I'.[26] And is it not a reasonable conjecture that it represents *a reference to* the Danielic phrase (just as, independently, and for a different purpose, the phrases

---

23 'The Use of *br nš/br nš*' in Jewish Aramaic', in M. Black, *An Aramaic Approach to the Gospels and Acts* (Oxford, ³1967), pp. 310 ff. (315).

24 *C.B.Q.* 30 (1968), 417 ff. (424 ff.).

25 '... in the Qorban grave inscription datable to the 1st century AD (*R.B.* 65 (1958) 409, *J.B.L.* 78 (1959), 60–5) *'nš* is the form for "man" and not *nš*, as in the scroll [= the Genesis Apocryphon]. This is a matter of importance in connection with discussion of the "Son of Man" question in the Gospels; any material quoted bearing the phrase in the form *br nš* or *br nš*' must be regarded as later than the 1st century AD and strictly irrelevant, since *br 'nš* was its 1st century AD form' – B. S. Sheret, 'An Examination of Some Problems of the Language of St Matthew's Gospel' (unpublished Oxford D.Phil dissertation, 1972), p. 47 (by permission of the author).

26 For such renderings, see J. Y. Campbell, 'The Origin and Meaning of the Term "Son of Man"' (*sic!*), *J.T.S.* 48 (1947), 145 ff. Reprinted in *Three New Testament Studies* (Leiden, 1965), pp. 29 ff., and Vermés, 'The Use of *br nš/br nš*'.

[* This point is not reckoned with in G. Vermés. critique in 'The Present State of the "Son of Man" Debate', *J.J.S.* 29 (1978), 123 ff.]

83

in I Enoch 37–71 do also)? In Dan. vii. 13 the phrase is anarthrous: *kbr 'ns, 'an* apparently human figure'. But if Jesus chose to take that figure as a symbol for his vocation – the vocation to *be* God's true people, going to any lengths of suffering in loyalty to his will, and ultimately to be vindicated in the heavenly court – might he not have referred to it as '*the* human figure', *brh dgbr'*, ὁ υἱὸς τοῦ ἀνθρώπου?[27] And if that is, in fact, what he did, then it is also conceivable that he applied it not only to some transcendental future, but to his authority wherever it was exercised in his capacity as the focus of God's dedicated people, both on earth and through his sufferings and beyond them in his ultimate vindication. This, in essence, is what M. D. Hooker has argued with reference to the Marcan usage.[28] It is, so far as I can see, equally conceivable that Jesus used it sometimes as a collective term (meaning, as in Dan. vii. 22 ff., 'the loyal people')[29] and thus as a symbol for the vocation which he called on his disciples to share, but sometimes also for himself as the heart and nucleus and brilliant focal point and alone the fully representative part of that collective entity; and even that, on occasion, he used it, as *though* of someone other than himself, when he wished to stress the ultimate, eschatological character of the final vindication and of the verdict on others which that vindication would constitute. I am not in this arguing for the dominical character of all the instances of 'the Son of Man' in the Gospels, but only for

27 In an unpublished essay (written with assstance from Mr H. St J. Hart of Queens' College, Cambridge) Mr D. R. de Lacey of St John's College, Cambridge† (to whom I am indebted for permission to quote his observations), points out that in the Ethiopic Enoch there are three distinct phrases for 'the Son of Man' or 'that Son of Man'; and that, while the Peshitta of the Gospels uniformly uses *brh d'nš*, the Old Syriac uses three (or, if one is a mistake and needs to be emended away, two) distinct phrases. These are: (I) most often, *brh d'nš*; (II) in Mk. viii. 38 (S:C is not extant), Lk. vii. 34 (S and C), Lk. ix. 26 (C: S is illegible), Lk. ix. 48 (C), Jo. xiii. 31 (S: C is not extant) *brh dgbr'*; (III) in Lk. xxii. 48 (S), *lbr d'nš'*. This is ungrammatical. Burkitt conjectured *lbr 'nš'*, which would still constitute a third form; but de Lacey suggests that an *h* had been elided, and that it should be *brh d' nš'* (= (I)).

Thus the case is strengthened for the view that the figure in Dan. vii could have been alluded to by various specific Aramaic phrases such as might be rendered into Greek by the single (and highly peculiar) phrase with the definite article.

28 *The Son of Man in Mark.*

29 See, e.g. Manson, *B.J.R.L.* 32, 2 (1950), and *The Teaching of Jesus* (Cambridge, 1935), pp. 211 ff. This conclusion does not depend on Manson's view of the chronological arrangement of Mark.

[† Now Dr de Lacey of Ridley Hall, Cambridge.]

the plausibility that some sayings of all three of the familiar categories – relating to present circumstances, to future suffering, and to future glory – are genuinely dominical and applied by Jesus to himself and his vocation. It is difficult, in my opnion, to accept Jeremias' suggestion[30] that only those Son of Man sayings are original and authentic which are not paralleled by a similar saying without a 'Son of Man' formula. The use of this criterion leads to such otherwise improbable candidates for authenticity that one wonders whether the assumption that 'the Son of Man' would be more likely to be added than to be subtracted can be right.

### III

But if the plausibility of what I am suggesting be granted, then it is possible to see the Johannine use of 'the Son of Man' (or, once, 'Son of Man', without the article)[31] as an extension of the Synoptic and genuinely dominical use. To this extent, at least, I can claim support from the Jubilar's article, 'Der Menschensohn im Johannesevangelium', and from his commentary.[32] The Fourth Gospel uses 'the Son of Man' with reference to suffering (at least by implication) and glory. In this respect it is like the Synoptists, although its manner of using it is distinctive and different. But to these more or less synoptic usages, it adds reference to 'the Son of Man' coming down from heaven or ascending up to heaven or being in heaven, and this is not synoptic.[33] This might well represent a Christian doctrinal development of the Daniel–Synoptic tradition[34] comparable to the (probably non-Christian) development of the Daniel tradition in I Enoch 37-71. The Johannine occurrences are set out on p. 86, with an attempt to arrange them in categories, which however, are inevitably unstable and overlapping. The fourth category ('use as a mere title') is comparable to such passages in the Synoptic Gospels (probably not genuinely dominical) as contain 'the Son of Man' simply as a designation of Jesus without any evident reference to an intelligible function (e.g. Matt. xvi. 13). Bracketed references indicate

30 'Die älteste Schicht der Menschensohnlogien', *Z.N.W.* 58 (1967), 159 ff.
31 See the valuable review by Ruckstuhl, *Die johanneische Menschensohnforschung.*
32 *N.T.S.* 11 (1965), 123 ff.; *Das Johannesevangelium* (Freiburg i. Br., 1965), Exkurs V.
33 For a different view, see S. S. Smalley, 'The Johannine Son of Man Sayings', *N.T.S.* 15 (1969), 278 ff.
34 Cf. Ruckstuhl, *Die johanneische Menschensohnforschung*, especially pp. 192 f., and (for Schnackenburg's view) p. 274.

association with the category in question by implication rather than explicitly.

| glorification | suffering | preexistence | use as a mere title (?) |
|---|---|---|---|
| i. 51 | – | – | – |
| iii. 13 | – | iii. 13 | – |
| iii. 14 | (iii. 14) | – | – |
| v. 27 (anarthrous) | – | – | – |
| – | – | – | vi. 27, 53 (but suffering) |
| vi. 62 | – | vi. 62 | – |
| viii. 28 | (viii. 28) | – | – |
| – | – | – | ix. 35 |
| xii. 23 | – | – | – |
| xii. 34 | (xii. 34) | – | – |
| xiii. 31 | (xiii. 31) | – | – |

## IV

If, now, looking back over what has been suggested, one asks What, then, on this showing, would the most controverted Son of Man sayings in the Synoptic Gospels have meant? The answer might be as follows. Mk viii. 38 would mean: 'for whoever is ashamed of me and mine[35] (that is, of true Israel, or mankind fulfilling its destiny, and of me as the heart and centre and focal-point of this) in this adulterous and sinful generation, will turn out, in the end, to be judged and repudiated by true Israel, or mankind fulfilling its destiny and by me as the heart and centre and focal-point of this (that is, by me and mine), when this is ultimately seen vindicated in the court of my Father in heaven'.

Mk xiv. 62 would mean: 'I am the Messiah'; (and then, *more suo*, Jesus amplifies and corrects the easily misinterpreted 'Messiah' language by a different sort of language, and adds:) 'and you will see true Israel (in me, its head and representative) vindicated, as in Daniel's vision...'

Lk. ix. 58 would mean: 'anybody fulfilling the destiny of true Israel as I am, by loyal obedience to God's will, must endure hardship and homelessness...' All the other Son of Man sayings in the Synoptists,

35 If, as is possible, it is correct, with Mk, to omit λόγους. But the reading 'me and my words' can almost equally well be brought inside this interpretation: it only makes Jesus, as the focal centre of the loyal Israel, less explicitly associated with his circle.

except those which appear to be due to an editorial introduction of the term as a mere title (e.g. Matt. xvi. 13), are amenable to the same sort of interpretation, namely, one which starts from the assumption, not that the term denotes an individual, apocalyptic figure, but that it is a symbol for Israel's (and so for Man's) vocation, and, *imprimis*, for Jesus as epitomizing and perfectly achieving this. The term sums up the vocation of Jesus to be (or to be the head and centre of) Israel truly fulfilling its destiny (and thus 'the Son of God', or Mankind as properly related to God); as such, he is authoritative, challenged, persecuted, destined to be put to death, and ultimately to be vindicated.[36] (In that last condition, he is, of course, an apocalyptic figure.) And it is worth noting, in passing, that there is no need to invoke Isa. liii for the suffering element in the picture, if Daniel's 'apparently human figure' means the vindication of *martyr-*'saints' after their suffering.

If this is how Jesus used the term, it becomes intelligible why the term was scarcely ever used except in sayings attributed to Jesus himself; for it was not properly a *title*, by which post-Easter Christians might allude to Jesus or hail him. It was not a title so much as a description; and a description more of his martyr-ministry on earth in the past and of his heavenly vindication looked for in the future than of his present position 'seated at the right hand of God', for which 'Son of God', 'Lord', or 'Christ' were more appropriate. Therefore, only in the context of suffering witness and martyrdom (e.g. Stephen's), to which it *was* appropriate, or in the recalling of Jesus' own description of himself would it have been naturally applied. And, despite what is often alleged, there is no independent evidence that it was a title popularly applied to Jesus by the early Church, still less that it was actually invented at that stage and artificially attached to the sayings of Jesus. The only substantial development beyond what can plausibly be attributed to the setting of the ministry of Jesus himself is, as has already been said, the Johannine 'preexistence' type of Son of Man saying; and this can be explained as a sort of retrojection of the Synoptic usage back from the vindication at the end to a preexistence in glory. This would still constitute no evidence for a popular use of the term as a title for Jesus among Christians. It would simply be a transcendentalizing of the person of Jesus, in keeping with the Johannine Christology as a whole and rather in the manner of certain Jewish speculations about the Torah. Outside orthodox Christianity and in Gnostic circles, admittedly, the phrase was, to some extent, exploited, as F. H. Borsch shows. But

36 Cf. Hooker, *The Son of Man in Mark*: see p. 84 above.

even there, many examples of the distinctively Christian usage, with the definite article, are in virtual quotations from Gospel sources.[37]

## V

The non-use of the term as a title by the later Church is borne out by F. H. Borsch's interesting study.[38] He points out[39] that Tatian's *Diatessaron* seems to have preferred 'I' or 'he', in reference to Jesus, to 'the Son of Man'; that *Didache* xvi,[40] though full of reminiscences of eschatological sayings in the Gospels, avoids it, except in the (secondary) Georgian version, once; that there is a similar tendency in II Clement and in the Apocalypse of Peter;[41] and that there are certain passages in Justin (to whom we must return in a moment) where 'the Son of Man' might have been used but is not (e.g. *Dial.* li.2 and xlix).[42]

The anarthrous form occurs in a few passages, so far as the subapostolic and early patristic literature is concerned; but it seems to refer to Christ's humanity, or else to be a direct quotation from the Old Testament, e.g. Barn. xii.10a,[43] and Ign. *Eph.* xx.2.[44] (In the latter passage the apparently definite form is not to be misunderstood: the definite article is clearly used retrospectively, as a substitute for a relative clause: . . . Ἰησοῦ Χριστῷ τῷ κατὰ σάρκα ἐκ γένους Δαυείδ, τῷ υἱῷ ἀνθρώπου καὶ υἱῷ θεοῦ means, as the absence of article before the genitives confirms, '. . . Jesus Christ who, physically, was of David's tribe, who was Son of Man and Son of God'.)

The form with the article, however - ὁ υἱὸς τοῦ ἀνθρώπου -, does occur in a limited number of passages. An interesting example is in the traditions of the death of James the Lord's brother retailed from Hegesippus by Eusebius in *H.E.* ii. 23.13, where James is represented as referring to Jesus as 'the Son of Man'. This, in a martyrdom story, is analogous to Stephen's use in Acts vii. 56. Justin, whose writings contain the other most conspicuous examples, presents a complicated usage, sometimes with the definite article, sometimes without. But Borsch's review of the facts[45] seems to point to an explanation. Justin uses both the Old Testament and the Gospels, but without himself appearing fully to understand the meaning of the Gospels' usage, nor

---

37 *The Christian and the Gnostic Son of Man*, pp. 58 ff. However, due weight must be given to his important conclusion on p. 114: '. . . a significant number of the gnostic references to the Son of Man ought not to be regarded as stemming from the influence of canonical materials'.

38 *Ibid.* 29 ff.    39 *Ibid.* 36, n. 19    40 *Ibid.* 39 ff.    41 *Ibid.* 34 ff.
42 *Ibid.* 47.    43 *Ibid.* 37.    44 *Ibid.* 38.    45 *Ibid.* 43 ff.

the distinction between theirs and Daniel's usage. Thus. I *Apol.* li.9 (anarthrous) is a conflation of Christian and Danielic elements, and the anarthrous form there seems to be due simply to Justin's failure to realize that the definite form is distinctive of the Gospels. He uses the definite form only when he is influenced by straight, uncontaminated quotation from the Gospels. Accordingly, 'wherever Justin refers to the hero of Daniel's prophecy, and on the two occasions [*Dial.* lxxvi.1, c.3] when he goes on to explicate the title as it is used in Gospel sayings, he does so in terms of ὡς υἱὸς ἀνθρώπου [cf. *Dial.* xxxi.1, xxxii.1], but when quoting from the Gospels [as in *Dial* lxxvi.7, c.3, from Mk viii. 31] he speaks of the figure as ὁ υἱὸς τοῦ ἀνθρώπου.[46] All in all, Justin's 'uses of the title reveal no contact with any continuing tradition which spoke of the Son of Man in worship or creed'.

In G. W. H. Lampe's Patristic Lexicon,[48] the article 'υἱός', under heading 'D.', shows how widely thereafter, in the subsequent patristic literature, the anarthrous form was used in Christological controversy for the humanity of Christ. The definite form scarcely occurs in the Lexicon article (though see the entry from Marcellus. The story of James is not included in the references).

## VI

To sum up: the purpose of these reflexions is, without going over the familiar story of current exegesis, simply to underline the plausibility of a hypothesis which, when attempting to understand Synoptic usage, starts, not from the supernatural figure but from the symbol for God's loyal people. If it be granted that Dan. vii is patient of such an interpretation, and that Jesus himself could have adopted it, alluding to the Danielic symbol as 'the Son of Man', then the strange fact that this definite form, 'the Son of Man', is almost invariably used in the Gospel traditions (as also in the comparable adaptation of Dan. vii in I Enoch 37-71), and is found virtually nowhere before them is explained; the use of the term in the various Gospel categories becomes intelligible; and at least some light may be thrown also on the selectivity of subsequent Christian usage.

The wider importance of this for New Testament interpretation is obvious. If the position here adopted held good, we should have a remarkable instance of Jesus' interpretation of Scripture, constituting an important '*Anstoss*' on our understanding of his meaning for us. One or

46 *Ibid.* 43.    47 *Ibid.* 49.    48 *A Patristic Lexicon* (Oxford, 1961).

two writers[49] have pointed out that, according to the traditions reflected in the New Testament, Jesus' use of the Old Testament was, far more often than not, on a deeper level than that merely verbal use which pleased many of the New Testament writers themselves (witness the 'formula-quotations' of Matthew, and a good deal else in the New Testament that makes play with verbal coincidence). By contrast to these, Jesus himself is represented as caring most about that in the Old Testament which reflects the true relationship between God and man. And of this, his use of 'the Son of Man' becomes a signal example, if it can be interpreted as a description, drawn from Daniel, of his vocation to be the nucleus of a right relation to God. C. H. Dodd, to whose interpretation of 'the Son of Man' I owe an immense debt, although he must in no way be held responsible for some of the details of what I have said in this article, wrote as follows:

> To have brought together ... the Son of Man who is the people of the saints of the Most High, the Man of God's right hand, who is also the vine of Israel, the Son of Man who after humiliation is crowned with glory and honour, and the victorious priest-king at the right hand of God, is an achievement of interpretative imagination which results in the creation of an entirely new figure. It involves an original, and far-reaching, resolution of the tension between the individual and the collective aspects of several of these figures, which in turn makes it possible to bring into a single focus the 'plot' of the Servant poems of II Isaiah, of the psalms of the righteous sufferer, and of the prophecies of the fall and recovery (death and resurrection) of the people of God, and finally offers a fresh understanding of the mysterious imagery of Apocalyptic eschatology. This is a piece of genuinely creative thinking. ... To account for the beginning of this most original and fruitful process of rethinking the Old Testament we found need to postulate a creative mind. The Gospels offer us one. Are we compelled to reject the offer?[50]

49 See, besides Dodd, quoted next, S. L. Edgar, 'Respect for Context in Quotations from the Old Testament', *N.T.S.* 9 (1962), p. 55 ff. But *contra* Hartman, 'Scriptural Exegesis', 151.
50 *According to the Scriptures*, pp. 109 f.

# 7

## The Individualism of the Fourth Gospel
### for E. Stauffer

I

Individualism was more at home in the 'Liberal Protestant' world than it is in the present climate of theology. For the 'Liberal Protestant' frame of thought it was easy to recognize the kingship of God in each individual who accepted the will of God, but harder to grasp the idea of Christianity as incorporation by baptism into membership of the Body of Christ - a corporate existence, entered upon and maintained sacramentally and institutionally. It is one of the results of the revival of 'biblical theology' that, of the two, the latter emphasis - the corporate and the sacramental - has come to be widely recognized as closer to the roots of authentic Christianity.

But this recovery of a theology of the Church has tended to swing the pendulum too far, sometimes actually to distort the picture and to engender an unwarranted suspicion of anything that sounds 'individualistic'. The famous Lucan saying (Lk. xvii. 21) about the kingdom of God being ἐντὸς ὑμῶν is today generally so interpreted as to rescue it from the unacceptable inward and individual sense; or, if there were an acceptable alternative today, it might be to blame 'Luke the Hellene' for introducing an alien individualism into the doctrine of the kingdom. It is almost a slur on a biblical writer - or else on his expositor - if an individualistic note is detected.

That may be a caricature of the situation. But if it contains even a modicum of truth, then perhaps it is not untimely to enter a plea for a reappraisal of the Johannine outlook in this particular respect. To that end I offer this essay, uncertain whether it will meet with approval from the distinguished scholar in whose honour it is presented; certain only that I am deeply indebted to him, both for warm personal friendship when I stayed at Erlangen in 1952, and for all that I have learnt from the publications he has generously presented to me, including a copy of his important *Theologie des Neuen Testaments.* Since the essay was first drafted, my attention has been drawn to an early paper by

91

another very good Erlangen friend, Dr G. Stählin (now of Mainz), which in part anticipates my theme, and to which I am indebted for further insights.[1] Something of my viewpoint is also shared with Dr E. Schweizer in the works cited below.

My thesis is that the Fourth Gospel is one of the most strongly individualistic of all the New Testament writings, and that the 'realized eschatology' which is so familiar a feature of this Gospel is the result rather of this individualism than of anything more profound or radical in its thought. This may sound a foolish thesis. St John's Gospel is generally thought of as one of the chief documents of Christian unity and organic life. One's thoughts immediately fly to the temple of Christ's body, to the Shepherd and the one flock, to the vine and the branches, to the *ut omnes unum sint*.[2] Of course! But is that the whole story?

## II

Picking up the point about 'realized eschatology' first, I begin from xiv. 21–23, which, I submit, is a far more explicitly individualistic type of eschatology than even the Lucan ἐντὸς ὑμῶν interpreted in the 'inward' sense. The immediate antecedents of this passage are a reference to a return of Christ after his departure (*v.* 18 οὐκ ἀφήσω ὑμᾶς ὀρφανούς, ἔρχομαι πρὸς ὑμᾶς), and the interpretation of his return not as a public manifestation to the whole world but as a manifestation to the disciples only (*v.* 19 ὁ κόσμος με οὐκέτι θεωρεῖ, ὑμεῖς δὲ θεωρεῖτέ με). For them, admittedly, it will be an understanding of something that seems emphatically 'corporate' – the 'mutual coinherence' of Christ and the Father and of Christ and the disciples (*v.* 20 γνώσεσθε ὑμεῖς ὅτι ἐγὼ ἐν τῷ πατρί μου καὶ ὑμεῖς ἐν ἐμοὶ κἀγὼ ἐν ὑμῖν). And yet, this seems to be immediately interpreted (in keeping with *v.* 19) in such individualistic terms that one of the disciples, Judas (not the Iscariot) is scandalized. Jesus says that he will love and manifest himself (ἐμφανίσω . . . ἐμαυτόν) to anyone who loves and obeys him. Judas exclaims, 'But

---

1 G. Stählin, 'Zum Problem der johanneischen Eschatologie', *Z.N.T.W.* 33 (1934), 225.

2 'Nun gibt es freilich im Neuen Testament kaum eine Schrift, die die Einheit der Kirche so stark betont wie gerade das vierte Evangelium (x. 16; xvii. 20 f.)' – E. Schweizer, 'Der Kirchenbegriff im Evangelium und den Briefen des Johannes', in *Studia Evangelica* (*Texte und Untersuchungen* 73. Band = V. Reihe, Band 18, 1959), p. 372 ('The Concept of the Church in the Gospel and Epistles of St John', in *New Testament Essays*, ed. A. J. B. Higgins (Manchester, 1959), p. 236).

what has happened, that you should manifest yourself to us and not to the world?' In reply, Jesus simply reiterates (*v.* 23) that the Father and he will come (ἐλευσόμεθα) and stay with anyone who loves and obeys. That could be interpreted - whether rightly or not remains to be seen - as a 'realized eschatology' indeed, but one which finds its realization only on the level of the individual. The Fourth Evangelist habitually makes his point by a dialogue containing a misunderstanding and its correction; and here, by means of Judas' misunderstanding, the point seems to be deliberately sharpened that, insofar as there is any 'coming' to be realized in the near future, it is essentially not a world-wide mani-festation but a secret, private coming to each individual as he realizes the fact of the resurrection, loves God in Christ, and accepts him.

It is perhaps not inopportune at this point to make the observation that indeed any eschatology that is to be immediately 'realized' must, of necessity, be only partial or 'inaugurated' or '*sich realisierende*'; and is therefore inherently bound to show an individualistic tendency: the more fully realized, the narrower the scope. Is it not, then, proper to ask whether the widely recognized emphasis of the Fourth Gospel on the realization of the coming as already about to take place is not largely achieved by a corresponding individualism?[3] Similarly the rabbis, as we know, sometimes spoke of individuals 'accepting the yoke of the kingdom' - that is, accepting God's will and conforming to his sover-eignty.[4] But any realization of the kingdom of God in a fuller, more nearly total, more corporate sense was, for rabbinic thought, an expec-tation only for the future. Whether there is here a clue to the Evange-list's milieu, who can say? In the Jerusalem of our Lord's time, there were probably rabbinical views such as this, side by side with Zealot revolutionary ideals, apocalyptic hopes, and many others.[5] But equally at Ephesus, near the end of the first century, there was no doubt a motley variety of religious views - individualistic gnostic types of thought, millennarianist ideals, and a host of others. It would be too much, therefore, to hope to find in this eschatological saying a clue to the Gospel's provenance.

But to return: are there any other passages in the Fourth Gospel that redress the balance in the direction of a less individualistic eschatology? The references to judgement or acquittal as having already taken place

---

3 As G. Stählin puts it in *Z.N.T.W.* 33 (1934), John, as contrasted with Paul, lacks 'Telosstrebigkeit': his thinking is, in that sense, more static; but this does not mean that he is without a futurist expectation.

4 References in S.-B. i. 608 ff., on Matt. xi. 29.

5 See E. Stauffer, e.g. *Jerusalem und Rom* (Bern, 1957), *passim*.

(iii. 18, v. 24), and to the passing from death to life as a *fait accompli* (v. 24), are in terms of individuals, except when it is the judgement of the world or of its ruler, which is accomplished by Christ's death (xii. 31, xvi. 11). Conversely, the only quite clearly 'collective' and 'corporate' allusion (other than these allusions to Christ himself and his conquest of cosmic powers) is in terms not of 'realized eschatology' but of the 'orthodox' future event, not yet realized (v. 28 f.). This confirms the view that the only 'realized eschatology' in the Fourth Gospel is on the individual level; and such a type of 'realized eschatology' so far from *replacing* a futurist eschatology, need be only its correlative. Indeed, in vi. 40, 44, 54 it is possible to see the two together, side by side: ... ἵνα πᾶς ὁ θεωρῶν τὸν υἱὸν καὶ πιστεύων εἰς αὐτὸν ἔχῃ ζωὴν αἰώνιον, καὶ ἀναστήσω αὐτὸν ἐγὼ ἐν τῇ ἐσχάτῃ ἡμέρᾳ, etc.; cf. xi.24.

## III

This leads to an observation on the relation between Luke and John. It is often said that the eschatology of the Fourth Gospel is in sharp contrast with that of Luke-Acts. It is a familiar fact that in other respects there are striking traces of a common tradition between Luke and John (e.g. the traditions of the Bethany family); but it is usually held that, in their theological approach and outlook, the two writers are vastly different, and, in particular, that their attitude to history and to eschatology sets them at a distance from one another. If Luke-Acts strings out the events, narrative-wise, in a sequence of 'moments' - the ministry, the death, the resurrection, the ascension, the coming of the Spirit, and (in the future) the coming again of Christ - the Fourth Evangelist, it is said chooses instead to present the great verities in their mutual relationship as a single, indivisible unity: the entire ministry is the self-giving; the exaltation on the cross is the exaltation in glory; the Spirit is Christ's own *alter ego*; and there is no concern about a future παρουσία, for the coming of the Spirit is 'the coming', absolutely.

Now, obviously there is a measure of truth in this. Luke is essentially a narrator, and, whatever his theological intention, he achieves it through the use of at least a seeming chronology. John, by contrast, thinks 'theologically' and is ready to fuse different members of his structure together by the use of multivalent words like ὑψοῦν in such a way that there might seem to be less place in his treatment of his theme for time-sequences or successiveness.

And yet, to leave such a statement unqualified is to simplify deceptively, and means ignoring the fact that, seldom though this is observed, Luke and John have something in common even in the territory of such themes as ascension and the doctrine of the Spirit and of eschatology. John alone, it must be remembered, shares with Mk xvi and Luke-Acts an explicit reference to ascension in addition to the resurrection. Jo. xx. 17, whatever its obscurities, clearly represents the already risen Christ as declaring that he is also 'ascending' or about to 'ascend': that is, it distinguishes ascension from resurrection, and underlines ascension as though it added something of theological significance to the resurrection. It is another matter to determine the meaning of the *noli me tangere*, especially when contrasted with the express injunction to Thomas to feel the Lord. But it is very difficult, in my opinion, to believe (with C. H. Dodd and others, *in loc.*) that the Evangelist intends us to understand that, between the meetings with Mary and Thomas, the 'ascension' has somehow been consummated and that it is this that explains the contrast between the 'touch me not' to Mary and the 'reach hither thy finger...' to Thomas. It is surely much simpler to explain the words to Mary to mean that she need not cling to the Rabbi, for he really is still 'with' her and not yet withdrawn from sight. By contrast, then, what Thomas needs is to be met upon his own ground and, since he has resolved to demand tactual evidence, to be offered it - if only to convince him, in the very act, that it may be dispensed with. On this showing, the contrast lies entirely in the needs and circumstances of the two disciples, and not in any difference in the state of the Lord as between the two encounters. In that case, this Evangelist, like Luke, is recounting certain 'resurrection-appearances' as taking place between the resurrection and the ascension. This interpretation of the words spoken to Mary Magdalene fits, incidentally, with the Matthaean picture of the women approaching Jesus and grasping his feet (ἐκράτησαν αὐτοῦ τοὺς πόδας, Matt. xxviii. 9) and being told μὴ φοβεῖσθε - meaning, perhaps, again, that they need have no misgivings, for it is really the Lord whom they see: he has not yet ascended, he is no phantom.

But returning to the allusion to resurrection, we must recognize, of course, that the word ἀναβαίνειν (apart from its uses with reference to going up to Jerusalem) is used earlier in the Gospel also, and in a striking way. Is this compatible with so 'Lucan' an interpretation as I have just offered? In iii. 13 the words are: καὶ οὐδεὶς ἀναβέβηκεν εἰς τὸν οὐρανὸν εἰ μὴ ὁ ἐκ τοῦ οὐρανοῦ καταβάς, ὁ υἱὸς τοῦ ἀνθρώπου ὁ ὢν ἐν τῷ οὐρανῷ (if, with A Θ 1 etc. 13 etc. 579 and others, we read this last difficult clause). It is simplest to accept this (which would otherwise be a hopelessly dark and oracular saying) as a post-resurrection formulation of the Church's faith.[6] For the post-resurrection Church, Christ is both the one who came down from heaven and also the only one who has returned thither. If the last clause is indeed original and if this is a post-resurrection point of view, then it is not irrelevant to our enquiry that Christ is spoken of as *now in heaven*: that is precisely in line with the *Lucan* eschatology, and by no means conforms with what is usually (but I suspect not quite correctly) thought of as the eschatology of the Fourth Gospel. On the Lucan view, Christ, seated at the right hand of God in heaven, is represented on earth by the Spirit; and that, I suspect, is in fact the Fourth Evangelist's 'pattern' of thought also. The other comparable use of ἀναβαίνειν is in vi. 62 ἐὰν οὖν θεωρῆτε τὸν υἱὸν τοῦ ἀνθρώπου ἀναβαίνοντα ὅπου ἦν τὸ πρότερον. But here there is no reason, as far as I can see, to look further than the most obvious sense – that the Son of Man, now ἐπὶ τῆς γῆς (to use the Synoptic phrase) will soon be exalted and vindicated (cf. Mk xiv. 62): it is simply an anticipation of that for which the ascension stands, and thus fits into the same comparatively simple 'pattern' of resurrection and ascension which we have seen implied in the post-resurrection narratives both of Luke and John. Certain peculiarities in the use of the term 'the Son of Man' will be discussed later. For the moment, the result of the enquiry is, I suggest, to confirm the thesis that John shares, substantially, Luke's 'pattern' of ideas.

With much less confidence, and only as a tenative suggestion, it may now be asked whether the σύ μοι ἀκολούθει of Jo. xxi. 22b may not be brought within the same scheme. Of course if we regard Jo. xxi as an extraneous addition, any affinities it may show to the standard 'pattern' which we are calling Lucan will be irrelevant to the authentic Johannine viewpoint. But there is little or nothing *in style* (to the best of my knowledge) to distinguish it from the rest of the Gospel;[7] and if it is pronounced unauthentic it will be mainly for three reasons: first, because of the obvious climax in xx. 30 f. (but that only means that xxi is an addition, not necessarily that it is by another hand); secondly, because of the possibility that, since xxi. 24 f. is manifestly by another hand, the whole chapter may be by another hand (but that is only a possibility); thirdly, because of the alleged incongruity of its eschato-

6 E. M. Sidebottom, *The Christ of the Fourth Gospel* (London, 1961), p. 120, proposes to translate 'No one has ascended ... but one has descended'; but, while I agree that εἰ μή need not mean 'except', I cannot see how ὁ καταβάς can thus be turned into an indicative clause.

7 See Cassien, Evêque de Catane, 'Saint Pierre et l'Eglise dans le N.T.', *Istina* 3 (1955), 291 f. and literature cited.

logy. But if the eschatology of the preceding chapters is, after all, compatible with the standard Lucan type, which reckons with post-resurrection appearances followed by a final withdrawal from sight (ascension), then even the 'follow thou me' might refer less to a spiritual, 'unearthly' leadership than to the leading of the disciples up to Jerusalem by the risen Lord for Pentecost which (as I am beginning to suspect) the Acts narrative implies. If such an idea is ruled out, it will be only on the grounds of the unacceptability of such crass, physical literalism, not on the grounds of language. Now Luke certainly did entertain such literalistic ideas: the post-resurrection accounts demonstrate this clearly – so much so that I am inclined (in parenthesis) even to accept the συναλιζόμενος of Acts i. 4 as = συναυλιζόμενος – Jesus bivouacking with the disciples.[8] But what is interesting for the present purpose is that John also exhibits a physical literalism about the post-resurrection appearances, for is it not he alone who expressly mentions the stigmata (xx. 25-27)? Luke's allusion to the hands and the feet (Lk. xxiv. 39) reaches the same result, but only by implication.

Further, before we leave the subject of the resurrection appearances, it is worth while to observe that St John is quite careful about the timing of them. The first (xx. 14) is in the continuous context of the early morning visit to the tomb (xx. 1); the next is οὔσης ὀψίας τῇ ἡμέρᾳ ἐκένῃ τῇ μιᾷ σαββάτων (xx. 19); the next, μεθ' ἡμέρας ὀκτώ (xx. 26), i.e. the following Sunday. Only the appearance in Galilee in xxi is more vaguely dated as μετὰ ταῦτα. There is not much here, I submit, to encourage the notion that John is concerned only to fuse together into a sequence-less unity all the timeless 'moments' of his theological interpretation. Not a whit less than Luke, he gives us a narrative sequence.[9]

## IV

Next, the 'going and coming' terminology of this Gospel must be examined. The relevant phrases are set out in the accompanying conspectus (pp. 105 ff.). So far as they refer to Jesus, they seem, for the most part, to fall into three main categories – allusions to the coming or coming forth or coming down from heaven, allusions to the going or the departure from sight or the ascending to heaven, and allusions to the coming or coming again or return to visibility. It is that third, of

8 See C. F. D. Moule, 'The Ascension', *Exp. T.* 68. 7 (April 1957, 205 ff. [pp. 54 ff. above].

9 My colleague M. F. Wiles has pointed out, however, that, if the point about Thomas is to be made at all, there must be a time interval: and what more theologically apt than that between Sunday and Sunday?

course, that is generally treated as taking the place of the παρουσία at the end of time. Now I suggest that the simplest possible way to interpret these phrases is to apply the first category to the incarnation, the second to the death, and the third to the resurrection, the return from death.

It is manifestly impossible to remain content with so simple an identification, because the second category certainly includes phrases which seem to refer to going in terms of going back to the Father, ascending to heaven, and so forth; while the third appears to include a mystical return such as is not to be identified *tout court* with reappearance after death: there is xiv. 3 πάλιν ἔρχομαι καὶ παραλήμψομαι ὑμᾶς πρὸς ἐμαυτόν, and there is the already-discussed xiv. 21 ff. which seems to describe an inward and spiritual coming to individuals. Moreover, further complexity is imparted to this third category by the introduction of the sayings about the coming of the Paraclete side by side with references to the coming of Christ.

It is this overplus to the simple going and coming categories, together with such phrases as 'the hour cometh *and now is* . . .', which lends plausibility to the idea that the Fourth Gospel is describing the death and resurrection as themselves the ultimate coming of Jesus – and that, in terms of the Spirit. The extreme form of such an interpretation would be that, for this Evangelist, there is no παρουσία at the end, nor even a strictly time-involved sequence of resurrection appearances, but rather a single coming – the incarnation – which is seen to be final and decisive because of the triumph through death. The triumph through death, releasing the Spirit, marks the beginning of the era of realized eschatology; and this 'coming' is the only coming that matters. For Dodd (*in loc.*) the 'ascension' is complete or consummated by the time of the appearing to Thomas and in the ascension is completed also the true *coming*.

But since we have already seen with what care the Evangelist describes and dates the resurrection appearances, is such a notion really in keeping with his own frame of thought? There are, so far as I can see, no references to the Spirit's coming which show decisively that the Evangelist intended to substitute the Paraclete for the παρουσία. xiv. 16 is the most that might be quoted to support such a thesis – ἄλλον παράκλητον δώσει ὑμῖν ἵνα ᾖ μεθ' ὑμῶν εἰς τὸν αἰῶνα. But εἰς τὸν αἰῶνα need only mean 'for good and all' in a purely relative sense (cf. Exod. xxi. 6, Philem. 15, etc.) and in contrast to the transitory, earthly ministry of Jesus which was about to be terminated. There is scarcely here sufficient evidence to show that the coming of the Spirit is conceived in any other way than as Luke – or, for that matter, Paul – conceives it, as the abiding presence of God with his Church on earth and as the first fruits or pledge of a consummation yet to come. What is more, the only other guides we possess in the New Testament point decisively away from the assumption that the presence of the Spirit is to be equated with the final consummation. Not only does St Paul notoriously call the Spirit only the first fruits and *pledge* of something yet to come (Rom. viii. 23, etc.); I John itself, recognizing the presence of the Spirit (iii. 24), adds, iii.2, . . . ἐὰν φανερωθῇ . . . Why, then, should it be assumed (unless there is cogent evidence) that the Fourth Gospel takes a different view? As for the 'now is' sayings (iv. 23, v. 25), these only represent the combination of realized with future which is a recognized phenomenon also in the Synoptists.[10] It is certainly true, however, that the coming or return of Jesus is described in terms which cannot be altogether confined to the mere post-resurrection appearances, just as also the 'going away' evidently contains in some instances a more pregnant idea than that merely of temporary departure in death. 'To go to the Father', 'to go to prepare a place for you', clearly mean a consummation corresponding more closely to the ascension than to the death alone. As G. B. Caird well says, 'on the Cross Jesus goes to the Father not as an individual resuming a place which He relinquished when He came down from heaven, but as the representative of those who are to share with Him this place He constantly occupied' ('The will of God: II. In the Fourth Gospel', *Exp. T.* 72, 4 (Jan. 1961), 115 ff.).

Yet such phrases by no means have the monopoly in the category of 'going'; and in the 'coming' or 'returning' category they are represented only by xiv. 2, 21 ff. It looks, then, as though St John were working with what I have called the ordinary 'Lucan' pattern, but sometimes adding phrases which transcend it in such a way as to suggest that the going in death and the return in the resurrection are actually fraught with greater, indeed with ultimate, significance[11] – that his going in death is also a return to the Father, in the sense that it represents the completion of Christ's earthly ministry, and that the return from death means the taking of the disciples up into the heavenly life of the new age (cf. xvii. 24). As Bengel says, on xiv. 18, 'Adventus primi *continuationes* sunt ceteri potius, quam iterationes'. But neither of these pregnant uses precludes the holding of a 'normal' expectation of a future consummation in addition. It is not a realized eschatology in exchange

10 Cf. Stählin, *Z.N.T.W.* 33 (1934), 257 f.
11 '. . . alles Entscheidende schon geschehen ist', E. Schweizer, *Gemeinde und Gemeindeordnung im Neuen Testament* (Zürich, 1959), p. 105.

for a futurist, but merely an expression of that element of the realized which inheres in any Christian eschatology (cf., as noted above, vi. 40, 54).

## V

And in fact one only has to read I John to see how the eschatology of the Fourth Gospel works out in post-resurrection terms. It is often said that the eschatology of the Johannine Epistles is more 'temporal' than that of the Gospel – that is, that it fits more directly into the 'orthodox', Lucan time-scheme ('die Mitte der Zeit'), looking back to the ministry of Jesus and forward to his reappearing. But two questions need to be asked before one concludes that this eschatology is therefore essentially different: (1) Is not the more 'temporal' factor due simply to the more corporate setting of the thought? (2) Is there anything in the eschatology of I John which is actually incompatible with the Gospel's teaching?[12] One may freely admit that there is no explicit parallel in the Gospel to the references in I Jo. ii. 28, iii. 2 (cf. ii. 18, iv. 17) to the coming (again) of Christ. But if it be once allowed that the Gospel recognizes an *ascension* (in the 'Lucan' manner), it is not going beyond the evidence to say that this also implies a *return*. Otherwise, why did not the Fourth Evangelist remain content with a more timeless, a more 'mystical', a more theological ascension?[13] The epistle's conception of a return of Christ, and its recognition of the presence of the Spirit meanwhile (iv. 13) are not essentially out of harmony with the presuppositions of the Gospel. For the rest, it shares with the Gospel the conception of Christ as sent by the Father (iv. 9, 14), as coming or appearing from heaven (iii. 8), as bringing victory over the world (ii. 13, iv. 4); and it has as much – and as little – as the Fourth Gospel about 'realized eschatology'. If in the Gospel's prologue the true light was just coming into the world (for so, perhaps, it is best to interpret Jo. i. 9), in the epistle that true light is already shining (ii. 8); the recipients of the epistle have, like the believer of the Fourth Gospel, already passed from death to life (iii. 14); they are already sons of God (iii. 1); already the expectations about the Spirit's instruction are being fulfilled (ii. 20 ff.). Perhaps most significant of all, the very same kind of realized eschatology is recognized as we examined in Jo. xiv. 21 ff.: in I Jo. iv. 12 f.

---

12 Cf. F. M. Braun, *Jean le Théologien* (Paris, 1959), p. 105.

13 If there is ἀρχή, is it mistaken to assume τέλος? cf. Stählin, *Z.N.T.W.* 33 (1934), 255 f. This is where perhaps J. A. T. Robinson, in *Jesus and His Coming* (London, 1957), over-estimates the alleged 'distortion' of a Johannine theological unity by the other writers (see e.g. p. 165).

'No one has ever seen God', but God does abide within the Christian community if its members love one another, and the token of this is the presence of the Spirit. That is only one degree less 'individual' than the Gospel passage: the 'presence' is confined to the community of believers; it is invisible; it is achieved in terms of the Spirit. All this goes to confirm that this degree of 'realized' eschatology is perfectly compatible with a vivid expectation of a *future* consummation; and that there is no need to find a frame of reference for the Fourth Gospel other than that of the epistle – or of St Luke. It may well be that the Johannine Epistles were a corrective, in some respects, to the Gospel, or to a misreading of the Gospel, and that part of the correction was in the direction of a greater stress on the corporate, leading to a correspondingly greater explicitness about the future consummation.[14] But, if so, this only confirms the thesis here advanced.

## VI

If, as I believe, the significance of the choice of the word παράκλητος is that the Spirit is viewed as the Vindicator or Champion of the cause of God, as the Advocate, pleading God's cause against disobedience everywhere, first in the Church and next (through the Church's obedient acceptance of God's judgement) in the world, then this, again, is exactly in line with the picture presented by the Acts.[15]

My conclusion thus far,[16] then, is that the Fourth Evangelist's eschatology is much more 'normal' than is often assumed;[17] and that, where it is of an emphatically realized type, there the individualistic tendency of this Gospel is also at its most prominent; and that the peculiar *depth* of the Fourth Gospel lies largely in its penetrating analysis of the meaning of individual relations with God in Christ.

14 Cf. Schweizer, *T.U.* 73 (1959), 376 (*N. T. Essays*, p. 235).
15 As Bengel says on Jo. xvi. 8: 'Hujus loci impletio habetur in Actis Apostolorum. Vide ibi exemplum elenchi, de *peccato infidelitatis*, c. 3, 13 s. de *justitia*, c. 13, 39. cum antecedenti: de *judicio*, c. 26, 18'. I would not have chosen these passages; but if we substitute (i) v. 4, 9; (ii) iv. 13–16; (iii) xix. 13–20, we get the same results.
16 With which cf. the thesis of Stählin, *Z.N.T.W.* 33 (1934).
17 There is, I think, no necessity to read Jo. xix. 37 as an instance of realized eschatology. The 'looking' of Zech xiii. 10 is not here (I would believe) intended to have been already fulfilled by the Roman soldier and his companions: only the piercing is fulfilled, in order that, on the *future* occasion of Christ's return, it may be upon him whom they pierced that his enemies must gaze.

## VII

All this being said, we may now go back for a while, behind the eschatological question, to note how often, throughout the Fourth Gospel,
it is the individual who is in question. As E. Schweizer has reminded
us,[18] the Fourth Gospel is practically without the words ἐκκλησία,
ἀπόστολος (only xiii. 16), ἅγιος (only πάτερ ἅγιε, xvii. 11); and only
once is there any mention of the Twelve (vi. 67). That might be taken
as a mere chance of vocabulary, were there not other, more unmistakable, indications pointing in the same direction. In the Synoptists, the
term 'the Son of Man' is used in a way which is at least compatible with
the 'human' figure in Daniel – the figure which stands for the group of
loyal Jews who chose martyrdom rather than surrendering their faith.
But in the Fourth Gospel generally, the nearest approach[19] to this is
only in the 'Jacob's ladder' saying (i. 51), where the corporate reference
is perhaps obliquely hinted by the substitution of the Son of Man for
Jacob (= Israel). Otherwise, the Son of Man is a pre-existent figure –
and presumably therefore an individual: he is nearer, at least in this
respect, to what we find in I Enoch 37–71 (although I am far from
convinced that those chapters were extant in the time of Christ).[20] Here,
then, instead of the true Israel, who, in the last analysis, is true Man,
including and comprehending man, we meet something more like an
individual Saviour.[21] Again, the Fourth Gospel is full of encounters

18 *T.U.* 73 (1959), 370 f. (*N.T. Essays,* p. 235); and *Gemeinde und Gemeindeordnung,* pp. 110 f.
19 On this passage see E. Schweizer, 'Die Kirche als Leib Christi in den paulinischen Homologoumena', *T.L.Z.* 86(1961), no. 3, Sp. 169. I doubt whether
C. H. Dodd's ingenious linking of Jo. xv. 1 ff. with the Son of Man via Ps.
lxxx (*The Interpretation of the Fourth Gospel,* Cambridge, 1953) is really
convincing.
20 Yet, note in I Enoch 42 that Wisdom found no place to dwell among men,
so returned to take her seat among the angels. This is strikingly parallel to
'his own received him not' (i. 11), and 'having come forth . . . he returned'
(xiii. 3); and the taking of his own to the dwelling-places (xiv. 2 f.) follows
very naturally. See Dodd, *Fourth Gospel,* p. 275 for other parallels from
the Wisdom Literature.
21 I do not, of course wish to deny that Jesus was 'the true self of the human
race' (Dodd, *Fourth Gospel,* p. 249), but I do question whether such a
conclusion is justly extracted from the use of the term 'Son of Man' in the
Fourth Gospel; and I am inclined to think that, even if the conclusion,
more broadly based, is a true one, it scarcely represents the *prevailing
emphasis* of this Gospel. It better describes St Paul's outlook.

between Jesus alone with an individual or with very small groups: two disciples (i. 38), Peter (i. 42), Philip (i. 43), Nathanael (i. 47), Nicodemus (iii), the Samaritan woman (iv), the infirm man (v), the brothers of Jesus (vii. 6), the blind man (ix), the Bethany family (xi, xii), the Greeks (xii).

Springing from these encounters are numerous sayings about the relation between Jesus and individuals: life belongs to anyone who believes; such a one has passed from death to life; anyone who drinks the living water will find thirst satisfied, whoever eats the living bread will not go hungry; the true worshipper is the one whose worship is not localized in a temple but is inward and spiritual. And is it not, perhaps, significant that what appears to be, short of the death and resurrection itself, the greatest of all the σημεῖα - the crown of the whole series - is the restoring to life of one individual, Lazarus? It is clear enough that for Paul the resurrection of Christ is an inclusive event as wide as Mankind: for Paul the resurrection of Christ is *the* resurrection at the last day, not the resuscitation of one individual; and it is difficult to imagine that Paul would have been content to use any merely human individual's restoration to life as a symbol for this essentially *final* and *all-inclusive* event. For Paul, Christ is the first-fruits of the whole human race; Paul's Christology is of the size of an anthropology. But when the Johannine Christ is shown as anticipating the final resurrection, it is on an individual scale. Martha says that she knows that her brother will be raised at the last day. Jesus replies that he himself *is* the resurrection, he *is* life. But what follows suggests that this is in the sense not that in him the total resurrection of man is included, but rather that each individual who puts his trust in him becomes possessed of an unassailable life. It is a one-by-one salvation that is here envisaged. It could very easily give rise to that individualistic heresy alluded to in II Tim. ii. 18 - that the resurrection had already taken place. Even when Christ is the Vine,[22] it is a matter for each branch, individually, to remain or to be detached. When he is the good Shepherd, it is the individual sheep who listen and respond or who are deaf to his voice. This is not, of course, to deny that the fact that disciples are spoken of as *in Christ*, and Christ is *in God* (xvii. 21, etc.) bears witness to that mysterious inclusiveness - that 'corporate personality' - which is characteristic of the New Testament

22 And I have no wish to controvert the assumption that behind this figure lie the characteristically corporate and collective Hebrew ideas associated with the vine as representing Israel. See E. Schweizer, 'Die Kirche als Leib Christi in den paulinischen Homologoumena', *T.L.Z.* 86 (1961), Spp. 168 ff.

estimate of Christ generally: it is merely to affirm that in this Gospel it is the individual relationship that is the more prominent.

Perhaps E. Käsemann was right, then, in picturing the Elder of the Johannine Epistles (and I am ready to believe, with him, that this is also the author of the Gospel) as the anti-ecclesiastical, pietistic believer;[23] and perhaps the Evangelist (though, in my opinion, no anti-sacramentalist, *pace* Bultmann, but, on the contrary, constantly alluding to the sacraments) is more interested in the great realities that underlie all sacraments – and, indeed, all life – than in their more narrowly sacramental embodiment and their corporate, ecclesiastical regularization. In other words, perhaps the Fourth Evangelist is consciously and deliberately interpreting the sacraments themselves in terms of other categories, rather than interpreting other categories by means of the sacraments. And even if one allows a very direct allusion to the sacraments in this Gospel, it is noticeable that the Pauline idea of incorporation in Christ in his death and resurrection is not made explicit: instead, it is rebirth by water and Spirit (iii), or enlightenment (ix). The nearest we come to a hint of baptismal incorporation is at xiii. 8 ἐὰν μὴ νίψω σε, οὐκ ἔχεις μέρος μετ᾽ ἐμοῦ: but that is still a long way from the Pauline idea of the death of Christ as 'the one baptism',[24] involving the baptism of all by incorporation: here is no Pauline sacramentalism in terms of entry into the Body of Christ crucified and raised.

## VIII

If there is any truth in these observations, they will help to explain why it is that the Fourth Gospel is so particularly precious to all pastors and evangelists who set store by personal dealing. This is the Gospel, *par excellence*, of the approach of the single soul to God: this is the part of Scripture to which one turns first when trying to direct an enquirer to his own, personal appropriation of salvation. Here, then, is an emphasis which is precious in the extreme. Only, it is not a total, inclusive view. It is as one-sided (in depth) as Luke-Acts tends to be (in breadth). The thinker who most organically and most profoundly combines the two planes is Paul. His doctrine of the Spirit not only as Advocate and

23 'Ketzer und Zeuge' in *Exegetische Versuche und Besinnungen* (1960), pp. 168 ff. (first published in *Z.T.K.* 48 (1951), 292 ff.).
24 See O. Cullmann, *Die Tauflehre des Neuen Testaments* (Zürich, 1948), pp. 18 ff. etc.; J. A. T. Robinson, 'The One Baptism as a Category of New Testament Soteriology', *S.J.T.* 6, 3 (Sept. 1953), 257 ff.; cf. W. Nauck, *Die Tradition und der Charakter des ersten Johannesbriefes* (Tübingen, 1957), pp. 179.

Champion pleading our cause, but also as Christ's sonship crying in us the 'Abba' of Christ's filial obedience, and yet, still only the 'first fruits' of a consummation in the future, goes further than John or Luke to combine depth and perspective. The function of Luke and John, in the divine dispensation, seems rather to be to stress each one side of the picture, although Luke's picture happens to be in the nature of a two-dimensional map into which it is possible to introduce the great depth of the Fourth Evangelist's insight – possible, because it is the same 'map' that he himself also accepts and uses.

Thus, each writer has his special vocation in the Lord, and each must be balanced by the other.[25] It is in the New Testament collectively that we find reflected ἡ πολυποίκιλος σοφία τοῦ θεοῦ.

### Coming, going, and returning in St John's Gospel (mainly xiii–xvii)

| Coming (from pre-existence) | Going (? in death) | Returning |
|---|---|---|
| i. 9 ἦν τὸ φῶς τὸ ἀληθινόν, ..., ἐρχόμενον εἰς τὸν κόσμον. | | |
| i. 11 εἰς τὰ ἴδια ἦλθεν. | | |
| iii. 2 ἀπὸ θεοῦ ἐλήλυθας διδάσκαλος. | | |
| iii. 13 | οὐδεὶς ἀναβέβηκεν εἰς τὸν οὐρανὸν εἰ μὴ | |
| ὁ ἐκ τοῦ οὐρανοῦ καταβάς, ὁ υἱὸς τοῦ ἀνθρώπου. | | |
| iii. 19 τὸ φῶς ἐλήλυθεν εἰς τὸν κόσμον. | | |
| iii. 31 ὁ ἄνωθεν ἐρχόμενος ... ὁ ἐκ τοῦ οὐρανοῦ ἐρχόμενος. | | |
| vi. 14 ὁ προφήτης ὁ ἐρχόμενος εἰς τὸν κόσμον. | | |
| vi. 33 ὁ γὰρ ἄρτος τοῦ θεοῦ ἐστιν ὁ καταβαίνων ἐκ τοῦ οὐρανοῦ. | | |
| vi. 38 καταβέβηκα ἀπὸ τοῦ οὐρανοῦ. | | |
| vi. 46 ὁ ὢν παρὰ τοῦ θεοῦ. | | |
| vi. 50 f. ὁ ἄρτος ὁ ἐκ τοῦ οὐρανοῦ καταβαίνων. ... ὁ ἄρτος ὁ ζῶν ὁ ἐκ τοῦ οὐρανοῦ καταβάς. | | |

25 'Vielleicht gibt es keine anderen Schriften im Neuen Testament, die derart anregend und fruchtbar werden können wie gerade diese [d. h. Joh.]. Aber sie [d. h. die Kirche] hat sie neben die anderen Schriften gestellt, neben die Synoptiker und die Paulusbriefe. Nur mit ihnen zusammen und von ihnen her auch modifiziert und interpretiert ist Johannes zu hören.' – E. Schweizer in *T.U.* 73 (1959) (*N.T. Essays*, p. 243).

| Coming (from pre-existence) | Going (? in death) | Returning |
|---|---|---|
| vi. 58 ὁ ἄρτος ὁ ἐξ οὐρανοῦ καταβάς. | | |
| vi. 62 | ἐὰν οὖν θεωρῆτε τὸν υἱὸν τοῦ ἀνθρώπου ἀναβαίνοντα ὅπου ἦν τὸ πρότερον; | |
| vii. 28 ἀπ' ἐμαυτοῦ οὐκ ἐλήλυθα. | | |
| vii. 33 ff. | ἔτι χρόνον μικρὸν μεθ' ὑμῶν εἰμι καὶ ὑπάγω πρὸς τὸν πέμψαντά με ... ὅπου εἰμὶ ἐγὼ ὑμεῖς οὐ δύνασθε ἐλθεῖν ... ποῦ οὗτος μέλλει πορεύεσθαι ...; | |
| vii. 39 | | [τοῦ πνεύματος] οὐ ἔμελλον λαμβάνειν οἱ πιστεύσαντες εἰς αὐτόν· οὔπω γὰρ ἦν πνεῦμα, ὅτι Ἰησοῦς οὐδέπω ἐδοξάσθη. |
| viii. 14 οἶδα πόθεν ἦλθον ὑμεῖς δὲ οὐκ οἴδατε πόθεν ἔρχομαι | καὶ ποῦ ὑπάγω· | |
| viii. 21 f. | ἢ ποῦ ὑπάγω. ἐγὼ ὑπάγω καὶ ζητήσετέ με ... ὅπου ἐγὼ ὑπάγω ὑμεῖς οὐ δύνασθε ἐλθεῖν. ὅπου ἐγὼ ὑπάγω ὑμεῖς οὐ δύνασθε ἐλθεῖν. | |
| viii. 42 ἐγὼ γὰρ ἐκ τοῦ θεοῦ ἐξῆλθον καὶ ἥκω· οὐδὲ γὰρ ἀπ' ἐμαυτοῦ ἐλήλυθα, ἀλλ' ἐκεῖνός με ἀπέστειλεν. | | |
| ix. 39 εἰς κρίμα ἐγὼ εἰς τὸν κόσμον τοῦτον ἦλθον. | | |
| xii. 47 οὐ γὰρ ἦλθον ἵνα κρίνω τὸν κόσμον, ἀλλ' ἵνα σώσω τὸν κόσμον. | | |
| xiii. 1 | εἰδὼς ὁ Ἰησοῦς ὅτι ἦλθεν αὐτοῦ ἡ ὥρα ἵνα μεταβῇ ἐκ τοῦ κόσμου τούτου πρὸς τὸν πατέρα ... | |
| xiii. 3 εἰδὼς ὅτι ... ἀπὸ θεοῦ ἐξῆλθεν | καὶ πρὸς τὸν θεὸν ὑπάγει ... | |
| xiii. 33 | ἔτι μικρὸν μεθ' ὑμῶν εἰμι· ... ὅπου ἐγὼ ὑπάγω ὑμεῖς οὐ δύνασθε ἐλθεῖν ... | |
| xiii. 36 f. | κύριε, ποῦ ὑπάγεις; ... ὅπου ὑπάγω οὐ δύνασαί μοι νῦν ἀκολουθῆσαι, ἀκολουθήσεις δὲ ὕστερον. διὰ τί οὐ δύναμαί σοι ἀκολουθῆσαι ἄρτι; τὴν ψυχήν μου ὑπὲρ σοῦ θήσω. | |

# The individualism of the Fourth Gospel

| Coming (from pre-existence) | Going (? in death) | Returning |
|---|---|---|
| xiv. 2 ff. | πορεύομαι ἑτοιμάσαι τό-πον ὑμῖν· καὶ ἐὰν πορευθῶ καὶ ἑτοι-μάσω τόπον ὑμῖν, | πάλιν ἔρχομαι καὶ παρα-λήμψομαι ὑμᾶς πρὸς ἐμαυ-τόν, ἵνα ὅπου εἰμὶ ἐγὼ καὶ ὑμεῖς ἦτε. |
| | καὶ ὅπου ἐγὼ ὑπάγω οἴ-δατε τὴν ὁδόν. οὐκ οἴδαμεν ποῦ ὑπάγεις ... ἐγώ εἰμι ἡ ὁδὸς ... οὐδεὶς ἔρχεται πρὸς τὸν πατέρα εἰ μὴ δι᾽ ἐμοῦ. | |
| xiv. 12 | ὅτι ἐγὼ πρὸς τὸν πατέρα πορεύομαι. | |
| xiv. 16 ff. | | ἄλλον παράκλητον δώσει ὑμῖν ἵνα ᾖ μεθ᾽ ὑμῶν εἰς τὸν αἰῶνα, τὸ πνεῦμα τῆς ἀλη-θείας, ὃ ὁ κόσμος οὐ δύναται λαβεῖν, ὅτι οὐ θεωρεῖ αὐτὸ οὐδὲ γινώσκει· ὑμεῖς γινώσ-κετε· αὐτό, ὅτι παρ᾽ ὑμῖν μέ-νει καὶ ἐν ὑμῖν ἔσται. οὐκ ἀφήσω ὑμᾶς ὀρφανούς, ἔρχομαι πρὸς ὑμᾶς. |
| | ἔτι μικρὸν καὶ ὁ κόσμος με οὐκέτι θεωρεῖ, | ὑμεῖς δὲ θεωρεῖτέ με, ὅτι ἐγὼ ζῶ καὶ ὑμεῖς ζήσετε. ἐν ἐκείνῃ τῇ ἡμέρᾳ γνώσεσθε ὑμεῖς ὅτι ἐγὼ ἐν τῷ πατρί μου.... ἐμφανίσω αὐτῷ ἐμαυτόν. |
| xiv. 23 | | πρὸς αὐτὸν ἐλευσόμεθα καὶ μονὴν παρ᾽ αὐτῷ ποιησό-μεθα. |
| xiv. 26 | | ὁ δὲ παράκλητος, τὸ πνεῦμα τὸ ἅγιον ὃ πέμψει ὁ πατὴρ ἐν τῷ ὀνόματί μου ... |
| xiv. 28 | ὑπάγω ἐχάρητε ἂν ὅτι πορεύομαι πρὸς τὸν πατέρα ... | καὶ ἔρχομαι πρὸς ὑμᾶς ... |
| xv. 22 εἰ μὴ ἦλθον καὶ ἐλάλησα αὐτοῖς ... | | |
| xv. 26 | | ὅταν ἔλθῃ ὁ παράκλητος ὃν ἐγὼ πέμψω ὑμῖν παρὰ τοῦ πατρός, τὸ πνεῦμα τῆς ἀλη-θείας ὃ παρὰ τοῦ πατρὸς ἐκπορεύεται ... |

| Coming (from pre-existence) | Going (? in death) | Returning |
|---|---|---|
| xvi. 5 | νῦν δε ὑπάγω πρὸς τὸν πέμψαντά με, καὶ οὐδεὶς ἐξ ὑμῶν ἐρωτᾷ με· ποῦ ὑπάγεις ; | |
| xvi. 7 f. | συμφέρει ὑμῖν ἵνα ἀπέλθω. | |
| | ἐὰν γὰρ μὴ ἀπέλθω, | ὁ παράκλητος οὐ μὴ ἔλθῃ πρὸς ὑμᾶς. |
| | ἐὰν δὲ πορευθῶ, | πέμψω αὐτὸν πρὸς ὑμᾶς, καὶ ἐλθὼν ἐκεῖνος . . . |
| xvi. 10 | πρὸς τὸν πατέρα ὑπάγω καὶ οὐκέτι θεωρεῖτέ με. | |
| xvi. 13 | | ὅταν δὲ ἔλθῃ ἐκεῖνος, τὸ πνεῦμα τῆς ἀληθείας . . . |
| xvi. 16 f. | μικρὸν καὶ οὐκέτι θεωρεῖτέ με, | |
| | | καὶ πάλιν μικρὸν καὶ ὄψεσθ με. |
| | μικρὸν καὶ οὐ θεωρεῖτέ με, | καὶ πάλιν μικρὸν καὶ ὄψεσθ με; καὶ |
| | ὅτι ὑπάγω πρὸς τὸν πατέρα; | |
| xvi. 19 f. | μικρὸν καὶ οὐ θεωρεῖτέ με, | καὶ πάλιν μικρὸν καὶ ὄψεσθ με; |
| | ὑμεῖς λυπηθήσεσθε, | ἀλλ᾽ ἡ λύπη ὑμῶν εἰς χαρὰ γενήσεται. |
| xvi. 22 f. | νῦν μὲν λύπην ἔχετε· | πάλιν δὲ ὄψομαι ὑμᾶς, κ χαρήσεται ὑμῶν ἡ καρδία καὶ τὴν χαρὰν ὑμῶν οὐδεὶ αἴρει ἀφ᾽ ὑμῶν. καὶ ἐν ἐκε νη τῇ ἡμέρᾳ ἐμὲ οὐκ ἐρωτ σετε οὐδέν. |
| xvi. 25 ff. | | ἔρχεται ὥρα ὅτε οὐκέτι παροιμίαις λαλήσω ὑμῖ ἀλλὰ παρρησίᾳ περὶ τοῦ π τρὸς ἀπαγγελῶ ὑμῖν. ἐν ἐκείνῃ τῇ ἡμέρᾳ ἐν τ ὀνόματί μου αἰτήσεσθε . . . |
| | ἐγὼ παρὰ τοῦ θεοῦ ἐξῆλθον. ἐξῆλθον ἐκ τοῦ πατρὸς καὶ ἐλήλυθα εἰς τὸν κόσμον· | πάλιν ἀφίημι τὸν κόσμον καὶ πορεύομαι πρὸς τὸν πατέρα. |
| xvi. 30 | ἀπὸ θεοῦ ἐξῆλθες. | |
| xvii. 8 | παρὰ σοῦ ἐξῆλθον . . . | |
| xvii. 11 | | καὶ οὐκέτι εἰμὶ ἐν τῷ κόσμῳ . . . κἀγὼ πρὸς σὲ ἔρχομαι. |
| xvii. 13 | | νῦν δὲ πρὸς σὲ ἔρχομαι, καὶ ταῦτα λαλῶ ἐν τῷ κόσμῳ . . . |

## The individualism of the Fourth Gospel

| Coming (from pre-existence) | Going (? in death) | Returning |
|---|---|---|
| xvii. 24 | θέλω ἵνα ὅπου εἰμὶ ἐγὼ | κἀκεῖνοι ὦσιν μετ᾿ ἐμοῦ [?] |
| xviii. 37 εἰς τοῦτο ἐλήλυθα εἰς τὸν κόσμον . . . | | |
| xx. 19 | | ἦλθεν ὁ Ἰησοῦς καὶ ἔστη εἰς τὸ μέσον . . . |
| xx. 24 | | ὅτε ἦλθεν ὁ Ἰησοῦς. |
| xx. 26 | | ἔρχεται ὁ Ἰησοῦς . . . καὶ ἔστη εἰς τὸ μέσον . . . |
| xxi. 22 f. | | ἐὰν αὐτὸν θέλω μένειν ἕως ἔρχομαι . . . ἐὰν αὐτὸν θέλω μένειν ἕως ἔρχομαι . . . |

109

# Two Studies in the Epistles

# 8

## The Problem of the Pastoral Epistles: A Reappraisal[1]*

The primary purpose of this lecture is simply to give further definition to the long-standing problem of the Pastoral Epistles. I am inclined to think, though this is a harsh remark, which may recoil, that there is no area of New Testament investigation where theories are proposed with greater inattention to the difficulties attaching to them. It may, therefore, be of some service – however negative – to the cause of scholarship if the difficulties can be clarified. Whether I shall be able also to contribute anything positive towards a solution I doubt (and here, indeed, my strictures are almost bound to recoil), although anyone who underlines a problem is almost under an obligation to make some attempt to find a possible way through it or round it.

It was one of my proudest moments when I received the invitation to give this lecture. Although, early in my university days, T. W. Manson examined me for a university prize and wrote me a characteristically kind note afterwards, in his beautiful hand, it was not until towards the end of his life that I began to know him personally, as a colleague in the making of the New English Bible. But even those few years were enough to kindle in me, in addition to the profound admiration I had already conceived for him as an exact scholar of great erudition, that

1 The Manson Memorial Lecture delivered in the University of Manchester on 30 October 1964.
[* Among publications since the date of this lecture, note especially: A. Strobel, 'Schreiben des Lukas? Zum sprachlichen Problem der Pastoralbriefe', *N.T.S.* 15 (1969), 191ff.; J. D. Quinn, 'P46 – the Pauline Canon?', *C.B.Q.* 36 (1974), 379 ff.; *idem*, 'Ministry in the New Testament', in M. Ward, ed., *Biblical Studies in Contemporary Thought* (Somerville, Mass., 1975); *idem*, 'The Last Volume of Luke: the Relation of Luke-Acts to the Pastoral Epistles', in C. H. Talbert, ed., *Perspectives on Luke-Acts* (Edinburgh, 1978), pp. 62 ff.; *idem*, 'Paul's Last Captivity', in E. A. Livingstone, ed., *Studia Biblica* III = *Journal for the Study of the New Testament, Supplements* 3 (Sheffield, 1980), 289 ff.; *idem*, *I and II Timothy and Titus*, Anchor Bible (Garden City, New York; forthcoming); S. G. Wilson, *Luke and the Pastoral Epistles* (London, 1979).]

genuine affection for him as a friend which he won, I think, from all who had the privilege of personal acquaintance with him. So, although I know that, with his clear and penetrating mind, he would quickly have found the weak spots in this little edifice of mine, I know also that, when he demolished it, it would have been in the kindest way and with a disarming smile. I know moreover that the subject, if not my treatment of it, would have been congenial to him. Therefore with just that modicum of confidence and with great pride and gratitude, I dedicate this essay to his memory.

I

I think I should like first to take you for a rapid walk round this little building that I have tried to erect, in order that you may see its shape; and then, so far as time allows, I shall invite you to come inside and see what you think of the structural details.

First, I want to repeat an observation, made long ago[2] and often reiterated by scholars ever since, that there are not inconsiderable pointers to some connexion between the Pastoral Epistles and the author of Luke and Acts. I think I may be able to add a few hitherto unnoticed scraps of evidence to reinforce this conclusion.

But suppose this connexion were even positively established, and not merely a well-based conjecture: it is one thing to establish a connexion between the Pastorals and Luke, and quite another to find any plausible explanation for it: and here we begin to run into the familiar problem of the Pastorals, which, as I say, it is my chief intention to throw into clearer relief than ever.

There are many features, particularly evident in I Timothy but not absent from II Timothy and Titus, which make it intensely difficult to believe that these letters are fully Pauline. I know that there are distinguished attempts, not least in very recent days, to rehabilitate their Paulinity.[3] But do they really carry conviction? Of course we know that writers change their style and their vocabulary, not only with advanc-

---

2 P. N. Harrison, *The Problem of the Pastoral Epistles* (Oxford, 1921), p. 52, cites 'forsitan Lucas' from H. A. Schott, *Isagoge Historico-Critica in Libros Novi Foederis Sacros* (1830), p. 325.

3 Besides E. K. Simpson, *The Pastoral Epistles* (London, 1954), and D. Guthrie, *The Pastoral Epistles* (Tyndale New Testament Commentary, London, 1957), there is now, from a quite different tradition, J. N. D. Kelly, *The Pastoral Epistles* (London, 1963). Among Roman Catholic publications, the most noteworthy defence of the genuineness of these epistles is C. Spicq's *Les Epîtres Pastorales* (*Etudes Bibliques*, Paris, 1947).

ing years but with changing situations; and there is no cogent reason for denying Pauline authorship to a letter, merely because its vocabulary and style mark it as different from others which are firmly established as genuine. It is possible, therefore, that, on such grounds, one might argue that the greetings, for instance, with which the Pastorals open are not necessarily unPauline although they are quite different from anything else we attribute to Paul. It is possible, again, that one might explain changes of emphasis in the doctrine of the person of Christ or of the Holy Spirit as due to a changed situation. I have myself recently argued that the shape of St Paul's eschatological teaching varied not in an evolving chronological sequence but rather in relation to successive situations.[4] It is possible, once more, that the ecclesiastical situation which the Pastorals reflect (if that is not too lucid a metaphor for so dim an image) is not incompatible with a setting in the life of Paul. But the problem of the Pastorals is constituted primarily by much more far-reaching differences than change of phrase or change of emphasis or change of situation. It is constituted by a change of mentality. The powerful mind and the daring thought behind Romans and Galatians or even I and II Thessalonians is, in the Pastorals, replaced by a concern for orthodoxy and for decorum. And as for I Tim. i. 8 ff. – it is astonishing that anyone could seriously attribute to Paul at any stage of his life the definition there offered of wherein the goodness of the law lies: 'We all know that the law is an excellent thing, provided we treat it as law, recognizing that it is not aimed at good citizens, but at the lawless and unruly, the impious and sinful.' The law, meant to be 'lawfully' (νομίμως) used, as a restraint, to prevent excessive sin! In what a different world of thought this stands from the noble Pauline conception of the law as the revelation of God's will and character, liable to abuse precisely when it is used 'lawfully'! It is when a change of mentality like this is added to the differences of vocabulary and expression, that the difficulty of accepting the Pastoral Epistles as wholly Pauline seems practically insuperable.

But as soon as one has decided that the difficulties in the way of accepting these writings as entirely, if at all, Pauline, are insuperable, one is confronted with the corresponding difficulty of imagining a situation in which they could have been created. Barrett's suggestion[5]

---

4 'The Influence of Circumstances on the Use of Eschatological Terms', *J.T.S.*, n.s. 15 (1964), 1 ff. [below, pp. 184 ff.]; cf. my 'The Influence of Circumstances on the Use of Christological Terms', *J.T.S.*, n.s. 10 (1959), 247 ff. [below, pp. 165 ff.].

5 C. K. Barrett, *The Pastoral Epistles* (New Clarendon Bible, Oxford, 1963), pp. 16 ff.

that the Pastorals are an attempt on the one hand to defend Paul against Judaistic detractors and, on the other, to show that he does not belong among the gnostics, is, in itself, plausible enough. But it hardly explains the peculiar features of these writings. It is these that constitute the impasse – an impasse that fragment-theories like P. N. Harrison's do little or nothing, as it seems to me, to remove.

For we are not confronted with a case of mere pseudonymity. If that were all, the problem might be more amenable. That all three epistles expressly claim to be by Paul, is, in itself, no difficulty to those who believe in what may be called well-intentioned pseudonymity. With no intention to deceive, they would say, the pseudonymist writes in the name of the apostle, genuinely believing that he is conveying a message that would have been acceptable to the master, and with the master's posthumous authority. And it may be that a writing like II Peter practically demonstrates that such a practice was followed at a comparatively early period – though the evidence for its being frequently followed in that period is not so convincing. But even so, the problem remains: how explain the circumstantial references in the Pastorals to the apostle's movements and plans? Critics who rightly or wrongly defend the naturalness and the honesty of pseudonymity in general, too often ignore this particular problem. II Peter can say that the apostle is about to die: that is an obvious and quite natural setting for weighty last words. But what would a posthumous pseudepigraph want with the cloak left at Troas, or (still odder!) with an expectation of speedy release? C. K. Barrett, although in part sharing with P. N. Harrison a view which demands belief in the insertion of Pauline fragments, rightly calls these alleged Pauline fragments 'artless – and in some ways pointless – scraps' (*Pastoral Epistles*, p. 11). They are worse than pointless. It seems gratuitously ironic – not to say callous – for an imitator of a deceased master to say, in his name, that he is hoping soon to come and visit the recipient. And the P. N. Harrison type of theory, which finds these to be genuine Pauline fragments incorporated by the pseudonymist, has to face the difficulty[6] of explaining the origin of these floating scraps of Pauline messages, and how and why they were

6 This difficulty remains, even when the number of scraps is reduced and their size correspondingly increased, as in *Paulines and Pastorals* (London, 1964), p. 10 (cf. Harrison's article, 'The Pastoral Epistles and Duncan's Ephesian Theory', *N.T.S.* 2, 4 (May 1956), 250 ff.). The same difficulty attaches to G. S. Duncan's suggestion of a *Sitz im Leben* for II Tim. iv, 'Paul's Ministry in Asia – the Last Phase', *N.T.S.* 3, 3 (May 1957), 211 ff., and 'Chronological Table to illustrate Paul's Ministry in Asia', *N.T.S.* 5, 1 (Oct. 1958), 43 ff.

pieced together in this most extraordinary way. What evidence is there that Paul ever wrote such brief, detached messages? And who in the world would make an implausible pastiche of them with the hope of conveying verisimilitude?

It seems to me, therefore - and here I come to my own desperate effort to suggest a way through the impasse - that we are driven to a theory of free composition (in the case of I Timothy, very free composition) by an amanuensis during the apostle's lifetime. In this case, we have to resort, once more, to the postulate - as old as Eusebius (*H.E.* ii. 11.1)[7] that Paul was released from prison and did the travelling implied by the Pastorals if they do belong to his lifetime, and was subsequently reimprisoned.

My suggestion is, then, that Luke wrote all three Pastoral epistles. But he wrote them during Paul's lifetime, at Paul's behest, and, in part (but only in part), at Paul's dictation.

The least Pauline of the three is I Timothy. It would be tempting, therefore, to place this last of all, at the end of the apostle's life and at a time when he was preoccupied with his trial, or even after his death. Indeed, I have suggested elsewhere[8] that the Christological titles of the Pastorals collectively may suggest a situation in which emperor worship had developed further than in Paul's lifetime. But perhaps this is not a necessary conclusion. Though, admittedly, the Pastorals' terms are more specialized,[9] rivalry with the Emperor is already implied in Luke's Gospel (e.g. ii. 11, 'a deliverer . . . the Messiah, the Lord') and in Acts xvii. 7 ('They all flout the Emperor's laws, and assert that there is a rival king, Jesus') - and Luke and Acts are seldom placed as late as the open clash between Christianity and the imperial cult. And, on the other side, there is also Titus iii. 1 to be remembered ('Remind them to be submissive to the government and the authorities . . .').[10] But, in any

---

7 I have not been able to see J. McRay's 'The Authorship of the Pastoral Epistles', *Restoration Quarterly* 7 (1963), 2 ff., which, I understand, is relevant here. Eusebius's own speculations, it must be admitted, are expressly deduced only from the text of II Tim., apart from his mere mention of tradition (λόγος ἔχει).

8 'The Influence of Circumstances on Christological Terms', *J.T.S.*, n.s. 10 (1959), 247 ff., see p. 262. [below, pp. 165 ff. (pp. 181 f.).

9 For the incidence of such phrases in ruler cults, see G. A. Deissmann, *Light from the Ancient East* (E.T., London, 1927), pp. 343 ff., and C. D. Morrison, *The Powers that Be* (London, 1960), pp. 131 ff.

10 O. Roller, *Das Formular der paulinischen Briefe* (*Beiträge zur Wissenschaft vom alten und neuen Testament*, ed. A. Alt, R. Kittel, 5 Folge, Heft 6, Stuttgart, 1933), p. 97, who suggests placing Titus before both I and II

case, the two references in I Timothy (iii. 14 and iv. 13) to Paul's impending visit to Timothy would, as I have said, be a sort of mockery if I Timothy were posthumous. Perhaps, instead, I Timothy was written just as Paul, about to be temporarily released, was busy with the negotiations involved in the release. This would admirably fit the allusions, and the epistle's ending without autograph. Might it not be that Luke wrote it for the apostle and in his name but very much in his own, not the apostle's, manner of thinking; and, finding a suitable messenger just leaving for Ephesus, sent it off before the apostle had read, corrected, or signed it? There was no time to be lost, if Paul himself was really so soon to follow. The other two epistles would then be also by Luke as amanuensis, but with more apostolic control, though, again, without Paul's autograph.

I cannot pretend that an amanuensis' freely drafted and uncorrected letter is an easy thing to conceive of; but I do not find it impossible; and I find it less difficult to imagine than either that the whole of these epistles was written at the direct dictation of Paul or that they are artificial, posthumous compositions with genuine Pauline fragments set into them like a mosaic. I find it easier to believe that the personal messages were actually given by Paul to Luke.

Perhaps the hardest feature to fit into the setting I am proposing is the portrait of Timothy himself. Defenders of the genuineness of the Pastorals have little difficulty in this respect with his youth, for they are able to show that νεότης is a relative term.[11] But the real problem was well expressed by B. S. Easton when he wrote:[12] '... to these years of close and affectionate intercourse [between Timothy and Paul] there is not the slightest allusion in 2 Timothy. Timothy is said, indeed, to have witnessed Paul's sufferings - but the sufferings (3.11) are those at Antioch, Iconium and Lystra, all of which occurred before Timothy's call!' The only answer I can propose to that is that, if Luke was responsible for the drafting of these epistles, it is, perhaps, intelligible that, in his reverence for Paul, he magnified the apostle's authority and seniority over against the younger man in a way in which Paul himself would not have.

Tim., thinks that the most likely moment for this sentiment would be just before Paul's presumed release from his first imprisonment, and before the Neronian edicts.

11 E.g. E. K. Simpson, *The Pastoral Epistles* (London, 1954), p. 8; J. N. D. Kelly, *The Pastoral Epistles* (London, 1963), p. 104.

12 *The Pastoral Epistles* (London, 1948), p. 10; cf. pp. 235 ff., and C. K. Barrett, *The Pastoral Epistles* (New Clarendon Bible, Oxford, 1963), pp. 9 f.

If one could concede this much, then one might perhaps be ready to take one further step, which concerns the Pauline corpus. My proposal is that after Paul's death, Luke, who knew better than most how many letters the apostle had written, set to work to collect these – his companion's and leader's authentic writings. It might well be, if so, that such a collection stood for some time separate from these three last letters which Luke himself had so freely composed and might not have troubled to retrieve from their recipients. This might help to account for the shorter corpus without the Pastorals, which is reflected both in p⁴⁶ and in Marcion.

That, in outline, is my suggestion.[13] At very best it is a sorry attempt to make the best of a bad job, and I shall not be surprised if I carry no one – perhaps not even the whole of myself – along with the argument. What I hope, however, is that there may at least be some value in this attempt to force a recognition of the difficulties attaching to orthodox solutions, and in the material I now present in relation to it.

II

Let me first go into a little more detail about the matter of authorship. I have already indicated why I side with those who find it almost or quite impossible to attribute the whole of these epistles to Paul. It is not merely a matter of vocabulary. Although the evidence of vocabulary is not to be ignored, and, in a moment, I am going to use it myself, it is a limited evidence because the problems it is supposed to solve are much too complex. It is much more significant that ways of thinking about fundamentals are different in the Pastorals from anything that we find in the acknowledged Paulines. I have mentioned the definition of the uses of law. This is not the time or place for a full review of other alien features. I will recall only two significant facts.[14] The first is that the famous Pauline phrase 'in Christ' (etc.), although used in the Pastorals, is not used in connexion with a directly personal relationship, but only with non-personal words such as 'the faith', or 'the life that is in Christ Jesus' (I Tim. iii. 13; II Tim. i. 1, etc.). The second is that the word 'Spirit' (πνεῦμα) is only comparatively rarely used in the Pastorals, and only twice of the Spirit of God given to Christians (II Tim.

13 The amanuensis theory is accepted in principle by J. Jeremias, *Die Briefe an Timotheus und Titus* (*N.T.D.*, Göttingen, 1953), pp. 7 f.
14 See W. G. Kümmel (Feine-Behm-Kümmel), *Einleitung in das neue Testament* (Heidelberg, ¹³1964), p. 278.

119

i. 14; Tit. iii. 5). Without going any further, we find ourselves thus confronted with something subtly but decidedly different in atmosphere
from the Paulines.

If, then, the case is pretty heavily loaded against, at any rate, total
Pauline authorship, the favourites among alternative names are Tychicus
and Luke. Jeremias, who believes the Pastorals to be genuinely Pauline
but written by an amanuensis, asserts roundly[15] that Luke is certainly
excluded by II Tim. iv. 11 which says 'Luke alone is with me', and he
chooses Tychicus. He means, I suppose, that the amanuensis, whether
he remained anonymous or, like Tertius in Rom. xvi. 22, declared
himself, would at any rate not speak of himself in the third person –
and in a rather complimentary way at that. But to speak of oneself in
the third person seems to me not unnatural when one is not writing in
one's own name; and to say that he is the only one still with the apostle
is, if it is a fact, hardly over boastful. I cannot see that II Tim. iv. 11
excludes Luke's pen from that epistle – let alone from the others. And,
although M. Albertz[16] also comes down, albeit tentatively, on the side
of Tychicus, there are others who favour Luke. Besides H. A. Schott,
quoted above, P. N. Harrison cites J. D. James, *Genuineness and Authorship of the Pastoral Epistles* (London, 1906), p. 154: ' "Only Luke is
with me" – stares us on the written page.' Robert Scott, to whom I
shall return directly, made out a considered case for him a few years
later (1909);[17] and Sir Robert Falconer, whose commentary[18] contains
a very elaborate partition theory of the Pastoral Epistles, attributes
certain sections to Luke. It is the case for Luke's immediate authorship
of all three epistles that I want now to try to reinforce, while, at the
same time, suggesting that they were written in Paul's lifetime and at
his behest, though not entirely at his dictation.

I have said that I do not put much faith in the statistics of vocabulary. This is not because I am adverse to the use of figures carefully
compiled by humans or by computers – being congenitally lazy, I am
always eager for whatever help, human or mechanical, may be available.[19] It is merely because I doubt whether linguistic statistics can take

15 *An Timotheus u. Titus*, p. 8.
16 *Die Botschaft des neuen Testaments*, i. 2 (Zürich, 1952), pp. 217–19.
17 *The Pauline Epistles* (Edinburgh, 1909), pp. 329 ff.
18 *The Pastoral Epistles* (Oxford, 1937).
19 K. Grayston and G. Herdan, 'The Authorship of the Pastorals in the light
   of Statistical Linguistics', *N.T.S.* 6 (1959–60), 1 ff., rightly complain
   against objections to applying statistical methods, as such, to literary
   problems.

us very far towards solving a problem in which a whole series of different factors must be taken into account - age, environment, situation, and so forth. One must ask how far the words in question are significant words; and - even more important - with what ideas they are associated. I am therefore far more inclined to take account of the character of words, and of themes, images and ideas than of the mere numerical totals.

However, so far as indiscriminate word-counts do take us, it seems to me they take us, or at least allow us to go, in the direction of Luke. Every student of this question is indebted to the late Dr P. N. Harrison for his invaluable[20] tables, added to, at the end of his long life, in a posthumously published volume.[21] Sir Robert Falconer's commentary[22] and, more recently, R. Morgenthaler's splendid statistical tables[23] are also of great value.

The main result of statistical work on the vocabulary of the Pastoral Epistles is to associate them rather with the Hellenistic and sub-apostolic writers than with Paul. But the same might be true, I suspect, of Luke's writing, if we had enough of his own to test by. As it is, Luke-Acts is too full (in all probability) of sources for that particular test to be particularly easy. Luke is widely recognized as having used sources (especially in the Gospel) and as having assumed styles from the Septuagint when he deemed it appropriate to do so. But equally, he is recognized as capable, on occasion, of writing in the manner of a Hellenistic historian. If any test were to be applied to him, it should probably be on the last eight chapters of Acts, which look like his own independent, eye-witness narrative. I suspect that it would bring him out with much the same affinities as the Pastoral Epistles. It is true that P. N. Harrison maintains that it is the period A.D. 95-170 to which they belong, and that he shows that, of the words in them not found elsewhere in the New Testament, nor in the Apostolic Fathers, nor in the Apologists, very few can be dated earlier.[24] But that is hardly convincing proof

20 This, in spite of any criticisms to which he may be open. See criticisms in B. M. Metzger, 'A Reconsideration of Certain Arguments against the Pauline Authorship of the Pastoral Epistles', *Exp. T.* 70 (1958-59), 91 ff.; Grayston and Herdan, *N.T.S.* 6 (1959-60).
21 His earlier work, *The Problem of the Pastoral Epistles* (Oxford, 1921), has just been crowned by *Paulines and Pastorals* (1964), a supplementary volume. Dr Harrison died, after a short illness, on 23 August 1964, and his son, J. G. Harrison, helped him through the publication of this book.
22 *The Pastoral Epistles.*
23 *Statistik des neutestamentlichen Wortschatzes* (Zürich, 1958).
24 See *The Problem*, pp. 82 ff.; *Paulines and Pastorals*, pp. 19 ff.

that they could not have been written by a Hellenistic writer in about A.D. 60.

So far as I know, the following two sets of figures have not been isolated by the scholars just mentioned: (1) the number of words in the Pauline epistles (excluding the Pastorals) found elsewhere in the New Testament only in Luke-Acts; (2) the number of words in the Pastorals found elsewhere in the New Testament only in Luke-Acts. With the help of the tables already available, I have attempted to obtain these figures, and the result (unless I have miscalculated) gives a distinctly, though admittedly not vastly, higher figure, proportionately, as an average per page, for the second group. As far as it goes – though this is, no doubt, not far – this reinforces the case for Lucan authorship. A further step, presumably, would be to compare with these figures the ratio between the Luke-Acts vocabulary and that of the non-Paulines. Not being a statistician, I only ask (it is not within my competence to answer) whether this type of investigation, carried out scientifically, might not yield some significant results.

The strongest evidence from mere vocabulary-counts that I have met against Lucan authorship is the dearth of Lucan particles, etc., from the Pastorals.[25] Most noteworthy of all is the lack of σύν and the dearth of σύν-compounds.[26] That the Pastorals are more sparing in Septuagint words than are the other epistles[27] need not be so significant. Luke's Septuagintalisms are, one suspects, a 'turn' that he could put on at will. There is no reason why he should do this when writing a letter.

Taking the statistics all round, then, I cannot see that – unless the argument based on the particles is decisive – there is anything but encouragement for the Lucan theory.

But I said that it was significant words that must carry the weight, together with themes, images, and ideas. What happens, then, by such a test? Years ago I published a very slight sketch of what seemed to me to be traces and echoes of Gospel parables, sayings, and scenes in the New Testament epistles.[28] My intention then was simply to see whether we could detect traces of the more descriptive and pictorial side of the Gospel traditions lurking in the words of the epistles. I did not immediately notice, as I have more recently, that, when I had done my best,

25 *The Problem*, p. 53.        26 Barrett, *The Pastoral Epistles*, p. 6.
27 Kelly, *The Pastoral Epistles*, p. 23.
28 'The Use of Parables and Sayings as Illustrative Material in early Christian Catechesis', *J.T.S.*, n.s. 3 (1952), 75 ff. [above, pp. 50 ff.]. See also H. Riesenfeld, 'Le Langage Parabolique dans les Epîtres de Saint Paul', *Recherches Bibliques*, 5 (1960), 47 ff.

a considerable proportion of the alleged Gospel echoes were in the Pastoral Epistles, and were echoes, moreover, from the material peculiar to Luke. Later, I went on to make a collection of all the parallels I could find between Luke and the Pastorals. These I mentioned in a short excursus to my book, *The Birth of the New Testament*;[29] and then I found that I had been anticipated by Robert Scott of Bombay. In a book, *The Pauline Epistles: a Critical Study* (Edinburgh, 1909), he made an attempt to detect, within the collection of writings canonically attributed to Paul, four groups, only the first of which was directly and immediately Pauline. This was, of course, nothing new in principle, even at that date. But Scott is important for the present purpose, partly because of his emphasis upon the fact that it does not require *lapse of time* to account for differences of phrase and theme, but only *a difference of culture and outlook* (pp. 351 f.), and partly because Scott was, perhaps, the earliest critic to exhibit in considerable detail a number of parallels between the Pastorals and Luke-Acts. I owe my own discovery of his book to D. Guthrie's *New Testament Introduction: the Pauline Epistles* (London, 1961), p. 235, n. 3. Putting my collection and Scott's together, rejecting some of Scott's as (to me) unconvincing, and adding some further items to my own collection, I now have what seems to me a not unimpressive list.

I will not weary you with a recitation of it all – I will select some specimens to show you the kind of thing I mean. Let me group my specimens in three broad categories, A, B, and C, although there will be a measure of overlapping between them.

First, A, the category of significant words, or uses of words:

(1) I have never been much impressed by the alleged medical language of Luke. H. J. Cadbury, I think, exposed the weaknesses in the reasoning of Hobart and Harnack when they tried to build upon it.[30] But it is, possibly, significant, nevertheless, that both νοσεῖν 'to be ill', and ὑγιαίνειν, 'to be well', are *metaphorically* used (of doctrinal error or soundness) only in the Pastorals (νοσεῖν, I Tim. vi. 4, ὑγιαίνειν, I Tim. i. 10, vi. 3, II Tim. i. 13, iv. 3, Tit. i. 9, 13, ii. 1, 2). (As a matter of fact, this is the only New Testament occurrence of νοσεῖν; and ὑγιαίνειν, even in its literal sense, only comes in Lk. v. 31, vii. 10, xv. 27, and in III John 2; but that, I think is not significant. νόσος (νοσώδης does not occur) and ὑγιής (ὑγίεια does not occur) have a

29 London, 1962, pp. 220 f.
30 *The Style and Literary Method of Luke (Harvard Theological Studies*, 6, 1920), pp. 39 ff.

rather wider currency.) It must be added that, as P. N. Harrison shows,[31] Philo uses the terms ὑγιαίνοντες λόγοι (*de Abrahamo*, 223) and ὑγιὴς λόγος (*somn.* i. 79).

(2) Luke and the Pastorals almost possess a monopoly within the New Testament, of the word-group εὐσεβ-, denoting piety or godliness: εὐσέβεια, outside Acts iii. 12 and the Pastorals, occurs only in II Peter (thrice); εὐσεβεῖν occurs only in Acts and I Timothy (once each); εὐσεβής occurs twice in Acts (x. 2, 7) and once in II Peter (ii. 9); εὐσεβῶς comes only at II Tim. iii. 12 and Tit. ii. 12.

(3) The interesting compounds ζωγρεῖν, (Lk. v. 10, II Tim. ii. 26), 'to catch alive', and ζωογονεῖν (Lk. xvii. 33, Acts vii. 19, I Tim. vi. 13), 'to preserve alive', are both confined to the Lucan writings and the Pastorals.

(4) περιποιεῖσθαι, 'to acquire, get hold of' or 'save, preserve' occurs only at Lk. xvii. 33, Acts xx. 28, I Tim. iii. 13 (though the noun, περι-ποίησις, is quite differently distributed).

(5) Finally, so far as 'A' is concerned, the word τιμή which, in the New Testament, mostly means 'honour', is used just twice in the sense honorarium or material gift or reward, namely, at Acts xxviii. 10 (of the gifts given to the shipwrecked Christians by the Maltese) and at I Tim. v. 17 (of the stipend, or honorarium, of elders).

In category B I place what may be called significant phrases, or collocations of words. My meaning will be obvious enough as we look at them.

(1) In I Timothy vi there is a good deal of moralizing against love of wealth. In verse 10 it is called φιλαργυρία, 'love of money'; in verse 17, when the theme is taken up again, Timothy is told to charge his flock μὴ ὑψηλοφρονεῖν - 'not to be proud'. Now, in Lk. xvi. 14, the Pharisees (surprisingly, and I do not know how correctly[32]) are described as φιλάργυροι, 'lovers of money'; and in the next verse, Jesus is represented as saying to them that what is lofty, ὑψηλόν, among men is abominated by God. Is this collocation fortuitous? φιλαργυρία and ὑψηλο-φρονεῖν, it may be added, come, in the New Testament, only at I Tim. vi. 10, 17; φιλάργυρος comes only at Lk. xvi. 14 and II Tim. iii. 2; ἀφιλάργυρος - the opposite adjective - comes only at I Tim. iii. 3 and Heb. xiii. 5. Here, then, is a group of words which might have been

---

31 *Paulines and Pastorals*, pp. 135 f.
32 But see J. Jeremias, *Jerusalem zur Zeit Jesu*² (Göttingen, 1958), II.A, 28–30, where there is evidence for cases of greed, coupled with a lack of affluence.

split up and quoted separately in group A, but which receive added significance by this collocation.

(2) Still on the subject of true and false riches, it is Luke's gospel which, more than the others, elaborates the theme of the folly of laying up treasure on earth, but not being (as the phrase has it) rich 'in the sight of God' (μὴ εἰς θεὸν πλουτῶν, Lk. xii. 21); and it is that same passage in I Tim. vi that takes up these phrases also: men are to be exhorted (verses 18 f.) 'to hoard a wealth of noble actions' (πλουτεῖν ἐν ἔργοις καλοῖς), 'which will form a good foundation for the future' (ἀποθησαυρίζοντες ἑαυτοῖς θεμέλιον καλὸν εἰς τὸ μέλλον). The themes of the distinctively Lucan parables of the rich fool and the dishonest bailiff are clearly audible here.

(3) In II Tim. ii. 12 comes the aphorism: 'if we endure we shall share his Kingdom' (εἰ ὑπομένομεν, καὶ συνβασιλεύσομεν). In Luke alone comes the saying of Jesus (Lk. xii. 28 f.), 'You are the ones who have persevered with me in my testing times, and I covenant to give you a kingdom' (ὑμεῖς ... ἐστε οἱ διαμεμενηκότες μετ' ἐμοῦ ἐν τοῖς πειρασμοῖς μου· κἀγὼ διατίθεμαι ὑμῖν ... βασιλείαν).

(4) In the Gospel saying about the labourer being worthy of support, the Matthaean form (Matt. x. 10) has 'worthy of his keep' (τῆς τροφῆς αὐτοῦ). Luke (x. 7) has 'of his pay' (τοῦ μισθοῦ), and so does the version of the saying in I Tim. v. 18.

(5) Next, there is a linked complex of sayings about Christ as destined to be judge of all alike, of the whole world, of both living and dead. The cliché 'living and dead' is peculiar, within the New Testament, to II Tim. iv. 1 and Acts x. 42. (The nearest approach is Rom. xiv. 9, where it is in the reverse order, 'dead and living'.) If we place these two passages, II Tim. iv. 1 and Acts x. 42, side by side, and add a third, from Paul's Areopagus speech in Acts xvii, we can see some suggestive links:

Acts x. 42: καὶ παρήγγειλεν ἡμῖν κηρύξαι τῷ λαῷ καὶ διαμαρτύρασθαι ὅτι οὗτός ἐστιν ὁ ὡρισμένος ὑπὸ τοῦ θεοῦ κριτὴς ζώντων καὶ νεκρῶν.

II Tim. iv. 1: διαμαρτύρομαι ἐνώπιον τοῦ θεοῦ καὶ χριστοῦ Ἰησοῦ, τοῦ μέλλοντος κρίνειν ζῶντας καὶ νεκρούς, ...

Acts xvii. 31: καθότι ἔστησεν ἡμέραν ἐν ᾗ μέλλει κρίνειν τὴν οἰκουμένην ἐν δικαιοσύνῃ, ἐν ἀνδρὶ ᾧ ὥρισεν, ...[33]

(6) Finally, there is a striking metaphor – the metaphor of the athlete finishing his race – shared in common between Paul's farewell address

33 Cf. Acts xxiv. 15.

to the elders of Ephesus, in Acts xx, and what reads like his farewell message in II Timothy:

Acts xx. 24: 'For myself, I set no store by life; I only want to finish the race' (ὡς τελειώσω τὸν δρόμον μου) 'and complete the task which the Lord Jesus assigned to me ...'.

II Tim. iv. 7: 'I have run the great race' (τὸν καλὸν ἀγῶνα ἠγώνισμαι), 'I have finished the course' (τὸν δρόμον τετέλεκα), 'I have kept faith.'

It is to be observed that only once again does δρόμος, 'racecourse', occur in the New Testament, and this, too, is in a Pauline speech, in Acts xiii. 25: 'And when John was nearing the end of his course' (ὡς δὲ ἐπλήρου Ἰωάνης τὸν δρόμον), ... The simplest explanation of this phenomenon, obviously, is that all three passages are genuinely Pauline; but I think it proper to include it here, in case it is deemed that the Acts speeches are Lucan.

My last group, C, may be headed significant ideas. Once again, there is a certain overlapping, for the athletic metaphor we have just been considering as a significant phrase could be classed also as an idea. But I distinguish, in this third section, something more far-reaching than mere phrases – what can only be called ethical or theological ideas; and of these I offer two.

(1) The first is the so-called 'angelic trinity' – that is, a phrase which, instead of the late, credal Trinity – Father, Son, and Holy Spirit – speaks of God or the Father, Christ or the Son of Man, and the angels. I do not of course, mean that the triple phrase is intended metaphysically or is really comparable to trinitarian terms, as though it were an early and undeveloped form of these. It is merely a convenient designation for a triple phrase of majesty in which the angels figure side by side with God and Christ.

In Lk. ix. 26 there is the saying, 'whoever is ashamed of me and mine, the Son of Man will be ashamed of him, when he comes in his glory and the glory of the Father and the holy angels'.

In I Tim. v. 21, 'Before God and Christ Jesus and the angels who are his chosen, I solemnly charge you ...'.

(2) Peculiarly clear in Luke (if, for a moment, we leave the Pastorals out of reckoning) is a quantitative, retributive notion of justice and responsibility, coupled with a theory of the veniality of unwitting sin. At Lk. xii. 47 f. comes the saying, peculiar to Luke, about the one who sins in ignorance deserving a less severe beating than the one who sins with his eyes open, and about the man of many gifts being correspondingly the more responsible. At Lk. xxiii. 34 (if it is the true reading, though this is doubtful) is the prayer of our Lord as he was fastened to

126

the cross: 'Father, forgive them; they do not know what they are doing'; and at Acts iii. 17, Peter excuses the Jews for the death of Christ because they did it in ignorance (a very rare note in the New Testament). Where else is this weighing of guiltiness expressed? Surely at I Tim. i. 13, 'But because I acted ignorantly in unbelief I was dealt with mercifully' (ἠλεήθην, ὅτι ἀγνοῶν ἐποίησα). One may add, in passing, that without any such condition, the dying Stephen prays, at Acts vii. 60, 'do not hold this sin against them'; and similarly at II Tim. iv. 16 we find 'I pray that it may not be held against them'.

Other ideas might be adduced, not least in the Christological realm, but I leave you with these two examples, only adding that there is an indication of more that might be said in C. K. Barrett's remark (*Luke the Historian in Recent Study*, 1961, p. 62 f.) that Luke 'shares the attitude of the Pastorals, though he is prevented by his subject-matter from uttering the explicit: O Timothy, guard the deposit, and turn away from profane babblings, and the contradictions of falsely so-called *gnosis* (1 Tim. vi. 20).'

### III

Supposing, then, that, for the sake of argument, we accept the hypothesis that Luke may have been the 'framer' (shall we say?) of these epistles. We must now examine more narrowly the question I have already formulated: In what circumstances can we conceive of this taking place? Writings under an assumed name – pseudepigraphs – are, for obvious reasons, normally composed after the death of the bearer of the name. Otherwise there would be no point in the fiction. There are plenty of pseudepigraphical books attached to great Old Testament names like Daniel, Enoch, Moses, Solomon and Esra which were written centuries after the period of the real or mythical figures who are their alleged authors; and a spate of fiction under apostolic names, too, sprang up some century and a half or two cenuries after the apostles. A writing like II Peter, inside the New Testament canon, which is widely believed to be a pseudepigraph, is, if so, exceptionally close to its alleged author's actual date; and K. Aland has plausibly suggested[34] that the earliest stage of Christian pseudonymity was an oral stage, when an actual disciple of an apostle spoke in the apostle's name under the influence of a prophetic afflatus. Nobody was at the time deceived: they recognized

34 'The Problem of Anonymity and Pseudonymity in Christian Literature of the First Two Centuries', *J.T.S.*, n.s., 12 (1961), 1 ff.

this as – say – a Petrine message through an inspired disciple of Peter's and gladly accepted it for what it was. It was only later, when such a message came to be written down, and when the generation who knew the speaker had passed, that the speaker's words, still bearing not his name but his master's, might be mistaken for literally the apostle's work – or as purporting to be such.

I am proposing, however, to treat the Pastorals as Luke's work, but written in the apostle's life-time and at his behest. The chief reasons that drive me to this odd conclusion are these (I have already alluded to the first of them): (1) I can understand a pseudepigrapher representing the apostle, as in II Pet. i. 14, as standing near the end of his life. It is a perfectly intelligible device to add weight to the message by presenting it as the apostle's last words. But I find it harder to conceive of an apostle's disciple pretending, after his master's death, that he was still shortly coming to visit his addressee. Twice in I Timothy this note is struck: iii. 14 f.: 'I am hoping to come to you before long, but I write this in case I am delayed . . .'; iv. 13 'until I arrive . . .'.[35] Some may say that this is an obvious device to lend verisimilitude, and I know that judgements of this sort are difficult to assess objectively. I can only say that to me it seems a piece of gratuitous irony and in bad taste.

(2) On the other hand, in II Tim. iv. 6 ff. where there is indeed a 'last words' setting, perfectly suited to a pseudepigraph, the effect is gratuitously ruined by the introduction of those extraordinary snippets of trivial detail, about the cloak and the books. It is hard enough to understand what Paul would want with them if he really thought that he was soon going to be executed. But it is still harder, in my opinion, to see why a pseudepigrapher should invent details so little consistent with an idealized scene of martyrdom. Surely, of the two, it is easier to believe that Paul really did send a message to Timothy (by Luke's pen, as I am suggesting) to this effect, either because he had a secret hope he might be reprieved and outlast the winter, or because he did not know that there would not be a long delay before the execution, even if he were condemned.

(3) The P. N. Harrison type of solution, of course, has its answer to this problem. These – and other bits of all three letters – really are genuine scraps of Pauline 'personalia', but they belong at a quite different stage of his career and have simply been posthumously incorporated – both to preserve apostolic material and to lend verisimilitude

35 Whether this ἕως ἔρχομαι goes with what follows, as N. Turner, in Moulton-Howard's *Grammar*, iii (Edinburgh, 1963), p. 344, holds, or with what precedes, does not alter the case.

- by the imitator. I must confess that it amazes me that such a solution has gained wide currency, for it presupposes (what, to the best of my knowledge there is not a shred of evidence to support) that Paul wrote these little scraps on separate, detached papyri; and, even if that could be established, it requires us to believe that they were kept by the recipients - another improbable assumption; and finally, it asks us to picture an imitator going round and collecting them and copying them into the letter he has fabricated at points so captiously selected that they have puzzled commentators ever since. Incidentally, it has been pertinently asked why the compiler did not put any of these fragments in I Timothy.[36] What seems to me fatal to the scrap theory (this stromatic theory, if I may coin the term!) is that it requires so much credulity on all sides.

For such reasons, I suggest, it is worth while to hunt for a more plausible explanation. The phenomenon to be explained - supposing I am right in my analysis of it - is a series of writings written in the name of Paul, but bearing, at various points, non-Pauline characteristics such as I have listed, yet containing also phrases and statements about Paul, which, whether in Paul's own actual words or not, are difficult to account for, and seem to be aimless, unless Paul himself prescribed them at those points. It is at this stage that I join with many before me who have invoked Otto Roller's celebrated work.[37] This is an investigation of the Pauline corpus in the light of methods of letter writing in antiquity - the use of amanuenses, and so forth; and it reaches the conclusion that, unless one had a professional stenographer and high quality papyrus, one would be unlikely to dictate verbatim. Verbatim dictation would need to be so slow and laborious that it would, in fact, become dictation syllable by syllable, and the composer's style (especially if he were a torrential thinker like Paul) would be gravely hampered. Much more likely alternatives are either that the apostle would write with his own hand - as he evidently did at the end of Galatians, if not throughout that letter, and as I strongly suspect he did at a certain point in II Corinthians, where the style is more intensely Aramaic than anywhere else[38] - or else that he would tell a friend what he wanted said and let the friend frame it in his own words, using, no doubt, as much of the apostle's actual words as he remembered. The apostle

36 See D. Guthrie, *New Testament Introduction: The Pauline Epistles* (London, 1961), p. 224 f.; J. N. D. Kelly, *The Pastoral Epistles* (London, 1963), p. 29; cf. W. G. Kümmel, *Einleitung*, p. 279.
37 *Das Formula.* Cf. J. Jeremias, *An Timotheus und Titus*, p. 7.
38 E.g. in II Cor. viii. 23 f. there is not a single main verb. [see pp. 158 ff. below.]

would then read it through to alter or emend before he added his signature or, at any rate, his autograph.

Some of Roller's details have been challenged, and I am told that he overdraws the picture of the slowness and difficulty with which the non-professional amanuensis might write. But I am not aware that his main conclusions need to be altered.[39]

If so, I repeat the suggestion of many before me, that a solution to our problem might be found by postulating Luke as the amanuensis; and I would assume a rather exceptional range of fluctuation between, on the one hand, the very free composition, embodying little more than the subjects and general lines of exhortation which the apostle had directed (I Tim.), and, on the other, the much more nearly verbatim reproduction of his phrases (II Tim.).

The non-Pauline characteristics are spread over all three epistles,[40] but it is widely agreed that I Timothy looks the least Pauline of all, and it contains the highest concentration of the sort of features I have illustrated, while II Timothy, by contrast, is by some, accepted as at least containing much that is fully Pauline. It would, as I have said, be easy to propose that this only means that I Timothy is a posthumous pseudepigraph, even if II Timothy (and possibly Titus) are not; but I have already pointed out the difficulties in the way of treating I Timothy so. Instead, we have to find a setting in which I Timothy could have been freely composed by Luke shortly before Paul was, in fact, released. And why not? It has been pointed out by several writers that there is no radical objection to the old theory (as old at least as Eusebius)[41] that Paul was released from imprisonment in Rome and only later reimprisoned. Is it not conceivable that, just before this release, he needed to send messages to Timothy in a hurry – pastoral directions as well as personal messages – but had not the leisure from preoccupations (including, it might be, the actual judicial proceedings immediately preceding the release) to devote to working out his themes in detail? In such circumstances, might not Luke have worked up this pastoral letter

39 W. G. Kümmel, p. 176, surely dismisses Roller too lightly when he objects that the frequent breaks and interruptions in the Pauline letters imply dictation, and appeals to the consistency of style. Has not the uniformity of style (as contrasted with thought) in the epistles been exaggerated? It does not seem to me to be true that (to quote Grayston and Herdan in *N.T.S.* 6 (1959–60), 15) 'if ever a writer was in the grip of his own words, it was Paul'. More realistically, Roller (p. 148) speaks of the 'Timotheisch-Paulinisch Mischstil' of Paul's letters.
40 See e.g. Kelly, *The Pastoral Epistles*, pp. 22–4.
41 See above, p. 117.

for his friend and master, using his own phrases and his own examples and his own reasoning (or lack of it) as best he could?[42] And might it not have been that he found a suitable messenger just leaving for Ephesus, and decided that, since there was no time to lose, it had better go off, even though the apostle had not read and signed it? C. Spicq, in a recent article,[43] has collected from the non-literary papryi some reference to just such opportunist seizing upon messengers to carry letters. Objectors will, no doubt, taunt me by asking whether Paul was so busy packing his valise that he could not sign his letters.[44] But I do not think that the situation I have sketched is really so implausible.

I do not think that I Tim. i. 3 compels us to postulate that Timothy had only *recently* been left at Ephesus when this letter was written. It is not incompatible with a much longer interval than either Paul or Timothy had expected when they parted (perhaps at the point indicated by Acts xx. 15 f.). The letter to Titus will have to have been written, again by Luke at Paul's behest but unsigned by Paul, from somewhere along Paul's route between Crete and Nicopolis, during the interval between the release and the reimprisonment; while II Timothy must have been written, also by Luke, during the second imprisonment and near the apostle's death, in different circumstances, and with much closer attention to the details of the apostle's messages, though still with a certain admixture of Luke's own style and ideas, and still without an autograph - this time, perhaps, because the apostle did not survive to add it. This means a thoroughgoing reinstatement of the old-fashioned theory of a journey to Crete and perhaps to Spain and all the rest of it. But why not? Objections are fashionable, but not, I think, cogent.

I have one final suggestion to fling out for your consideration. The collecting of the Pauline epistles is a notorious enigma. How did it take

42 Roller, *Das Formular*, pp. 147 ff., notes the official character of I Tim. (especially). Is not this just how a disciple, impressed by his master's authority would have written?

43 'Pèlerine et Vêtements (à propos de *II Tim.* iv, 13 et *Act.* xx, 33)', in *Mélanges Eugène Tisserant*, i (*Studi e Testi*, 231) (1964), 389 ff. (see p. 298 and n. 25).

44 Barrett, *The Pastoral Epistles*, p. 7, says that if the secretary was responsible for such un-Pauline writing he was not a secretary but an author. So be it! I do not wish to press the secretarial term; all I require is a trusted writer, writing for the apostle in the apostle's lifetime. In a review of J. N. D. Kelly, *J.T.S.*, n.s. 15, 2 (Oct. 1964), Barrett writes (p. 377): 'The impression given by the Pastorals is precisely that of an essay in Paulinism written by one who was not Paul'.

place – gradually, snowball-wise, or at the initiative of one man?[45] E. J. Goodspeed's most ingenious theory[46] that Onesimus was the initiator of it has been trenchantly criticized.[47] But I am not convinced that the only alternative is to postulate not the work of a single person but a gradual, snowball growth. Suppose we offer St Luke as a candidate. Goodspeed thought that Onesimus was led to his work of going round and collecting the epistles by reading Acts, which brought it to his attention that there must be epistles at the Pauline centres there described. But the one thing Acts does not refer to is that Paul wrote any letters to his churches. Surely it is far more plausible – if we are looking for a single person's initiative at all – to choose not the reader but the writer of Acts. Though Acts mentions no Pauline epistles, Luke as Paul's companion knew of them; and as the biographer of Paul (if I may be allowed a phrase which, I know, is not a strictly correct description of the Acts), he is the sort of person who might have thought of making such a collection. There is some degree of doubt whether the Pastorals formed part of the earliest Pauline corpus.[48] Suppose they did not, what more likely than that Luke, if he had written them himself, should deem them less important than the others, knowing, in any case, that whenever he did need them he could probably retrieve them from Timothy and Titus? It would be the earlier letters he would go for first.

I said at the beginning that theories about the Pastoral Epistles are too often put forward with too little attention to the difficulties attending them. I have tried to be fair to the difficulties attending the theory I have advanced, but I dare say that I am still unaware of their size. My main question is only whether the difficulties attending others are not even greater.

45 See C. L. Mitton, *The Formation of the Pauline Corpus* (London, 1955).
46 *New Solutions to New Testament Problems* (Chicago, 1927), *The Meaning of Ephesians* (Chicago, 1933), *The Key to Ephesians* (Chicago, 1956).
47 See, especially, G. Zuntz, *The Text of the Epistles: a Disquisition upon the Corpus Paulinum* (British Academy, *Schweich Lectures*, 1946, 1953), esp. pp. 276 f.
48 That they were not in Marcion's canon is interpreted by Tert., *adv. M.* v. 21, to mean that he had *rejected* them, not that they were not known by then, but this is not necessarily true. Tatian, however, knew and (according to Jerome (pref. to Tit.)) denied the authenticity of I Tim. on ascetical grounds, but accepted Titus. From the end of the second century (Murat. Canon, Iren., Tert.) they are recognized as Pauline. That p[46] does not contain them may not prove that they were never there (the question of space is not certain).

# 9

## The Nature and Purpose of I Peter

This article springs in part from a critical consideration of Professor sor F. L. Cross's *I Peter, a Paschal Liturgy* (London, 1954), and is an attempt, first, to define difficulties which seem to me to stand in the way of accepting his thesis, and then to offer an alternative suggestion. But first of all, I must express my gratitude to Dr Cross for the stimulus of his lecture and my admiration for the skill and brilliance with which he handles the material. My only hope is that my own attempts at a solution of the problem of I Peter are advanced with anything like as much modesty as his: for I have no doubt that they will need the more clemency.

### I

The data with which we have to work are notoriously complicated. Stripping them down to the minimum, there are the following, which I present in two groups.

(A) (1) The writing declares itself to be from the Apostle Peter, from Babylon, to Christian communities in specified parts of Asia Minor.

(2) Eusebius classes it as among the writings which were never in any doubt.

On the other hand,

(3) demonstrable traces of its use apparently only date from Polycarp of Smyrna (*c.* 135); the Muratorian Canon omits it (though that may be due only to the corrupt nature of that document); and it was not in the canon of the Syriac-speaking Church in Mesopotamia as late as *c.* 350 – though this applies equally to James and I John, not to mention the smaller Catholic Epistles (see W. Bauer, *Der Apostolos der Syrer* (1903), pp. 40ff.).

(4) Moreover, the language and ideas of I Peter have convinced many that it is post-Pauline (see F. W. Beare's commentary, (Oxford, 1947), p. 9); and one asks, in any case, whether a Galilean apostle could possible have written so.

(5) Its references to suffering *as a Christian* (iv. 16) have led some to conclude that its date is likely to be under Trajan (98–117), in whose time Pliny in Bithynia writes about indictments of Christians *as such*, as though this presented a new problem.

Those who adhere to belief in its Petrine origin have to attribute (3) (late evidence of use) to chance. (4) can be met, I think, partly by recognizing that there was a common framework of catechetical instruction, sufficient to explain similarities without requiring literary dependence on Paul.[1] Attempts have been made to meet it also partly by postulating mediation by Silvanus as an amanuensis (so Selwyn etc.).[2] (5) (the question of persecutions) is not, I think, conclusive: to this we shall return later.

(B) Meanwhile there is another set of data to be reckoned with – the form and contents of this writing. These will be alluded to in more detail later, but the outstanding feature is the difference between the first, and larger, section and the second which starts at iv. 12, after a very evident break marked by the doxology and 'Amen' of iv. 11.

This has led to many partition theories, of which two are instanced, while this article ventures to add one more, but of a different sort.

Streeter[3] conjectured that this so-called Epistle comprised (a) a sermon to a group of baptized persons (i. 3–iv. 11), (b) a letter of encouragement in time of persecution (iv. 12–v. 11). Both, he thought, might have been by the Elder Aristion (*c.* 90), who may have been Bishop of Smyrna at the time of the persecution there referred to in Rev. ii. 10. Later, these two documents were turned, Streeter conjectured, into a 'Petrine' epistle by someone, possibly at Sinope in Pliny's time, who added the address (i. 1 f.) and the salutation (v. 12–14). The church order implied in the writing is, Streeter held, far in advance of that implied in the Paulines: elders are in danger of 'lording it over the flock', Christ is spoken of as Shepherd and Episcopus, etc.; and the

---

1 See P. Carrington, *The Primitive Christian Catechism* (Cambridge, 1940), and Selwyn's commentary; and a useful summary of the position in Bo Reicke, 'The Disobedient Spirits and Christian Baptism', *Acta Sem. Neot. Upsal.* 13 (1946), 229. But see also the serious difficulties in the way of this argument regarding I Peter exposed by C. L. Mitton, 'The Relationship between I Peter and Ephesians' (*J.T.S.* n.s. 1, 1 (1950), 67 ff.). He argues for the dependence of I Peter on Ephesians. Yet, are his examples conclusive?

2 But, as W. L. Knox pointed out (reviewing Selwyn in *Theology*, 49 (1946), 343), if Silvanus drafted the Thessalonian Epistles, it is hard to believe that he was up to the style of I Peter.

3 *The Primitive Church* (London, 1929).

gulf between the Pauline situation and that implied for Asia by Ignatius and Polycarp might be bridged, he suggested, by just such leaders as the Elder John for Ephesus and the Elder Aristion for Smyrna. His other arguments for a comparatively late date turn on his answers to the problems presented by the data under (A) above, though he does not wish to place any part of the writing as late as Trajan, except the epistolary greetings and farewell.

Beare, in his commentary, likewise makes a sharp distinction between what he regards as the real epistle (i. 1 f., iv. 12–end) and the much more formal homily, i. 3 to iv. 11. He, too, is inclined to allow that the two parts are by one writer; and he, too, is convinced (by his answer to the data under (A)) that this was not St Peter.

## II

We turn, now, to another type of approach. H. Preisker, in his additions to the posthumous edition of H. Windisch's commentary (3rd ed., Tübingen, 1951), offers a liturgical solution to the problem presented by the apparent discrepancies between, and within, the sections of the epistle. In treating it as liturgical, he had been anticipated (as Dr Cross points out) by Perdelwitz (*Die Mysterienreligion und das Problem des I. Petrusbriefes* (1911)) and Bornemann ('Der erste Petrusbrief - eine Taufrede des Silvanus?', *Z.N.T.W.* 19 (1919), 143 ff.). But Preisker's presentation of the liturgical idea constitutes the most important antecedent to Dr Cross's work.

Preisker found in I Peter a baptismal liturgy, with the following sections and sub-sections.

(1) i. 3–iv. 11 is for the baptizands, and consists of:

    (i) *A Prayer-Psalm*, i. 3–12, strongly eschatological; φρουρουμένους (*v*. 5) is a reference to the *coming* safety of the baptizands.

    (ii) *Instruction*, i. 13–21 (cf. Lev. xix. 2), with formal, credal phrases (*vv*. 17, 18 f., 21). Γενήθητε (*v*. 15) points to the imminent baptism. Law and Gospel are here combined; eyes are turned to the glorious End.

    (iii) Between i. 21 and 22 *the baptism* itself takes place, for n.b. the tenses and the phrases of *vv*. 22 f.

    (iv) *Baptismal Dedication*, i. 22–5 (note the solid morality of it, avoiding mere ecstasy and exaltation).

    (v) *A Festal Song* in three strophes ii. 1–3, 4 f., 9 f. (contributed by some inspired member of the congregation).

(vi) *Exhortation*, ii. 11-iii. 12, including (ii. 21-4) a Song about Christ (perhaps derived from elsewhere).

(vii) *A Revelation*, iii. 13-iv. 7a (with peculiarities of style).

(viii) An epistolary equivalent to the *Closing Prayer*, iv. 7b-11c. The newly baptized are here no longer guests but active participants in the spiritual gifts and duties.

(2) iv. 12 ff. is a Closing Service for the whole congregation (note, now, the reference to actual sufferings, while previously they had been alluded to as only potential):

(i) *A Revelation*, iv. 12-19 (ideas from iii. 13-17, iv. 1-7a are renewed).

(ii) *Exhortation*, v. 1-9.

(iii) *Closing Blessing*, v. 10.

(iv) *Closing Doxology*, v. 11.

i. 1 f. and v. 12-14 provide opening and closing epistolary formulae.

Thus Preisker sought to explain the apparent discrepancies within I Peter - in particular the changes of tense, and the fact that iv. 12 alludes to actual sufferings, whereas until then the suffering is only potential: it is only when the whole congregation is addressed that the sufferings, which do not belong to those outside the Church, are spoken of as a fact.

In short, it is a Roman Baptismal Liturgy, which was eventually written down and of which the several parts were put together by Silvanus (a second or third generation Christian). St Peter had been martyred within recent years, and the Roman Christians send this liturgy (in the Apostle's spirit, as they believe) as a greeting to the Churches of Asia which had known him.

Dr Cross's thesis (*I Peter*), advanced with the greatest modesty and caution, is an expansion of Preisker's: not only is I Peter a Baptismal Liturgy; it is substantially the celebrant's part of the Baptismal Eucharist of the Paschal Vigil.

He was led thus to connect it with the Paschal season by noting the remarkable frequency of πάσχω, πάθημα and recalling the way in which (e.g.) Melito of Sardis makes use of the paronomasia πάσχω and πάσχα. If it is difficult to find a satisfactory 'setting in life' for the suffering (until as late as Trajan), may not the suffering motif be due rather to the *Pasch* setting?

Following this clue, Dr Cross finds other references both to the paschal season and to the baptismal practice of the Church (e.g. i. 13 girding up the loins, iii. 3 the deposition of ornaments before going down into the bath), as well as agreeing with Preisker in locating the baptism itself between *vv.* 21 and 22 of Ch. i; and he shares with certain others the suspicion that ἐγεύσασθε in ii. 3 may be an allusion to the Baptismal Eucharist.

## III

For my own part I whole-heartedly agree that I Peter is concerned with baptism - who, indeed, could deny it? But this much is true, of course, of many other parts of the New Testament (Rom. vi, Col. ii, Heb. vi, to go no further), and, in itself, it proves no more than that the early Church writers continually had the 'pattern' of baptism in mind, and often cast the Gospel into that dramatic form. The sacraments were vehicles of the Gospel and the Gospel was sacramental, and the two are virtually inseparable.

It is another matter to detect here an actual liturgy - the words used actually at a celebration of a baptism or a baptism-and-eucharist; and it is there that I still find myself unconvinced, even allowing for the fact, as Dr Cross justly points out, that at this early stage of development a clear distinction between liturgy and homily could not have been drawn.

The following are my reasons.

(1) The 'suffering' allusions can be more convincingly accounted for than by the paschal paronomasia. Of this, more anon.

(2) I do not find it easy (as Preisker and Cross apparently do) to conceive how a liturgy-homily, shorn of its 'rubrics' (which, of course, were probably oral), but with its changing tenses and broken sequences all retained, could have been hastily dressed up as a letter and sent off (without a word of explanation) to Christians who had not witnessed its original setting.

(3) If the Exodus-motif is really as strong as the paschal thesis requires, why did the Celebrant miss the golden opportunity of applying the Wilderness figures to baptism (the cloud and the sea, as in I Cor. x), and, instead, use the far less appropriate figure of the Flood?

(4) Bornemann (*Z.N.T.W.* 19 (1919), 146 ff.) noted the prominence of Ps. xxxiv (LXX xxxiii) in the epistle. He suggests (p. 161) that it was actually read before the homily which I Peter represents, and he draws up an impressive list of parallels, including the following (the Petrine reference in each case is followed by the verse or verses of the Psalm in the LXX): i. 3/2; ii. 3/9; ii. 4/6; ii. 6/6; iii. 10-13/13-17; v. 5/19; and other echoes are noted on pp. 149 f. But there appears to be, Miss A.

Guilding of Sheffield University tells me, 'no evidence for the paschal connexion of Ps. xxxiv (nor indeed for its connexion with any other Jewish feast), except that in Midrash Rabbah *v.* 9 of the Psalm is connected with Exod. xii. 22 and *v.* 23 . . . is connected with the first Passover and the redemption of the firstborn'.[4] This does not, as it seems to me, encourage the connexion of I Peter as a whole with a paschal setting, though of course there is no knowing what liberties the Christian calendar had already begun to take with the Jewish festival traditions.

(5) There are certain smaller details also where I fail to find Dr Cross convincing:

(a) On p. 20 he argues that the theological significance of iv. 1b ('he that hath suffered in the flesh hath ceased from sin') requires the paschal context to bring it out. But this verse is in a context which (as I have agreed) is already baptismal; and baptism itself is quite sufficient without the special Pasch motif to explain it. Christians knew that they must suffer, if not literal death, at any rate that death and burial with Christ which are baptism.

(b) On p. 21 he argues that to give ὑπομενεῖτε in ii. 20 the moral connotation of 'take it patiently' (so English versions) it is necessary to presuppose the religious basis of all suffering by the Christian - namely its relation to Christ, the archetypal Sufferer. Granted: but that does not require a paschal context, any more than II Thess. iii. 5, II Tim. ii. 10, 12, Rev. i. 9. And I doubt very much whether, in i.11, τὰ εἰς Χριστὸν παθήματα can conceivably be taken (p. 22) as 'the sufferings of Christ's people in mystical union with Him'. Neither this, nor the interpretation in Selwyn's commentary ('the sufferings of the Christward road') is nearly as natural as to take the prophets of i. 10 as prophets of the old dispensation, and τὰ εἰς Χριστὸν παθήματα as the sufferings which were destined for Christ.

(c) on pp. 23 f. Cross argues that the paschal setting is required to explain the startling combination of joy and suffering. In reply, need one do more than point to Acts v. 41 and all the passages of which that is typical? Is there any more obvious characteristic of Christianity at all times and not alone at Pasch?

(d) On p. 25, discussing the ἀναζωσάμενοι τὰς ὀσφύας of i. 13, Cross claims Lk. xii. 35 as the only other New Testament use of the verb ζώννυμι (here περιζώννυμι) used for 'girding up'. But has he not forgot-

4 Miss Guilding has a very interesting suggestion to make about I Peter in relation to Psalms and lections: but I will not spoil her story by telling it prematurely. It does not substantially alter mine.

The nature and purpose of I Peter

ten Acts xii. 8 ζῶσαι καὶ ὑπόδησαι τὰ σανδάλιά σου and Eph. vi. 14 περιζωσάμενοι τὴν ὀσφὺν ὑμῶν ἐν ἀληθείᾳ? Incidentally, Acts xii. 8 is in a confessedly paschal context (v. 3), and in both Acts and Ephesians we are given not only girding but also shoes! I Peter can provide no paschal shoes upon the feet!

(e) The intrusion of the mention of baptism into a credal passage is claimed (pp. 28 f.) as pointing to an occasion when baptism was actually in view. But in the New Testament, the theme of baptism and the creed are constantly linked: if baptism is credal, the creed is also baptismal; and the conjunction does not prove the enactment of an actual baptism (see above, p. 137).

(f) Dr Cross agrees (p. 30) with Preisker that the νῦν of i. 12, ii. 10 (bis), 25, iii. 21, the ἄρτι of i. 6, 8, and the ἀρτιγέννητα of ii. 2 help to indicate that the rite is actually in progress, 'now'. He admits that the argument has been over-pressed. But will it, in fact, bear any weight at all? The first two ἄρτι passages are concerned with the present suffering and walking by faith, as contrasted with the glory to come; they are thus irrelevant. Of the νῦν passages, the first is irrelevant if (as seems natural - see above, p. 138) the passage is interpreted of Old Testament prophecy in contrast to the new Christian era. The other four occurrences would certainly fit perfectly well into a baptism actually in progress - especially iii. 21 (ὃ καὶ ὑμᾶς ἀντίτυπον νῦν σώζει βάπτισμα). But not one of them is out of place in a simple 'dispensational' view of things as in i. 12: once thus, now thus; once the Flood, now (in the present dispensation) baptism.

There remains the ἀρτιγέννητα βρέφη of ii. 2. This is by far the best for Dr Cross's purpose (as Bornemann, Z.N.T.W. 19 (1919), 155 f., had shown). And it is perfectly true that the other two instances of γάλα used metaphorically in the New Testament, I Cor. iii. 2, Heb. v. 12 f., are of young or 'arrested' believers. Yet not even this phrase, ὡς ἀρτι-γέννητα βρέφη τὸ λογικὸν ἄδολον γάλα ἐπιποθήσατε, as it seems to me, need necessarily mean more than 'long for spiritual nourishment as eagerly as newly born babies do for physical nourishment'. After all, of any Christians it may be said that they have been reborn (i. 3); and is I Pet. ii. 2 saying more than Jas i. 21 δέξασθε τὸν ἔμφυτον λόγον? No doubt both passages are baptismal in reference; but is there any need to press the ἀρτι- , to imply that baptism took place a moment ago? The argument is certainly not without force, and I admit that it would be impressive cumulatively. But it needs more grains to go with it before it forms a heap. In passing, the τέκνα ὑπακοῆς of i. 13 could easily be translated 'obedient children', in line with the theme of new birth; but

139

it could equally well mean (by the familiar Semitic idiom) simply 'obedient people'.

(g) On p. 34 Cross suggests that i. 23 διὰ λόγου κ.τ.λ. and i. 25 τὸ ῥῆμα τὸ εὐαγγελισθὲν εἰς ὑμᾶς may be allusions to the baptismal formula. But it is wildly improbable that this would be spoken of as εὐαγγελισθέν, 'proclaimed as good news'; while 'the word of God' is a perfectly natural description of the Gospel (cf. Jas i. 18).

(h) On the same page he most ingeniously relates the passage about the women's ornaments (iii. 3 ff.) with the Hippolytean rules for women preparing to go down into the baptismal bath. But the parallel is not really very apt; for the Petrine theme is 'not gold but good character' (exactly as in I Tim. ii. 9 f.), which would fall rather flat if the women were shortly going to *resume* their finery after baptism.

(i) On p. 39, returning to the association of πάσχω with Pasch, Cross translated iii. 14 as 'But if ye should *suffer* for Righteousness sake'. But the words are ἀλλὰ εἰ καὶ πάσχοιτε which clearly mean 'but if ye *should* suffer. . .' (in contrast to the preceding καὶ τίς ὁ κακώσων ὑμᾶς. . .). The passage quite clearly means 'If you are good citizens you are not *likely* to be molested; but if you *should* suffer - provided it is in a good cause - it is only cause for gladness'. There is no 'mystical' sense here, but a straightforward allusion to the possibility of actual suffering.


IV

If, for all these reasons, the case for an actual baptismal liturgy seems precarious, is there any more plausible thesis? It is for others to judge whether what is here suggested takes us any nearer to a solution. In brief my suggestion is as follows:

I Peter is genuinely epistolary and was written specifically for the communities indicated in the greeting; but since some of these communities were actually suffering persecution, while for others it was no more than a possibility, the writer sent two forms of epistle, one for those not yet under actual duress (i. 1-iv. 11 and v. 12-14), and the other - terser and swifter - for those who were in the refining fire (i. 1-ii. 10, iv. 12 to v. 14). The messengers were bidden to read the appropriate part to each community according to the situation;[5] and it is not difficult to imagine that ultimately, when apostolic writings were

5 A partial parallel is to be found in the Epistle to the Romans, if (as T. W. Manson argued in *B.J.R.L.* 31, 2 (Nov. 1948)) it was used both for Rome and, with ch. xvi added, for Ephesus.

being collected, the two 'insets' were copied continuously, one after the other, within the common framework of salutation and farewell. Some points of detail may now be taken up.

(1) Regarding the nature of the persecution implied by I Peter, it is sometimes argued that the terms are too close to the situation implied by Pliny's correspondence for them to be construed as anything but a reference to official indictment. In particular, iv. 15 f. is appealed to: you must not suffer as a *criminal, ὡς φονεὺς ἢ κλέπτης ἢ κακοποιὸς ἢ ὡς ἀλλοτριεπίσκοπος· εἰ δὲ ὡς χριστιανός, μὴ αἰσχυνέσθω, δοξαζέτω δὲ τὸν θεὸν ἐν τῷ ὀνόματι τούτῳ*. This, it is urged, puts the being a Christian on the same level as those criminal offences, as an indictable charge, and cannot date earlier than the time when Christianity as such was a crime. Moreover, Professor J. Knox of Union Theological Seminary, New York, has pointed[6] to a further parallel with the Pliny situation. Pliny speaks of obstinacy *(pertinacia)* as deserving to be punished, whether or not Christianity as such ought to be indictable. This, suggests Knox, is perhaps the point of I Pet. iii. 16 *ἀλλὰ μετὰ πραΰτητος καὶ φόβου*: the Christians are to give a clear account of what they stand for - but with such humility and deference that, if they are condemned, it will be abundantly clear that it is for their faith and nothing else whatever, not even obstinacy.

Despite this, it seems to me that all the requirements of these passages are equally well met by postulating 'unofficial' persecution - harrying by Jews and pagans. The fact that *ὡς χριστιανός* is parallel to *ὡς φονεὺς ἢ κλέπτης* (whatever the other words in that list may mean - which is obscure) does not in the least compel the conclusion that to be a Christian was officially a crime in the same category as the indictable offences. Even if all the other words mean indubitable crimes, all that the Greek says is, if you have to suffer, suffer as a Christian, not as a criminal. It does not specify the nature of the suffering in the parallel clauses.

It was possible to suffer *ὡς χριστιανός* from the moment that the name was given (Acts xi. 26): the Christians did not escape that sort of suffering even before it was an officially recognized offence. And it seems as natural to postulate 'private' persecutions here ('pogroms', so to speak) as it is in I Thess. ii. 14-16, Heb. x. 32-9,[7] xiii. 7. I put forward this view in the *J.T.S.* n.s. 1 (Apr. 1950) and, in this regard, I am supported by Dr E. G. Selwyn in *S.N.T.S. Bulletin* (Oxford,

6 *J.B.L.* 72, 3 (1953).
7 In *v.* 34 the δέσμιοι need only be those imprisoned by Jewish authorities (Acts v. 18).

1950), p. 46 and by Dr W. C. van Unnik in *N.T.S.* 1, ii (Nov. 1954), p. 102. It may be noted also that Dr E. Stauffer, *Die Theologie des Neuen Testaments* (Stuttgart, 1948), note 65, points out how readily the Jews of Asia Minor could instigate a rising in the days of Polycarp (*Mart. Polyc.* xiii. 1), though of course that was much later. It is worth while to note that in I Pet. iv. 4 there is a reference to precisely such social ostracism and unpopularity as might lead to open persecution of this sort, without any state intervention.

As for the use of 'Babylon' (v. 13), unless, with some, we take it literally, there is no need to deduce from it that Rome is the arch-enemy and that the Christian writer needs to conceal his whereabouts from persecuting officials by this cryptogram. As a matter of fact, if the writing had fallen into the hands of a Pliny, what he would have read would have been loyal exhortations to good citizenship (ii. 13–17): so there were no security reasons for the term. Rather, the motive is homiletic: Rome is called Babylon as the place of exile; for the Christian, in the metropolis of the civilized world, is a πάροικος καὶ παρεπίδημος.

(2) Postulating, then, a situation of actual persecution or the threat of it, but not necessarily State persecution, it is easy to find abundance of parallels from similar situations:

| | | |
|---|---|---|
| Matt. x. 16ff. etc. | I Pet. iii. 15 f. | Gentle but firm |
| John xv. 18 ff. | I Pet. v. 9 | ὁ κόσμος the opponent |
| Acts iv. 31; v. 41 | I Pet. iv. 13 f. | πνεῦμα and χαρά |
| I Cor. xii. 3 | I Pet. iv. 4 | βλασφημεῖν |
| Gal. iv. 29 | I Pet. iv. 3 f. | Persecution by the 'un-spiritual' |
| I Thess. i. 6 | I Pet. iv. 13 f. | πνεῦμα and χαρά |
| I Thess. ii. 14–16 | [See notes] | General (private) persecution |
| I Thess. iii. 3 | I Pet. ii. 21 | εἰς τοῦτο κείμεθα |
| II Thess. iii. 5 | I Pet. ii. 20 | ἡ ὑπομονὴ τοῦ Χριστοῦ |
| Tit. ii. 8[8] | I Pet. iv. 4 | Vituperation |
| Heb. ii. 18; iv. 15 | I Pet. iv. 12 | πειρασμός |
| Heb. vi. 6, 9–11; x. 26–31 | I Pet. i. 17–19 | The terror of apostasy |
| Heb. x. 32–9 | I Pet. v. 9 | The fellowship in sufferings |

This, it seems to me, suggests how much can be explained by postulat-

8 See Bo Reicke, *Acta Sem. Neot. Upsal.* 13 (1946), 226.

ing harrying by local opponents, sometimes leading to imprisonment by local authorities or even (as in the case of Stephen) death.[9]

(3) The one New Testament document which quite evidently is concerned, at least in part, with State persecution is the Apocalypse. Not that even there there are not also the signs of less official action – e.g. by the Synagogue of Satan (iii. 9). But few would doubt that in this writing we are confronted by persecution of a more official type – though even this, more likely, was under Domitian than under Trajan. Selwyn (*S.N.T.S. Bulletin*, p. 46) reminds us that Pliny himself bears witness to persecution in Asia Minor twenty years before the time at which he writes.

Yet even so the general circumstances are the same; and there are other special parallels betweeen the Apocalypse and I Peter, bearing out the thesis that the latter is addressed to a situation of real distress, while not compelling us to regard the persecuting powers as identical in the two writings:

| | | |
|---|---|---|
| Rev. ii. 2; iii. 10, etc. | | ὑπομονή |
| Rev. i. 6 | I Pet. ii. 9 | Royal priesthood (for the slaves and the unpriested sufferers!) |
| Rev. i. 9 | I Pet. v. 1 f. | Witness and participator in the sufferings and kingdom |
| Rev. ii. 10; iii. 11 | I Pet. v. 4 | στέφανος |
| Rev. ii. 23 | I Pet. i. 17 | God the all-knowing |

The Shepherd-theme is in both, but I doubt if that is relevant. Incidentally, Revelation is *clearly* paschal (xv. 3), where I Peter is less clearly so.

(4) But in particular it is significant that, in the Letters to the Seven Churches, some are actually under persecution (ii. 13), while others are only under the threat of it (ii. 10, iii. 10); and the letters are adapted accordingly. This, it seems to me, provides an exact parallel to the two letters which I find within I Peter (cf. also Heb. x. 33 τοῦτο μὲν ... τοῦτο δέ). And here is the solution to the perennial problem of the 'break' between the two sections and of the two doxologies.

(5) It remains to point out that if the two specialized parts of I Peter

---

9 Mr H. Chadwick* remarks that there is plenty of evidence that, after A.D. 64, the Christians were liable at any time to be arrested; but that whether this happened or not depended on the whim of the Governor. E.g. Origen, *In Matt. Comm. Ser.* 120, discusses whether a pagan Governor who exercises his discretion so as to protect the Church will be rewarded by admission to heaven.

[* Now Professor Chadwick.]

are set side by side, they prove to contain a good deal of the same material, although the one addressed to the Churches actually suffering persecution is (as is fitting) terser; and the order is not identical (but why should it be, in two freely written letters?). Common to both is i. 1 f. (or such parts of the combined greetings as were thought suitable), 3 to ii. 10. Then come the specialized parts:

Letter I, to those not yet under actual persecution

| | | |
|---|---|---|
| (1) | ii. 11 | Address, ἀγαπητοί. |
| (2) | ii. 11-17 | Exhortation to convince detractors by good life (καλὰ ἔργα, ἀγαθοποιεῖν). |
| (3) { | ii. 18-25 | Servants to be in subjection (ὅτι καὶ Χριστὸς ἔπαθεν). |
| | iii. 1-6 | Wives be in subjection. |
| | iii. 7 | Men behave rightly to women. |
| | iii. 8-12 | All be rightly disposed to one another (ὁ γὰρ θέλων . . . Ps. xxxiv). |
| (4) { | iii. 13-iv. 6 | If you *should* have to suffer, μακάριοι (ὅτι καὶ Χριστὸς . . . ἀπέθανεν or ἔπαθεν): a theme leading into the theme of baptism. |
| (5) | iv. 7-11 | Judgement is imminent: therefore be alert and keep love fervent, and minister to one another in God's |
| (6) { | | name - to whom belongs glory, for the ages of the ages, Amen. |

Letter II, to those in the 'refining fire'

| | | |
|---|---|---|
| (1) | iv. 12 | Address, ἀγαπητοί. |
| (4) | iv. 12-19 | Do not be surprised at the πύρωσις: you are μακάριοι if reviled for Christ's sake; but be sure your life is good. |
| (5) | | Judgement there must be: |
| (2) | | trust God and do good (ἀγαθοποιΐα). |
| (3) { | v. 1-5 | Minister to one another, younger in subjection to elders, with mutual regard (ὅτι ὁ θεὸς ὑπερηφάνοις ἀντιτάσσεται . . ., Prov. iii). |
| (5) { | v. 6-11 | Commit yourselves humbly to God; be vigilant; resist |
| (4) { | | the devil. You are not alone. God will bring you through - |
| (6) | | to him belongs strength for the ages of the ages, Amen. |

144

Common to both is v. 12–14, farewell: unless, indeed, v. 12 (with its reference to brevity and its exhortation to firmness) belongs exclusively to the shorter form. Both contain an opening address and a closing ascription, a macarism, an appeal to scripture, a reference to the imminence of judgement, and an exhortation to commit one's cause to the Lord.

The only problem in this analysis, as I see it, is that *within* Letter I there are parallels – especially the two appeals to the example of Christ (ὅτι καὶ Χριστὸς...., ii. 21, iii. 18). But this, I suggest, is intelligible in view of the first of these appeals being introduced with special reference to the servants. It is inserted for their benefit, and is part of the *Haustafel*, ii. 18 to iii. 7. In the tenser situation of actual persecution, this special appeal and the whole *Haustafel*, can be dispensed with: all the Christians alike are 'up against it', and all the exhortation they need is that they should be loyal to their leaders.*

(6) As for the baptismal theme, which, as all are agreed, is prominent, there is an obvious congruity between this and the theme of suffering. Suffering is connected with baptism (through Christ's baptism which meant the cross), and baptism is an epitome of the Christian doctrine of suffering. There is no context where Christian thought more naturally takes baptismal shape than the context of persecution: once again, Heb. vi. 4–6 is an obvious parallel. The argument there is 'Think of your baptism before you dare apostatize'.

(7) It may be added, finally, that Ps. xxxiv, which, as has been shown, clearly lies behind the epistle, is eminently appropriate to the same situation: its theme is 'God protects or rescues the loyal sufferer'.

No attempt is here made to discuss the authorship of the epistle. But if there is anything in the contention (supported by Dr Selwyn and Dr van Unnik) that the persecutions need not be 'official', then the way is open, so far as chronology goes,[10] for apostolic authorship. Also, I am in whole-hearted agreement with the last two pages of Dr Cross's lecture, where he argues that at any rate the theology, the ethics, and the 'tone' of the writing are all in keeping with an early period of the Christian Church's existence.

10 Unless I Peter is demonstrably dependent on Ephesians: see Mitton in *J.T.S.* 1, 1 (1950).

* The theory of §(5) was in part anticipated by J. H. A. Hart's commentary in W. R. Nicoll ed., *The Expositor's New Testament* (London, 1910), pp. 29 f.

# Two Linguistic Studies

# 10

## Death 'to sin', 'to law', and 'to the world':
## A Note on Certain Datives*

### for B. Rigaux

There are certain passages in the New Testament where a verb connoting dying is followed by ἁμαρτία (or ἁμαρτίαι) or νόμος in the dative, and one further passage with a similar construction but other words. There is no lack of comments on these passages in the standard commentaries, but this essay is an attempt to reinvestigate the lines along which interpretation may be sought. In particular, it gives a conspectus and offers a classification of the passages in question, and tries to determine what part, if any, is played in these datives by the idea of discharging an obligation. The passages are here shown in three categories, (a) to (c), followed by two other passages (group (d)) which may be relevant although they do not contain such datives.

(a) Rom. xiv. 7 f. οὐδεὶς γὰρ ἡμῶν ἑαυτῷ ζῇ,
        καὶ οὐδεὶς ἑαυτῷ ἀποθνῄσκει ·
        ἐάν τε γὰρ ζῶμεν, τῷ κυρίῳ ζῶμεν,
        ἐάν τε ἀποθνῄσκωμεν, τῷ κυρίῳ ἀποθνῄσκομεν.
        ἐάν τε οὖν ζῶμεν ἐάν τε ἀποθνῄσκωμεν,
        τοῦ κυρίου ἐσμέν.

(Cf. II Cor. vi. εἷς ὑπὲρ πάντων ἀπέθανεν ·
14b, 15   ἄρα οἱ πάντες ἀπέθανον ·
      καὶ ὑπὲρ πάντων ἀπέθανεν
      ἵνα οἱ ζῶντες μηκέτι ἑαυτοῖς ζῶσιν
      ἀλλὰ τῷ ὑπὲρ αὐτῶν ἀποθανόντι καὶ ἐγερθέντι.)

(b) Rom. vi. 2 οἵτινες ἀπεθάνομεν τῇ ἁμαρτίᾳ,
      πῶς ἔτι ζήσομεν ἐν αὐτῇ;

Rom. vi. 10 f. ὃ γὰρ ἀπέθανεν, τῇ ἁμαρτίᾳ ἀπέθανεν ἐφάπαξ ·
      ὃ δὲ ζῇ, ζῇ τῷ θεῷ.

* Viro doctissimo magnanimoque parvula quidem commentatio sed cum gratia amice dedicata.

149

οὕτως καὶ ὑμεῖς λογίζεσθε ἐαυτοὺς εἶναι
νεκροὺς μὲν τῇ ἀμαρτίᾳ
ζῶντας δὲ τῷ θεῷ ἐν χριστῷ Ἰησοῦ.

I Pet. ii. 24 ὃς τὰς ἀμαρτίας ἡμῶν
αὐτὸς ἀνήνεγκεν ἐν τῷ σώματι αὐτοῦ ἐπὶ τὸ
ξύλον,
ἵνα ταῖς ἀμαρτίαις ἀπογενόμενοι
τῇ δικαιοσύνῃ ζήσωμεν . . .

(c) Rom. vii. 4 . . . καὶ ὑμεῖς ἐθανατώθητε τῷ νόμῳ,
διὰ τοῦ σώματος τοῦ χριστοῦ,
εἰς τὸ γένεσθαι ὑμᾶς ἐτέρῳ . . .

Rom. vii. 6 νυνὶ δὲ κατηργήθημεν ἀπὸ τοῦ νόμου,
ἀποθανόντες ἐν ᾧ κατειχόμεθα . . .

Gal. ii. 19 ἐγὼ γὰρ διὰ νόμου νόμῳ ἀπέθανον
ἵνα θεῷ ζήσω.
χριστῷ συνεσταύρωμαι . . .

Gal. vi. 14 ἐμοὶ δὲ μὴ γένοιτο καυχᾶσθαι
εἰ μὴ ἐν τῷ σταυρῷ τοῦ
κυρίου ἡμῶν Ἰησοῦ χριστοῦ, δι' οὗ ἐμοὶ κόσμος
ἐσταύρωται κἀγὼ κόσμῳ.

(d) Rom. vi. 6b, 7 . . . ἵνα καταργηθῇ τὸ σῶμα τῆς ἀμαρτίας,
τοῦ μηκέτι δουλεύειν ἡμᾶς τῇ ἀμαρτίᾳ·
ὁ γὰρ ἀποθανὼν δεδικαίωται ἀπο τῆς ἀμαρτίας . . .

I Pet. iv. 1 χριστοῦ οὖν πάθοντος σαρκὶ
καὶ ὑμεῖς τὴν αὐτὴν ἔννοιαν ὁπλίσασθε,
ὅτι ὁ παθὼν σαρκὶ πέπαυται ἀμαρτίας,
εἰς τὸ μηκέτι ἀνθρώπων ἐπιθυμίαις,
ἀλλὰ θελήματι θεοῦ,
τὸν ἐπίλοιπον ἐν σαρκὶ βιῶσαι χρόνον.

How are the datives in (a), (b), and (c) to be interpreted? Perhaps
the most important observation that can be made as a start was made
by Mr A. J. M. Wedderburn[1] (now a Research Student working under
my supervision)[*] in an unpublished essay. There he claims that the

1 To whom I am indebted also for useful criticism of an earlier draft of this
essay.
[* Now (1980) Dr Wedderburn, a University Lecturer in the University of St
Andrews.]

phrase 'to die to . . .' (we need not yet ask whether 'to' is the right English preposition, but use it simply to indicate the dative) is a syntactical novelty, and he suggests that it was formed by Paul on the analogy of 'to live to . . .', which is a comparatively common expression. He further points out that Rom. xiv. 7 f. (see under (a)) contains, side by side, both this comparatively common expression with 'to live' (οὐδεὶς γὰρ ἡμῶν ἑαυτῷ ζῇ . . . τῷ κυρίῳ ζῶμεν, cf. II Cor. v. 15) and the rarer phrase with 'to die' (καὶ οὐδεὶς ἑαυτῷ ἀποθνῄσκει . . . τῷ κυρίῳ ἀποθνῄσκομεν), and he suggests that it may have been the parallelism that led Paul to adopt this rarer phrase.

It is difficult to deny the claim that 'dying to . . .' is a syntactical novelty. Wettstein, who has plenty of parallels for 'living to . . .', adduces, for 'dying to . . .', only (on Rom. vi. 10) Quintilian *Decl.* 332, 'tibi vixi, tibi moriturus fui, nulli alii in hoc pectore locus fuit', and (on Rom. xiv. 7) Plut. *Cleomen. et Agid.* p. 819 F (= 52 (31), 10), δεῖ γὰρ τὸν αὐθαίρετον θάνατον οὐ φυγὴν εἶναι πράξεων ἀλλὰ πρᾶξιν· αἰσχρὸν γὰρ [καὶ] ζῆν μόνοις ἑαυτοῖς καὶ ἀποθνῄσκειν· [820 A] ἐφ' ὃ νῦν σὺ παρακαλεῖς ἡμᾶς, σπεύδων ἀπαλλαγῆναι τῶν παρόντων, καλὸν δ' οὐδὲν οὐδὲ χρήσιμον ἄλλο διαπραττόμενος. (Cleomenes in a rebuke to Therukion: I have transcribed more of the context than Wettstein did.) Both of these are close to the usage of Rom. xiv. 7 f., and represent only the barest departure from the common 'living to . . .' idiom. Very recently, Mr Wedderburn has called my attention to Ps.-Philo *Bib. Ant.* xxviii, 10:[2] 'Si sic est requies iustorum posteaquam defuncti fuerint, oportet eos mori corruptibili seculo, ut non videant peccata'. (The speaker is 'Cenez', i.e. Kenaz, who, for Ps.-Philo, takes the place of Othniel as the first of the judges.) This, it seems to me, represents a stage nearer than the other two quotations to the peculiar usages we are investigating.

But even the phrases with 'to live to . . .' are not all on the same level of meaning. In the citations from Quintilian and Plutarch, as in Rom. xiv. 7 f., the datives may reasonably be represented by the preposition 'for', and classified (in respect of the verb 'to live', as well as 'to die') as datives 'of advantage': it is for his own sake that the selfish person lives and dies, and for God's sake or for a friend's sake that the dedicated person lives and dies. But the commentators on Gal. ii. 19 appeal to IV Macc. xvi. 25, and here the dative is different. Of the martyrs it is here said that διὰ τὸν θεὸν ἀποθανόντες ζῶσιν τῷ θεῷ; and, in IV Macc. vii. 19, similarly, θεῷ οὐκ ἀποθνῄσκουσιν. So, exactly, Lk. xx. 38: πάντες γὰρ αὐτῷ [*sc.* θεῷ] ζῶσιν. In these cases, the datives

2 Text from Guido Kisch's edition (Indiana, 1949).

seem to need to be described as datives 'of relation' or 'of respect' or 'of reference'. It is not *'for* God' but *in God's sight*, or *in relation to* him, that the martyrs, or the departed patriarchs, are alive: which is not the same as the 'dative of advantage' or 'ethical dative' in living (or dying) *for the sake* of God.

But, if so, what about the dative when not only is the verb not 'living' but 'dying', as in (a), (b), (c), but the noun is not 'self' or 'God' but 'sin', as in (b), or 'law' or 'the world', as in (c)? Even if the origin of such expressions may very plausibly be traced to analogy with the positive phrase ('live to God', etc.) we are still left asking what, precisely, they mean when they reach such a form as this. What exactly does 'dying to sin' or 'dying to law' or 'being crucified to the world' mean – or, for that matter, Ps.-Philo's 'dying to the corruptible age'? Is this, too, a dative of relation? Or is it of advantage? Or what?[3]

The answer, probably, is that these are, in some sense, datives of relation. But before finally attempting a decision, we must consider group (d). Here, both phrases – that in Rom. vi. 7 and that in I Pet. iv. 1 – have been interpreted to mean 'Death pays all debts'. On I Pet. iv. 1, F. W. Beare[4] tentatively suggests this sense, and, on Rom. vi. 7, Sanday and Headlam[5] paraphrase: 'a dead man has his quittance from any claim that Sin can make against him'; and K. E. Kirk[6] and C. K. Barrett[7] recognize this among the possible meanings. On this showing both passages are saying that you cannot pay more than your life; and, therefore, when you have parted with your life, you are quit. The maximum fine, as it were, has been paid. And the Christian has parted with his life by sacramental union with Christ in his death; incorporated in Christ, the believer has served the ultimate sentence. (In parenthesis, it may be said that the passages cited by Strack-Billerbeck (iii. 232) from Sabb. 151[b] Bar. and Pesiq. 200[b] (∥ Sabb. 30[a]), which are often adduced by commentators, to the effect that a dead man is freed from the obligations of the Law (something of a truism!), do not seem to be particularly apposite, despite the similarity of language.) On I Pet. iv. 1, K. H. Schelkle[8] is hesitant of finding, in this particular context, the Pauline

---

3 One is reminded of the English phrase, 'dead to the world'. I do not know the origin of this unless it be in Gal. vi. 14. *The Oxford English Dictionary*, III (1933), 57*c* (s.v. 'Dead') quotes from a work of 1340 (Dan Michel's Ayenbite of Inwyt, 240): 'He ssel by dyead to þe wordle, and libbe to god'.

4 *The First Epistle of Peter* (Oxford, ²1968).

5 W. Sanday – A. C. Headlam, *The Epistle to the Romans* (Edinburgh, 1895).

6 *The Epistle to the Romans* (Oxford, 1937).

7 *A Commentary on the Epistle to the Romans* (London, 1957).

8 *Kommentar zum Neuen Testament*, Herder, XIII, 2 (Freiburg/Basel, 1961).

idea of sacramental union with Christ in his death. But the alternative – that literal, physical suffering (not death) subdues the flesh or purifies from sin – seems even less appropriate; and the aorist, παθών, and perfect, πέπαυται, appear to indicate that it is not a process of suffering but a completed condition, while the phrase καὶ ὑμεῖς τὴν αὐτὴν ἔννοιαν ὁπλίσασθε (a close parallel to the λογίξεσθε of Rom. vi. 11) makes the idea of sharing Christ's position virtually inescapable.

In view, then, of group (d), it is tempting to suggest that the datives following the words for death in groups (b) and (c) (omitting, for the moment, Gal. vi. 14) may spring from the same notion of discharging an obligation. Does 'dying to sin' or 'to law' mean meeting, by the extreme cost of death, the penalties or sanctions for sin? In the case of Christ, the situation was that one who was not himself a sinner, and therefore who gave no hostages to sin, was able, by going to death as representative Man, to clear Adam's debt. This is why, for Christ, the death is ἐφάπαξ. The representative Man, the ultimate Adam, by accepting, though not guilty and not indebted, the old Adam's predicament, discharges, absolutely, Adam's accumulated debt.[9]

That this kind of transactional language was actually in the mind of at least one New Testament writer is suggested by Col. ii. 14 f., where the death of Christ is described in terms of the cancelling of a debt and the holding up of opponents to ignominy. It is conceivable therefore, that elsewhere, too, the death of Christ was thought of as the 'payment in full', as it were, of the penalty incurred by 'Adam' collectively, and, thus, the gaining of complete quittance and release for man. Jesus 'died *to sin*' in the sense that he did not evade but fully reckoned with the consequence of sin. And it is equally intelligible to represent this as a 'dying *to law*', since it is God's moral law that is violated in sin and that prescribes the penalty. J. A. T. Robinson, by using the odd phrase 'Christ died out on' the forces of evil,[10] seems to be hinting at this idea: Christ gives all that can be demanded; the evil forces have no more that they can ask: they have fired their last shot. And in keeping with the implied classification of the datives as datives of obligation is J. A. T. Robinson's ingenious suggestion[11] that, in Col. ii. 14, the dative, τοῖς δόγμασιν, might be due to the meaning of obligation in χειρόγραφον:

9 It is true that Paul does not himself use Adam-language in this particular connexion, though he does in connexion with Christ's total rightness (Rom. v. 18). But it is clear from, e.g. Gal. iii. 13, Col. ii. 14 that Christ is seen as representative.

10 *The Body: a Study in Pauline Theology* (London, 1952).

11 *Ibid.*, 43, n. 1.

the 'bond' was an undertaking to keep the *dogmata*: it placed us under an obligation to them; signed, like an 'I.O.U.', by our own conscience, it is adverse to us because we have broken the bond. At any rate, the result - freedom from sin (the debt fully discharged), and obligation to God - is precisely what becomes explicit in the latter part of Rom. vi. Thus, a case might seem to be made for calling the datives in groups (b) and (c) 'datives of obligation'.

But doubt is thrown on this category from within group (c) itself. In the notoriously tortuous passage in Rom. vii. 1 ff., Paul seems to be saying:

(1) A woman is under legal obligation to her husband only so long as he is alive. If he dies, she is free.

(2) We are under obligation to the Mosaic law only so long as (and here comes the paradox!) we are alive. If we die, we are discharged from obligation (cf. the rabbinic opinions cited above). Paul has reversed the parts. It is not the law that dies, but we. And what he calls *our* death - that which releases us from obligation - is *Christ's* death as 'sacramentally' shared and entered into by us. Our death occurs (*v.* 4) διὰ τοῦ σώματος τοῦ χριστοῦ, i.e. through Christ's physical body surrendered to death for us, and through his risen body of which we are made part.

But is it 'obligation' that is represented by the datives here? The marital analogy behind Rom. vii. 6 seems to answer No. It seems to compel us to reject the idea of obligation in favour, simply, of relationship. There is plenty of obligation, plenty of indebtedness; but the point of the datives here is not that the demands of the law have been met with a costly death, but that we have been placed where the law no longer operates: 'we are dead' (*v.* 6), or 'we have been put to death' (*v.* 4) *so far as law is concerned, with reference to law*; our relationship with the law has been annulled (*v.* 4, κατηργήθημεν ἀπὸ τοῦ νόμου), just as a woman's relation with her husband is - for legal purposes - annulled by death.

If this happens διὰ τοῦ σώματος τοῦ χριστοῦ in Rom. vii. 4, in Gal. ii. 19 the same condition (νόμῳ ἀπέθανον) is described as διὰ νόμου. Many interpretations have been offered for this latter expression. An ancient one (in the Ambrosiaster and others) is that the νόμος in question is not the Mosaic law but 'the law of the Spirit', the new (Christian) way of things. But this, rightly, is almost universally rejected now. Rather, it seems that what is likely to be meant is that the law was instrumental in bringing Christ to his death. By pronouncing the sentence of death, the law annihilates the offender so that he ceases to exist within its reach. Paul believed that Jesus had himself been subjected to the sentence of the law on Man's sinful condition (Gal. iii. 13). And the Christian is united sacramentally with the death of Christ. Consequently, the paradox arises that the law is intrumental in the removal of the sinner from its own jurisdiction. Hence, Gal. ii. 19 can say διὰ νόμου νόμῳ ἀπέθανον. It is this uniting of the believer with Christ's body in baptism that, as has already been suggested, is alluded to in the other passage from Romans in (c), when Rom. vii. 4 says ἐθανατώθητε τῷ νόμῳ δια τοῦ σώματος τοῦ χριστοῦ. On this showing, the two passages are closely parallel. In both, the believer becomes virtually non-existent so far as the law is concerned because, through Christ's body (killed 'through the law'), the believer has been, in this sense, 'annihilated'. In his very careful discussion of the Galatians passage,[12] H. Schlier writes: 'Es ist das Gestorbensein und nun Totsein für das Gesetz, so dass das Gesetz an mir nur einen Toten hat, so dass ich für das Gesetz nur als Toten da bin, der für seine Wirksamkeit objectiv nicht mehr in Frage kommt'. E. de W. Burton, in his admirably clear discussion,[13] thinks that διὰ νόμου is by no means equivalent to διὰ τοῦ σώματος τοῦ χριστοῦ and he refers διὰ νόμου not to what the law did to Christ, but to Paul's personal experience of the law's stringency, which had caused Paul to take the step of going beyond the law. But does this interpretation do justice to ἀπέθανον, which it is difficult to interpret otherwise than in the drastic sense of 'baptismal death' (or, at any rate, 'conversion death')? At any rate, the datives seem to be 'relational'. All this, finally, is clinched by the other Galatians passage, Gal. vi. 14, where St Paul, stretching his curious phrase almost to breaking-point, declares that through the instrumentality of the cross (δι' οὗ, as commentators rightly note, refers not to Christ but to the cross) the world has been crucified to him and he to the world. This must, as it seems, mean that St Paul's union with Christ in his sufferings and death have led to the abolition of 'the world', in the sense (defined by Burton)[14] of 'the mode of life characterized by earthly advantages' (cf. Ps.-Philo, *ut supra*), and his own abolition so far as 'the world' is concerned. By using the verb σταυροῦν and applying it to κόσμος as well as to ἐγώ, St Paul emphasizes the instrumentality of the cross in this complete annihilation of any relationship he might have had apart from Christ.

12 *Der Brief an die Galater* (Göttingen, 1962), pp. 98 ff.
13 *The Epistle to the Galatians* (Edinburgh, 1921), pp. 132 ff.
14 *Ibid.*, p. 354.

On the whole, then, it seems less likely that, even in (b) and (c), the datives are datives of obligation, than that they are simply datives of relationship, though, as Burton observes,[15] when it is ἵνα θεῷ ζήσω the dative of relation has turned into a dative of advantage. Even though the notion of paying the law its dues - of serving the full sentence - is not absent from New Testament thought about the death of Christ, it is not this that the datives are expressing, but, rather, the resulting condition: non-existence so far as law is concerned, or sin, or the world. The idea of non-existence seems to be particularly emphatic in I Pet. ii. 24, under (b), where the comparatively rare ἀπογενόμενοι is perhaps used deliberately to this end: 'ceasing to exist' so far as sins are concerned.[16]

And if we now return to group (d), the question arises whether, in spite of what was said before, even these two passages really move in the realm of 'satisfaction'. After all, πέπαυται in I Pet. iv. 1 does not, strictly, mean more than 'he has ceased (or been caused to cease) from sin', and it probably fits better into the purely relational category than into an 'obligatory' one. Perhaps Rom. vi. 7 remains the only phrase in our 'exhibit' which carries a definite allusion to the clearing of the debt. Even in Rom. vi. 7, it may be just possible that δεδικαίωται means 'has been vindicated against' rather than 'acquitted in respect of (by payment of the dues)'. In the preceding verse, sin is a slave-master. It is only when the sin-dominated body is abolished (ἵνα καταργηθῇ τὸ σῶμα τῆς ἁμαρτίας) that we are no longer in servitude to sin (τοῦ μηκέτι δουλεύειν ἡμᾶς τῇ ἁμαρτίᾳ). It is, perhaps, possible, then, that the seemingly proverbial phrase that follows (ὁ γὰρ ἀποθανὼν δεδικαίωται ἀπὸ τῆς ἁμαρτίας) means, in the context, 'once you have died, you are vindicated against sin', in the sense that there is no longer anything left for sin to get a grip of. But in the only other New Testament instance of δικαιωθῆναι ἀπό, in Acts xiii. 38, it seems to mean 'be cleared (acquitted) of', and, although it is not necessary for the sense of the verb to be identical in both cases, it is more rational to give it the same meaning in Rom. vi. 7 (*pace* Zahn).[17]

15 *Ibid.*, p. 134.
16 For details of the incidence of the word, see F. Büchsel, in *T.W.N.T.* i. 685.
17 *Der Brief des Paulus an die Römer* (Leipzig, 1910), *in loc.*, where he also contrasts Sir. xxvi. 29 (οὐ δικαιωθήσεται κάπηλος ἀπὸ ἁμαρτίας), Hermas, *Vis.* iii. 9.1 (... ἵνα δικαιωθῆτε καὶ ἁγιασθῆτε ἀπὸ πάσης πονηρίας καὶ ἀπο πάσης σκολιότητος'), and Test. Sim. 6.1. - Since writing this article, I have seen the note by E. Klaar, 'Rm 6⁷: Ὁ γὰρ ἀποθανὼν δεδικαίωται ἀπὸ τῆς ἁμαρτίας', *Z.N.T.W.* 59 (1968), 131 ff., in which he argues that the distinction between the aorist ἀποθανὼν and the perfect δεδικαίωται has

## Death 'to sin', 'to law' and 'to the world'

If this reasoning is right, the result is this: the phrases using a verb of dying, with the dative, may indeed have been created by analogy with phrases using a verb of living, with the dative; but the meaning is extended beyond the 'dative of advantage' to a 'dative of reference' or 'relation' (Burton),[18] so as to open up a whole range of phrases very different in key and motif from the originating phrases. It is not, however, legitimate to press beyond this 'dative of reference' to a 'dative of obligation'. The theological idea that would be indicated by such a dative is indeed present within New Testament though; but the temptation to read it into this particular type of phrase should probably be resisted.[19]

> been too little observed, and that ὸ ἀποθανών (which is not the same as ὸ νεκρός) means one who has accepted death; and that δεδικαίωται refers to release from servitude to sin. He paraphrases: 'Denn der das . . . Sterben auf sich nahm – perfektive erledigt ist der Rechtsanspruch der Sündenmacht an ihm (auf weiteren Sklavendienst)'.

18 Burton, *Epistle to the Galatians*, 355.
19 F. M. Abel, *Grammaire du Grec Biblique* (Paris, 1927), p. 196, § 45 (*i*), places Rom. vi. 10; xiv. 7; II Cor. v. 15 under 'le datif d'intérêt' and characterizes them as 'avec une nuance plus accentuée du rapport'. R. W. Funk's revision of Blass-Debrunner (Cambridge, 1961), 101, § 188. 2, says, of Rom. vi. 10 f., vii. 4; II Cor. v. 15; I Pet. ii. 24, 'the dat. expresses more than the possessor'.

# 11

## Peculiarities in the Language of II Corinthians
### for B. Reicke

This short note is, at best, of minor importance; but I offer it, with admiration, congratulations, and affection, to a scholar who, in the midst of important and influential studies, is not above enjoying a digression after something of sheer curiosity.

II Cor. viii contains a number of sentences without any main verb, including at least one which uses a participle – the δεόμενοι of *v.* 4 – in lieu of an indicative.

Now, Rom. xii contains, as is well known, a large number of sentences without a main verb, involving the use of two adjectives and some seventeen participles (not to mention two infinitives) where one would expect imperatives. The same 'imperatival' participles and adjectives are found also in I Peter several times, and occasionally elsewhere in the New Testament; and a classic article by D. Daube[1] showed, as against J. H. Moulton's claim[2] that it was a genuine Hellenistic idiom, that, in all probability, it was not native to *koine* but was derived from a Tannaitic usage, by which general injunctions are expressed by participles.

In II Cor. viii itself, there seems to be an instance of the imperatival participle, namely, the ἐνδεικνύμενοι of *v.* 24. Daube ('Participle and Imperative', 481) thinks that AB may be right in reading ἐνδείξασθε but this is surely an obvious correction (in mss. which do tend to contain intelligent 'improvements') of an original *difficilior lectio.*[3] I find it hard to follow Daube also when he says (*ibid.*) that, even if we read the participle, 'it is best explained as loosely connected with the εἰς ὑμᾶς of verse 22'. I would, therefore, be inclined to see in II Cor. viii. 24 one

---

1 'Participle and Imperative in 1 Peter', an appended note in E. G. Selwyn, *The First Epistle of St Peter* (London, 1946), pp. 467 ff. See also my *An Idiom Book of New Testament Greek* (Cambridge, ²1959), pp. 179, 208.
2 *A Grammar of New Testament Greek* i, *Prolegomena* (Edinburgh, 1908), pp. 180 ff., 223 ff. (not 232 ff. as in Daube's reference).
3 So Moulton, *Grammar*, p. 181.

## Peculiarities in the language of II Corinthians

more example of the 'Tannaitic' imperatival participle. The participles in II Cor. ix. 11, 13 may (I agree with Daube) be explained as virtually in construction with neighbouring main verbs. But the δεόμενοι of II Cor. viii. 4 is different, and so are three other participles in II Cor., namely, διδόντες in v. 12, θλιβόμενοι in vii. 5, and φανερώσαντες in xi. 6. These are in narrative, and can hardly represent anything but indicatives, and they cannot, therefore, be accounted for by Daube's category. In addition, there are in II Cor. viii many other sentences without a main verb. Most of these require to complete them only the verb 'to be', and the omission of this is, of course, very common all over the New Testament and in many other literatures. Without going further than II Corinthians, one may note striking examples in v. 13, 17; and there are quantities besides. But there is, all the same, an exceptionally high concentration of such sentences in this one chapter. Besides the passages in which occur the δεόμενοι of v. 4 and the ἐνδεικνύμενοι of v. 24, the remainder are as follows (shown, to save printing unnecessary quantities of Greek, by minimal indications, together with supplied verbs in English): 11, καθάπερ (was present) . . . οὕτως (may be present); 12 (is) εὐπρόσδεκτος; 13 (it is) οὐ γὰρ (a matter of) ὑμῖν θλίψις ἵνα (there may be) ἄλλοις ἄνεσις· ἀλλ' (it is a matter of) ἐξ ἰσότητος; 14 (so that) τὸ ὑμῶν περίσσευμα (may go);[4] 16 χάρις (be); 18 ὁ ἔπαινος (is); 19 (he was) χειροτονηθείς; 23 (he is) κοινωνὸς ἐμὸς . . . (they are) ἀπόστολοι.

Altogether, then, including δεόμενοι but excluding ἐνδεικνύμενοι (so as to give the benefit of the doubt either to an alternative to the imperatival explanation of the participle or to the alternative reading) here are ten or eleven sentences in twenty-four verses without a main verb – a concentration enough to pull at least one reader up with a jerk every time he reaches this passage when reading continuously through the New Testament. Minor 'jerks' of the same sort are encountered at v. 12 and vii. 5, as has been already noted.

There is at least one other curiosity in the Greek of II Corinthians as a whole, namely, the almost obsessive frequency with which the word πρόσωπον occurs. The word does not occur in Romans, Ephesians, Philippians, or the Pastoral epistles. For the rest of the Paulines, the figures are: I Cor. 2, II Cor. 12, Gal. 3, Col. 1, I Thess. 3, II Thess. 1. Thus, II Corinthians has 12 out of 22 occurrences in the Pauline corpus. Of these 12, 4 are accounted for by Ch. iii, with its theme of radiance

---

4 Even in the second limb of the sentence the γένηται is omitted by p⁴⁶. I owe this observation to Dr W. Horbury of Clare College, now Dean of Corpus Christi College, Cambridge.

reflected in the face; and a fifth is at iv.6, which is still on the same theme; and J. Louis Martyn has made the interesting suggestion[5] that Paul's opponents may have made some special boast about an authenticating radiance of countenance. If so, this single fact might account for these five. But the remaining seven instances are, at least in the main, unrelated, and represent a variety of senses, including the merely prepositional. Besides those in Chh. iii and iv, the references are i. 11, ii. 10, v. 12, viii. 24, x. 1, 7, xi. 20.

It is a common experience, probably for most persons, that they get into the habit of over-working certain words or expressions, and continue to do so until they realize for themselves what they are doing or are laughed out of it by others. Is it possible that the proliferation of πρόσωπον-phrases in II Corinthians is due largely to some psychological chance of this kind?

The two phenomena of verbless sentences in II Cor. viii and a special frequency in the use of πρόσωπον all over this epistle raise the time-honoured question how much of the Pauline epistles represents Paul's very words and how much is paraphrase by an amanuensis.[6] If Paul was in what we may be permitted to call a πρόσωπον phase, any amanuensis could easily have caught and reproduced the frequency of its use.[7] But an amanuensis, if writing freely and not slavishly following dictation, would be less likely to produce such a crop of Semitic constructions, unless, of course, he were himself as Semitic as the Apostle. At any rate, it remains remarkable that so conspicuous a lack of main verbs should have occurred in this one chapter of the epistle. It is tempting, then, to imagine that Paul himself, for some reason, picked up the pen and wrote this section in his own hand. Unfortunately for this theory,

---

5 'Epistemology at the turn of the ages: 2 Cor. 5:16', in W. R. Farmer, C. F. D. Moule, R. R. Niebuhr eds., *Christian History and Interpretation* (Cambridge, 1967), pp. 269 ff.

6 See, e.g. Otto Roller, *Das Formular der paulinischen Briefe* (Stuttgart, 1933).

7 Not all πρόσωπον-phrases are necessarily Semitic. Dr Horbury points out to me that J. C. Wolf [*Curae philologicae* (Hamburg, ²1732) *in loc.*] cites G. Raphelius as rendering the εἰς πρόσωπον of II Cor. viii. 24 by *erga*, and as adducing Eusebius *H.E.* vii. 30: διαχαράξαντες ἐπιστολὴν εἰς πρόσωπον τοῦ τε ῾Ρωμαίων ἐπισκόπου Διονυσίου καὶ Μαξίμου . . . The Loeb version by Lawlor and Oulton, however, renders the phrase in Eusebius by 'personally'.

I am particularly indebted to Dr Horbury for reading an earlier version of this note with great care, and saving me from several errors, as well as adding valuable observations.

the only part of the Pauline corpus (apart from signatures at I Cor. xvi. 21, Col. iv. 18, and II Thess. iii. 17) which is self-confessed autograph, namely, Gal. vi. 11 ff., is impeccable in the supply of main verbs, whatever other roughnesses there may be. Besides, there are, as we have seen, those other 'indicatival' participles outside this passage. The peculiarities of II Cor. remain – to me, at least – unexplained.

Studies Exegetical, Doctrinal, Ethical

# 12

## The Influence of Circumstances on the Use of Christological Terms

Much attention has always been paid by New Testament theology to the names and titles applied to Jesus. Dr Vincent Taylor's monograph on *The Names of Jesus*[1] is a recent example of this approach, and still more recently, Dr Oscar Cullmann's work on Christology[2] has in some respects followed the same method. The intention of this essay, however, is not to traverse precisely this ground once more, but rather, moving selectively over parts of it, to inquire into the reasons for the appearance and disappearance, for the advance and retreat, of one title and another. In other words, it will try to relate the names and designations of Jesus to the circumstances and conditions of their use.[3]

Two notoriously difficult problems in this connexion are, of course, the strikingly limited occurrence of the term 'the Son of Man', and the comparative rarity with which the figure of the suffering Servant is applied to Christ. Why, for instance, is there in early Christian apologetic outside the gospels no application to Jesus of a full-length testimonium from Dan. vii? Or again, Isa. liii is almost the only Old Testament passage which seems to recognize innocent suffering as possessing redemptive power. Why, then, are direct references to Isa. liii in the gospels so very rare? Why are the occurrences scarcely less meagre in the whole of the rest of the New Testament? And – most surprising of all – why are the explicitly *redemptive* phrases from Isa. liii only quoted once or twice in all?

These, and others like them, are the familiar questions behind this essay; and, although no claim can be made to have found answers, the

1 London, 1953.

2 *Die Christologie des Neuen Testaments* (Tübingen, 1957).

3 Dr Vincent Taylor's *The Person of Christ in New Testament Teaching* (London, 1958) came into my hands after this essay had been drafted. In a valuable chapter (xv, 'The Christology of the Primitive Christian Communities') he examines the terms under some such sections as I do here (Preaching, Teaching, Worship, etc.). But the questions which I have tried to formulate remain, I believe, still worth investigating.

hope is that some progress may eventually be made towards the understanding of the selection and use of christological terms in the New Testament period by the method here advocated and illustrated. The method in question is the simple one of inquiring about the circumstances and setting of each phrase or term examined. Certain factors, in particular, it will be argued, need to be taken into account in any attempt to explain the vocabulary we are to study, namely the requirements of liturgy, and of explanation (that is, in admonition, teaching, and apologetic). Another factor, which is not here pursued, is locality. It is evident that, to some extent, local habits of language and thought may account for the prevalence of a term in some writings and not in others.[4]

## THE INFLUENCE OF LITURGY ON THE SELECTION AND USE OF CHRISTOLOGICAL TERMS

The first factor which may be looked to for some explanation of the selectiveness of the New Testament's vocabulary may be described as the demands of adoration and worship.

Here, the prevailing tendency seems to be to adhere almost exclusively to directly honorific terms. St Francis of Assisi has been called *il poverello*, the poor man; and Jesus may well have thought of himself as God's suffering Servant (cf. Lk. xxii. 27) – possibly even as God's πτωχός, although II Cor. viii. 9 (ἐπτώχευσεν) is the nearest that the New Testament comes to applying this term to Jesus (cf. Phil. ii. 7). At any rate, it seems (despite the arguments of some scholars against this conclusion) that he thought of himself as the persecuted Human Figure (Son of Man) of Dan. vii, who was destined in the end to triumph and to be vindicated. Perhaps he also saw in himself the Shepherd, that is, the leader of God's People, who faces martyrdom.[5] He may also have thought of himself as the defenceless lamb, to which Jeremiah likened himself (Jer. xi. 19, cf. Isa. liii. 7), although no such saying is actually attributed to Jesus. Yet – and this is the point – terms such as these are only very rarely used of Jesus in the New Testament *in a context of adoration*.

In considering the evidence, it needs to be remarked that, in any case, ·

4 See, for instance, J. Daniélou, *Théologie du Judéo-Christianisme* (Tournai, 1958), p. 50, on the theological terms of Syrian Christianity.

5 For there is not only Jo. x, but also Mk xiv. 27 = Matt. xxvi. 31 with its reference to Zech. xiii. 7, with which theme are also linked Matt. xxiv. 30, Jo. xix. 37, Rev. i. 7.

*direct* address to Jesus in worship or invocation is, in the New Testament, exceptional. As early as the beginning of the second century (if Pliny is to be trusted in this detail) Christians were hymning Christ as divine. But within the New Testament, instances may be counted on the fingers of one hand. The few that may be found, however, are nearly all directly honorific, scarcely ever using terms which relate to the humiliation or suffering of Christ. The only New Testament titles of Jesus which occur in the vocative or quasi-vocative, besides his personal name⁶ (and the ῥαββουνί of Jo. xx. 16, recalling a pre-resurrection habit of address), are the Aramaic μαρανα (probably), κύριος, and (perhaps) θεός.⁷ *Marana* (I Cor. xvi. 22, *Didache* x. 6) is an honorific address not unsuitable to a human rabbi or honoured teacher; but, combined as it is with the imperative *tha*, 'come!', it inevitably becomes an invocation of one who, though dead, is believed to be alive and destined to return.⁸ Its Greek equivalent is, clearly enough, the ἔρχου κύριε 'Ιησοῦ of Rev. xxii. 20. (Even if we divide the words *Maran atha*, 'our Lord has come', it still, in its context, yields an unmistakably transcendental meaning for *maran*.) Whether any early Christian communities speaking a semitic language followed the clue of Ps. cx and actually addressed Jesus as *Adon*, it is impossible to say.⁹ But again the Greek translation is κύριος; and κύριος it is which swallows up the other titles. The only exception to the exclusive use of honorific titles is the direct address to Christ in Rev. v. 9 ("Αξιος εἶ . . .), which, although using no vocative noun, alludes in a subordinate clause to the sacrificial death of Christ.

6 Outside the gospels, the vocative 'Ιησοῦ occurs only in Stephen's invocation, Acts vii. 59, and at Rev. xii. 20, and both times with κύριε.
7 It is strange that the vocative χριστέ does not occur in the N.T. For the obscure history of the earliest occurrences of χριστὲ ἐλέησον see E. Bishop's *Liturgica historica* (Oxford, 1918), especially p. 123. As for κύριε ἐλέησον, it was, he writes, 'a pre-Christian religious invocation. It found its way into public Christian services soon after the triumph of the Church, that is, in the course of the fourth century' (*ibid.*, p. 135). Note its occurrence in *Peregrinatio Etheriae*, 24 (ed. H. Pétré, *Sources chrétiennes* no. 21 (Paris, 1948) p. 192). See further E. Peterson, ΕΙΣ ΘΕΟΣ (Göttingen, 1926).
8 For the supernatural associations of *adventus* see E. Stauffer, *Christ and the Caesars* (E.T., London, 1955), pp. 38, 86 ff. And for the possibility that *Marana tha* is originally an address to God from Jewish liturgy see R. Bultmann, *Theologie des N.T.*³, p. 55. Indeed, *Marana* (even without 'come!') appears sometimes to have been used as a divine title on heathen Syriac coins: see the evidence alluded to in F. J. Foakes Jackson and K. Lake (edd.), *The Beginnings of Christianity* (London, 1929), i, p. 410.
9 For the periods at which *Adoni* may have been current see *T.W.N.T.* iii, p. 1082 f.

It is immediately picked up again in the third person in *v.* 12: Ἄξιός ἐστιν τὸ ἀρνίον. ... But this, as will be remarked later, is in a special category, belonging to a martyr-context. Thus, practically all titles of direct address are exclusively honorific. Is it possible that the reason is that to allude, in direct address to Christ, to his abasement belongs to a rather more sophisticated stage in Christian consciousness? It is true that it was not very long before the cross itself began to be adored;[10] and as early as the *Gloria in Excelsis* there is a signal instance of adoration of Christ in terms of his suffering, not to mention such later forms as the *Te Deum*. Indeed, this stage has already been reached by the thought of the fourth gospel. But it does not seem to have taken liturgical shape among the New Testament writers; even the Apocalypse does not actually use the *Agnus Dei* as an invocation. The focus of worship (in direct adoration of Christ) is, for the New Testament, the 'majesty' rather than the crucifix.

But what of allusions to Christ in prayer directly addressed to God? Here one might have expected to find thanksgivings for his gracious self-abasement. But in fact the same reserve seems largely to obtain. Even in the martyr-context[11] of I Peter it is the resurrection, not the death, for which God is blessed (i. 4). The sufferings of Christ do not explicitly come in until a more descriptive and prosaic passage has been reached (i. 11).[12] The most powerful single influence on the shaping of early Christian titles for Christ was probably the Psalter and one might have expected expressions of abasement to have been borrowed from it. But the New Testament bears witness to a certain selectiveness even here. Κύριος is prominent enough. It has already been alluded to as having 'swallowed up' other titles for Christ. This was not only because it happened to be a translation for both *Mar* and *Adon*, but also because,

---

10 See, for instance, E. Peterson's article 'La Croce e la Preghiera verso Oriente' (*Ephemerides Liturgicae*, 59 (1945), pp. 52 ff.) to which Dr H. Chadwick calls my attention. Cf. also the *Gospel of Peter* and *Barnabas*, etc., alluded to in this connexion by Daniélou, *Théologie du Judéo-Christianisme*, pp. 32, 290 ff. The traces of a cross on a wall in Herculaneum seem to be variously interpreted: see A. Maiuri, 'La croce di Ercolano' in *Rendiconti della Pontificia accademia romana di archeologia* (1939), pp. 193–218 (picture in *Amer. J. Arch.* 1st series, 5 (1889), pl. lxxxviii), criticized, in the course of a discussion of the Sator-Rotas square, by J. Carcopino, *Etudes d'Histoire chrétienne* (Paris, 1953), pp. 48 ff. I owe these references to Professor E. C. Ratcliff.

11 For such I still believe it to be: see *N.T.S.* 3, (Nov. 1956), pp. 1 ff. [pp. 133 ff. above].

12 Eph. i. 7 (in a clearly liturgical passage) makes only a fleeting reference to the *blood* of Christ; there is none in Col. i. 14.

standing in the Greek Scriptures for the divine name,¹³ it was a ready-made bridge between the *Marana* of primitive address to Christ and the divine name¹⁴ in Jewish hymnody and worship. To become a worshipper of God is 'to invoke the divine name', in Greek ἐπικαλέσασθαι τὸ ὄνομα κυρίου (see Acts ii. 21, citing Joel); but quickly (it appears) Christians became known in a special sense as 'those who invoke the name (of Jesus or of the Lord Jesus)', Acts ix. 14, 21, xxii. 16, I Cor. i. 2 (cf. Stephen in Acts vii. 59); and the distinction between κύριος meaning God and κύριος Ἰησοῦς was rapidly blurred. Just as 'the Name' was a pious Jewish surrogate for God, so for Christians 'the Name' came to be that of the Lord Jesus.¹⁵ This fusion of the applications of κύριος is so obvious that it requires no exhaustive illustration.¹⁶ One very striking instance (though not from the Psalter) will suffice. In Phil. ii. 10 f. there are unmistakable echoes of Isa. xlv. 23; but that is a passage where God, in a monologue, is represented as claiming for himself alone the bending of every knee in adoration. That such a passage should be transferred to Christ is indicative of what was happening: so much so, that in Heb. i. 10 ff. a great act of adoration to God as Creator is daringly lifted from Ps. cii and applied to Christ, just as (on a quite possible interpretation) a divine invocation from Ps. xlv is similarly applied in the preceding verses (Heb. i. 8 f.). Only ὕψιστος and παντοκράτωρ seem – for obvious reasons – to have been reserved for God alone: though even παντοκράτωρ came eventually – outside the New Testament period – to be transferred to Christ.¹⁷

13 C. H. Dodd, *The Bible and the Greeks* (London, 1935), pp. 3 ff., discusses the names of God, and shows how the choice of κύριος by the LXX to represent the personal name of God 'amounted in itself to a manifesto of monotheism'. See also *T.W.N.T.* iii. 1081. Note that E. Peterson, ΕΙΣ ΘΕΟΣ, p.165, n. 2, writes: 'Aus dem akklamatorischen Charakter der κύριε ἐλέησον-Formel möchte ich es auch erklären, dass es zur Hauptbildung von κύριε ἐλέησον und nicht etwa von θεὲ ἐλέησον o. ä. gekommen ist. Das Wort κύριος ist in Akklamationen beliebt.'

14 But it must be remarked that, according to *T.W.N.T.* iii. 1049, κύριος is not naturally applied to a god in pure Greek, but gains this colour rather from the usage of non-Greek religions.

15 Daniélou, *Théologie du Judéo-Christianisme*, pp. 50, 199 ff., argues that τὸ ὄνομα was a designation for the Word or Son of God in early Hebrew Christian thinking. But it is difficult to be confident that the N.T. itself shows any signs of this.

16 See in this connexion the discussion of the λέγει κύριος formula in E. E. Ellis, *Paul's Use of the Old Testament* (Edinburgh, 1957), pp. 107 ff.

17 It would be interesting to know at what point the μόνος ὅσιος of Rev. xv. 4 came to be transferred, illogically, to Christ, as in the *Gloria*.

It may be added that, as soon as Christian thought began to associate 'Wisdom' terms - σοφία, πνεῦμα, λόγος - with Jesus, his connexion with the creative activity of God was strengthened, and creation-passages (such as Ps. cii) might the more naturally be applied to him. The question why σωτήρ is not more freely transferred from God to Christ through the use of the Psalter has already been raised and is discussed further in a subsequent section of this essay.

There are other titles - also honorific - derivable from the Psalter; but as they are not used in express adoration, they do not immediately concern us. But it was not the Psalter alone - or even only the Scriptures as a whole - that influenced early Christian worship. There were also the current Jewish extra-biblical liturgical forms.[18] One particularly interesting example may be noticed. David was called God's servant in certain Jewish prayers, namely the fifteenth of the Eighteen Benedictions (in the Babylonian recension) and - especially significant - in the paschal *Haggada* before the fourth cup.[19] This suggests that if the Christians modelled their grace before meat, and especially their eucharistic prayers, on this pattern, they found themselves faced with a striking parallelism imposed on them by their faith - the parallelism between God's Servant David, and 'David's greater Son', who was God's Servant in a unique degree, and was also God's Son. The result was the kind of thing which the *Didache* has preserved: εὐχαριστοῦμέν σοι, πάτερ ἡμῶν, ὑπὲρ τῆς ἁγίας ἀμπέλου Δαυειδ τοῦ παιδός σου, ἧς ἐγνώρισας ἡμῖν διὰ Ἰησοῦ τοῦ παιδός σου· σοὶ ἡ δόξα εἰς τοὺς αἰῶνας (ix. 2; cf. x. 2, I Clem. lix. 2, 3, 4, *Mart. Polyc.* xiv. 3, xx. 2, Barn. ix. 2, ? vi. 1). And it is difficult to doubt[20] that the same Messianic parallel explains the use of παῖς in reference to Jesus in Acts iv. 27, 30 (very close to Δαβὶδ παιδός σου in *v.* 25), whether or not it is the Isaianic suffering Servant who is intended in that other passage, Acts iii. 13, 26. And if it is the suffering Servant in Acts iii and the royal Servant in Acts iv, this is in

18 Possibly one may have to add also esoteric Jewish teachings. See Daniélou's *Théologie du Judéo-Christianisme, passim.*
19 See W. Zimmerli and J. Jeremias, *The Servant of God* (E.T., London, 1957), p. 48, n. 184.
20 *Pace* J. Jeremias, *Servant of God*, p. 86, and O. Cullmann, *Petrus* (Zürich, 1952), p. 70. Professor E. C. Ratcliff points out to me that the description of the *puer* (= παῖς) in the Verona Latin version of the Anaphora of the Apostolic Tradition as *angelus voluntatis tuae* (= ἄγγελος βουλῆς σου) indicates the thought of Isa. ix. 5 (LXX) and not of Isa. liii. He notes, incidentally, that the Anaphora, when it comes to deal with the Passion, does not echo Isa. liii, although Justin Martyr had interpreted Isa. liii as a prophecy of the Passion.

keeping with the contention that it is the latter - the more honorific - which has its place in worship.²¹

In other words, it seems that, when the term Servant was applied to Jesus in prayer, in the early days of Christianity, it was by analogy with a Jewish form, and in description, not direct address to Jesus, and in the sense of the royal rather than the suffering Servant; and, moreover, that, if παῖς, not δοῦλος, was used, it may have been because it was capable of carrying also the more exalted connotation of Son.²²

The subject of Messianic designations of Jesus in prayer to God raises the question why βασιλεύς is not a more widespread title. This will be considered again later in this inquiry; but it remains puzzling that there is not more of the transference to Christ of the address to God as King (e.g. from the Psalter), analogous to the transference of κύριος and even θεός. C. C. Oke, it is true, argued in a recent article²³ that the noble doxology of I Tim. i. 17 (τῷ δὲ βασιλεῖ τῶν αἰώνων...) is addressed to Christ; but it is difficult to be convinced by this. It is strange, in this connexion, that, whereas the phrase ὁ βασιλεὺς τῆς δόξης (as in Ps. xxiv (LXX xxiii)) is not applied to Christ, the phrase ὁ κύριος τῆς δόξης, which is applied to Christ in I Cor. ii. 8, is not a septuagintal term, although its equivalent occurs in Enoch.²⁴

Finally, before leaving the subject of liturgy, we must consider the use and avoidance of the formula 'through' or 'in the name of Jesus' in prayer. As for avoidance, one of the most astonishing facts in the history of Christian prayer is the avoidance of specifically Christian additions to the Lord's Prayer. Even the doxology, although (in its extant forms) it is widely held to be an addition to the original, is a 'unitarian' one.²⁵ F. H. Chase, at the end of the discussion of the doxology,²⁶ wrote:

> To sum up, the evidence which we have considered seems to show that several different forms of doxology, ultimately to be

21 Which it denotes in I Clem. lix. 2–4 and in the martyr-context of *Mart. Polyc.* xiv. 1–3, xx. 2, it is difficult to decide.
22 δοῦλος is used of David several times, including use in a prayer to God in I Macc. iv. 30; cf. Ps. lxxxviii (M.T. lxxxix). 4, 21, II Esdras iii. 23; and of Moses in, e.g. Rev. xv. 3; but never of Jesus except in the special context of Phil. ii. 7.
23 *Exp. T.* 67, 12 (Sept. 1956), pp. 367 f.
24 See J. Héring, *I aux Corinthiens* (Neuchâtel/Paris, 1949).
25 That it is not christianized is the more remarkable in that 'power, honour, and dominion', are exactly what belong to the Son of Man in Dan. vii. 14.
26 'The Lord's Prayer in the Early Church', in *Text and Studies*, (ed. J. A. Robinson, Cambridge, 1891), p. 176.

171

traced to the Old Testament, were in common use in the earliest years of the Church's life ...; that from the first the Lord's prayer, like other prayers, had attached to it now one doxology, now another; that, as the *Didache* in particular seems to suggest, the Lord's Prayer was in this way frequently adapted for use at the Service of Holy Communion; finally, that one form of the doxology, which appears to be a conflation of two distinct forms, was added to the Prayer in the 'Syrian' text of St. Matthew's Gospel and so has remained the common conclusion of the Prayer since the fourth century.

There are, as Chase noted, three forms of doxology even within the *Didache*:

(1) σοὶ ἡ δόξα εἰς τοὺς αἰῶνας (ix. 2, 3, x. 2, 4);

(2) σοῦ ἐστιν ἡ δόξα καὶ ἡ δύναμις διὰ Ἰησοῦ Χριστοῦ εἰς τοὺς αἰῶνας (ix. 4);[27]

(3) σοῦ ἐστιν ἡ δύναμις καὶ ἡ δόξα εἰς τοὺς αἰῶνας (viii. 2, x. 5).

But it is the last (3) which goes with the Lord's Prayer, not the Christian form (2) (even supposing this to be authentic);[27] and not, it would appear, until Gregory of Nyssa (and then in his exposition of the Lord's Prayer, not necessarily in a form for liturgical use) does Chase find a Christian doxology – indeed, a trinitarian one – attached to this prayer: ... ἀπὸ τοῦ πονηροῦ τοῦ ἐν τῷ κόσμῳ τούτῳ τὴν ἰσχὺν κεκτημένου, οὗ ῥυσθείημεν χάριτι τοῦ χριστοῦ, ὅτι αὐτῷ ἡ δύναμις καὶ ἡ δόξα ἅμα τῷ πατρὶ καὶ τῷ ἁγίῳ πνεύματι νῦν καὶ ἀεὶ καὶ εἰς τοὺς αἰῶνας τῶν αἰώνων· ἀμήν (Migne, *P.G.* xliv. 1193).

Can the explanation be that Jesus himself used a doxology (though not, in view of the textual variations, that of the Matthean version in any of its extant forms), and that reverence for the tradition of his words prevented the Christian Church from altering it in its essential contents?[28]

Even for other prayers, however, the evidence for a formula with the

27 J.-P. Audet, *La Didaché* (*Etudes bibliques*, Paris, 1958), p. 403, expresses doubts as to the authenticity of διὰ Ἰησοῦ Χριστοῦ here.

28 That some doxology was attached by Jesus himself has already been suggested in my hearing by J. Jeremias. Yet the variations in the Lord's Prayer (as in the Words of Institution) show (as G. Bornkamm observes in *Jesus von Nazareth* (Stuttgart, 1956), p. 125) 'wie wenig die Gemeinde ein Interesse daran hatte, auch solche Worte Jesu gleichsam archivarish zu hüten'. Note that a form of doxology containing a reference to the *Kingdom* goes back at least as far as I Chron. xxix. 11, and may have been current among the Jews. See Chase, 'The Lord's Prayer', pp. 168, 175; and B. F. Westcott, *Hebrews* (London, 1889), pp. 464 f.

name of Jesus is not plentiful in the New Testament. The most explicit allusion to such a usage in the Pauline epistles is perhaps II Cor. i. 20, where St Paul seems to be appealing to a liturgical use of διὰ Χριστοῦ Ἰησοῦ (or an equivalent phrase) with ἀμήν to support his affirmation that Christ is the 'amen' to God's promises. Elsewhere there are some instances of thanksgiving and doxology in this form: Rom. i. 8, vii. 25, xvi. 27, Eph. v. 20, Col. iii. 17, I Pet. iv. 11 (and cf. ii. 5), Jude 25. More important still, for the historian of the practice, would be the Johannine allusions, if only it were clear what was their purpose. In Jo. xiv. 13 f., xv. 16 the potency of prayer in Christ's name is fairly simply affirmed (whether or not the difficult reading ἐάν τι αἰτήσητέ με ἐν τῷ ὀνόματί μου in xiv. 14 should be accepted does not directly affect the present question). But in xvi. 24, 26 stress is laid on the fact that the use of the name of Jesus in petition is a new thing, a practice of the future (from the standpoint of the farewell address). This seems to imply that the fourth evangelist recognized the practice as something which began immediately after the resurrection, to which the futures in the farewell address must be meant (at least in the first instance) to point. If so, it makes the paucity of early instances even more surprising.

Outside the New Testament, in the Apostolic Fathers, there are such examples as *Didache* ix. 4 (already cited), I Clem. lxi. 3 (cf. lix. 2, 3, 4, though these are not quite so clear), and *Mart. Polyc.* xiv. 3, xx. 2.

To conclude, the titles of Jesus in prayer, whether in direct address to Jesus or as allusions in address to God, were probably controlled partly by a sense of adoration, which tended to exclude terms relating to his humiliation (except in special circumstances), and partly by the already existing Jewish Psalter and other liturgical forms. The measure of adaptation applied to these was controlled by the tension set up by the growing tendency to transfer κύριος-passages (and even θεός-passages) to Jesus while, at the same time, retaining a recognition of the role of Jesus as Messiah and Son of God. That 'Christ' never occurs in the vocative* in the New Testament may or may not be significant. One has to remember all the time how slender in any case is the material for studying prayer and adoration, especially that addressed to Jesus himself.

## EXPLANATION: ADMONITION, TEACHING, AND APOLOGETIC

If the demands of worship provide an important clue to the understanding of the processes of selection in the use of titles and names for Christ, so do the requirements of teaching the faith to inquirers and

[* Save in the mocking, Matt. xxvi. 68.]

defending it against critics. And whereas it appears – so far as our rather meagre evidence goes – that worship, in the early days, only called into play a comparatively narrow range of words, there are other, more specialized terms demanded by this parallel activity of evangelism and witness.

The study of this subject suggests one general principle – obvious enough, but important – namely, that each several explanation of the faith or defence of it is likely to run along rather particular lines, according to circumstances. In other words, it may be assumed that, although this activity, taken as a whole, has added considerably to the range of the Christian vocabulary, each separate manifestation of it is likely to be specialized and aimed at solving only one or two particular problems or meeting certain specific objections; and it is here that an explanation may reasonably be sought for some of the curious selectiveness of the New Testament. A Christian theologian, attempting to give as comprehensive an account as possible, may be surprised at the absence of one term or another; but the evangelist, or – still more – the apologist, may well need to concentrate on one or two aspects only and hammer home certain particular truths alone.[29]

In the New Testament the allusions to Christ's humiliation and suffering occur mainly not in prayer but in exhortation or explanation, and are chosen according to the circumstances. It is as example that he is referred to (in II Cor. viii. 9, Phil. ii. 5 ff., I Pet. ii. 21 ff.) as self-beggared and suffering; only in Rev. v (already alluded to) is there an exception. As for explanation and apologetic, St Paul's extant polemics are chiefly concerned with two great matters – faith-works controversy and the false estimate of Christ which is combated in Colossians. For the former, the most telling categories may well have been those of free-gift, sacrifice, and verdict of acquittal; for the latter, the Wisdom-vocabulary of Judaistic cosmogony. So with the writer of the Epistle to the Hebrews, it is obviously the Mosaic and the priestly analogies which are going to be the most effective for his type of argument.

To say this is only to indicate that the titles and descriptions of Christ in admonition and in controversy may well be not only different from those used in worship and in more general allusion, but also themselves limited by careful selection for the immediate purpose in hand. But admittedly this is still no adequate explanation of the very sparing use of Isa. liii already alluded to;[30] for both St Paul and the writer to

---

29 Cf. Taylor, *The Person of Christ*, Ch. xvi.

30 Especially when in so early a writing as I Clem. it is extensively applied (I Clem. xvi).

the Hebrews might have been expected to find in Isa. liii exactly the meeting-place of sacrificial and personal terms that they needed. It is strange that in Heb. x, when the climax is reached and the tremendous truth is enunciated that the offering presented by the real High-priest is *his own self*, the passage of Scripture requisitioned is Ps. xl (in its famous σῶμα-form) and not Isa. liii; and strange indeed that St Paul does not bring Isa. liii into Rom. iii or viii.

Be that as it may, it is easier to understand how 'the Son of Man' at any rate came to be restricted chiefly to the explanation of the meaning of martyrdom. The term does not greatly help to explain *how* salvation comes by Jesus; but it does provide a perfect symbol for the conviction that the oppressed and eclipsed martyr (or martyr people) is to be ultimately vindicated and seen 'coming with clouds' – that is, moving about as heavenly beings move (Ps. civ. 3) – and exalted in the glory of the divine favour. And although it would be inappropriate in the vocative as an adoring invocation, it is eminently suitable first on the lips of Jesus himself, and then afterwards as a reminder to martyrs of the 'pattern' of triumph through death, exemplified by the Archmartyr, the faithful and true μάρτυς. It is exactly consistent with this that the only occurrences of the term, other than on the lips of Jesus himself in his ministry, are in martyr-contexts – the account of the death of Stephen[31] and the Apocalypse. It might, on this showing, have been expected in I Peter. Instead, the writer uses the symbol of the stone – the stone rejected by the expert builders, but vindicated as indispensable; the stone on which faith can build, but over which unfaith stumbles; in fact, the *Kephas* which may be a sound foundation or a hindrance according to circumstances. He also calls Jesus the Chief Shepherd (v. 4, with possibly an allusion to the martyr-pastor of Zech. xiii): and he contrasts suffering in the flesh with vindication in the Spirit (iii. 18, cf. iv. 1; and I Tim. iii. 16). Perhaps it is mere chance, but it is worth

---

31 M. Simon, *St. Stephen and the Hellenists* (London, 1958), pp. 73 f. feels 'rather inclined to think that the term was used in the early Church, and perhaps especially in Jewish-Christian quarters, as a kind of *terminus technicus* to describe the exalted and eschatological Christ and that, consequently, there is nothing specific about it as used by Stephen'. I believe however, that, for St Luke at least, its use is significant in the way here indicated. And M. Simon does add (p. 74): 'It is perhaps used just here because this is the only account, in the whole New Testament, of a martyr's death, and because to martyrs only the privilege was granted to see the Son of Man exalted as he himself had announced he would henceforth be, and to proclaim him as such.'

noting that all these ideas are elsewhere associated with Peter (Matt. xvi. 18, 23; Acts iv. 11; John xxi. 15; Mk xiv. 38).

But, returning to the Son of Man, there may be a contributory reason, over and above its limited application to martyrdom, for the rarity of its occurrence outside the gospels. This is, that half its content was already a thing of the past, and half was – at any rate in the eyes of the early Church – yet in the future. Jesus had been ὁ υἱὸς τοῦ ἀνθρώπου ὁ ἐπὶ τῆς γῆς – the Son of Man in his humiliated, eclipsed, veiled, suffering aspect. He had shown in his ministry that even ἐπὶ τῆς γῆς he already possessed ἐξουσία (Mk ii. 10): there was, even then, some anticipation of the exalted condition described in the vision of Dan. vii. But then had come the crisis: he had been put to death, his work ἐπὶ τῆς γῆς had been terminated. And now, although he was raised and vindicated (yes – with clouds, Acts i. 9!), still the Church as a whole did not recognize him as having yet 'come with clouds' in the apocalyptic sense in which they took the words. The whole 'narrative' of Daniel's vision is in the past, it is true, and in the past it ought perhaps, to have been understood by the Christians in reference to Christ. But, whether rightly or wrongly, they took the coming with clouds to be still future.[32] The 'angels' of the ascension in the Acts story tell of his destined return in the same way as he had just gone; Mark xiii, and its parallels, speak of the future coming of the Son of Man; and the risen Lord of the Apocalypse announces that he is coming. And wherever this view prevailed, there it was naturally assumed that the Church was in a *Zwischenzeit*, between the going and the return; and what relevance has the term Son of Man to that? Far more relevant is the term Lord which, with its associations with Ps. cx, exactly fits the heavenly session. Ps. cx is, accordingly, one of the most frequent of all *testimonia*. It is in keeping with this explanation of the non-use of the title 'the Son of Man' that the exceptions are essentially apocalyptic[33] – Stephen's vision, and the advent message of the Apocalypse. It is appropriate to the past and the future; but not to the present except when the future is projected by an apocalyptic vision into the present.[34]

---

32 It is only necessary to turn the words of Dan. vii into one of the ordinary testimonium forms to see how difficult it would have been to recognize it as already accomplished. Thus: οὗτός ἐστιν ὁ υἱὸς τοῦ ἀνθρώπου περὶ οὗ γέγραπται ἵνα ἐλθῇ ἐν νεφέλαις καὶ ἵνα δοθῇ αὐτῷ ἡ ἀρχὴ καὶ ἡ τιμὴ καὶ ἡ βασιλεία, καὶ ἵνα πάντες οἱ λαοί, φυλαί, καὶ γλῶσσαι δουλεύσωσιν αὐτῷ. This had not yet literally taken place.

33 For Heb. ii (Ps. viii) see below.

34 It is, perhaps, still surprising that the term does not appear, as in the gospels, so also in a *retrospective* passage like Phil. ii. 5–11. But σχήματι

With this 'past and future but not present' conception of the Son of Man may perhaps be compared the apocalyptic use of the Shepherd figure already alluded to. If the mysterious martyr-Shepherd of Zech. xii, xiii is behind this idea, then it becomes intelligible that Jesus is thought of as the Shepherd who *was* 'pierced' (Jo. xix. 34), and who *will be* seen again (Matt. xxiv. 30, Jo. xix. 37).[35] The fact that this conception is combined with the Son of Man's clouds in both Matt. xxiv. 30 and Rev. i. 7 shows how closely the two figures were connected in the minds of Christians; and the same explanation as has been offered for the sparing use of the Son of Man may apply to the Shepherd also. It is consistent with this that the Chief Shepherd of I Pet. v. 4 is in a future, apocalyptic context (φανερωθέντος τοῦ ἀρχιποίμενος).

To say what has just been said about the limitations of the term 'the Son of Man' is to recognize that it was felt to be a term less appropriate to the Church, or to mankind collectively, than to Christ and to individual martyrs. Why this was so remains still unexplained. Apart from Heb. ii, where the term (in Ps. viii) is (most probably) applied to humanity, the word generally used for the collective body is ἄνθρωπος or Ἀδάμ or (in appropriate contexts) Ἰσραήλ, or (in some contexts) σῶμα. The suffering Church, entering into the afflictions of Christ (cf. Col. i. 24), might well have been styled the Son of Man: but by now

εὑρεθεὶς ὡς ἄνθρωπος (*v.* 7) is not far off it, and if the actual phrase Son of Man is avoided, it may be only for the sake of mainly Gentile hearers. Lohmeyer, *in loc.*, notes that ὡς must go with the noun, not the verb; and that ὡς ἄνθρωπος is exactly כבר אנש. E. Stauffer, *Jesus, Gestalt und Geschichte* (Berne, 1957), p. 122, suggests that the early Church avoided the term 'als tabuhafte Selbstpraedikation Jesu Christi'; but the reasons I have suggested both for its sparing use and for its avoidance seem to me to point away from this (and cf. Bornkamm, *Jesus von Nazareth*). On the next page, Stauffer argues very interestingly for the avoidance of the term in Jewish writings as a conscious reaction against Jesus' use.

35 I do not believe that the ὁ ἑωρακώς of Jo. xix. 34 is meant to be taken as a reference to the fulfilment of the ὄψονται of the Zecharian passage cited in xix. 37; the subject of the ὄψονται is the *opponents* of the pierced one (cf. Mk xiv. 62, Rev. xi. 12), and they have yet to 'see' their error and condemnation. If this is the force of the testimonium, it is not already fulfilled in Jo. xix, even by the fact that 'they who pierced' Jesus (the Roman soldier and his colleagues) did, there and then, of course 'see' him. 'Seeing' must mean seeing him vindicated and seeing themselves correspondingly in the wrong. The Massoretic reading in Zech. xii. 10 admittedly has 'they shall look to *me*' (וְהִבִּיטוּ אֵלַי); but it is not certainly correct; and although the LXX reflects this (ἐπιβλέψονται πρός με), Christian interpretation at any rate seems to have accepted the third person. Besides the canonical passages, see *Didache* xiv. 7, Justin, *I Apol.* lii.

the title was evidently, for whatever reason, too exclusively appropriated for Christ alone.

A limited and special significance, again, attaches to the Lamb (ἀρνίον) of the Apocalypse and perhaps to the Lamb (ἀμνός) of the fourth gospel. The former, at any rate, seems to be an appropriate symbol for the triumph of Christ's death: it is the sacrificial animal which is also the triumphant leader of the flock. As such – apart from any use in the context of the actual ministry of Jesus, or in apologetic to explain his death (Acts viii. 32 uses πρόβατον from Isa. liii) – it is appropriate only where it occurs, in a martyr-context. This is possibly the explanation of the fact that only here in the New Testament is the term used also in adoration. Some other instances of the influence of the persecution setting of the Apocalypse fall for consideration below.

The category of terms applied to special circumstances or used with some particular teaching in view may be held to include δεσπότης, which is applied explicitly to Christ in Jude 4 and may be used of Christ in II Pet. ii. 1.[36] Elsewhere in the New Testament it is applied either to God (Luke ii. 29, Acts iv. 24, Rev. vi. 10, perhaps II Pet. ii. 1)[37] or to slave owners; and the application to Christ seems to be part of the specially pointed teaching that Christians have been 'purchased' into Christ's ownership – teaching particularly appropriate in combating antinomianism. It is comparable to the absolutism of St Paul's use of δοῦλος and αἰχμάλωτος of Christians in their relation to Christ. That non-biblical Greek uses it of gods may also help to explain its occurrence in so Hellenistic a context as II Peter, by way of contrast.

It may be recorded at this point that the term λυτρωτής is not only not applied to Christ at all within the New Testament, but apparently is not found in secular Greek either. In the LXX it occurs twice, in both cases applied to God (as גאל), in Pss. xviii (M.T. xix). 15, lxxvii (M.T. lxxviii). 35. Its only occurrence in the New Testament is of Moses in Acts vii. 35. The verb λυτροῦσθαι, however, occurs in the significant phrase ὁ μέλλων λυτροῦσθαι τὸν Ἰσραήλ in the Emmaus story (Lk. xxiv. 21); and it is possible that the word ἄρχων, used of Moses in the same passage of Stephen's speech (Acts vii. 35) as the word λυτρωτής, may be echoed in the ἀρχηγός so notably applied to Christ in Acts (iii.

36 *T.W.N.T.* ii. 48 notes that the use of οἱ δεσπόσυνοι for members of the Lord's family (Eus., *H.E.* i. 7. 14) reflects the use of δεσπότης for Christ.
37 Cf. the frequent use of ὁ δεσπότης for God in I Clem., and some examples also in Barnabas, *Diognetus*, and Hermas. See Bauer s.v. See also the verb δεσπόζειν, in (e.g.) Ps. lxxxviii (M.T. lxxxix). 10.

15, v. 31) and Hebrews (ii. 10, xii. 2). In other words, Moses-typology may be behind the choice of some of the terms for Christ, despite the non-use of λυτρωτής itself.

The situation created for Christian apologetic by the Emperor cult certainly seems to explain some of the New Testament terminology, and it will be convenient to discuss this next, via the question of the translation of Semitic terms into Greek. Outside the gospels no actual Semitic title of Jesus survives except the *Maran(a)* which has been discussed. *Adon, Adoni,* if implied by Ps. cx, at any rate does not actually occur; and *Messias* only occurs within the narrative of the ministry in the fourth gospel. Practically everything, that is to say, has been turned into Greek. Χριστός is the most nearly Semitic term left. It is a literal translation of the Semitic *māšîah* or *mešîhâ'*, and, in the Greek world, would (except when recognized as a foreign term) mean absolutely nothing except 'anointed' or 'smeared' (as of a sore which had been treated medicinally with an emollient) or 'smeared on' (as of the ointment itself – χριστός, 'for external application', as distinguished from πιστός 'for internal use'). As a technical term of Jewish religious king-making it must have been quite alien to the Greek world. When it was understood at all, it was used, as it were, in inverted commas: ' "Christ", a King' (Lk. xxiii. 2); and, as we know, it was also misunderstood and corrupted, by false analogy, to χρηστός, or turned into a term of ridicule or satire in χριστιανοί.[38] Accordingly, it is at first sight surprising that it survived in the Christian non-Palestinian vocabulary.

In St Paul's writings it is all but a proper name – though never quite: though not interchangeable with κύριος, as a sheer title, neither is it interchangeable with 'Ιησοῦς as a mere proper name. It still carries some flavour of function and of Israelite divine destiny.[39] But in so far as it is nearly a personal name, its retention might be explained. In the Acts sermons, however, it is more than this. It here seems to retain still its sense as a title: that 'Jesus is ὁ χριστός' (Acts ix. 22) seems to have been as much a clause of the primitive confession for Jewish Christians as was, for Gentiles, the confession of Jesus as κύριος. Possibly, therefore, when χριστός was a real title it was used by Greek-speaking Jews,

38 See especially H. B. Mattingly, 'The Origin of the Name *Christiani*', *J.T.S.*, n.s. 9, 1 (April 1958), 26 ff.
39 F. Neugebauer, in a very acute analysis of the meaning of the Pauline ἐν-phrases ('Das Paulinische "In Christo"', *N.T.S.* 4, 2 (Jan. 1958), 124 ff.), finds a distinction between 'in Christ Jesus', etc. as concerned with the *indicative* of the Kerygma, and 'in the Lord' as concerned rather with the ethical *imperative*.

on the analogy of the Septuagint. It was a technical term of Jewish-Christian religion. As has been observed already, the Psalter by itself might have been sufficient to give it considerable currency.[40]

But if it survived in certain circles, whether as intelligible to readers of the Jewish scriptures in Greek or as virtually a personal name, it remains surprising that elsewhere it is not rendered simply by βασιλεύς. The description of God as βασιλεὺς τοῦ αἰῶνος, מלך העולם,[41] would be familiar to Jews, as were 'the Great King' (Mal. i. 14, Pss. xlvii. 2, xlviii. 2, xcv. 3, cf. Matt. v. 34) and 'the King of glory' (Ps. xxiv (LXX xxiii), cf. Acts vii. 2, ὁ θεὸς τῆς δόξης).[42] The Psalms of Solomon use βασιλεύς freely for Messiah. The divinization of the Emperor would have made it easy for the Gentile to find in βασιλεύς a suitable aura of divinity. It might, therefore, have been almost as substantial a 'bridge'-word as κύριος. But very seldom is Christ described so.[43] Within the gospels βασιλεύς is applied to Christ from the quotation of Zech. ix. 9 at the triumphal entry, and occasionally by opponents as a charge of sedition; and in the fourth gospel, of course, it is used by Jesus himself and his friends. The verb βασιλεύειν is used, with Jesus as subject, in Lk. i. 33 and I Cor. xv. 25.[44] Otherwise, if we exclude I Tim. i. 17 (see above, p. 171), the words, so used, are confined to the Apocalypse. Thus, the total is tiny in proportion to χριστός or κύριος, until, in the Apocalypse, the sonorous title βασιλεὺς βασιλέων twice meets us, xvii. 14, xix. 16, and the verb three or four times. Of this, more directly. Perhaps the fact is that βασιλεύς was too human and secular,[45] despite

40 It is extremely interesting that, in the Johannine epistles, where χριστός is used as a high christological title, interchangeable with ὁ υἱὸς τοῦ θεοῦ, κύριος is totally absent. Titus (see below, p. 181, n. 52) and the Johannine epistles are the only N.T. writings in which κύριος is not found at all (see Taylor, *The Person of Christ*, pp. 144 ff.).

41 Cf. I Clem. lxi. 2.

42 Cf. ὦ μέγιστε βασιλεῦ θνητῶν καὶ ἀθανάτων, Philo, *Flacc.* 123.

43 Note that in the 'Q' passage, Matt. xi. 25, Lk. x. 21, God is addressed as κύριε τοῦ οὐρανοῦ καὶ τῆς γῆς; contrast the phrase 'King of heaven and earth' cited by Jeremias (*Jesus' Promise to the Nations*, p. 14) from Siphre Deut. 313 (to Deut. xxii. 10).

44 In a striking passage of *Mart. Polyc.* the verb is used in deliberate imitation of the method of dating by secular rulers (xxi βασιλεύοντος δὲ εἰς τοὺς αἰῶνας Ἰησοῦ Χριστοῦ); but that is later even than the original story of Polycarp: see H. von Campenhausen, 'Bearbeitungen und Interpolationen des Polykarpmartyriums', *Sitzungsberichte der Heidelberger Akademie der Wissenschaften*, 1957, Abh. 3.

45 May it be also that, since it had actually been used in the accusations against Jesus and in the 'title' on the cross, it was studiously avoided as too closely

its Jewish use for God (cf. Philo, as well as LXX), whereas the word κύριος was felt to be safer, because (although beginning to be used for the Emperor - Bauer says it began with Claudius, and Acts xxv. 26 is a rare and early example)[46] it was widely associated with deity or divinity in paganism (even if not in native Greek usage)[47] and in Greek-speaking Judaism (cf. I. Cor. viii. 5).[48]

As for the terms applied in adulation to the deified emperors of Rome or kings of the Levant, these were probably felt by most of the New Testament Christians to have been dragged in the dust by this very circumstance, and therefore did not really take root in the religious vocabulary, despite the considerable use of σωτήρ for God in the Psalter, and the etymological association of the name Jesus with Salvation. But there are two notable exceptions to this tendency - the Pastoral Epistles and the Revelation.[49] It is possible[50] that ὁ κύριός μου καὶ ὁ θεός μου (Jo. xx. 28) may be an allusion to the proclamation of Domitian as 'Lord and God'. But otherwise, it is in the Pastorals and the Revelation that there seem to be clear and deliberate allusions to the imperial cult. Even here there is no use of εὐεργέτης[51] or σεβαστός; nowhere in the New Testament is ἡγεμών used of Christ, although Philo uses it of God. But the Pastorals make free use of the ideas ἐπιφάνεια and σωτήρ (I Tim. vi. 14, II Tim. i. 10, iv. 1, 8, Tit. i. 4, ii. 13, iii. 6, cf. II Pet. i. 1, 11, ii. 20, iii. 18; also note φῶς, ζωή, ἀφθαρσία, II Tim. i. 10);[52] and the descriptions of Christ in the Apocalypse are strongly reminiscent of the terms of the Emperor-cult. Hanns Lilje, in

associated with misleading charges? Jo. xviii. 33–40 is obviously designed to underline the fact that Christ's kingship was not of a sort to rival the Emperor's. Indeed (as Professor E. C. Ratcliff points out to me) the stress is on the fact that Jesus is μάρτυς (v. 37) rather than on his kingship.
46 See also *T.W.N.T.* iii. 1053: *Mart. Polyc.* viii κύριος καῖσαρ.
47 See also *T.W.N.T.* iii. 1049, cited above, p. 169, n. 14.
48 It is to be noted that υἱός (and cp. ἀγαπητός) is also used here and there in contexts which link it with the address in the Psalter to the *royal* Son of God: Acts xiii. 33, Rom. i. 4, perhaps Heb. i. 2 (cf. 5). The deeper, more theological significance of the term, in Paul, John, and Hebrews, is another matter. See the valuable tables in Taylor, *The Person of Christ*, pp. 143 ff.
49 Unless the word παρουσία must be included among those dangerously close to imperial vocabulary (cf. p. 167, n. 8 above). But it is used so often in other, non-technical, senses that it does not in fact seem to be such.
50 So G. Stählin in a recent broadcast in Germany.
51 But see Tit. iii. 4.
52 It is interesting that κύριος is totally absent from Titus. See Taylor, *The Person of Christ*, pp. 145 f. It is, incidentally, in Tit. ii. 13 that μέγας θεός occurs (of Christ?). This is a very rare phrase whether for God or Christ, and may owe its use here, again to the Emperor cult.

his commentary on the Revelation,[53] heads the section on Rev. i. 9–20 *Christus Imperator*; and E. Stauffer offered a brilliant and dramatic interpretation of the Apocalypse in terms of the Roman games.[54] It is in this part of the New Testament, as has just been said, that the title βασιλεὺς βασιλέων occurs.[55] Similarly, only once in the whole New Testament is ἄρχων applied to Christ,[56] and that in the polemical context of the Apocalypse (i. 5 ὁ ἄρχων τῶν βασιλέων τῆς γῆς).

Thus the vigorous and daring use of Roman imperial language, where it does occur, seems to be explainable in terms of the special situation. If Emperor-cult terms are generally avoided, the case is different when there is direct conflict. Here the most effective apologetic may well be boldly to use as many cult-terms as possible, challenging the enemy on his own ground. Hence the spate of such language in the Apocalypse (and to some extent in the Pastorals) in contrast to the rather studious avoidance of it elsewhere. Does its virtual absence from I Peter suggest an early date, and does its presence in the Pastorals and the Apocalypse confirm a later date for them? [cf. p. 117 above.]

Finally, it must be recalled that only in the prologue of the fourth gospel is λόγος used in an unequivocally Christological way.[57] In Colossians and Hebrews there is a λόγος-Christology, but without the actual term. Is the explicit use in the Johannine prologue conditioned simply by the interests of the readers to whom the gospel is addressed? This familiar problem, however it is solved, is one more illustration of the relevance of the method of inquiry here advocated.

53 *Das letzte Buch der Bibel* (Hamburg, 1955).

54 *Christ and the Caesars*, pp. 179 ff.

55 See Stauffer, *Christ and the Caesars*, p. 190. For the wider history of the term see J. G. Griffiths, 'βασιλεὺς βασιλέων: remarks on the history of a title', *Class. Philol.* 48, 3 (July 1953), pp. 145 ff. It is noteworthy, however, that (ὁ) κύριος τῶν κυρίων and κύριος τῶν βασιλέων are biblical terms for God; see Ps. cxxxv. 3 (LXX), Deut. x. 17, Dan. x. 47. In both Rev. xvii. and xix. 16 κύριος κυρίων accompanies the βασιλεύς-phrase; and in I Tim. vi. 15 there is βασιλεὺς τῶν βασιλευόντων καὶ κύριος τῶν κυριευόντων.

56 Though see the remarks above (pp. 178 f.) about ἀρχηγός as possibly equivalent to a *Mosaic* figure.

57 I do not include Rev. xix. 13, for it seems to me that it represents a personification of God's *fiat* as a victorious warrior, closely comparable to the passage in Wisdom; and if so, it does not belong to a genuine Logos-Christology in the ordinarily accepted sense. I John i. 1 has a far stronger claim to be included; but even that is not as inevitable as the use in the fourth gospel.

Throughout this inquiry the attempt has been made to account for the use and non-use of titles and epithets from the circumstances and objects of the writings in which they occur. The reader may well detect special pleading and far-fetched suggestions, and the writer is less concerned to defend himself against such a charge than to maintain that it is a sound principle to examine the 'Sitz im Leben' of the titles, with special attention to the distinction between liturgy and 'explanation'. This is only a preliminary groping after a clue. Further investigation along these lines may, it is to be hoped, lead to a fuller understanding of early Christian thinking.

# 13

## The Influence of Circumstances on the Use of
## Eschatological Terms[1]

The literature on New Testament eschatology is vast and daily vaster, and I make no pretence to have mastered it. All that I venture to offer in this paper is the suggestion that, in some of the learned discussions, an obvious but important fact is overlooked. This is the fact that, in all that they wrote about what we call eschatology, St Paul and the others were confronted - always, and not at one time any more than another - by a complex situation. That situation, from first to last, was invariably held within the tension of the incarnation itself - a tension which, by definition, can never be resolved in this life and is never amenable to progressive adjustments. The situation, therefore, always, from the very first, presented a wide variety of needs and a diversity of questions which were potentially simultaneous. It is, I suggest, when this constant fact is forgotten that theories of successive phases of thought and even of evolutionary stages of development gain more plausibility than they deserve. In an article in the *J.T.S.* not long ago,[2] I tried to show that christological formulations were dominated first by one emphasis, then by another, not always according to chronological sequence but rather according to their particular purposes, whether it was worship and adoration, explanation and defence, or, perhaps, even attack. What I shall try to do now is to apply the same kind of considerations to eschatological formulations, by asking: What particular conviction did this one and that one aim to safeguard? In thus offering a classification according to the convictions that needed protecting, I want to suggest that the need or the appropriateness of that other kind of classification according to successive phases of development is correspondingly weakened, and even that the search for consistency or uniformity at any given stage is partly obviated.

1 The Presidential Address delivered to the Oxford Society of Historical Theology on 25 October 1962.
2 'The Influence of Circumstances on the Use of Christological Terms', *J.T.S.* 10 (1959), 247 ff. [See pp. 165 ff. above.]

This idea, although I have been arriving at it, I think independently, is of course, not original: it is sponsored by others also, at least in part. In a paper read before this very Society on 9 May 1940, and later published in the *J.T.S.*,[3] Dr John Lowe presented a view which, in some respects, though by no means all, is close to mine. Much more recently - in last year's session - Dr G. B. Caird read a fascinating paper ('The Linguistics of New Testament Eschatology')[4] which he has been kind enough to lend me, and with which my own (though drafted before I had read it) concurs in important respects. To these articles I shall return later. Then, to quote only two others from among the more recent examples, L. Cerfaux speaks of three different 'scenarios' for Paul's eschatology, in I Thassalonians, II Thessalonians, and I Cor. xv;[5] and L. van Hartingsveld, writing of Johannine eschatology, says: 'Man wird von jedem Versuch der Systematisierung absehen müssen. Ein einheitliches System gibt es nicht'; and adds: 'Auch das übrige N.T. kennt verschiedene eschatologische Begriffe, ohne dass diese systematisch eingeordnet werden'.[6] Later, in a footnote, he writes: 'An sich ist das Fehlen der Apokalyptik kein Argument, das Joh. Evang. und die Joh. Apok. verschiedenen Autoren zuzuschreiben. Wieviel Vorsicht man walten lassen muss, kann man aus den Briefen des Paulus ersehen. Diese haben auch nicht immer die gleiche Thematik und sind untereinander sehr verschieden. Der Römerbrief und der Brief an Philemon sind nicht vergleichbar. Dennoch stammen sie vom selben Autor.'[7] All this already anticipates just the kind of observation that I want now to make; but it is, I think, worth while to reiterate this untidy view of things and to reinvestigate it, if only because attempts continue to be made to give a neat and orderly account of the steady evolution of eschatological thought, and New Testament scholarship is still coloured to a surprising extent by the assumption that such an account can be given.

A caricaturish and over-tidy presentation of such an orderly account might run something like this:

(1) The earliest understanding of all drew no dividing line between

3 'An Examination of Attempts to Detect Developments in St. Paul's Theology', *J.T.S.* 42 (1941), pp. 129 ff.

4 Cf. his article 'On Deciphering the Book of Revelation: III. The First and the Last' in *Exp.T.* 74, 3 (December 1962), pp. 82 ff.

5 *Le Christ dans la théologie de Saint Paul* (Paris, 1954), p. 45.

6 *Die Eschatologie des Johannesevangeliums* (Assen, 1962), p. 154.

7 *Ibid.*, p. 169, n. 1. Note also N. A. Dahl's essay on 'The Particularity of the Pauline Epistles' in *Neotestamentica et Patristica* (Leiden, 1962, *Supplements to Nov. Test.* 6, for Cullmann), pp. 261 ff. (especially p. 271).

the incarnation and its sequel: Christians were participating in a single, indivisible event – the coming of Christ.

(2) Then quickly came the sense that there had been an interruption, and that an interval was taking place, with the conviction, however, that it would be a very brief interval: Christ would return at any minute, and the whole of God's purposes would then be consummated.

(3) As time passed without this happening, compensations were invented or discovered. One was *Heilsgeschichte* – the incorporation of the interval into a recognizable divine pattern of salvation; another was the recognition of the presence of the Holy Spirit in the Messianic Community, a foretaste and pledge of the consummation and an interim consolation.

(4) Finally, this coming of the Holy Spirit came to be identified, without remainder, with the consummation: it *was* the return of Christ. Such a view carried with it, no doubt, implications of a more evolutionary and progressive, a less cataclysmic, conception of the final dénouement itself.

I called this outline caricaturish. But in fact it is such only, perhaps, in its simplicity and neatness. One could quote chapter and verse from recent writers – let alone those, like E. F. Scott, of a rather earlier generation – for substantially each of these stages. Dr J. A. T. Robinson[8] holds, if I mistake not, that no. 1 is really not only the most primitive Church-view, but also the dominical view; that no. 4, accordingly, represents the profoundest and most dominical way of translating this into the language of the Church's life; and that the rest was brought upon the Church by its inability, as time passed, to resist the temptation to divide the indivisible. Dr Dodd, in a celebrated essay,[9] and elsewhere, has argued for successive changes, at least in emphasis, within Paul's own thinking. Starting from an early emphasis on the immediacy of the consummation and on judgement for the reprobate, Paul's thought moved through to a revaluation of the natural order – indeed to universalism. Dr Dodd throws considerable stress, as we know,[10] upon a believed crisis in St Paul's life, which makes this anything but an even or a steady evolution; but an evolution it remains, however jerky. Not long afterwards, Dr Wilfred Knox argued[11] for a change, as he put

8 See, for example, *Jesus and His Coming* (London, 1957).
9 'The Mind of Paul: Change and Development' in *B.J.R.L.* 18, I (1934), pp. 69 ff; reprinted in *New Testament Studies* (Manchester, 1953).
10 'The Mind of Paul, a Psychological Approach' in *B.J.R.L.* 17, I (1933), pp. 91 ff.
11 *St. Paul and the Church of the Gentiles* (Cambridge, 1939).

it in his chapter-heading, 'from Omega to Alpha', in Paul's teaching. Under the pressure of Hellenstic influence, and especially the Colossian situation, Paul found himself, Knox thought, driven from apocalyptic back to cosmogony: from Christ the Omega to Christ the Alpha. Once again, it is a change precipitated, in part abruptly, by circumstances; but still it is a permanent movement out of one position into another. As for the idea that the Johannine coming of the Paraclete replaces the *parousia*-hope, that is a commonplace of interpretation.[12]

In reaction against the evolutionary view of Pauline thought, the late Dr John Lowe's paper, already mentioned, maintained that virtually no alteration or development whatever could be established in the eschatology (or, for that matter, the christology) of the Pauline epistles: Galatians may be early, but is without apocalyptic; Philippians is late, yet expects the Lord from heaven.

I do not myself hold that there is no case for a progressive sequence of changes in emphasis; but my thesis is that the chief explanation of the variations (which are great) in New Testament eschatological formulation is to be sought not primarily in successive compensations for the delay of the *parousia*, nor yet in incalculable changes of mood or in the mere hyperbole of a vehement Oriental (to which Dr Lowe gave a good deal of weight in his paper), nor even in the special characteristics of oriental thought, so satisfyingly illuminated by Dr Caird's paper, but in the fact that the New Testament writers - and notably Paul - were content to be torn by a dilemma, and were aware of it in a way which some of their interpreters refuse to recognize. In all fairness to Dr Lowe's paper, this, be it said, is his own last and crowning point. I want to try to show that, both in the Pauline letters and elsewhere, formulations are found which may be both mutually incompatible, and, equally, incapable of being plausibly arranged as successive stages in an evolutionary order of development; and that they are best explained as the result, simply, of the unmanageable dimensions of the Christian verities. These being great beyond expression, all that Paul can do is to nail down or 'peg' first one insight and then another, as need arises, without

12 Dr Dodd, for instance, speaks of the Fourth Evangelist's 'reinterpretation, or transmutation, of popular eschatology'; 'the true *parusia*', he says, 'is to be found in the interchange of divine ἀγάπη made possible through Christ's death and resurrection' . . . 'It appears . . . that the evangelist had the intention to interpret the event which he is about to record in Chs. xviii-xx - the death and resurrection of Christ - as the eschatological Event in the fullest sense.' *The Interpretation of the Fourth Gospel* (Cambridge, 1953), pp. 395 f.

attempting a coherent, architectonic scheme or a logical series. The 'pegs', if I may pursue the metaphor, were driven in - as, indeed, actually happens with tent-pegs - not in a developing sequence all round, but on opposite and complementary sides, preferably simultaneously, or at least alternately.

In handling the greatest and most paradoxical convictions of the Christian faith, something like this is bound to happen: we have to drive in pegs for guy-ropes on opposite sides.[13] This, be it observed, holds good for western thought quite as much as for oriental. Among the characteristics of oriental thought named by Dr Caird in the paper I have referred to are two: the use of absolutes, and the putting of these absolutes starkly side by side unreconciled. But, while wholly agreeing, I venture to suggest that the nature of the incarnation forces the same situation, at certain levels, on any formulation, even if it is a westerner's. I expect we all find ourselves questioned by inquirers, from time to time, about the central puzzle - freewill versus predestination - and about what Christianity teaches concerning heaven and hell. In such cases, I often find myself driven to make two antithetic, yet complementary, affirmations in quick succession - first, that there is no language even remotely big enough to describe the gravity of our responsibility for free choice, except the language of heaven and hell; and, then, that the love of God is such that I cannot conceive of its being ultimately defeated, or failing to bring everyone in fact to choose heaven by his own free choice in the end: that God's love is such that it could neither be itself if it did not respect a person's freedom of choice, nor yet if a single soul were ultimately left to choose hell. This is what, rightly or wrongly, I understand to be the position of Dr Robinson's book, *In the End, God . . .* (London, 1950).

Now, in the same way, there are, as we know, within the New Testament statements about the last things which it is difficult to fit into a single system; and my point is not only that these are incapable of being built into a single system, but also that they have, intrinsically, no

13 In another connexion, M. E. Dahl writes admirably: 'The Hebrew asserts both the immanence and transcendence of God and is stubbornly *consistent* in maintaining this "inconsistency". Over human personality he employs a great number of apparently contradictory expressions and ideas, thereby showing inconsistency. But he *is* consistent in refusing to allow his ideas of human personality ever to fall into a "consistent", systematic way of conceiving it . . . if we are to understand the Bible, we must look for a number of intuitional insights which together build up a meaningful pattern, but which discourage systematization.' *The Resurrection of the Body* (London, 1962), pp. 85 f.

logical sequence or successive order of evolution, but may arrive on the scene at any moment, and in almost any order, whether to 'peg' two opposite ends of a paradox or to defend different aspects of the truth as they chance to come under attack. They are produced (to use Papias' celebrated phrase) πρὸς τὰς χρείας, to meet each need as it arises. There are aspects oī eschatology which have to be stated and then simply balanced by their opposites or complements. So vast are the purposes of God that the human mind can only adumbrate bits of them as thesis and antithesis, never, in this life, reaching synthesis; and, consequently, it is not surprising if a single thinker is found using antithetic formulations at one and the same period of his own development. Van Hartingsveld[14] recalls W. F. Howard's striking citation[15] of two of Charles Wesley's hymns – the first containing such phrases as:

> Never in the whirlwind found,
> Or where earthquakes rock the place,
> Still and silent is the sound,
> The whisper of Thy grace;

the second:

> Come, Thou Conqueror of the nations,
> Now on Thy white horse appear;
> Earthquakes, dearths, and desolations
> Signify Thy Kingdom near. . . .

It is true that, in this case, seventeen years divide the two; but they both belong to a single mind, and the one follows the other not in the order of an evolution from a primitive apocalypticism to a mature mysticism, but in the reverse order; and they appear to have been controlled by circumstances rather than by any permanent change of outlook.

With this in mind, let me attempt some classification of the variety of formulations demanded of a Christian by various situations.

(1) Where personal decision is at issue, there, as we have said, the symbols of the Great Assize and of the alternatives, salvation and damnation, are perhaps the only symbols even remotely big enough to carry the gravity of the situation. Von Dobschütz was not far off the mark when he wrote (in 1908):[16] 'Of course, in His addresses to the people

14 *Die Eschatologie*, p. 180, n. 3.

15 *Christianity according to St. John* (London, 1943), p. 202.

16 *The Eschatology of the Gospels* (addresses at the Third International Congress for the History of Religions, Oxford, 1908, published by Hodder and Stoughton in 1910), p. 20.

[Jesus] speaks as the missionary; there is the need to be watchful, for the great moment will come shortly, suddenly'; but went on to contrast this with Jesus' language to those who had decided to accept him - 'the intimate circle of His followers', where 'there is no anxious self-preparation for judgment to come, but a happy enjoyment of all blessings which God's grace has vouchsafed to them in Jesus'. We do not need to endorse this particular classification or description of the sayings of Jesus to recognize the force of such a distinction. Similarly, van Hartingsveld[17] (surely rightly) attributes the language of judgement and resurrection in St John to the setting of conflict with the Jews, as against a different set of symbols in the discourses with the disciples.

If one thus distinguishes between language for the uncommitted and language for the committed, another significant distinction will be between the individual and the collective.

Thus, (2) on the level of the individual, or even of the comparatively small and homogeneous group, it is possible to speak in terms of realized eschatology.[18] His choice once made - or in so far as his choice is made - an individual may be said already, here and now, to have passed from death to life, or to have been judged and condemned, as the case may be. Either way, he is 'beyond judgement'; and where there still remains futurity for the individual, the day of death can, in a sense, be substituted for a world-cataclysm or a collective Day of Judgement, as a symbol for the climax of the process.

But (3) it is different for humanity viewed collectively. The more the group overlays the individual, the less appropriate do terms of realized eschatology seem to be, and the less adequate is the aggregate of individual deaths as a symbol of the consummation. Of a believing individual you may say that he has already 'seen the light', 'accepted life', 'passed from death to life', or (*judaice*) 'accepted the yoke of the Kingdom'; and, at death, he may even be conceived of as being taken forthwith into the immediate presence of God.[19] But when the departed individual is viewed in relation to a larger group, he has to be conceived of as 'sleeping' or somehow 'waiting' - as though not yet in the immediate Presence, so that he without us should not be made perfect. And

17 *Die Eschatologie*, pp. 168 f.
18 I do not say 'it is necessary', for of course there is often a strong note of futurity for individuals (e.g. in parables enjoining alertness).
19 Thorleif Boman, whose essay 'Hebraic and Greek Thought-Forms in the New Testament' contributed to *Current Issues in New Testament Interpretation* (essays in honour of O. Piper, ed. W. Klassen and G. F. Snyder, London, 1962), seems to me open to question in some respects, makes this point convincingly (pp. 8 f.).

of the group as a whole you can scarcely affirm realization. The group, unless it is exceptionally homogeneous and pure, is bound to be, in some measure, a *corpus permixtum*, awaiting a unification and purification and consummation still in the future. The only language appropriate to its destiny is that of futurist eschatology. Wheat and tares must grow together *until* the harvest. *Parousia* is mostly a collective word, describing the arrival of the King to the city or community, who receive him with mingled joy and fear, according to each individual's condition.[20] Strictly speaking, the difference between circumstances (2) and (3) is the difference between being fully *committed* one way or the other, and not being committed; but it remains true that, in practice, committal becomes less obvious and more diffused, the larger and looser the group becomes.

(4) Then, yet again, one might distinguish questions about human destiny from questions about the destiny of the whole of creation. About man's destiny it may be possible – just because he is man and is personal – to speak in terms quite free of apocalyptic. Of man's destiny one may use terms of personal relationship and character – the growing up into mature selfhood, the attainment of a right relationship with God; and, as a means to this end, one may recognize evangelism as an eschatological activity of great significance. But about the future of the entire cosmos, if one speaks at all one must speak not in personal but in the mythical and quasi-physical language of apocalyptic.

(5) Or, again, apocalyptic has its value simply in emphasizing the transcendent and the 'vertical', as against the 'horizontal' and merely human. Ultimately, I believe that anthropomorphic language goes deeper into divine mysteries than any other terms, because the fully human is nearer than anything else in our experience to the divine. But nevertheless it may be that the mythical is, in certain circumstances, the only means of emphasizing the 'otherness' of God and his transcendence. It is rather like abstract art in contrast to naturalism – it introduces mystery and transcendence into a scene that may be in danger of becoming earth-bound and photographic. Conversely, when myth and a cataclysmic conception of the End threaten to induce a fatalistic resignation, and when one is in danger of forgetting God's creatorhood and the goodness of the created world and God's redemptive purposes towards it, then it is time to abandon myth and apocalyptic again in favour of moral progress and social development. A recent example of a bid to retrieve the latter values in the teaching of Jesus himself is S.

20 So exactly Chrysostom, *Hom. in ascens.* (*P.G.* 1. 450–1, cited by Cerfaux).

191

Aalen's treatment of the Theme of the Kingdom in his paper ' "Reign" and "House" in the Kingdom of God'.[21] There he maintains that Jesus deliberately abandoned the normal Jewish conception of the 'revealing' of the Kingdom of God as a transcendent manifestation of God's power and glory, in favour of the idea that the Kingdom was not manifested, but simply 'came': 'the Kingdom', he writes, 'is sent into the scene of history, or into the world as the scene of mankind. And history is here, in accordance with Old Testament thought, conceived as a linear stream running towards a goal.'[22] While impressed by this article, I am not myself fully persuaded by the whole of it; but I cite it simply as an example of an interpretation of the Kingdom in terms which are not apocalyptic.

(6) Viewing the this-worldly and the human from a slightly different angle again, one may say that there are times when the emphasis falls on human responsibility in the working out of God's design. Then it is that the missionary task of the Church (already alluded to) comes into the foreground, and eschatological statements take the form: 'but first must the gospel be preached to all the nations'. A stress on the suddenness of the coming and the foreshortening of the time, while logically contradicting this, is primarily a way simply of emphasizing the opposite or complementary truth of the divine control of the design.

(7) Finally, any distinctively Christian account of God's purposes is bound to take cognizance of two facts: first, that, with the incarnation, a new era has begun; but, secondly, that it has not yet been consummated; and the language may vary considerably according as the stress falls upon the newness or upon the incompleteness. The distinction here will overlap in part with the distinction from which we began – namely, that between the realization for the individual and the futurism for the group.

Now I do not pretend that this sevenfold classification of aspects of eschatology or types of eschatological statement is either exhaustive or successful; but I hope it is sufficient to show that different formulations have to be enlisted in the service of different affirmations, all of which may prove to be simultaneous aspects of a single great conviction too large to be expressed coherently or singly. If so, I need not weary you by attempting a complete exemplification from the New Testament of each of these aspects. I propose, instead, merely to recall the existence of examples of a certain number, while selecting only a few special cases to look at in rather more detail. We can easily enough

21 *N.T.S.* 8, 3 (April 1962), 215 ff.        22 *N.T.S.* 8, 3 (1962), 226.

think of a large number of judgement-sayings couched in apocalyptic language from one end of the New Testament to the other.

About these we need, at present, do no more than observe, that, even within this category, there are different aspects to be detected. The parable of the wheat and the tares speaks, so far as its distinctive element goes, to the problem of the impurity of the Church collectively, and warns against hasty judgement before the time: it is like St Paul's μὴ πρὸ καιροῦ τι κρίνετε (I Cor. iv. 5). The twin parable of the dragnet, on the other hand, affirms nothing except that there *is* a judgement and a separation coming. The story of Dives and Lazarus underlines, for the individual, the irrecoverability of lost opportunity and the transitory character of this life's conditions.

Then, over and above the judgement sayings, the parables of growth affirm various further aspects of God's way. I do not, myself, believe that they all say only one thing, namely, that the harvest is here. Each has a different aspect to present. The Kingdom of God is secret but potent; it is alive, with a life that man cannot fabricate for himself. On the other hand, like any living, growing thing, it is, in an extraordinary way, at the mercy of man, to help or hinder. The size and quality of the crop depends in part upon the way in which the message is received and responded to: and so forth.

But, instead of dwelling longer on these sides of New Testament eschatology, perhaps it will be worth while to pause a little over certain less frequently noticed aspects of it in the light of our classification.

One is simply this (to reiterate what I have already stated): the 'realized' type of formulation tends to apply to individuals. As I have argued elsewhere,[23] the well-known difference between the Gospel and the First Epistle of St John in respect of eschatology lies precisely here. The realized eschatology of the Gospel is for the individual believer: it is by no means exclusive of futurist language for the group; and when, as in the Epistle, a group is being addressed, the futurism becomes more pronounced. Van Hartingsveld is absolutely right in reminding us that there are futurist-sayings in the Gospel, and I think his observation (already alluded to) that they occur in dialogue with antagonistic Jews is significant.[24] Conversely, it is, of course, true that, even in the Epistle, there are collectively applied 'realized' statements such as 'we have passed from death into life' (I John iii. 14). But nevertheless the two tendencies are, I think, distinguishable. Exactly so with Paul. He can

23 'The Individualism of the Fourth Gospel' in *Nov. Test.* 5, 2–3 (1962), 171 ff. [pp. 91 ff. above].    24 *Die Eschatologie*, p. 153.

speak, on a comparatively individual level, of having died with Christ and even (if we so interpret Rom. vi. 8–11 and if we accept Colossians as Pauline)[25] of having been raised with him; but if anyone says that 'the Day' is here (II Thess. ii. 2), or that the resurrection has taken place already (II Tim. ii. 18), or – which comes to the same thing – that there *is* no resurrection such as Paul would recognize, but only a private, individual, spiritual resurrection (I Cor. xv. 12), that is a dangerous deceit.[26] Similarly, speaking on the individual level, death may mean being with the Lord (Phil. i. 23); but, when the whole Church is in view, then, as I have said, the individual who dies has to be conceived of as waiting or sleeping, and the being with the Lord is something only realized at the end (I Thess. iv. 13 ff., II Thess. ii. 1).[27]

Incidentally, it is the recognition of this kind of duality of expression (as well as linguistic considerations) that disposes me to be still so old-fashioned as even to entertain the possibility that ἐντός in Lk. xvii. 21 means 'within', and that the point at issue there is simply the invisible, inward and spiritual character of the kingdom.[28] It is, after all, very much like Rom. xiv. 17, 'the Kingdom of God is righteousness, peace and joy in the Holy Spirit'. Be that as it may, it seems to be particularly noteworthy that not only St John (as just noted) but also St Paul demonstrably contains within a single writing both non-apocalyptic and apocalyptic eschatologies. I refer, of course, to the Epistle to the Romans. Whatever may be said of the provenance of Rom. xvi. 20

25 See G. R. Beasley-Murray, *Baptism in the New Testament* (London, 1962), p. 139.

26 H. Köster has recently argued ('The Purpose of the Polemic of a Pauline Fragment (Phil. iii)' in *N.T.S.* 8, 4 (July 1962), 317 ff.) that the opponents attacked in Phil. iii were Jewish–Christian missionaries who believed that they already had the eschatological promises in full, including resurrection. If so, this helps, on my showing, to explain the vigorously futurist eschatology of Phil. iii. 20.

27 This, it seems to me, is a more realistic interpretation of the facts than to attempt to attach a particular *stage* in human destiny to the being σὺν Χριστῷ (as, for example, is done by P.-H. Menoud, *Cahiers Théologiques* (Neuchâtel, 1945), p. 9). Cf. M. Bouttier, *En Christ* (Paris, 1962), pp. 38 ff., for a useful discussion.

28 See, long ago, von Dobschütz, *Eschatology*, p. 13, n. 1; and Aalen, *N.T.S.* 8, 3 (1962), 223, n. 1, has a non-committal note; and now J. A. Baird is arguing in great detail for the meaning 'within' (*The Justice of God in the Teaching of Jesus*, London, 1963, pp. 169 ff.). Dr Caird, in conversation, has pointed out to me that objections to ἐντός = 'within' still remain, in that Luke – who places his material carefully – follows the verse with *apocalyptic* material, and in that it is difficult to find a parallel for the *generalizing* use of 'you' demanded by the sense 'within'.

('the God of peace will grind Satan under your feet speedily'), at least it will scarcely be doubted that the strongly apocalyptic formulations of Rom. ii. 1 ff. and xiii. 11 ff. belong to this epistle. Yet equally integral is Rom. viii; and here a majestic eschatology is unfolded which is essentially non-apocalyptic. I know that in fact the actual words ἀποκαλυφθῆναι and ἀποκάλυψις do occur (*vv.* 18 f.); I am well aware also that a cosmic, and not only a human, perspective enters in (*vv.* 19 ff.). But the values throughout the chapter are personal values and are expressed in terms, not of myth and apocalypse, but of personal relationship - especially sonship. Only at the very end do 'supernatural' terms make their appearance (*vv.* 38 f.); and then it is only a dramatic way of emphasizing the invincibility of the love of God - the most personal of all his manifestations. It seems to me that the presence of ch. viii side by side with ch. ii and xiii makes it perfectly clear that Paul uses apocalyptic and non-apocalyptic language according to his theme, not according to the stages of his theological development.

Very striking also is the fact that, although Ephesians is so elaborate in its demonology, its eschatology is essentially that of Rom. viii: it is in terms of the growing up of the entire people of God into mature personhood. Whether this is Pauline or not, it is, in this particular respect, similar to Rom. viii. Furthermore, the gap of time between I Cor. xv and II Cor. iv-v is, on any calculation, short: yet here, again, one finds, side by side, a fully apocalyptic eschatology (I Cor. xv, directed, probably, against mystical individualism) and an eschatology of individual growth in character. I am not denying that St Paul may have undergone some decisive experience between the two. Indeed, I believe that - if one goes no further - it is at least true that, up to and including I Corinthians, he seems to count on his own survival to the *parousia*, whereas afterwards there is no evidence that he does so. But I am not sure that the change in II Corinthians is itself due to this. For II Cor. iv-v is, I believe, a profound meditation on the necessity for accepting one's creatureliness. The unspiritual man is the possessive man, who tries to win immortality by clinging to life and behaving as though he were not a mortal. The spiritual man is the one who, accepting his mortality, dares to believe that it is precisely by 'letting go', by detachment, that he will find - not 'nakedness', but a heavenly clothing.

I am well aware that this is a questionable interpretation, and that the passage has recently been put right back into the melting-pot of critical discussion.[29] It would take us too far from the main point to

29 See for example, A. Feuillet, 'La Demeure Céleste et la Destinée des

attempt a detailed justification of my exegesis now. I will only say that, as I see it, the crucial questions for exegesis are: (1) What is the reason for the 'groaning' in II Cor. v. 2, 4? (2) What is in view in the famous phrase εἴ γε καὶ ἐνδυσάμενοι οὐ γυμνοὶ εὑρεθησόμεθα (v. 3)? (3) What is meant by the clause beginning ἐφ' ᾧ οὐ . . . (v. 4)? I side with those commentators who believe that Paul is *not* dealing here with the problem of death before the *parousia*: and I believe, instead, that he is, throughout this passage, speaking of the difference between a wordly and vain attempt to *cling* to the transitory, and the Christian way, which means *using up* the transitory in the construction of what is enduring. The 'groaning', as in Rom. viii, is due to the natural hatred of parting with the transitory – we groan *because we do not like* (R.S.V. 'not that we would . . .' is wrong) the hateful process of 'taking off' comfortable old clothes in exchange for the new and the unknown: we all prefer to put on more clothes on top, like a pullover (ἐπενδύσασθαι v. 3). There are times when the terrifying thought overtakes us, '*Is* what we are offered in exchange real at all, or is it a cruel hoax, and shall we be found naked?' But no! (v. 5), God has created us for precisely this exchanging process: the transitory is *meant* to be used up and parted with in the good cause of entering upon the permanent, the home from heaven.

If this is a fair interpretation of this notoriously controverted passage, here, very near to the apocalyptic of I Cor. xv, is an eschatology of individual growth towards maturity, parallel to the non-apocalyptic corporate eschatologies of Rom. viii and Ephesians. I have no wish to deny that a crisis occurred in Paul's life between I and II Corinthians; but I do not think that this need be invoked as the explanation of this particular change. It is simply a difference of theme.

Now, the tension in which all these ideas are held, and by which they may be co-ordinated (though not logically reconciled), is that of the central affirmation of the Christian faith, the incarnation. As I said at the outset, I have no wish to deny that there was change and development in the eschatological thinking of the New Testament. What I have been questioning is the extent of its relevance to much of the formulation of such thought; and I hold that the heart of the problem is not the delay of the *parousia* but the nature of the incarnation, which,

Chrétiens, Exégèse de II Cor., v, 1-10 et contribution à l'étude des fondements de l'eschatologie paulinienne', in *Recherches de Science Religieuse*, 44 (1956), 161 ff., 360 ff.; R. F. Hettlinger, '2 Corinthians 5. 1-10' in *S.J.T.* x. 2 (June 1957), 174 ff.; E. E. Ellis, 'II Cor. v. 1-10 in Pauline Eschatology' in *N.T.S.* 6, 3 (April 1960), 211 ff. [Add pp. 200 ff. below.]

from early to late was an invariable factor. On the Christian estimate, the incarnation of the Word of God marks the opening of the new age, the inauguration of the new covenant. But it does not abolish imperfection, and St Paul is nothing if not realistic on this score. Schweitzer, through wildly false exegesis of Rom. iii. 25, gravely erred in imagining that, in the eyes of Paul, 'Christ's atoning death has reference only to sins committed in the old condition of existence, that is to say, before baptism';[30] and H. J. Schoeps has unhappily followed Schweitzer in this misconception.[31] But this seems to me to be blindness to words and tenses. St Paul himself is perfectly well aware that at present there is sin; the present age is an evil age; at present, we see in a mirror, enigmatically; so far, the Spirit's presence is only a firstfruits and a pledge. Just as Yahweh was married to Israel, but found his spouse unfaithful, so Christ, who loved the Church and made her his bride, has not yet finished freeing her from every spot and wrinkle. The Church is the temple of the Holy Spirit, but still needs cleansing; God lives and walks among his people, but the unclean is yet to be removed. The bride in her perfection, the abode of God in its absolute purity, are a vision of what is yet to be. At present Jesus is reigning as Messiah, but his enemies are not yet all reduced: only when his reign is fully implemented will it become the reign of God[32] And any exegesis which turns a blind eye to the presence of this tension is likely to be unsound. I believe Cullmann is perfectly right in his insistence[33] that the development of New Testament theology was conditioned far more by what had already happened, the incarnation, than by hopes - expectant or flagging - about the future, or by the delay of the *parousia*. The constant and really influential factor is the tension between the already and the not yet; and the long and the short of New Testament eschatology, at almost any period, is the 'Become what you are!' - 'thy kingdom come, for thine is the kingdom!', 'Christ our Passover is sacrificed for us, therefore let us keep the Feast'.

Here I gratefully quote from the closing paragraph of Dr Lowe's paper: '. . . the most satisfying reason of all for much of Paul's mutability, the real justification for his apparent inconsistencies, is the

30 *The Mysticism of Paul the Apostle* (E.T. London, 1931), p. 220.
31 *Paul* (E.T. London, 1961), pp. 196 f.
32 There is a superbly clear analysis of this in A. Robertson's 1901 Bampton Lectures, *Regnum Dei* (London, 1901), pp. 54-8 (and, for the Gospels, pp. 72-7).
33 E.g. in 'Parusieverzögerung und Urchristentum' in *T.L.Z.* 83, 1 (Jan. 1958), 1 ff., and 'Unzeitgemässe Bemerkungen zum "historischen Jesus" der Bultmannschule' (from the Evangelische Verlagsanstalt, Berlin, 1960).

inherently paradoxical character of the Gospel which he preaches. When one's religion proclaims "Become what you already are", it is impossible to avoid falling into verbal contradiction.' The two halves of that proclamation may be momentarily taken apart, so that 'what you are' may at one moment be the dominant thought, and 'become!' at another moment. But there is absolutely no reason why the one should follow the other in any logical evolution. The constant datum is the incarnation;[34] and, given this, the rest may be affirmed simultaneously or successively and in either order.

The problem - so far as the shaping of theological thought is concerned - is not primarily the delay of the *parousia*. So far as I can see, II Pet. iii is unique within the New Testament in this respect. II Pet. iii contains a considered reply to scoffers who say that things have gone on so long without any sign of the coming that there are obviously no grounds for believing in a coming at all. To this 'time-scale' type of objection it is difficult to find any satisfactory reply in kind. All that can be said, as long as one stays on the same level as the objector, is that God's time-scale is not man's time-scale: and that, alas, is the very lame argument adopted. It is a relief that the New Testament nowhere else adopts it. For elsewhere in the New Testament I can think of nothing like this. There are affirmations that the end will be within that generation (notably Mk xiii. 30),[35] or that it will be very soon (Lk. xviii. 8; Rom. xiii. 11 ff.; xvi. 20; etc.); there are affirmations that it will not be as soon as some expected (Mk xiii. 7; Lk. xix. 11; II Thess. ii; I Cor. xv. 25; etc.); and there are sighs and longings for its hastening (Lk. xviii. 7; Rev. vi. 10; etc.). But nowhere, I think, is there evidence that the Church's prolonged existence without its arrival has either altered the programme of expectation or very much changed the shape of theological thinking. There is a sustained yearning for the coming; there are few signs of a change in the expectations or in the various affirmations of basic conviction. Most of the passages that may be cited for 'anxiety over the delay' are from outside the New Testament: from non-Christian Judaism, there is Isa. xiii. 22 (LXX); Hab. ii. 3 (with 1 QpHab. vii. 7; and from Christian documents I Clem. xxiii. 3 f.; Barnabas xix. 5; Hermas, Vis. iii. 4. 3; II Clem. xi. 2 f.; Tert., *de patient.*

34 Cf. Von Dobschütz, *Eschatology*, p. 30; Robertson, *Regnum Dei*, p. 47.
35 I am weary of reading comments which stress the confession, in *v.* 32, of ignorance of the precise date, but ignore this affirmation of certainty that it will be within that generation.

2. 7.[36] P. Minear, in a recent essay,[37] seems to have made a very good case for the view that this time-scale type of calculation was utterly remote even from the mind of the author of the Apocalypse, whose viewpoint (if Minear is right) was infinitely more spiritual.

The real problem, therefore, is the far profounder problem of a perfect Head united to an imperfect body; and all the incomplete fragments of a solution are concerned with him who is Saviour as well as Judge, who is individual as well as inclusive, and who is the Omega because he is Alpha.

36 I owe these references to Dr E. Bammel, but he did not intend them as an exhaustive list. See, further, A. Strobel, *Untersuchungen zum eschatologischen Verzögerungsproblem* (Leiden, 1961).

37 'The Cosmology of the Apocalypse' in the O. Piper *Festschrift* (Klassen and Snyder, *New Testament Interpretation*), pp. 23 ff.

# 14

## St Paul and Dualism: The Pauline Conception
## of Resurrection*

Everybody knows that the relation between Paul's beliefs and expectations about life beyond death and those of his contemporaries is obscure and hotly disputed. Everybody knows, too, about the debate over the origins of gnosticism and the extent to which Paul shared its dualism; and I am not so simple as to imagine that I can provide clarity and precision where great scholars, past and present, have confessed to bewilderment. In discussing Paul's attitude to the material world, all that I shall attempt is, after defining certain areas of the problem, to defend Paul's basic consistency on certain particular issues; and, in this connexion, to suggest an interpretation of certain parts of II Cor. v which,[1] as I believe, throws light on his degree of consistency.

Before I outline my thesis about Paul's basic consistency, then, I must briefly attempt to define certain areas within dualism. W. Schmithals holds[2] that Paul inherited and accepted the sort of dualism that had

[* Among publications since this paper, note especially J.-F. Collange, *Enigmes de la deuxième épître de Paul aux Corinthiens* (Cambridge, 1972), and M. J. Harris, 'The interpretation of 2 Corinthians 5:1-10 and its place in Pauline eschatology' (unpublished dissertation, Manchester, 1969-70); *idem*, '2 Cor. 5:1-10: Watershed in Paul's Eschatology?', *Tyndale Bulletin* 22 (1971), 32 ff.; *idem*, 'Paul's View of Death in 2 Corinthians 5:1-10', in R. N. Longenecker and M. C. Tenney edd., *New Dimensions in New Testament Study* (Grand Rapids, 1974), pp. 317 ff.]

1 In discussing this famous passage, I am indebted not only to commentaries and to discussions, alluded to below, by J. N. Sevenster, M. E. Thrall, and E. E. Ellis, but also to the following, even where I reach different conclusions: A. Oepke, article γυμνός in *T.W.N.T.* i. (1933); A. Feuillet, 'La Demeure Céleste et la Destinée des Chrétiens, Exégèse de II Cor., v, 1-10 et contribution à l'étude des fondements de l'eschatologie paulinienne', *Recherches de Science Religieuse*, 44 (1956), 161 ff., 360 ff.; R. F. Hettlinger, '2 Corinthians 5. 1-10', *S.J.T.* 10, 2 (June 1957), 174 ff.

2 'Die Gnosis in Korinth', *F.R.L.A.N.T.* 48 (1956), 240 f. I had not access to the new edition when preparing this paper.

already deeply penetrated Judaism, but he adds that this was, of course, not a primal, metaphysical dualism. No Jew, he points out - not even a gnostic Jew - entertained a primal, metaphysical dualism: at the beginnings of things, God stands alone. But, he continues, even before creation, Satan fell out of the divine unity by trying to rival the Most High (cf. Isa. xiv. 14); and, as soon as a demonic rivalry of this kind is admitted, there is a virtual dualism, even if it is not strongly of the primal, metaphysical type; and a virtual dualism of this sort is common enough, both in non-Christian Jewish writings, such as Test. Asher 5. 1 (ἐν κατέναντι τοῦ ἐνός), and, equally, all over the Pauline epistles themselves, with their obvious demonology, not to mention so extraordinary and exceptional a phrase as ὁ θεὸς τοῦ αἰῶνος τούτου in II Cor. iv. 4.

Now, of course this is true; but it seems to me that this distinction between a primal, metaphysical dualism and a secondary, demonic dualism is not the most important distinction, at any rate where Pauline thought is concerned. What is even more important here is the distinction between a material dualism and a dualism of the will - a dualism of obedience and disobedience. The significant question is whether 'matter' is treated as, in itself, evil, or whether the evil is in disobedience. Does Paul set matter and spirit, 'body' and 'soul', in antithesis; or is it obedience and disobedience to the will of God that constitute his primary concern? If it is the latter, if it is essentially a moral antithesis that concerns him, then he can entertain a dualistic demonology (the disobedience of Satan set in opposition to the will of God) without having anything to do with a material dualism of matter against spirit. Provided there is no demiurge, to create an evil world, a demonology is no hindrance to a dualism essentially of the will.

Now, against this background, my concern is with Paul's treatment of matter; and my thesis is, first - and this is no new point, but an already familiar one - that Paul steered a remarkably consistent course between, on the one hand, a materialistic doctrine of physical resurrection and, on the other hand, a dualistic doctrine of the escape of the soul from the body; and that the secret of his consistency here is his tenacious grasp of the central theme: Jesus, Son of God. What controls his system of thought is not the antithesis between matter and spirit but that between disobedience and filial obedience. That relationship of son to father which is, for 'Adam', made possible only through 'the final Adam', Jesus Christ, is the key to eternal life. But, in holding to this, Paul did not hereby evade the problem of materiality and mortality. On the contrary, he formulates a view which was perhaps wholly novel and derived directly from his experience of Christ - namely, that

201

matter is to be used but transformed in the process of obedient surrender to the will of God. Matter (I am suggesting that Paul is saying) is not illusory, not unimportant, not even to be shunned and escaped from, nor yet exactly destined to be annihilated. All such views of matter belong to what I have called material dualisms. Paul's view is none of these. Yet neither does he believe that matter is to be preserved just as it is, as was, apparently, taught by a literalistic type of Pharisaism. Rather, matter is to be transformed into that which transcends it. But a final point in what I have to say - and this, perhaps, is less trite and more debatable - is that there is one important change of mind in Paul's presentation of his beliefs about matter. At an earlier stage - that reflected in I Cor. xv - he believed that matter would be included in, or enclosed and swallowed up by, a superimposed immortality. Latterly, however - as is reflected in II Cor. iv and v - he accepted, instead, a more drastic and more demanding expectation, namely, that matter must be consciously surrendered and released, in exchange for that which transcends it. The change in Paul's views is, on this showing, a change from the hope of addition to the acceptance of exchange.

I am well aware that, in attempting to formulate this thesis, I have, for convenience, been using modern terms - in part, the terms of physics - and that it is all too easy to fall into the mistake of modernizing Paul. For that matter, Paul does not so much as once use even the ancient term ὕλη in his extant writings. But the test of the validity of the thesis will be whether it emerges in the same essential form from investigation in its own terms and in its own historical setting.

Let me begin, then, by a brief statement, largely in Paul's own words, of his salient views, before I take up each of them in turn and try to elucidate them in relation to the views of his contemporaries or near contemporaries.

(1) Paul believed in the possibility of an ultimate transformation of the σῶμα. Our σῶμα, as it is at present (or, if that is too temporal a phrase, let us say our σῶμα in some respects or if left to itself - more will be said later about the time-factor) is a 'death-laden' body (τὸ σῶμα τοῦ θανάτου τούτου, Rom. vii. 24); it is mortal (νεκρόν, θνητόν, Rom. viii. 10 f.), perishable (τὸ φθαρτὸν τοῦτο, I Cor. xv. 53 f.; ἐν φθορᾷ, I Cor. xv. 42; ἡ φθορά, I Cor. xv. 50), merely 'animal' (σῶμα ψυχικόν, I Cor. xv. 44, 46); it is a humiliating and humiliated body (τὸ σῶμα τῆς ταπεινώσεως ἡμῶν, Phil. iii. 21): it constitutes a condition in which we groan (ἐν τούτῳ στενάζομεν, II Cor. v. 2, 4). But it is capable of being transformed into an imperishable, a spiritual and glorious body (ἐν ἀφθαρσίᾳ, ἐν δόξῃ, ἐν δυνάμει, σῶμα πνευματικόν, I Cor. xv. 42-4; ἀλλαγησόμεθα, I Cor. xv. 51 f.).

(2) If one asks, How is it to be thus transformed? Paul's answer is a wholly Christ-centred and a wholly moral one. If transformation is to take place at all, it is because God, by his glorious power, raised up Christ from among the dead, and, therefore, is able to raise up our mortal bodies also (Rom. viii. 10 f.; I Cor. xv. 22; Phil. iii. 21; Col. iii. 1–4); it is because Christ, thus raised, is able to transfigure our humiliating and humiliated bodies into bodies like his own glorious body; it is part of God's triumphant act of conquest in Jesus Christ (Rom. vi. 4: I Cor. xv. 26 f.). If one presses the question further, it is clear that Christ was raised because, as Son of God, he perfectly performed his Father's will (Phil. ii. 8 f. . . . γενόμενος ὑπήκοος . . . διὸ καὶ . . .); and the work of God in us which leads to our transfiguration is evidently viewed by Paul wholly in terms of conformity to God's will: it is a moral, not a physical or quasi-physical concern. The Spirit, for Paul, is the Spirit of God's Son; the Spirit's voice in us is the voice of filial obedience (Rom. viii. 15; Gal. iv. 6); and 'spiritual' (πνευματικός) is a word denoting a quality not of substance but of relationship (cf. Rom. xii. 2; II Cor. iii. 18). The process of transformation is variously described, and the metaphor of clothing is one which must engage our attention later, when we take up the points in more detail.

(3) If one asks, When is this transformation to happen? Paul's answers vary according to the different aspects of the question which are under consideration, and according to the degree of completeness contemplated; for it is at least capable of being regarded as a process already begun rather than an instantaneous event of the future. The completion of the process, admittedly, is not until the parousia (Rom. viii. 24; I Cor. xv. 23; Phil. iii. 20 f.; Col. iii. 4; I Thess. iv. 15 f.). And to say that it will be at the parousia is to say that it will not be until the general resurrection - of God's people, at least, if not of all mankind, both good and bad (? II Cor. v. 10). But meanwhile, the change is already anticipated, in so far as individual Christians begin to 'become' what they already 'are' in Christ (for Christ the change is already complete); and Paul seems to contemplate a whole range of stages and a progressive and gradual metamorphosis within this condition - a gradual 'becoming' what we already 'are' in Christ (see Rom. xii. 2; II Cor. iii. 18, already quoted).

(4) But, if there is a gradual process between the moment when a man comes to be in Christ and the moment of the parousia, it has to be admitted that, within this range, the moment of death (when he contemplates death at all as a possibility before the parousia) is, for Paul, a specially marked and critical one. It marks (apparently) the difference

between walking by faith and walking by sight (II Cor. v. 7); between being absent from the Lord (does Paul really mean *distant* rather than *absent*, or absent only *by comparison* with greater closeness?) and being present with him (II Cor. v. 6, 8; Phil. i. 23; I Thess. iv. 17; v. 10); between being ἐν σαρκί (Gal. ii. 20; Phil. i. 22), being flesh and blood (i.e. being nothing but a feeble mortal, I Cor. xv. 50), and being in some different state. Of this, more must be said later.

We return, now, to take up and elaborate these statements; and the first two concern the possibility and manner of an ultimate transformation of σῶμα. How far, if at all, may this conviction of Paul's be given precision by comparison with the beliefs of his contemporaries? He was a Pharisee, and there is no reason why the words given him in Acts xxiii. 6 should not be accepted as at least in character, if not *ipsissima verba Pauli*: 'I am a Pharisee . . . and the true issue of this trial is our hope of the resurrection of the dead.' But precisely what forms would this common hope of Pharisaism have taken at the time of Paul, and how did his own form of it compare with them?

There are fairly clear indications that contemporary Pharisaic beliefs varied, from the crassest materialism and literalism to an almost gnostic spiritualization. At the literalistic end of the spectrum, there is the familiar notion that God would ultimately reconstitute each dead body from the one indestructible bone, the *os sacrum*.[3] Or, again – even if the passages quoted for this are too late for our purposes – there are the literalistic sayings in II Maccabees, whose date is, probably, at any rate earlier than A.D. 100. In II Macc. vii. 11, the third of the seven martyr brothers bravely extends his tongue and hands for the torturers to cut off, saying defiantly: ἐξ οὐρανοῦ ταῦτα κέκτημαι καὶ διὰ τοὺς αὐτοῦ νόμους ὑπερορῶ ταῦτα καὶ παρ' αὐτοῦ ταῦτα πάλιν ἐλπίζω κομίσασθαι. In II Macc. xiv. 46, the patriot Razis with his dying breath calls upon the Lord of Life to give back to him again the internal organs exposed by his own suicidal sword-thrust (ταῦτα αὐτῷ πάλιν ἀποδοῦναι). So, too, the Dura-Europos paintings are cited, to confirm that the allegory of Ezekiel xxxvii was applied to the restoration of individual corpses.[4]

---

3 Lev. r. 18. 1 (in H. Freedman and M. Simon, *Midrash Rabbah translated into English*, London, 1939): '*And the almond tree shall blossom* [= Eccles. xii. 5] refers to the *luz* (nut) of the spinal column'; and then follows the story (which occurs also in Gen. R. 28. 3) of R. Joshua b. Hanania demonstrating to Hadrian the indestructibility of this bone.

4 K. Prümm, *Diakonie Pneumatos* (1960), II, 1, 171, n. 1 cites Comte du Mesnil du Buisson, *Les peintures de Doura Europos* (Rome, 1939), p. 99; and refers also to G. Delling, '*Speranda futura*. Jüdische Grabinschriften Italiens

In view of such evidence, G. F. Moore was probably justified in speaking of a 'mundane' restoration as representing the popular notion of the future life.[5] On the other hand, a significant compromise is represented by the much-quoted *Ap. Bar.* 1. 1-li. 10. Here, bodies are restored indeed, but only in order to enable their owners to be judged; after which, the evil deteriorate in appearance, whereas those who pass the judgement successfully are given a new, glorious appearance and new powers and are like the angels and the stars.[6] I know no reason for thinking that such a notion cannot have existed before the date of this writing (? about A.D. 132-5 - Eissfeldt, *Einleitung* (1934 ed.), p. 686); and W. D. Davies[7] is able, while endorsing Moore's view of the popular notion, to adduce, nevertheless, parallels from rabbinic sources to three important factors in Paul's hope; the analogy of the grain of wheat, the distinction between different kinds of flesh, and the reference to varying degrees of 'glory'. And he can go on to cite decidedly spiritual interpretations of the body of the future, leading to the conclusion (in H. St J. Thackeray's words) that: 'The more spiritually-minded of Jewish thinkers in the time of St Paul were familiar with the conception of a transfigured resurrection body.'

According to Matt. xxii. 30; Lk. xx. 35 f., Jesus himself declared that at the resurrection (Matthew), or among those who are deemed worthy of that age (Luke), there is neither marrying nor giving in marriage: they are like angels (Matthew, ὡς ἄγγελοι; Luke, ἰσάγγελοι). Billerbeck (S.-B. 1, 889 (*fin.*), 888 f.) maintains that this would have been alien to the Pharisees among Jesus' hearers, who associated this sexless state only with the interval between death and resurrection – that is, only with the world of souls. But I Enoch 51. 4 speaks of the risen righteous as becoming angels in heaven; and again, although the *status* of the departed may here not be the main point, there is a very close verbal parallel, as Dr Black points out to me, in the Qumran *Benedictions*, where (1Q Sb iv. 24, 25) it is said of the priest: 'May you be as an Angel of the Presence in the Abode of Holiness' (Vermés' translation). One cannot help suspecting that the more spiritualized and less

über das Geschick nach dem Tode', *T.L.Z.* 76 (1951), 521 ff. Delling concludes that the emphatic *Leiblichkeit* of the resurrection marks a deep gulf between New Testament thought and Hellenistic expectations (not to mention other contrasts – between being bound to history and sitting loose to it, between social thinking and individualism); and the Jewish hope, as evidenced by these inscriptions, in the same sort of way, stands over against the mystery religions.

5 *Judaism*, ii (²1950), 313.                     6 See S.-B. iii, 474.

7 *Paul and Rabbinic Judaism* (London, 1948), pp. 305 ff.

material notions were entertained by at least some Pharisees at the time. It would be interesting, incidentally, to know how Pharisees at the time of Christ were replying to the Sadducees' taunts.

It may be said in parenthesis that what matters most, as far as morals are concerned, and what the Pharisaic beliefs, both the more crude and the more refined, were evidently intended chiefly to safeguard, is continuity – the maintenance of identity between the life in this age and the life which was ultimately to be judged at God's tribunal. The connexion between resurrection and judgement comes out in II Clem. ix (which contains a kind of Christianized Pharisaism). In that passage it is the judgement that is the concern behind the terribly materialistic doctrine of fleshly resurrection, and it is the incarnation itself which is appealed to as authority for this fleshly life being the necessary sphere both of salvation and of judgement:

(1) καὶ μὴ λεγέτω τις ὑμῶν, ὅτι αὕτη ἡ σὰρξ οὐ κρίνεται οὐδὲ ἀνίσταται ... (5) εἰ χριστὸς ὁ κύριος, ὁ σώσας ἡμᾶς, ὢν μὲν τὸ πρῶτον πνεῦμα, ἐγένετο σάρξ καὶ οὕτως ἡμᾶς ἐκάλεσεν, οὕτως καὶ ἡμεῖς ἐν ταύτῃ τῇ σαρκὶ ἀποληψόμεθα τὸν μισθόν.

In this respect, it may be that the Pauline conception of metamorphosis (or transfiguration) was not necessarily alien to the underlying convictions of contemporary Pharisaism, whether in its more materialistic or its more refined form. For what Paul is stressing is the maintenance of personal identity ('somatic identity' as M. E. Dahl calls it),[8] and the importance of the present life as the scene in which we are assessed. We are to be judged by τὰ διὰ τοῦ σώματος (II Cor. v. 10), just as in Matt. xxv the nations are judged by what they did or failed to do for the needy in this life. That the mode of existence after judgement is conceived in spiritualized, angelic terms, is, for purposes of morals, of secondary importance. However, that was a parenthesis. What I am mainly concerned to point out now is that non-Christian Pharisaism did find room for a more spiritualized conception of resurrection.

But if both Paul and a section of non-Christian Pharisaism were ready to repudiate a fleshly materialism, how, we must now ask, was their end of the spectrum distinguished from gnosticism? Is a transformed, unfleshly body very different, after all, from a disembodied soul? Here we are fortunate to have, for comparison, the peculiarly interesting letter to Rheginus *de resurrectione* from Nag Hammadi, to add substance to our picture of the kind of speculation that may have obtained even in Paul's day.

8 *The Resurrection of the Body* (London, 1962), p. 94.

St Paul and 'dualism': the Pauline conception of resurrection

The most significant passage for the moment is the following (45. 14-46. 2), in the translation of R. McL. Wilson and J. Zandel:[9]

The Saviour swallowed up I death. You are not to be ignorant. I For he laid aside the I world (κόσμος) which perisheth. He changed I himself into an incorruptible aeon I and raised himself up, after he had I swallowed up the visible I by the invisible, I and he gave us I the way of our immortality. I But then as the Apostle I said, we suffered I with him, and we arose I with him, and we went to heaven Iwith him. But if we I are made manifest in I this world wearing (φορεῖν) I him, we are his beams (ἀκτίς) I and we are I encompassed by him I until our setting, which is I our death in this life (βίος). I We are drawn upward I by him like the beams I by the sun, without being held back I by anything. This is I the spiritual (πνευματική) I which swallows up the psychic (ψυχική) I alike with the fleshly (σαρκική). I

We are again faced with the problem of dating; and it is, admittedly, only speculation that precisely this view (if, indeed, precision appropriately describes it!) was current in Paul's day. But there is one aspect of it, at any rate, to which we do know his attitude, and it is immediately revealing as to the difference of the Pauline position. The *de resurrectione*, despite future tenses such as (46. 7 f.) 'He who is dead shall arise' (cf. 46. 10), really treates the resurrection of believers as a *fait accompli*. Besides the passage just quoted, there is also 49. 22 f., 'why dost thou not consider thyself I as risen (already) . . . ?' (cf. 48. 4 ff.).[10] This is just like the view attacked in II Tim. ii. 18 (ἀνάστασιν ἤδη γεγονέναι), which is, on any showing, probably nearer to Paul's own date; and, whether or not Paul consciously has similar views in mind in I Cor. xv, at least we can say with confidence that he would have maintained, against any such views, that the time-factor was of vital importance.[11] If Paul's conviction was that in Christ there was already a new creation, yet equally he believed that those who were in Christ had yet to become what they were; and that this would not take place in the present evil age, but only at the End, when everything had

---

9 *De Resurrectione (Epistula ad Rheginum)*, Codex Jung fo. xxii[r] to fo. xxii[v] (pp. 43–50), edd. M. Malinine, H.-C. Puech, G. Quispel, W. Till (Zürich and Stuttgart, 1963). The text it is here stated, is in subakhmimic, but is evidently a translation from Greek.

10 Cf. *The Gospel of Philip*, 21. 15 ff., 90. 1 ff., with comments in the edition by R. McL. Wilson (London, 1962).

11 Cf. W. Schmithals, *Die Gnosis in Korinth* (Göttingen, 1956), p. 137.

been ultimately subjected to Christ (or, at the very soonest, and then only on a private and individual level, at the individual's death). The *de resurrectione*, for all its talk about flesh and body, seems only to be saying that Christ *revealed* that the world is illusion[12] and that resurrection is real. And here I am anticipating other points of contrast; but, for the moment, it may be said that even the most spiritualized Pauline Pharisaism parts company with the type of gnosticism illustrated by the letter to Rheginus and indicated also by II Tim. ii. 18 and perhaps elsewhere in the New Testament, at the point where this latter ignores time, whereas Paul takes time very seriously.

But another distinctive factor – one which is even more vital – is Paul's consistently moral interpretation of the transformation of σῶμα, and, with it, the absence, from Pauline thought, of any estimate of matter as, in itself, evil. The fact that Paul's vocabulary does not even contain the word ὕλη at all need mean no more than that he was at no time concerned with the philosophical distinctions. but it is significant that even σάρξ is not treated by him as essentially evil. For Paul, evil is consistently identified as sin, or disobedience to God's will. Its antithesis is filial obedience. Indeed, in nothing, I suspect, is Paul more consistent than in his amazingly firm grasp of the personal and essentially relational character of what he calls 'glory'. 'Glory' is, of course, a physical metaphor, and one may safely assume that Paul had a more than metaphorical, an actually visual experience, of an intensely painful character, on the Damascus road, just as the Gospel tradition of the transfiguration of Jesus (alluded to, incidentally, in *de resurrectione* 48. 6 ff.) is in visual terms. But for Paul the visual is at most a sacrament and at least a metaphor denoting something not material or quasi-material but personal and moral. The glory of which all men are continually falling short is that perfect relation of sonship to God for which Adam was created. The fleshly outlook is the antithesis of this – it is self-centredness, it is Adam's refusal to accept his status as a creature: one might even say, paradoxically, that the φρόνημα τῆς σαρκός is the outlook that refuses to accept one's own σάρξ καὶ αἷμα, refuses to recognize one's mortal weakness and dependence on God and responsibility towards the creation of which one is part. Transfiguration from one stage of glory to a still higher stage of glory is by means of reflecting the glory of Christ, and his glory is the glory of obedient Sonship, the glory of the Son of God (here Paul could easily have

12 So, explicitly, 48. 15, 'the world (κόσμος) is an illusion (φαντασία)'; so, again, 48. 27 f.

accepted the Johannine phrase). For Christians to appear with Christ in Glory is the same thing as the manifestation of the sons of God. At every point, the process is in terms of filial obedience, not of an amoral, unethical, quasi-physical transformation. Man's predicament is not that he is ἐν σαρκί but that, *via* his σάρξ, sin has got hold of him.

That it is through the 'flesh' that sin most clearly gains access to a man explains why Paul sometimes speaks of flesh as a realm opposed to Spirit, and associates it closely with sin.[13] But his firm grasp on the reality of the incarnation would itself forbid us to imagine that he actually identified flesh with evil. The letter to Rheginus does not compare with Paul in this respect, in spite of its use of the word 'resurrection' and its references to Christ's flesh (44. 13 ff.). It is interesting to compare the outlook of the Qumran Sect also. For example:[14]

1QH iv. 29: '... what is flesh (to be worthy of this)? What is a creature of clay for such great marvels to be done, whereas he is in iniquity from the womb and in guilty unfaithfulness to his old age?'

1QS xi. 9: 'As for me, I belong to wicked mankind, to the company of ungodly flesh' (cf. IQM iv. 3).

1QS xi. 20-2: 'What shall one born of woman be accounted before thee? Kneaded from the dust, his abode is the nourishment of worms. He is but a shape, but moulded clay, and inclines towards dust.'

1QH i. 21 f. '... And yet I, a shape of clay kneaded in water, a ground of shame and a source of pollution, a melting-pot of wickedness and an edifice of sin...' (cf. 1QH iii. 23 f., x. 3 ff.).

Here, although *basar* is not invariably used (and, where it is used, it sometimes merely means mankind collectively), the pessimism of the estimate of man, as both frail and liable to sin, is more emphatic than Paul's.[15] On the other hand, admittedly, the ethical dualism of the Sect is expressed not in the antithesis between flesh and spirit but between the two spirits in man.

13 And σάρξ, of course, means, for Paul, more than we mean by the merely physical side of things. See E. Schweizer, article σάρξ, *T.W.N.T.* vii (1960), 98 ff.

14 For convenience, I use the translation by G. Vermés, *The Dead Sea Scrolls in English* (Harmondsworth, 1962), not, however, retaining his line-divisons, which do not correspond to the original, nor his capitals.

15 Cf. Marcion's derogatory descriptions of the body in Tert. *adv. M.* i. 29; iii. 10; iv. 21.

In both respects, Paul's outlook is different. First, as a matter of fact (as W. D. Davies observes),[16] he does not very often use σάρξ in a sense other than the physical; and, where he does, it is because of its association with sin rather than because of any evil actually inhering in σάρξ itself. And yet secondly, he never uses the Qumran terminology of the two opposed spirits, but speaks rather of σάρξ and πνεῦμα.[17]

While we are talking of Qumran, it is a remarkable fact that so far, to the best of my knowledge, no conclusive information has come to light about the Sect's ideas of life beyond death. Several passages are claimed, by some scholars, to point to ideas of survival, but few, if any, are necessarily more than an expression of hopes of victory and success in this life. None of them, as far as I can see, necessarily relates to a transcendental existence.[18] The nearest approach to this, as far as I know, is in the so-called Angelic Liturgy[19] This contains a series of magnificent blessings, among which occurs (again I quote from Vermés' translation, ignoring his line-division and capitals):[20] 'In the name [of the might of the God] of gods, the sixth sovereign Prince shall bless with seven words of his marvellous mighty deeds all who are mighty in wisdom. He shall bless all the perfect of way with seven marvellous words that they may stand with them that live for ever.' After the blessings, there follows a wonderful elaboration of the Ezekiel throne-

16 'Paul and the Dead Sea Scrolls: Flesh and Spirit', in *The Scrolls and the New Testament*, ed. K. Stendahl (1st British ed., London, 1958), pp. 157 ff. See p. 163. Cf. K. G. Kuhn, 'Fleisch der Schwachheit, Bösheit, Sünde', *Z.T.K.* 49 (1952), 200 ff. Kuhn makes the point that, whereas in rabbinic Judaism בשר ודם is the standing phrase for man (in his creatureliness and limitations), in the Qumran literature the single term בשר occurs, and can stand for evil, over against the good God.

17 Kuhn, *Z.T.K.* 496 (1952) rightly draws a parallel between the two-powers concept of Qumran, and the N.T. idea that temptation comes from the Devil and is a temptation to be disloyal to God. But the difference I have indicated still remains. Both alike are a moral dualism. but their conception is different.

18 The Reverend [now Dr] J. Pryke, in conversation, mentioned the following: CD iii. 20; 1QS iv. 7, 8; 1QS iii. 20 ff., vi. 29 ff.: 1QM i. But I do not feel fully convinced that phrases such as חיי נצח (CD iii. 20, 1QS iv. 7), באור עולמים (1QS iv. 8), מעפר לסוד עולם (1QH iii. 21) necessarily signify what we are looking for. See, however, M. Black's very important views to the contrary in *The Scrolls and Christian Origins* (London, 1961), esp. pp. 135 ff.

19 J. Strugnell, 'The Angelic Liturgy at Qumran', Congress volume, Oxford, 1959, *Supp. Vetus Test.* 7 (1960), 318 ff.

20 *Dead Sea Scrolls*, pp. 211 f.

chariot, which might not unjustly be called a description of Heaven: it is comparable, indeed, to Rev. iv.

In this fragment we do seem to have a description of Heaven combined with a reference – albeit an extremely fleeting and slightly defective one – to 'those who live for ever'. But the lack of any such theme in clearly transcendental terms elsewhere in this literature is striking, and the more so when Josephus' account of the Essenes is quite explicit about their belief in an after-life. This he presents in a thoroughly dualistic form, in terms of the release of immortal souls (ψυχαὶ ἀθάνατοι) from the prison-house and spell of the body (ὥσπερ εἰρκταῖς τοῖς σώμασιν ἴυγγι τινι φυσικῇ κατασπώμενοι (*Bell.* ii.154)); and although he also (ii. 153) says that, in bravely enduring tortures, they cheerfully resigned their souls (or lives?), confident that they would receive them back again (εὔθυμοι τὰς ψυχὰς ἠφίεσαν ὡς πάλιν κομιούμενοι), I suppose that this, in the context, must be interpreted in a dualistic way and not with the literalism attaching to the comparable sayings in II Maccabees.[21]

Even if Josephus on the Essenes could be accepted as filling a lacuna in the Qumran literature, we would still not have anything comparable to Paul's teaching, but only one more instance of the sort of dualism which he avoided. The *Wisdom of Solomon*, whatever its date, would come in the same category, except in so far as it may have been edited in a more orthodox direction in chapters i, ii, and xiii.[22]

All in all, Paul comes out of such comparisons with non-Christian literature as we can scrape together as free from a crass materialism, and yet outstandingly consistent in his seriousness about time, and in his adherence to a moral contrast between obedience and disobedience rather than a metaphysical or quasi-physical one between matter and spirit or even a demonic one between two spirits. Where demonology is concerned, the issue for Paul is still not between two spirits within man, but between all the disobedient spirits, on the one hand, and God on the other. And man's destiny is viewed in terms of a transformation of σῶμα by the Spirit of God, who produces, in man, the deeds and words of filial obedience.

We move on, then, to a further section in the elaboration of points

---

21 Cf. Eleazar's dualism in *Bell.* vii. 344 ff. (suicide as the release of the soul). D. Georgi, *Die Gegner des Paulus im 2. Korintherbrief: Studien zur religiösen Propaganda in der Spätantike (W.M.A.N.T.* 11, 1964), p. 144 n. 1, thinks that Josephus has deliberately put this heterodox speech in Eleazar's mouth to denigrate the *sicarii*; he contrasts Josephus' own monism in *Bell.* iii. 361 ff.  22 Georgi, *Die Gegner*, 144, n. 1.

3 and 4, namely, questions concerning the time-factor, the 'When?' of the transformation. Here, while reiterating the point about Paul's seriousness regarding the historical incarnation and about the End-time, I suggest that, between these two temporal points, Paul scarcely concerns himself with the 'When?' at all. I agree, on the one hand, with those who find a change in Paul's outlook between I Corinthians and II Corinthians.[23] On the other hand, I would look for this change in a rather different direction from what is usually suggested. I do not think that it is primarily a change in Paul's idea of *when* the ultimate transformation of σῶμα would take place. My suggestion, rather, is that the change is in Paul's ideas about the relation between the two phases of σῶμα – between σῶμα ψυχικόν and σῶμα πνευματικόν, between the body of humiliation and the body of glory, between 'the outward' and 'the inward man'.

Throughout his extant writings, Paul is consistent, I think, in holding that the individual's identity will be maintained. It is not that a soul escapes from the body's prison (still less that, by initiation, the transformation is already complete), but that an entire person, a σῶμα,[24] dies, and the same person is raised to life. It is not the same form: there is a radical transformation. He dies mortal and corruptible and is raised a glorious body; he dies animal and is raised spiritual. But always it is the same individual, just as the seed that is surrendered to the earth grows into a plant which is dramatically different, and yet continuous with the seed.[25]

But within this steady conviction of identity of person maintained

23 *Contra* R. Berry, 'Death and Life in Christ: the meaning of 2 Corinthians 5. 1–10', *S.J.T.* 14 (1961), 60 ff. Instead of a *change of mind* in II Corinthians, Berry finds merely that in II Corinthians Paul is in *two minds* about death – welcoming one aspect of it (nearness to Christ), dreading the other ('nakedness').

24 It is noteworthy that even in I Cor. v. 3 f., where Paul distinguishes his σῶμα (in which he will be absent from the Corinthian meeting) from his πνεῦμα (in which he will be present), he scrupulously reverts to the use of σάρξ in v. 5, when he says (with reference to the excommunicated man) '. . . for the destruction of the *flesh*, in order that the spirit may be saved on the day of the Lord'.

25 In urging this, I am not denying a point which is extremely well made by S. Laeuchli, 'Monism and Dualism in Pauline Anthropology', *Biblical Research* (Papers of the Chicago Society of Biblical Research), 3 (1958), 15 ff. This is a well-justified protest against any too rigidly monistic and Hebraistic interpretation of Paul's doctrine of man. Laeuchli rightly recognizes a degree of pluralism in Paul's descriptions of human personality, as against those who would tie him down to a completely consistent refusal to 'subdivide' personality into departments.

through change of form, there is room for a variety of ideas as to how this change takes place; and my suggestion is that the difference between I Cor. xv and II Cor. v concerns the manner, rather than the moment, of the change.[26] Whereas I Cor. xv implies that the new is *added to* the old and *superimposed upon* it, II Cor. iv, v implies that the new is received only *in exchange for the old.*

An important factor when one studies the evidence for this is the metaphor of clothing, of which Paul makes considerable use. It is, of course, a not infrequent metaphor in the Old Testament, from the dramatic use of לבש in, e.g. Judg. vi. 34 (the Spirit of Y" clothed itself with Gideon), to such contexts as those in which qualities or circumstances are described as garments. For example, in Ps. cix. 18 f. the psalmist says 'He clothed himself with cursing as his coat. . . . May it be like a garment which he wraps round him . . .!'; and, again, in *v.* 29, 'May my accusers be clothed with dishonour; may they be wrapped in their own shame as in a mantle!' And in Ps. cxxxii. 9 there is the prayer: 'Let thy priests be clothed with righteousness. . . .' I think that it is possible, incidentally, that Paul may have had one particular Old Testament passage in mind when, in I Cor. xv. 53, he wrote 'this corruptible must clothe itself with incorruption, and this mortal with immortality'. In Isa. lxi. 2 the Prophet uses a clothing-metaphor and applies it with a visual pun. He is describing the dramatic reversal of Zion's fortunes, and he says that God will give her פְּאֵר תַּחַת אֵפֶר - a glorious headband or scarf (*Kopfbinde*) in place of ashes. Paul does not indulge in so ingenious a pun, but he uses the forceful assonances – φθαρτόν Ι ἀφθαρ-σία, θνητόν Ι ἀθανασία.[27]

However that may be, outside the Old Testament, in the gnostic and other esoteric literatures, the metaphor is applied, conveniently, to a dualistic doctrine of the soul. For instance, in the *Gospel of Truth*, xx. 29 ff., occurs the following: 'O how great a Teacher, that he should lower himself even to death, although he was clothed with eternal life! After he had divested himself of the torn shreds, he put on eternity, of which there is none who can deprive him'.[28] There are examples, again, in the *Gospel of Philip*, such as (63. 16-21): '. . . While we are in this

26 I have no wish to ignore a further fact – that I Cor. xv and II Cor. v are distinguished also by the former being concerned with 'collective' eschatology, the latter with individual eschatology.

27 It is noteworthy, incidentally, that Paul did *not,* in Phil. ii. 7, make use of the ἐκδύεσθαι which he might have got out of the הֶעֱרָה of Isa. liii. 2, had he used Isa. liii more than he did, and used the M.T. of it.

28 My translation from the German of W. Till in *Z.N.T.W.* 50 (1959), 171.

world | it is fitting for us to acquire for ourselves the resurrection, | in order that when we strip off the flesh | we may be found in Rest and not | walk in the Midst. For many go | astray on the way.'[29] Thus, a metaphor which, before Paul, had been applied to reversals of fortune and to qualities of character and circumstance, appears again, subsequently, in connexion with dualistic ideas of a soul temporarily 'wearing' a body. What use does Paul himself make of it? He uses a considerable range of such words. In I Cor. xv. 49 he applies φορεῖν, 'to wear', with τὴν εἰκόνα τοῦ χοϊκοῦ and τὴν εἰκόνα τοῦ ἐπουρανίου as successive objects. In II Cor. iv. 10 he uses περιφέρειν in what, I suspect, is a similar sense: we go about 'wearing' the νέκρωσις of Jesus. Then, there is the extensive use of ἐνδύεσθαι both in the contexts which are our particular concern now, and also in the descriptions of the baptismal divestiture of the old life and investiture with the new, and in other metaphorical ways. The object of ἐνδύεσθαι as used by Paul is (in addition to the uses in I Cor. xv. 53 f., II Cor. v. 3 ff. (to which must be added also the double compound ἐπενδύεσθαι, II Cor. v. 2, 4)), sometimes the Christian's armour (Rom. xiii. 12; Eph. vi. 11, 14; I Thess. v. 8); once, qualities of character - σπλάγχνα οἰκτιρμοῦ, etc. (Col. iii. 12); and several times Christ, or the new man (Rom. xiii. 14; Gal. iii. 27; Eph. iv. 24; Col. iii. 10). Ἐκδύεσθαι is used by Paul only in II Cor. v. 4, though ἀποτίθεσθαι serves a similar purpose in Rom. xiii. 12; Eph. iv. 22; Col. iii. 8.

Now, it is Paul's conception of the process of transformation that we are investigating. And it is precisely in his application of the clothing-metaphor to this that I believe a change of view can be traced as between I Corinthians and II Corinthians. The clue, I believe - going to the far end of the process first, in II Corinthians - is in the use of that double compound, ἐπενδύεσθαι in II Cor. v. 2, 4. An ἐπενδύτης (Jo. xxi. 7) was an outer coat - an overcoat or top-coat, as we might say; ἐπενδύεσθαι means to put on additional clothing - a pullover, for instance, to use a modern analogy; and in II Cor. v. 2, 4 Paul says that we would *like* to put on the permanent clothing of eternal life like that - as an *additional* garment - without first divesting ourselves of anything. But, he says, we cannot. That is not God's plan for us. We should *like*,

29 From the translation by R. McL. Wilson (1962). Cf. C. J. de Cantanzaro in *J.T.S.* n.s. 13 (1962), 35 ff. See also *Asc. Isa.* ix. 9, and *Odes of Sol.* xv. 8 'I have put on incorruption through his name: and have put off corruption by His grace' (translation by J. H. Bernard, *Texts and Studies*, Cambridge, (1912)). We have already met the metaphor also in the Letter to Rheginus, 45. 30.

indeed, to add without subtracting; we groan at the painful, disagreeable process of divesting; we *want* to receive without first surrendering - *Anglice*, 'to have our cake and eat it'; we even have our agonizing moments of doubt when we wonder whether the very promise of new clothing is not itself a cruel hoax, and whether, having stripped, we shall not be left stark naked. But that, namely, the addition of clothing rather than exchange,[30] is not what God has made us for. God has designed[31] us for the process of exchange, not of addition; but, in requiring us to part with our present clothes, he has, nevertheless, given us a guarantee of something better to reassure us - the presence of the Holy Spirit.

This is the hard lesson which is reflected throughout the latter part of II Cor. iv and the first part of II Cor. v - the discovery that the Christian, and especially the apostle, has to accept 'wear and tear'. He has to accept ageing, bruising, weakness, decay, as part of the painful process of exchange, buoyed up, the while, by the conviction that this affliction is light in comparison with the eternal gain, and by the presence of the Holy Spirit as a reassuring pledge of God's good faith.

Indeed, where the dualistic philosopher complained of the soul's having to wear mortality like a cumbersome garment (νεκροφοροῦσα, ὁ περιφόρητος τάφος),[32] the Christian apostle is able to come to terms

30 It is on the understanding of ὁ δε κατεργασάμενος ἡμᾶς εἰς αὐτὸ τοῦτο θεός... (*v.* 5) that my interpretation largely turns. If *v.* 4 means 'we groan because we do not want to strip off but rather to add clothing', then *v.* 5 must mean, either (i) *'and* it is God who has made (?, see next note) us for this very thing, viz. to add clothing', or (ii) *'but* it is God who has made (?) us for this very thing, viz. to strip off clothing (and receive new clothing in exchange)'. Interpretation (i) seems to make nonsense of the groaning (if one gives ἐφ' ᾦ οὐ its proper meaning of 'because not' rather than 'not because'); therefore (ii) seems preferable.

31 The weakest part of this interpretation, linguistically, is the necessity of taking κατεργασάμενος to mean 'designed', 'created' - though, ironically enough, commentators who interpret the whole passage quite differently from me are ready to give it this sense. Héring *in loc.* renders: 'celui qui nous a formés pour cette destinée'; Lietzmann-Kümmel, 'dafür zubereitet hat'; New English Bible, 'shaped us for this very end'. But Bauer, *s.v. 3 jmdn. zu etw. instand setzen*, can quote no parallels except Hdt. vii. 6, 1, χρόνῳ δὲ κατεργάσατό τε καὶ ἀνέπεισε [Μαρδόνιος] Ξέρξην ὥστε ποιέειν ταῦτα, Xen. *Mem.* ii. 3. 11, εἴ τινα τῶν γνωρίμων βούλοιτο κατεργάσασθαι, ὁπότε θύοι, καλεῖν σε ἐπὶ δεῖπνον, and both of these seem clearly to mean not 'make' but 'prevail upon' - see L. and S. *s.v.** [* This remains, so far as I know, an unsolved problem.]

32 (ψυχὴ) νεκροφοροῦσα, Philo, *agr.* 25; *Corp. Herm.* xii, 2: πρῶτον δὲ δεῖ σε περιρρήξασθαι ὃν φορεῖς χιτῶνα, τὸ τῆς ἀγνωσίας ὕφασμα, τὸ τῆς κακίας

with this necessity through the revolutionary discovery that the mortality he is wearing is the very mortality of Christ himself: Christ himself submitted to this process - he has been that way ahead of us. And it is the νέκρωσις of the very Jesus of history that we are wearing; and therefore we can wear it not resentfully but triumphantly, knowing what Jesus has made of it. It is actually ἐν τῇ θνητῇ σαρκί that the life of Jesus may be manifested (iv. 11). Incidentally, by making this allusion to the death of Christ, Paul clinches his insistence on history, as against a gnostic timelessness.

I am here interpreting the passage without reference to the moment of the παρουσία. I am quite ready to believe that Paul had changed his mind about his own survival till the coming of Christ, and that, whereas he expected to survive for it when he wrote I Corinthians, he was now reckoning with death before it occurred. Further, I believe that the supervening of the παρουσία on the present life is the ideal image for that swallowing up of the old by the new and that addition of extra clothing that he was hoping for in I Cor. xv. Similarly, death before the παρουσία well focuses the painful process of divestiture with which, in II Cor. v, he is coming to terms. But I do not think that the 'When?' of the παρουσία is the real issue in II Cor. iv and v. Nor do I think that the 'groaning' Paul alludes to is because of being away from Christ[33] or because of a fear of not surviving till the παρουσία. The real issue is the recognition that the process of mortality - νέκρωσις, φθορά - has got to be accepted, and the garment of the old life progressively parted with, in exchange for the new. The old life is, in one sense, already taken off at baptism, when the new man, Christ himself, is already put on: hence the baptismal and ethical uses of this metaphor. In another sense, again, the individual's death may constitute a very important crisis in the process. But there is also the protracted and painful process of implementing what is done in baptism and is to be completed in the future; and it is this, I suggest, that is here in view, and this which causes the 'groaning', exactly as, in Rom. viii. 22 f., 'groaning' is due to corruption and mortality.

Now, although the double compound ἐπενδύεσθαι is not used in I

στήριγμα (Festugière, *support*), τὸν τῆς φθορᾶς δεσμόν, τὸν σκοτεινὸν περίβολον, τὸν ζῶντα θάνατον, τὸν αἰσθητὸν νεκρόν, τὸν περιφόρητον τάφον, τὸν ἔνοικον λῃστήν, τὸν δι' ὧν φιλεῖ μισοῦντα καὶ δι' ὧν μισεῖ φθονοῦντα. The notes in Nock-Festugière here allude to Empedocles *fr*. 126 Diels, but the words σαρκῶν . . . χιτῶνι there are sufficiently obscure.

33 *Pace* J. N. Sevenster, 'Some remarks on the ΓΥΜΝΟΣ in II Cor. v. 3', *Studia Paulina in hon. J. de Zwaan* (Haarlem, 1953), pp. 202 ff. (see p. 214).

St Paul and 'dualism': the Pauline conception of resurrection

Cor. xv, I do not think there is much doubt that Paul intended there to
affirm, what in II Cor. v he finds, after all, that he has to deny. In II
Cor. v Paul says that we would *like* to *add* more clothing (ἐπενδύεσθαι),
but that we cannot and must not do so. In I Cor. xv. 53 f. he speaks
clearly of the corruptible putting on incorruption and the mortal putting
on immortality: δεῖ γὰρ τὸ φθαρτὸν τοῦτο ἐνδύσασθαι ἀφθαρσίαν καὶ τὸ
θνητὸν τοῦτο ἐνδύσασθαι ἀθανασίαν - a phrase which caters not at all for
preliminary divestiture,[34] not at all for exchange; and, moreover, he
uses another metaphor, that of death being *swallowed up*: τότε γενήσε-
ται ὁ λόγος ὁ γεγραμμένος Κατεπόθη ὁ θάνατος εἰς νῖκος. The swallowing metaphor, borrowed here by Paul from Isa. xxv. 8, was widely used
in later literature, both gnostic and orthodox. The Nag Hammadi *de
resurrectione* itself several times employs it; e.g.: '... For incorrupti-
bility I de⟨scends⟩ upon the I corruption, and the light flows I down upon
the darkness, to I swallow it up, and the Pleroma I makes perfect the
deficiency ...' (48. 38 ff., cf. 45. 14, 20; 46. 1; 49.4).[35] And, as one
instance of the use of the metaphor in later orthodox Christianity, take
Basil's phrase[36] combining the metaphors of clothing and swallowing,
when he says that, in baptism, κατεπόθη τὸ θνητὸν ἐν τῷ τῆς ἀφθαρσίας
ἐνδύματι. But in I Cor. xv it seems to be particularly appropriate to this
hope that the mortal would be, as it were, overwhelmed and swallowed
up by an immortality superimposed upon it; and it is in that sense that
I suggest Paul chiefly intended it. If so, we have a definite contrast
between I Cor. xv and II Cor. v, not primarily in terms of an altered
chronology or παρουσία-expectation (although, as I have said, this does

34 We must not be deceived by Paul's use of γυμνός in the phrase (I Cor. xv.
   37) γυμνὸν κόκκον. In the context, this clearly means *'mere* grain', as contrasted with the plant into which it will be transformed; it does not indicate
   that Paul was, at this point, thinking of a preliminary *divestiture*. The
   κόκκος never has been other than γυμνός. The use of γυμνός in II Cor. v. 3
   is in a different context.
35 Malinine's note (pp. 26 f.) on *de resurrectione* 45. 14 cites Tert. *de resurr.
   mortuorum* 42 and 54, and Heracleon's use of I Cor. xv. 54 *apud* Orig. *in
   Joh.* xiii, 60 (59), 418, and compares *P. Oxy.* 2074 (? a fragment of
   Melito), if one accepts Campbell Bonner's proposed restoration of lines
   54 f. (*Melito of Sardis, The Homily on the Passion* (London, 1940), 54):
   [σὺ εἶ ἡ κα]ταπιοῦσ[α τὸ]ν [θάνατον] - with reference to the Truth, identified with Christ. And of course the idea of feeding on death which feeds on
   us is a philosophic commonplace: cf. Valentinus (?) *apud* Clem. Alex.
   *Strom.* iv. 13. 89: ... τὸν θάνατον ἠθέλετε μερίσασθαι εἰς ἑαυτούς, ἵνα
   δαπανήσητε αὐτὸν καὶ ἀναλώσητε....
36 Cited (without reference!) by J. H. Bernard in his note on *Odes of Sol.*
   xv. 8 (*Texts and Studies*, 1912, p. 79).

217

serve well to symbolize the change), but in terms of 'addition' in I Cor. xv, over against 'exchange' in II Cor. v.[37] On the basis of the interpretation I am offering, there is no need to think that in II Cor. v Paul introduces a further difference, namely, an expectation of an interval of 'nakedness' or disembodiment between his death and the παρουσία. Some scholars[38] have interpreted the allusion to nakedness in II Cor. v. 3 as an acceptance of a state which, although terrifying in respect of its disembodiment and inferior in comparison with the ultimate state, is, nevertheless, closer to Christ than this life and therefore not incompatible with the passage in Phil. i. 23, where Paul speaks enthusiastically of it as much better than his present state, and the verses in II Cor. v which immediately follow the passage we have been examining. But I believe, as I have said, that it expresses not a Christian expectation at all, but simply a spasm of unbelief which passes like a cloud across the sun but is also as parenthetic as the cloud.[39] And, if so, it does not constitute a new attitude to be reckoned with when we are comparing the two passages in the Corinthian letters.

A more formidable problem, for anyone who tries to win consistency out of Paul's thinking, is this business of departing this life, in II Cor. v.

37 The fact that the metaphor of 'swallowing up' is used in the Nag Hammadi *de resurrectione* also (albeit without reference to a future *parousia*) is a hint that Paul, at this stage, had come near to an unrealistic, gnostic attitude to matter. And the fact that 'swallowing up' is, in II Cor. v. 4, associated with precisely the hope that now has to be rejected, fits my theory of a change in Paul's perception at this point.

38 E.g. O. Cullmann, *Christus und die Zeit* (Zürich, [8]1962), p. 214; and J. N. Sevenster, 'Some remarks on the ΓΥΜΝΟΣ in II Cor. v. 3', pp. 202 ff.

39 Cf. J. A. T. Robinson, *The Body* (London, 1952), p. 77. My theory is not, I think, invalidated by the fact that the clause εἴ γε καὶ ἐνδυσάμενοι (ἐκδυσάμενοι, pace Bultmann's *Theologie* (Tübingen, [6] 1958), p. 203, is the less likely reading – see Lietzmann *in loc.*; and whether or not εἴπερ is preferable to εἴ γε makes little difference to the sense, though M. E. Thrall, *Greek Particles in the New Testament* (London, 1962), pp. 86 ff., points to some slight distinction. She argues for both particles as here expressing *confidence*) is attached to the expression of longing for an additional garment. Admittedly, it would have been more straightforward if Paul had attached the expression of fear not to ἐνδυσάμενοι but to ἐκδύσασθαι, as though to say 'We do not want to divest ourselves – that might mean stark nakedness'. But it is really more forceful if he is saying 'We want to add, not to subtract. *Even so*, we sometimes fear that it may be all a hoax'.* In

[* Nobody, to the best of my knowledge, has so far found any evidence to support the view that εἴ γε καὶ (as contrasted with plain εἴ γε) can express confidence rather than doubt.]

6 ff. If I am right in interpreting II Cor. iv–v in terms of process already begun rather than of crisis in the future – in terms of the painful process of using up one's strength and parting with one's physical health in obedience to the will of God and in such a way as to be progressively possessed of the new life, the new man, the inner man – then one would think that there would be no room, in such a scheme, for the idea that death, departure from this life, *ipso facto* brought one nearer to the Lord. The deeply moral dualism of obedience and disobedience, which, as I am maintaining, is the only dualism seriously entertained by Paul, seems here, disturbingly, to give way to a more gnostic dualism as between physical life and life in another sphere, and, in II Cor. v. 6–9 (cf. Phil. i. 23), we seem to be extremely near to a doctrine of the escape of the soul from the shackles of the body.[40]

In face of this, let me first try to reformulate the matter-affirming doctrine that I would like to attribute to Paul. I would like to believe that Paul actually conceived of the matter which is progressively surrendered by the Christian in the process of living, dangerously and laboriously, in the service of God, as being used, and used up in the creation of the new life, as fuel is used up to produce energy. This would mean that he placed a positive value on matter, as transitory and expendable indeed, but not useless – still less, essentially evil. The physical world, on that showing, is the good and purposeful work of the good Creator, not the evil work of a demiurge.

One must reckon, admittedly, with passages like I Cor. vi. 13, where Paul (or is it only a gnostic slogan which he is quoting?) says that God will destroy (καταργήσει) both foodstuffs (βρώματα) and the belly (κοιλία); or Col. ii. 22, where he says that foodstuffs, etc., are all destined for decay as they are used up (ἅ ἐστιν πάντα εἰς φθορὰν τῇ

the *Gospel of Philip*, 23. 26 ff., there is a striking passage beginning with the words: 'some are afraid lest they rise naked'; and it appears to urge that the only way to receive true clothing is to be unclothed. See the discussion in R. McL. Wilson's edition (London, 1962), pp. 87 ff.

E. E. Ellis, 'II Cor. v. 1–10 in Pauline Eschatology', *N.T.S.* 3 (1959), 211 ff., suggests that 'naked' means 'guilty, not having a wedding garment'; but this is scarcely plausible. His interpretation of ἐκδημεῖν as meaning 'casting off the securities of earthly existence' fits my scheme well.

40 It is interesting that a passage in the Nag Hammadi *de resurrectione* seems to be meeting the same anxiety as Paul expresses, about whether 'exchange' is not going to be for the worse, but meeting it in dualistic terms of 'departure': 47. 20–2, '. . . absence is an advantage. | For thou wilt not give up what is | better if thou shouldst depart.' This immediately follows the very negative sentence (17–19): 'The after-birth (χόριον) of the body (σῶμα) is | old age, and thou | art corruption.'

ἀποχρήσει). But both abolition (καταργεῖν) and decay (φθορά) can become part of a process of transformation: they can become purposeful and need not be simply negative and wasteful;[41] and, on the other side of the account, one has to reckon with the 'somatic identity' stressed in I Cor. xv - the continuity of identity as between seed and plant, as between the σῶμα that is buried and the σῶμα that is raised, and with the extremely positive valuation by Paul of what he calls (in II Cor. v. 10) τὰ διὰ τοῦ σώματος and ἃ ἔπραξεν - a man's use of his body and the things he has done with this life. Adam's disobedience brings death; but the last Adam's obedience can so use the death-laden, that God can raise it to life.

In view of this, may it not be that Paul describes departure from the body (II Cor. v. 8, ἐκδημῆσαι ἐκ τοῦ σώματος) as presence with the Lord (ἐνδημῆσαι πρὸς τὸν κύριον) in the sense that, for the individual, death marks the climax of that process of using up and letting go of the material which has been going on all the time? And may it not be that, conversely, he views presence in the body (II Cor. v. 6, ἐνδημοῦντες ἐν τῷ σώματι) as absence from the Lord (ἐκδημοῦμεν ἀπὸ τοῦ κυρίου) in the sense that, as long as this life continues the process is never complete?

On this showing, death, even in this passage, marks, not so much the escape of the soul from the prison of the body, as the completion of the transformation of the σῶμα ψυχικόν into the σῶμα πνευματικόν; and it would be for this reason that in Phil. i. 23 also Pauls speaks of it with longing as something eagerly desired.[42]

It is a pity that Paul did not know the physiological process by which an insect goes through its metamorphoses, forming the pupa beneath the larva form, forming the imago beneath the pupa and getting ready, at each successive stage, to let the old skin, from which all that is necessary has been used up, fall off and reveal the new stage. It might have been a useful analogy.

As it is, my suggestion is simply that the essential distinction between his positions in I Cor. xv and II Cor. v, is only that, in the former, he

---

41 Would Paul have said that, although the Lord did not see φθορά (Acts ii. 31), yet the physical body was *used* up in the resurrection? It seems to me that, so far from being unconcerned for the empty tomb, Paul actually suggests it when, in I Cor. xv. 4, he specifies καὶ ὅτι ἐτάφη.

42 Just so, in I Cor. xv, he was regarding the supervening of the παρουσία on this life as the climax of that putting on of Christ which had taken place at baptism, for each believer. Death is, as it were, the sacrament and summing up of the whole process of detachment, just as the παρουσία sums up the triumph of the new over the old.

too lightly looked for addition, whereas, by II Cor. v, he was more realistically reckoning with exchange; and that, throughout his thinking in the extant epistles, he maintains, with remarkable tenacity, a basic consistency regarding dualism. I would dare to trace this, at least in part, to the Damascus road discovery, that the Jesus who had suffered in a physical body had been raised in glory.[43] Although he ransacks and freely borrows from current gnostic and philosophic formulae, Paul really has no use for a dualism of matter and spirit, no room (despite his elaborate demonology)[44] for a demiurge creating an evil world, no ultimate antithesis except the moral antithesis between disobedience (which characterizes all the sons of darkness, angelic as well as human) and obedience. It is obedience, by the power of the Holy Spirit, which effects the metamorphosis of Christians (II Cor. iii. 18). The two 'sets of clothes' in the metaphor are, basically, the likeness of the first (disobedient) Adam and the last (obedient) Adam respectively (I Cor. xv. 49). But obedience, nevertheless, finds a positive use for the old clothes, since it can so part with them as to make them serve the purposes of the creation of the new. And that obedience is, for Paul, crystallized in the pregnant utterance of the Spirit of God's Son in us, crying the cry of trust and obedience - Abba! Νέκρωσις is Adam's lot; and the old Adam hates and resents it. But Jesus parted with his body in obedience to the Father. That is what makes his νέκρωσις a triumph, and enables his life to be expressed through mortal flesh.

43 Cf. J. Jeremias, 'The Key to Pauline Theology', *Exp.T.* 76, 1 (October 1964), 27 ff. (see p. 29b).
44 Cf. A. D. Nock, 'Gnosticism' (posthumously edited by Zeph. Stewart), *H.T.R.* 57 (1964), 255 ff. (see p. 271).

# 15

## A Reconsideration of the Context of *Maranatha*

It is widely held that the *marantha* of I Cor. xvi. 22 (construed as an imperative, 'O our Lord come!') is to be understood as an invocation of Christ to be present in the eucharist.[1] Support for this is sought in the fact that other words and phrases in the same context can also be interpreted eucharistically: the kiss (*v.* 20), the 'anathema' upon anyone who does not love the Lord (*v.* 22), and the grace (*v.* 23) can all be supposed to be among the preliminaries to the eucharist (in terms both of inclusion and of exclusion). Further, the *maranatha* also occurs in *Didache* x. 6, in a section connected at least in some way with the eucharist;[2] and the Greek equivalent, ἔρχου κύριε Ἰησοῦ, occurs in Rev. xxii. 20, together with amen (cf. *Didache* x. 6 again) and not far from what might seem to be a eucharistic 'invitation' (*v.* 17).

But how much of this is really cogent? If I Corinthians was really intended to be (as it were) the homily, leading on into the eucharist,[3] why is there so little trace of this in other New Testament epistles?[4] Why does the *maranatha* in I Cor. xvi. 22 come at this particular point, *before* the grace (and the apostle's love)? Why does it occur where it does in the *Didache*? In spite of all that is said,[5] is there sufficient evi-

1 See K. M. Hofmann, *Philema Hagion* (1938); A. J. B. Higgins, *The Lord's Supper in the New Testament* (London, 1952), p. 60; O. Cullmann, *Early Christian Worship* (1950; E. T. London, 1953), p. 13; J. A. T. Robinson, 'Traces of a Liturgical Sequence in I Cor. xvi. 20–24', *J.T.S.* n.s. 4, 1 (April 1953), 38 ff.; N. Clark, *An Approach to the Theology of the Sacraments* (London, 1956), p. 70.

2 Cf. H. Lietzmann, *Messe und Herrenmahl* (Bonn, 1926), pp. 236 ff.

3 See R. Seeberg in *Aus Religion und Geschichte* i (1906), pp. 118 ff. ('Kuß und Kanon'); Lietzmann, *Messe*, p. 229; Robinson, *J.T.S.* 4, 1 (1953).

4 The alleged traces in Rom. xv, alluded to by Robinson, *J.T.S.* 4, 1 (1953), are inconclusive.

5 See, besides Lietzmann, *Messe*, M. Dibelius, 'Die Mahlgebete der Didache', *Z.N.T.W.* 37 (1938), 40 ff.; G. Bornkamm, 'Das Anathema in der urchristlichen Abendmahlsliturgie, *T.L.Z.* 75 (1950), 4/5, 227 ff., reprinted (in a revised form) in *Das Ende des Gesetzes* (München, 1952), pp. 123 ff.; J.-P. Audet, *La Didaché* (Paris, 1958), p. 415.

dence to suggest that it was meant to lead straight into the eucharist proper? And is there anything obviously eucharistic in the context of Rev. xxii?

In view of so many doubts, it is perhaps worthwhile to revive and reconsider a different interpretation which was suggested, in substance, at least as early as E. Peterson's ΕΙΣ ΘΕΟΣ (Göttingen, 1926), pp. 130 ff.,[6] namely, that the *maranatha* (amen) is, in effect, part of the *anathema* – an element in the ban-formula. This is a less agreeable interpretation, but it is not to be lightly rejected. What if not only the *maranatha* of I Cor. xvi. 22 and *Didache* x. 6, but also the ἔρχου κύριε Ἰησοῦ of Rev. xxii. 20 are not (at least primarily) eucharistic invocations but invocations (primarily at least) to reinforce and sanction the curse or ban?[7]

In I Cor. xvi. 22 μαραναθα follows εἴ τις οὐ φιλεῖ τὸν κύριον, ἤτω ἀνάθεμα. In *Didache* x. 6 it follows εἴ τις ἅγιός ἐστιν, ἐρχέσθω· εἴ τις οὐκ ἔστι, μετανοείτω. In Rev. xxii. 20 the ἔρχου κύριε Ἰησοῦ follows the tremendous curse (*vv.* 18 f.), beginning μαρτυρῶ ἐγὼ παντὶ τῷ ἀκούοντι τοὺς λόγους ... ἐάν τις ἐπιθῇ ἐπ᾽ αὐτά, ... καὶ ἐάν τις ἀφέλῃ ἀπὸ τῶν λόγων ..., and (compatibly with the μαρτυρῶ there) the invocation formula begins λέγει ὁ μαρτυρῶν ταῦτα Ναί, ἔρχομαι ταχύ.

The formulae in such contexts are not difficult to interpret as Christian forms of the pagan 'sanction' formulae. W. Bauer[8] notes that Artemidorus (II, 70, p. 167, 25) begs the reader of his books μήτε προσθεῖναι μήτε τι τῶν ὄντων ἀφελεῖν and (p. 168, 2 ff.) entrusts his work to the protection of Apollo: that is not unlike the theme of Rev. xxii. Students of ancient cursing formulae will be familiar with the ἤδη ἤδη ταχὺ ταχύ of the impatient invocation (R. Wünsch, *Antike Fluchtafeln*, Kleine Texte 20, (Leipzig/Berlin, 1907), pp. 13, 25, etc.);[9] and in other types of magical papyri there are comparable formulae, for

6 And cf. W. Bousset's *Jesus der Herr* (Göttingen, 1916), p. 22 cited by Peterson, ΕΙΣ ΘΕΟΣ, as having been retracted by Bousset in his later *Kyrios Christos* (Göttingen, 1921), p. 84.

7 S.-B. in loc. (iii, p. 494) allude to the ingenious suggestion (whose?) that *maranatha* is an interpretation of *anathema* along the lines of analysing the rabbinic word שַׁמְּתָא ('ban') as שֵׁם אֲתָא 'the Name [of Yahweh] comes'. But they note that this cannot be substantiated from rabbinic writings.

8 *Zur Einführung in das Wörterbuch zum N.T.* (*Coniectanea Neotestamentica*, 15 (1955)), 26 (printed as the introduction to Arndt and Gingrich's version of Bauer).

9 It is perhaps significant that Peterson, ΕΙΣ ΘΕΟΣ, p. 233 (in a different context) is able to cite, from a Coptic amulet, an amen and a ταχὺ ταχύ in juxtaposition.

example, . . . τάχος, τῇ σῇ δυνάμει ἤδη ἔ[γγ]αιος, ναὶ ναί, φαῖνέ μοι θεέ (K. Preisendanz, *Papyri Graecae magicae* (Bonn, 1928), I, ll. 89–90). Nearer home is the Jewish usage illustrated by the prayers for vengeance incised on gravestones and ending with a call to God to avenge τὴν ταχίστην (see G. A. Deissmann, *Light from the Ancient East*, London, 1927 edn., pp. 413 ff.). But particularly significant is the Christian sepulchral inscription (IV/V A.D.) from Salamis (*C.I.G.* IV, 9303) calling down a curse on anyone who interferes with the remains, in the form ἀνάθεμα ἤτω μαρὰν ἀθάν. The comment on this in Moulton and Milligan (*s.v.* ἀνάθεμα) is: 'the meaning of the Aramaic σύμβολον [i.e. μαραναθαν] being wholly unknown, it could be used as a curse - like unknown words in later days!' But is it not more natural to suppose that the μαραναθαν was here not a σύμβολον but a genuine invocation, that its meaning was understood (the slight misspelling is hardly an argument for complete misunderstanding), and that it was deliberately used to sanction the anathema?

Not far from the same intention are such 'sanctioning' invocations as the following, from the New Testament itself: I Cor. v. 4 f. . . . σὺν τῇ δυνάμει τοῦ κυρίου ἡμῶν Ἰησοῦ . . . (in connexion with excommunication; cf. the phrase cited above from Preisendanz's collection); II Cor. i. 23 ἐγὼ δὲ μάρτυρα τὸν θεὸν ἐπικαλοῦμαι ἐπὶ τὴν ἐμὴν ψυχήν, ὅτι . . . (cf. the witness-motif in Rev. xxii); II Cor. xi. 31 ὁ θεὸς καὶ πατὴρ τοῦ κυρίου Ἰησοῦ οἶδεν, ὁ ὢν εὐλογητὸς εἰς τοὺς αἰῶνας, ὅτι . . . ; Gal. i. 20 ἰδοὺ ἐνώπιον τοῦ θεοῦ ὅτι . . . ; I Thess. v. 27 ἐνορκιζω ὑμᾶς τὸν κύριον. . . . There are also all the Old Testament imprecations and asseverations with such formulae as . . .כֹּה־יַעֲשׂוּן אֱלֹהִים וְכֹה יֹסִפוּן, . . .חַי יְהֹוָה. Perhaps one should add Zech. iii. 2 . . .יִגְעַר יְהֹוָה בְּךָ, cf. Jude 9.

That anathema occurs in both I Cor. xii. 3 and Gal. i. 8 without the *maranatha* is no proof that the latter, when it does occur, is not intended to sanction the curse. In the first instance (ἀνάθεμα Ἰησοῦς) it would in any case have been self-contradictory, and, besides, there is no reason why St Paul, in merely alluding to, not using, a shocking and blasphemous curse upon Jesus himself, should add a sanction. In the second, St Paul is admittedly pronouncing a solemn curse on false preachers (with, indeed, the εἴ τις formula); but he is only repeating what he appears to have established on some previous occasion (when he may have used the full sanction). The other occurrences of ἀνάθεμα in the New Testament (Acts xxiii. 14, Rom. ix. 3) are again in allusions, and are not relevant for the present purpose.

In recent allusions to Peterson's idea, K. G. Kuhn[10] and G. Born-

10 In *T.W.N.T.* iv, 470 ff.

kamm[11] agree with him to the extent of allowing that the *maranatha* does reinforce the ban. But they hold that he goes beyond the evidence in taking the *maranatha* (amen) as simply an apotropaic or exorcistic formula. They prefer to interpret it as the eucharistic invocation (or possibly affirmation, if the verb be construed as an indicative, not an imperative), and to find as it were incidental reinforcement for the ban in the conception of the Lord's eucharistic presence or coming. Against this, the purpose of this note is to show that, after all, Peterson's view is not without plausibility.

If, however, this is so, it does not necessarily mean, even now, that I Cor. xvi. 22 and (*a fortiori*) *Didache* x. 6 are not connected with the eucharist; only that, even if the contexts are eucharistic, the proper function of the *maranatha* is here not to constitute the eucharistic invocation but to sanction the preliminary 'fencing of the table'. As for Rev. xxii. 20, it may be, despite current opinion, that the phrase is not eucharistic at all, but is primarily a sanction for the ban on anyone who tampers with the book's integrity, while at the same time it echoes and reaffirms the theme of the whole Apocalypse.

It remains to ask in precisely what sense Jesus was expected to 'come' in answer to such an invocation. The pagan formulae no doubt imply the belief (or hope) that the god would forthwith come and smite the delinquent. In view, however, of the Biblical expectation of a future general day of judgement, it seems more likely that the Christian formulae were directed - primarily at any rate - towards this expectation, and that *maranatha* meant 'may the Lord *soon* come in judgement to redress wrong and establish right!'[12] This fits the appeal to repent (μετανοείτω) in *Didache* x. 6, which would be reinforced by the expectation of the coming of the Lord in the near future (though perhaps to construe *maranatha* as an indicative, 'the Lord is here', would be even more appropriate here). It is in line also with the full formula in Rev. xxii. 20: λέγει ὁ μαρτυρῶν ταῦτα ναί, ἔρχομαι ταχύ. ἀμήν, ἔρχου κύριε Ἰησοῦ. And it is in line with one other 'asseveration' formula in the New Testament, which has not so far been mentioned, namely II Tim. iv. 1 διαμαρτύρομαι ἐνώπιον τοῦ θεοῦ καὶ χριστοῦ Ἰησοῦ, τοῦ μέλλοντος κρίνειν ζῶντας καὶ νεκρούς, καὶ τὴν ἐπιφάνειαν αὐτοῦ καὶ τὴν βασιλείαν αὐτοῦ. ... It will be seen that this eschatological interpretation is, in effect, very nearly identical with that which sees the formula as a

11 *T.L.Z.* 75, 4/5 (1950), 227 ff.
12 Cf. canon 75 of the fourth Council of Toledo (A.D. 633), 'qui contra hanc nostram definitionem praesumpserit, anathema maranatha hoc est, perditio in adventu domini sit' (cited *T.W.N.T.* iv, 470).

eucharistic invocation. But there is this difference, that, while appropriate to the eucharist, it is not confined to it.

Alternatively, it is possible that at least in some contexts - and even, in a secondary way, in the others also - the invocation implied the immediate (unseen) coming of the Lord, not necessarily to strike, but to hear and see and bear witness.[13] Precisely this sense of standing in the presence of God and of Christ while making the asseveration is already explicit in the first words of the passage just quoted from II Tim. iv. 1; and it no doubt underlies all solemn religious oaths, as in the modern legal oath 'on the Bible'.

13 E. Käsemann, 'Sätze heiligen Rechtes im Neuen Testament', *N.T.S.* 1, 4 (May 1955), 248 ff., is ready to interpret the *maranatha* of I Cor. xvi. 22 in terms of an anticipation of the Last Day such that the delinquent is faced by the presence of the Judge, yet with time to repent (*loc. cit.* 251). In dealing with Rev. xxii. 18 f., however (256), he does not relate *v.* 20 to the ban.

# 16

II Cor. iii. 18b, καθάπερ[1] ἀπὸ κυρίου πνεύματος
for O. Cullman

The main conclusion reached in this note, completed in July 1970, though entertained by me for many years past (see note 29, p. 234), has now been anticipated in print by my friend and pupil, J. D. G. Dunn, in his article '2 Corinthians III. 17 - "the Lord is the Spirit"', *J.T.S.* n.s. 21 (1970), 309 ff. He there paraphrases II Cor. iii. 18b by: 'Such is the influence of the Lord, who, as we have already said, is Spirit' (318).

But perhaps it is still worth while for me to offer the note as originally drafted, partly because it shows that two students of Paul have, more or less independently, reached the same conclusion, and partly because my interpretation of the eschatological implications of this passage are not quite identical with Dr Dunn's.

The passage leading up to and including this cryptic phrase is one of the most elaborately studied of all New Testament *cruces*. (Incidentally, it should be recognized that the passage stretches to iv. 6.) One of the fullest and finest studies is that of Ingo Hermann;[2] but there is an immense literature on it, and it is no intention of this note to traverse all the ground again, nor to re-open the much-debated question of Paul's opponents and the setting of this chapter in his conflict with them.[3] All that is here offered, for the consideration of the reader, and particularly of the great scholar and friend in whose honour it is respectfully

1 Or, with B, καθώσπερ.
2 *Kyrios und Pneuma: Studien zur Christologie der paulinischen Hauptbriefe, Studien zum Alten und Neuen Testament*, hg. von V. Hamp und J. Schmid, Band II (München, 1961).
3 See, besides D. Georgi *Die Gegner des Paulus im 2. Korintherbrief* (Neukirchen, 1964) (and the literature there cited, especially S. Schulz, 'Die Decke des Moses', *Z.N.T.W.* 49 (1958), 1 ff, suggesting that Paul was replying to Jewish–Christian opponents by adapting to his own polemic an already exiting midrash of theirs), the essay by J. L. Martyn, 'Epistemology at the turn of the ages: 2 Cor 5:16' in *Christian History and Interpretation: Studies Presented to John Knox*, edd. W. R. Farmer, C. F. D. Moule, and R. R. Niebuhr (Cambridge, 1967), pp. 269 ff, and C. K. Barrett, 'Paul's Opponents in II Corinthians', *N.T.S.* 17 (1971), 233 ff.

presented, is one more attempt to interpret that cryptic phrase - or, rather, to ask a tentative question about it: Could the phrase possibly refer, not to the Lord Jesus but to 'the Lord God (Yahweh), *present as Spirit*'? To refer κύριος here to God rather than Christ is, though rarely adopted, not unprecedented.[4] But I am not aware that this has before been combined with construing πνεύματος in apposition to it.[5] For that very reason, it is all too likely to be impossible, for one suspects that all possible devices must have already been tried. But it is a ghost of a notion that has haunted me for too long, and this seems a good opportunity either to give it substance or (more probably) to get it well and truly laid.

Any plausibility that this at first sight implausible proposal may have is derived from the movement of the argument in this difficult chapter; and an annotated paraphrase of the whole passage will perhaps best serve to explain how it is arrived at.

(*Vv.* 1-3) The apostle, defending his authority, claims that his credentials are written, not on some inanimate material with ink but by the Spirit of the living God on tablets which are human hearts - the hearts of the Corinthian Christians.[6] In other words, Paul's credentials are not on paper but in persons. But these contrasts - not ink but the Spirit, and not dead material but living hearts - have brought to mind some Old Testament passages, expecially from Ezekiel and Jeremiah, in which contrasts of a rather different sort are drawn, namely, contrasts between dead stone and living flesh (Ezek. xi. 19, xxxvi. 26), and between an outward code written on stone (Exod. xxiv. 12) and an inwardly accepted obedience (Jer. xxxi [LXX xxxviii] . 33). The transition[7] from the contrast between letters of introduction written in ink (presumably on papyrus) and credentials consisting of human hearts, to that other contrast between a covenant written on tables of stone and a covenant written inwardly on the heart, is made in a quaintly syncopated way. You do not write on stone with ink but with incised letters; but Paul syncopates the transition in *v.* 3, by first contrasting

---

4 B. Schneider, O. F. M. 'Dominus autem Spiritus est' (Romae: Officium Libri Catholici, 1951) represents one instance.

5 Schneider takes κυρίου as depending on πνεύματος. But see, now, Dunn, *J.T.S.* 21 (1970).

6 Reading, in *v.* 2, ἐν ταῖς καρδίαις ὑμῶν with ℵ 33 against the majority reading ἡμῶν. The latter is very difficult to make sense of, for, while the apostle might use a plural pronoun of himself, he would hardly have a plurality of hearts; but if it is a genuine plural, who could be intended by '*our* hearts'?

7 See Hermann, *Kyrios und Pneuma*, 27 f.

228

ink with the Spirit (οὐ μέλανι ἀλλὰ πνεύματι Θεοῦ ζῶντος), but then going straight on with the contrast between stone tablets and tablets which are hearts of flesh (οὐκ ἐν πλαξὶν λιθίναις ἀλλ᾽ ἐν πλαξὶ καρδίαις σαρκίναις). The link that is common to both the situation at Corinth and the Old Testament passages is ἐγγεγραμμένη ἐν καρδίαις (*vv.* 2 f.). The transition, once made, leads on to a new formulation of the apostle's claims.

If he began by saying that his credentials were letters of introduction written on the hearts of men, he now says that the credentials consist, essentially, in the fact that he is a minister of the new, superior covenant – that new covenant of Jer. xxxi, which was to be written not on law-tables but inwardly on men's hearts. In the case of the Corinthians, he has heart-written credentials: in his ministry generally, he is the apostle of a heart-written covenant.

(*Vv.* 4-6) But since the heart-written covenant was that which, in Jer. xxxi, was prophesied as destined to supersede the old covenant, in this respect, Paul's ministry is superior to that of Moses himself.[8] Moses was a minister of a written law which could only pronounce sentence on the offender – it was mere writing, and it could only kill. Paul is a minister of the Spirit – that is, the inward law written on the heart by God's Spirit –, and that brings life.[9]

(*Vv.* 7-11) But even the ministering of the old, literal death-sentence was attended by glory: how much more, then, that of the new, spiritual, life-giving acquittal! That, in itself, is evidence enough of the apostle's high credentials. But with the word 'glory', Paul has introduced a further thought – the tale, in Exod. xxxiv, about Moses' face shining with the divine radiance which he had caught in the presence of Yahweh.[10] Yes, even the old law-giving was attended by glory. But it was a glory that faded from Moses' face: the glory gained from the divine confrontation on the mountain-top faded when he came down. (It is well known that Paul here reinterprets the story of the veil over Moses' face so as to make it a device not only for screening the Israelites from the intolerable brilliance of the glory,[11] but also for concealing its transiency.) By contrast, the glory of the new covenant is not a waning glory, but a permanent one. The key-note of this homily has thus become this contrast

8 Cf. J. Munck, *Paulus und die Heilsgeschichte* (Aarhus, 1954), Ch. II.
9 For the contrast, cf. Rom. ii. 29, vii. 6.
10 See T. F. Glasson, *Moses in the Fourth Gospel* (London, 1963), p. 69, for ancient comments on this, and for the suggestion that 'Moses and Jesus and glory' constituted a theme in the dispute between Christians and Jews.
11 As in Philo's interpretation, *vit. Mos.* ii (iii). 70 – though, as a matter of fact, the story in Exod. xxxiv itself does not make it altogether clear (see

between τὸ καταργούμενον (what is being abolished) and τὸ μένον (the permanent). As Moses' radiance faded, so is the Mosaic covenant one that is coming to an end. By contrast, the new covenant is permanent, and correspondingly more glorious.

(*Vv.* 12-15) Accordingly, the apostle has no need of a veil:[12] there is nothing to conceal; his credentials will bear open scrutiny. (This theme is taken up and developed in II Cor. iv. 2.) But - and here another theme comes on the scene, the familiar theme of the hardening of Israel[13] - the Israelites were callous and unperceptive. (Not that this is any part of Exod. xxxiv itself,[14] but it is implied by the story of the golden calf in Exod. xxxii, and is certainly a recurrent motif of the story of the wilderness wanderings - see, especially, in this context, Deut. xxix. 4;[15] also Ps. xcv, and, of course cf. Isa. vi.) And, right up to the present day, it is the same: non-Christian Israel is unperceptive; it fails to recognize the transiency of the Mosaic covenant. Indeed, one may say by a transference of the metaphor, that there is a veil over their own face. Moses concealed his face from the Israelites: the Israelites blindfold themselves from the truth. (Is there a fleeting reminiscence, at this point, of that other veil in scripture, the covering and the veil over the face of all peoples and nations, in Isa. xxv. 7? Neither of the words used here is the same as the word in Exod. xxxiv (M.T. in Isa. xxv. 7 has לוֹט and מַסֵּכָה as against the מַסְוֶה of Exod. xxxiv; LXX in Isa. xxv. 7 altogether otherwise, but κάλυμμα in Exod. xxxiv), but possibly the image is in Paul's mind.[16] This sort of veiling is further described in II Cor. iv. 3 f.: Israel fail to see that in Christ the old covenant is superseded. (There is no need to debate the exact syntax of *v.* 14b: see Hermann, *Kyrios und Pneuma*, pp. 36 f.).

especially *v.* 33) at what point the veil was put on, nor what its purpose was: but it is usually assumed that the Exodus story intends it to enable the Israelites to approach Moses without fear. See Schulz, *Z.N.T.W.* 49 (1958), 7 f.

12 W. C. van Unnik, '"With unveiled face", an exegesis of 2 Corinthians III 12-18', *Nov. Test.* 6 (1963), 153 ff, sees here a subtle connexion between παρρησία and its Semitic equivalents meaning 'unveiling', which he had established previously in *De semitische achtergrond von* ΠΑΡΡΗΣΙΑ *in het Nieuwe Testament* (Amsterdam, 1962).

13 See J. Gnilka, *Die Verstockung Israels, Isaias 6, 9-10, in der Theologie der Synoptiker, Studien zum Alten und Neuen Testament*, hg. von V. Hamp und J. Schmid, Band III (München, 1961).

14 See Hermann, *Kyrios und Pneuma*, p. 35.

15 Van Unnik, *Nov. Test.* 6 (1963), 163.

16 It is much less probable that there is a subtle allusion to the reverent veiling of the Torah roll in synagogues. See Schulz, *Z.N.T.W.* 49 (1958), 13, n. 65.

*II Cor iii. 18b, καθάπερ ἀπὸ κυρίου πνεύματος*

(*Vv.* 16-18) But - and here Paul reverts to his 'text' in Exod. xxxiv - 'whenever Moses returns to Yahweh he removes the veil again'. This interpretation is contrary to the prevailing opinion.[17] With most commentators, this clause is not treated as a repetition of the Exodus phrase; the subject of the sentence, unexpressed in the Greek, is taken, rather, to be not Moses but either Israel or else 'anyone' generally; and κύριος is taken to mean not Yahweh but the Lord Jesus Christ: the veil of obtuseness is going to be removed as soon as 'conversion' to Christ takes place.[18] But, despite the weight of opinion to the contrary, ἡνίκα ἐὰν[19] ἐπιστρέψῃ . . . περιαιρεῖται is most naturally read as a frequentative temporal clause meaning 'every time he returns . . . he removes . . .', rather than 'when' or 'as soon as he returns . . .'; and although admittedly (as Hermann and others observe) the words are not the same as those of Exod. xxxiv. 34, which uses narrative past tenses (ἡνίκα δ' ἂν εἰσεπορεύετο . . . περιῃρεῖτο, 'every time he went in . . . he used to take off . . .'), nevertheless it is plausible, if I am right in my analysis of Paul's train of thought thus far, to take the phrase as still frequentative and as intended to refer to Moses. The alteration of the past tense of the Exodus story into tenses capable of a repetitive present-and-future meaning need not divorce the clause from the Exodus context. The aorist subjunctive followed by the present indicative need only represent the equivalent (in a temporal clause) of a historic present; and this alteration could be explained by Paul's desire to make more vividly the point that return into the presence of God must always mean (whether for Moses, for Israel, or for anyone else) the end of the necessity to veil fading glory, since in the presence of God the glory is always renewed: 'whenever (Moses) returns into God's presence he always removes the veil'. (Note, incidentally, that the anarthrous κύριος used by Paul here is also used in Exod. xxxiv. 34: ἡνίκα δ' ἂν εἰσεπορεύετο Μωϋσῆς ἔναντι κυρίου.) But it is the interpretation of the next step in the argument that is most crucial for the view that is being advocated in this paraphrase. I suggest that Paul reaches the climax of his 'allegory' in *v.* 17a with ὁ δὲ κύριος τὸ πνεῦμά ἐστιν, meaning 'Now that κύριος - that Yahweh of the Exodus story - is (now, for us) the Spirit'. Hermann and most others reject the interpretation of κύριος here as Yahweh, in

17 See, however, Schulz, *Z.N.T.W.* 49 (1958), 151, and now Dunn, *J.T.S.* 21 (1970).
18 See, e.g. Hermann, *Kyrios und Pneuma*, p. 38, for his arguments against treating it as a virtual repetition of the Exodus phrase.
19 The only New Testament occurrence of this classical expression - Schulz, *Z.N.T.W.* 41 (1958), 13, n. 67, citing Windisch.

231

favour of interpreting it as the Lord Jesus Christ.[20] But the Yahweh-interpretation is not without its supporters, and it makes a remarkably coherent argument if we take the sense to be that the Yahweh[21] of the Moses story is no longer remote on the mountain top, but is (through Christ) present as the Spirit among his people. It is the eschatological fulfilment, in terms of the era of the Spirit, of the promise that Yahweh would dwell and walk among his people - Lev. xxvi. 12 (which, incidentally, is quoted in II Cor. vi. 16, though that, of course, may be a fragment of a quite different epistle from the one to which II Cor. iii and iv belong). And, if so, of course it follows that not only the apostle but all of us Christians (ἡμεῖς πάντες, v. 18) are continually in a position to reflect[22] the radiance of the divine Presence.[23] None of us Christians needs a veil to conceal a transitory splendour: the radiance we borrow from the Lord is not transitory, because we never need to come away from the Presence. Indeed, so far from waning, the glory actually waxes, increasing, as we are transfigured into God's likeness,[24] from one degree of glory to another. And so, the climactic phrase is reached: καθάπερ (or καθώσπερ, see note 1, p. 227) ἀπὸ κυρίου πνεύματος. My question is: May not this mean: *'This is in keeping with - this is what one would expect from - the glory being derived from a Yahweh who is (now with us as) Spirit'?*

I cordially agree with Hermann's view that πνεῦμα in this whole context constitutes a description of how the believer experiences the divine presence: '"Der Herr ist der Geist" ist also eine existentielle Aussage. Sie redet über das Verhältnis von Kyrios und Pneuma nicht in der Art einer spekulativen Wesensschau, sondern gibt eine Erfahrung wieder: für mich,

20 See Hermann's criticism of V. Holzmeister, K. Prümm and J. B. Nisius, *Kyrios und Pneuma*, pp. 39 ff. See also N. Q. Hamilton, *The Holy Spirit and Eschatology in Paul, Scottish Journal of Theology Occasional Papers* 6 (1957).

21 On this showing, the definite article, ὁ δὲ κύριος, would be the 'anaphoric' article or article of 'renewed mention' (Debrunner-Funk, *A Greek Grammar of the New Testament* (Cambridge, 1961), 252), and would simply take up the anarthrous κύριος of v. 16.

22 For κατοπτρίζεσθαι as = 'to reflect' (despite a strong trend towards taking it as 'to see'), see Chrysostom *in Epist. II ad Cor. Homil. VII*, 486 (*P. G.* 61, 448) and Theodoret, *interp. Epist. II ad Cor. III*, 307 (*P. G.* 82, 397D-400A); and W. C. van Unnik, *Nov. Test.* 6 (1963), 167.

23 van Unnik, *Nov. Test.* 6 (1963): '. . . permanently in the same situation which Moses, according to Exod. XXXIV, only temporarily enjoyed.'

24 But van Unnik *Nov. Test.* 6 (1963), 167 f., takes τὴν αὐτὴν εἰκόνα to mean that all Christians are transfigured not into the same likeness as God's, but into one and the same εἰκών.

auf mich hin ist der Herr das Pneuma, er stellt sich für mich als Pneuma dar'; but I believe that a case can be made for referring the divine presence to God rather than to Christ. Although of course it is through Christ that Paul experiences the spiritual presence (and this is made even more explicit in iv. 6), I suggest that the point he is making is that the Yahweh of the Exodus story is no longer remote on the mountain top (necessitating a waxing and waning glory as Moses goes to and fro) but is permanently present (through Jesus Christ) as Spirit (leading to an unintermittent – indeed, a constantly increasing – glory). The new covenant is contrasted with the old as more glorious because it belongs to the new era of the permanent presence of the Spirit. Of course the Old Testament does not consistently represent Yahweh as far away on the mountain top: his presence is frequently recognized, in the tabernacle, in the temple, and, indeed, already in the hearts of his people and in visitations of his Spirit.[25] But Paul is stylizing the situation by allegorizing the story in Exod. xxxiv, so as to highlight the new and distinctively Christian experience of God as Spirit. That this takes place through Jesus Christ goes without saying; and that κύριος, for Paul, usually means Jesus is undeniable.[26] But since II Cor. iii is a 'sermon' on Exod. xxxiv, it would not be surprising if Paul departed from his habitual usage. And it is to be remarked that, whereas Paul's usage when he applies κύριος to Jesus varies between arthrous and anarthrous, he nearly always uses it anarthrously when it is demonstrably in an Old Testament reference.[27] So far as the usage goes, therefore, it fits the assumption that the anarthrous κύριος in *vv.* 16, 18 means Yahweh, while the article is used in *v.* 17 purely because of 'anaphora' or 'renewed mention' (cf. n. 21, p. 232). Conversely, as for the application of πνεῦμα to the Lord Jesus, the only absolutely clear instance is in I Cor. xv. 45;[28] whereas it is precisely in a famous contrast between the localization of God on a mountain and his ubiquity that πνεῦμα ὁ Θεός occurs (Jo. iv. 24). If it be conceded, on such grounds as these, that the

25 Indeed, Num. xiv. 14 expressly says that Y" is seen in the community 'eye to eye'.

26 See, e.g. Hermann, *Kyrios und Pneuma* and E. Schweizer in *T.W.N.T.* vi, 416, where, in reference to this passage, he says 'κύριος (= Χριστός v. 14 wie stets ...)'.

27 The only virtually certain exceptions in the Pauline corpus (outside the Pastorals) are Rom. xv. 11, I Cor. x. 9, 22, 26, II Cor. x. 18.

28 As M. M. Bourke points out in 'The Eucharist and Wisdom in First Corinthians', *Analecta Biblica* 17–18 (Rome 1961), 367 ff. (379); cf. P. E. Hughes, *Pauls's Second Epistle to the Corinthians* (Michigan, 1962), 116.

reference of (ὁ) κύριος to God is not implausible, then the only serious difficulty encountered by the proposed interpretation is, as far as I can see, the necessity to fill out the sense of the two crucial clauses. ὁ δὲ κύριος τὸ πνεῦμά ἐστιν has to be interpreted by some such paraphrase as 'the Lord (of the Exodus story) is (now, for us, represented by) the Spirit'; and καθάπερ ἀπὸ κυρίου πνεύματος by 'as (is natural when the glory is) from a Lord (who is now experienced as) Spirit'. It seems to me that these paraphrases, though they admittedly appear to be supplying a great deal, are actually in keeping with the thrust of the argument and the context (including iv. 1–6, which clearly belongs to this section of the argument), and are not unjustifiably derived from them. But that, of course, is the debatable question, and I submit it for judgement by those more competent than I.[29]

29 I am indebted, for certain references and for valuable comments on these ideas, to the Reverend T. C. G. Thornton, who was discussing them and corresponding with me about them as long ago as 1961. In particular, I have notes from him on the meaning of κατοπτρίζεσθαι and on B. Schneider's monograph. For none of my vagaries is he responsible, but I am glad here to express my gratitude for his help. Professor C. K. Barrett and Dr A. J. M. Wedderburn have also been kind enough to read this note and make suggestions.

# 17

## Punishment and Retribution: An Attempt to Delimit
## Their Scope in New Testament Thought*

It is likely, I know, that many readers - perhaps most - will find them-
sevles in disagreement with the radical thesis I am about to present. But
my hope is that time will not have been wasted - whatever the conclusions reached - because the thesis leads us in any case to ponder, once
more, the very heart of the Gospel.

What I offer for your consideration is the thesis that the word
'punishment' and other words related to it (especially 'retribution')
have, if used in their strictly correct sense, no legitimate place in the
Christian vocabulary. The word 'punishment' is often loosely applied,
it is true, in modern parlance, to suffering inflicted for other purposes -
disciplinary or deterrent. But for such inflictions I believe that it is an
incorrect and misleading term. Similarly, in many places where the
notion of punishment (even if not the actual word) appears in the New
Testament, careful pondering shows that what is meant is, again, not
strictly speaking punishment. There is no denying, however, that there
are further passages in the New Testament where the idea of retribution
is most definitely and deliberately intended. But here, I would dare to
say, the essentially personal character of the Christian gospel is temporarily obscured. In other words, what I want to ask is whether suffering
inflicted for disciplinary and deterrent purposes (which are entirely relevant to the gospel) is not too lightly confused with suffering inflicted
for the purposes of punishment and retribution, so that the latter have
been dragged into a Christian context where they do not properly
belong.

Let me start from what, in England at any rate, is a widely held
view, among Christians as well as others, and from a formulation of it
by a distinguished British theologian, Dr Leonard Hodgson, formerly
Regius Professor of Divinity at Oxford. In his book, *The Doctrine of*

[* Among relevant publications since this paper, note especially W. Moberly,
*The Ethics of Punishment* (London, 1968) and E. Moberly, *Suffering,
Innocent and Guilty* (London, 1978). Cf. pp. 250 ff. below.]

*the Atonement* (London, 1951), embodying the Hale Lectures, Dr Hodgson devotes a considerable section of a chapter (Ch. III) to the subject of punishment and forgiveness. In the course of this he describes punishment as, essentially, the disowning by the community of evil done by its members (p. 57, etc.). By this I think we have to understand that, quite apart from anything that is done to rescue and reform the offender, and quite apart from any action that may be deemed likely to serve as a deterrent to prevent a repetition of the offence – over and above these, and distinguishable from them – Dr Hodgson maintains that a purely *punitive* duty is laid upon the community. Quite apart from their duty to try to reform the offender and their need to protect themselves from again becoming victims of his offence, the members of a society have to maintain the moral standards of that society by expressing their disapproval of the offence: they have formally to repudiate it as something they refuse to accept into their system, by judicially assessing it and awarding an appropriate penalty. Over against the offender's 'Yes' to the offence, the community has a duty to utter its equivalent 'No'.

In an entirely different context, here is a concrete example of the same attitude, though expressed very much more diffidently and without any confessedly Christian presuppositions. It is in a short book-review by Philip Toynbee, which appeared in *The Observer* for the 11th June, 1961. The book under review was *The Case of Adolf Eichmann* by Victor Gollancz – a moving plea against Eichmann's trial and, most of all, against his execution. The reviewer went a long way with Gollancz, but, at the end, came to precisely the point which I am raising. 'Mr Gollancz', he wrote,

> points out that it would be absurd to defend the trial of Eichmann on deterrent grounds: it would, I think, be almost equally difficult to defend it on reformatory grounds. But are there other legitimate grounds for the infliction of punishment by human beings on one of their kind? Retribution is an ugly and an arrogant word, but are we quite sure that punishment is morally improper simply *qua* punishment? Are we quite sure that our motives are *only* bad when we feel indignant that some evil-doer has 'got away with it'? Does Eichmann deserve at least his arrest and trial simply because it is, in however helpless a way, *fitting* that he should be exposed to the world for what he is or was? I can only say that I am *not* sure about these points . . .

Now, all of us, I know, can understand that reviewer's instinctive query and Hodgson's reasoned affirmation. But, nevertheless, I venture to think that this sense of the fittingness of retribution and the idea that punishment is proper, simply *qua* punishment, do need to be challenged in the name of personal values and, especially, in the name of the Christian gospel. I want to ask whether there is any room at all for this principle inside the good news of the death and resurrection of Jesus Christ, or, indeed, inside any relationship between persons as persons. May it not be one of those alien bits of secularism and sub-personal standards that still adhere to thinking that has got beyond their stage, and subtly cloud the issue?

The facts may, I hope, become clearer if, for a start, we look briefly at two famous New Testament themes - namely, the wrath of God, and sacrifice.

About wrath, ὀργή, it seems to me that three things may be said by anyone who presupposes the long and familiar debate round the word. The first is that it is probably a mistake to imagine that Paul - let alone any other New Testament writer - thought of ὀργή impersonally. As D. E. H. Whiteley, one of the most recent writers to discuss the word, says: 'When he [Paul] says "wrath", he means "wrath of God", though he seldom includes the words "of God". In referring to what *we* should call "impersonal, automatic" processes, he employs "personal" language'.[1] In this, Whiteley follows C. K. Barrett[2] and others against C. H. Dodd.[3] The second thing that may be said (again, with Whiteley)[4] is that - for Paul, at any rate, ὀργή relates not to a *feeling* (*affectus*) in God, but to his *action* (*effectus*). In this, Whiteley is in agreement with Dodd. Thus, thirdly, even if ὀργή is not merely some impersonal phenomenon but is *God's* ὀργή, we are still not compelled to assume that it must be retributive and punitive - least of all, if it denotes less a *feeling* than an *action*. If God has willed the dire consequences that ensue on sin, it does not necessarily follow that he has willed them retributively, punitively. It may be that he has willed them as the only way of doing justice to the freedom and responsibility of the human personality, as he has created it. There are, it is true, passages, as we shall shortly remind ourselves, where the sense seems, in fact, to be retributive, but they are strikingly few, and I shall argue that they are not really integrated with the logic of the gospel. Indeed, I suspect that, once we have eliminated *affectus* in favour of *effectus*, we have logically eliminated any need to associate punishment in its strict sense with ὀργή.

1 *The Theology of St Paul* (Oxford, 1964), p. 67.
2 *The Epistle to the Romans* (London, 1957), p. 33.
3 *The Epistle to the Romans* (London, 1932), pp. 21 f.    4 *Theology*, 69.

About sacrifice, I have written at some length elsewhere.[5] Very briefly, I would submit that, although it is *possible* to interpret the ritual and cultic offering to God of material objects - animal or other - as a gesture of pure adoration, it is, in the main, extremely difficult to dissociate from the word sacrifice, and from the action we so denote, the notion of bribery and barter and propitiation. If the word sacrifice has, in fact, been rescued from these associations, that is due to the astounding discovery that God himself initiates, provides, and, indeed, offers the sacrifice - the discovery adumbrated by Hebrew prophecy and implemented in Jesus Christ. But in so far as God's initiative does become evident - in so far as he is thus revealed as the subject rather than the object of the action - the notion of sacrifice, in any cultic sense, is correspondingly weakened. And precisely because the initiative is God's, it becomes impossible any longer at all to think of him as requiring to be propitiated or capable of being bribed. The language of sacrifice is, indeed, used metaphorically in the New Testament of the death of Christ, but comparatively seldom, and, in terms of Christ offering sacrifice to God, only in Eph. v. 2 and in Heb.[6] And the root ἱλασκ- is notoriously stood on its head by the New Testament, so that it can no longer logically be rendered by words of propitiation. Sacrificial language is used metaphorically also of the self-dedication of Christians to the service of God. But, for both these actions - Christ's and ours - the word 'sacrifice' tends to be misleading, because it is so heavily charged with notions of propitiation and satisfaction - terms which consort badly with an action initiated by God himself and effected at his own infinite cost.

It may be that the cultic language of sacrifice is still the only language which sufficiently preserves the idea of adoration and worship and dedication on man's side, but I have my doubts. Costly self-surrender must surely be capable of being described in other ways. Meanwhile, the matter is at any rate germane to our inquiry, because the more cleanly and clearly the notion of compensation and satisfaction is eradicated from the Christian doctrine of atonement, the less clouded will be the issue about the place of retribution inside the gospel. If words like 'compensation' and 'satisfaction' could be successfully specialized, so as to relate exclusively to what has to be done in order to restore the wrong-doer to his proper personhood, to his full stature and dignity as a responsible person, then they would be tolerable - perhaps even

5 *The Parish Communion Today,* ed. D. M. Paton (London, 1962), pp. 78 ff. [pp. 287 ff. below.]
6 ix. 14, x. 10, 14.

238

desirable. But it seems to me extremely difficult to detach them from the suggestion of compensation and satisfaction to a feudal lord for injuries done to him; and this is something which is alien to the gospel. With this preliminary, we come specifically to the question of rewards and punishments.

It seems, at first sight, that, in the Gospels, at any rate – most obviously in the parables, but also in many other contexts – we are moving in the realm of quantitative justice, and that the language of retribution, of penalty and punitive measures, as also of reward and merit, is here, at any rate, perfectly clear – indeed, inescapable.

Even here, however, in the Gospels, I question whether, on closer scrutiny, one is not driven to recognize that what is described (though less often than we sometimes think) in popular terms of reward and punishment is (usually, at least) something much more organically related to the actions and attitudes in question than these words suggest. It may be that the language of reward and punishment may only be used in these passages because it is the plain man's way of talking – perhaps the plain man's only way of understanding. But, if so, it is so rough and ready that it needs much qualification and amplification the moment one attempts to be more precise.

For instance, in Lk. xiv. 12–14 Jesus is represented as saying that one should give generous meals not to the rich who might offer hospitality in return but to the poor, because then one will be rewarded (ἀνταποδοθήσεται) at the resurrection of the just. But this is not necessarily different from saying that virtue is its own reward. 'Reward' in its normal sense is a mercenary word, and the mercenary-minded would be intolerably bored by the resurrection of the just – by heaven. The very notion of heaven compels us to transvalue the word 'reward' by some such paradox as this. Similarly, the so-called 'rewards' named in the beatitudes, and the so-called 'penalties' in the corresponding woes in the Lucan version, are not mercenarily or arbitrarily fixed. They are organically related to the attitudes for which they are so-called 'rewards' and 'penalties'. The avaricious, because they are avaricious, do not know how to enjoy anything other than material riches: they already have (ἀπέχετε, Lk. vi. 24 f.) the only 'reward' they are capable of receiving. Conversely, it is because the poor and the distressed may become thereby aware of their dependence on God that they, as a class, are capable of the permanent and inexhaustible riches of fellowship with him.

There are exceptions, and Luke, in particular is prone to quantitative ideas, but there are instances of the same paradoxical use of mercenary terms in Tannaitic literature. Morton Smith[7] quotes the saying: 'The pay for a commandment is a commandment, and the pay for a transgression is a transgression'. It is difficult, as matter of fact, to find more than a few parallels from the New Testament to the use of 'pay' in a sinister sense (*in malam partem*), to denote the results of sin. Acts i. 18 (Judas ἐκτήσατο χωρίον ἐκ μισθοῦ τῆς ἀδικίας) is not an instance, for there the μισθός evidently means the literal silver he was paid by the Jewish authorities for betraying Jesus; and II Pet. ii. 13 ἀδικούμενοι μισθὸν ἀδικίας is too obscure for us to be confident. I can think of no more than three clear examples – though two of them are very striking. The first is in Rom. i. 27, where homosexuals are described as τὴν ἀντιμισθίαν ἣν ἔδει τῆς πλάνης αὐτῶν ἐν ἑαυτοῖς ἀπολαμβάνοντες, '... paid in their own persons the fitting wage ...' (New English Bible). The second is in Rom. vi. 23, where the contrast between the two halves of the verse is instructive: τὰ γὰρ ὀψώνια τῆς ἁμαρτίας θάνατος, τὸ δὲ χάρισμα τοῦ θεοῦ ζωὴ αἰώνιος ἐν Χριστῷ Ἰησοῦ τῷ κυρίῳ ἡμῶν. This is perhaps a deliberate attempt to express the ruthlessly mercenary nature of sin as an employer and to contrast this with God's huge generosity which makes terms of merit or reward on God's side wholly ridiculous. The New English Bible translation sharpens the contrast: 'For sin pays a wage, and the wage is death, but God gives freely, and his gift is eternal life ...'. Thirdly, there is Heb. ii. 2, which says that, even under the Mosaic Law, every disobedience received its appropriate requital – ἔνδικον μισθαποδοσίαν. Of course, there are other passages where the same idea is expressed without precisely the 'pay' metaphor (e.g. II Thess. i. 6, ἀνταποδοῦναι). But these are not relevant to the present point.

Thus, the New Testament uses the 'reward' metaphor seldom for the consequences of evil; and whatever use it makes of it for good, is offset by such passages as the one just quoted from Rom. vi, where the utterly paradoxical, unmerited graciousness of God is stressed; and, in any case, the New Testament uses the metaphor in such a way as to show that it is really inadequate for its theme.

Even in the parables, where one might expect the vividly pictorial presentation to employ this sort of language extensively, it is comparatively restrained. To say, for instance, as in Lk. xvi. 19 ff., that a person who is blind to the needs of the beggar on his doorstep is bound to

---

7 'Tannaitic Parallels to the Gospels', *J. B. L. Monographs* 6 (1951), 64. For other similar sources, see the bibliography in R. Schnackenburg's *Die Sittliche Botschaft des Neuen Testamentes* (München, 1962), 122, n. 15, where Schnackenburg also criticizes Morton Smith.

suffer irreparable remorse - indeed, that regard would not otherwise have been paid to his responsibility as a person, and that there is no way of forcibly making a man do good without violating that personal responsibility - is not the same thing as saying that he *deserves* this pain *as a punishment*, or that it has been determined *as a punishment* for such conduct. Again, the parables of Matt. xiii merely describe consequences: the wheat is garnered and the weeds are burned; and 'that is where the weeping and the gnashing of teeth will be'. There are other parables in which the 'rewards' and 'punishments', so-called, are as thinly disguised as in the beatitudes. The parable of the money in trust, for instance, is - at least on its 'rewarding' side - notoriously like that Tannaitic saying I quoted just now. The 'pay' for the 'commandment' to use the money well, turned out to be another 'commandment' to exercise the same acumen and diligence in a still wider sphere. Virtue has, in that sense, become its own reward. Even in the allegory of the sheep and the goats, the two classes are merely invited into the kingdom or ordered off to misery. It is true that that misery is described as 'prepared' for them (τὸ πῦρ τὸ αἰώνιον τὸ ἡτοιμασμένον τῷ διαβόλῳ καὶ τοῖς ἀγγέλοις αὐτοῦ, Matt. xxv. 41, cf. 46);[8] and it is perfectly true that, in such a hint as this, and occasionally elsewhere, the dire consequences of wrong are described as penalties judicially imposed. For instance, two undeniable examples are Matt. xviii. 35, οὕτως καὶ ὁ πατήρ μου ὁ οὐράνιος ποιήσει ὑμῖν, i.e. something comparable to the enraged king who ordered the unforgiving servant off to the torturers; and the savage finale to Luke's version of the money in trust, Lk. xix. 27: πλὴν τοὺς ἐχθρούς μου τοὺς μὴ θελήσαντάς με βασιλεῦσαι ἐπ' αὐτοὺς ἀγάγετε ὧδε καὶ κατασφάξατε αὐτοὺς ἔμπροσθέν μου. Here, too, it must be added that Luke manifests (whether by selecting traditions or by his own shaping of them I will not here discuss) a clearer tendency towards a quantitative scheme of justice and responsibility than the others. Lk. xii. 47 f. definitely assumes degrees of responsibility and of deserts: to know one's duty and to neglect it deserves a severer flogging than unwitting failure. To have more gifts is to be more responsible. The same principle is implied in Acts iii. 17, where Peter says that he knows it was in ignorance that the Jews killed Jesus.[9] Again it is in Luke (if it

---

8 Cf. the similar use of ἐτοιμάξειν *in bonam partem*, in Matt. xx. 23, ‖ Mk x. 40.

9 D. Daube has observations on this principle in Judaism, e.g. ' "For they know not what they do": Luke 23, 34', in *Studia Patristica* IV = *T.U.* 79 (1961), 58 ff. But all this, I think, is exception rather than rule in the Gospels as a whole.

is an original reading - though this is doubtful) that we find (xxiii. 34), 'Father, forgive them, for they know not what they do' - a prayer which in this respect contrasts, as a matter of fact, with the unconditional prayer of Stephen (Acts vii. 60), 'Lay not this sin to their charge'. There is also, in Lk. xxiii. 41, the dying robber's statement that, while Jesus suffers innocently, he and his companion deserve all that they get (καὶ ἡμεῖς μὲν δικαίως, ἄξια γὰρ ὧν ἐπράξαμεν ἀπολαμβάνομεν). But I believe it is fair to say that this kind of thing is the exception rather than the rule, even in the realm of parable, where, in any case, we have learnt to accept the picture as a whole, and not press details in an allegorical spirit.

Thus far, our discussion of the language of reward and punishment in the New Testament has chiefly concentrated on the traditions of the words of Jesus. Apart from my excursion into the meaning of ὀργή and of sacrificial terms, I have stayed inside the dominical traditions. You will be asking when I am going to face the evidence of the rest of the New Testament. The answer is 'Now'; and my conclusion will be that there are passages, indeed, which are quite clearly retributive and even vindictive; but, once again, that they are fewer and more limited than is sometimes imagined; and, as I believe, peripheral and alien to a strict exposition of the Gospel.

Before we look at the passages in question, I beg you to remember that I am at no point denying - who in his senses could? - that, throughout the New Testament, dire consequences are attached to sin; neither am I saying that these are not 'willed' by God. That sin leads to suffering, and that, without suffering, there is no reconciliation, nobody could hope to deny. Precisely because God's grace is, by definition, respectful towards personality and recognizes the dignity and responsibility of a free person, it cannot 'pauperize' the recipient. Grace is stern, it is challenge and demand, precisely by reason of its generous concern for the whole, undiminished entirety of personhood. But to say that is not the same thing as saying that punishment, penalty, retribution belong within the compass of grace, any more than reward does, except in the extremely paradoxical senses already indicated.

With that reminder, we face the chief passages outside the Gospels in which punitive words are used with precision and cannot but imply a definite notion of retribution.

(1) In Rom. ii. 5-11 Paul is in what anyone belonging to a Reformed tradition might be tempted to call a distinctly unpauline mood. He speaks quite specifically in terms of retributive justice: *v.* 6, God will give everyone his due (ἀποδώσει), each in proportion to his deeds (κατὰ

τὰ ἔργα αὐτοῦ).¹⁰ To those who, by patiently doing good, seek glory and honour and immortality he will give eternal life; to those whose concern is nothing but self-interest (τοῖς ἐξ ἐριθείας) and who reject truth and accept falsehood he will give ὀργή and θυμός (v. 8) ... For God is impartial in his verdicts (οὐ γάρ ἐστιν προσωπολημψία παρὰ τῷ θεῷ, v. 11). In short, the theme of the whole paragraph is God's exact justice - δικαιοκρισία (v. 6). Well: justification by works! But it has always been recognized that, in these opening sections of his mightiest epistle, the Apostle is building up a massive indictment against mankind, Jew and Gentile alike, and is arguing from the premises accepted by anyone who recognizes a moral code.¹¹ It is not until we are shown to be all alike legally without defence that the good news of grace is introduced. In a sense, therefore, this section is deliberately taking up a pre-evangelic, pre-Christian standpoint.

I am not pretending by this that Paul at any point consciously repudiates the system of justice it implies; but it is worth observing that the point at which he develops to its extreme a system which, as I am arguing, has no real place within a fully personal relationship, is precisely the point at which he is consciously taking a pre-Christian stance - as it were, deliberately leaving the Gospel out of account for a while.

(2) Not so, however, the next passage, Rom. xii. 19-21. Whatever this means in detail, nobody can deny that it is firmly within a confessedly Christian standpoint. And it is here that the same note of retribution occurs, with a quotation again, as in Rom. ii, from the Old Testament; ἐμοὶ ἐκδίκησις, ἐγὼ ἀνταποδώσω is quoted (v. 19) with approval from the Pentateuch. It is perfectly clear that, while Christians are here forbidden to vindicate themselves by retaliation (μὴ ἑαυτοὺς ἐκδικοῦντες, v. 19), this is not because vindication, as such, is deemed undesirable, but because the proper person to achieve it is God himself. The phrase δότε τόπον τῇ ὀργῇ is extremely difficult to interpret in any sense except 'give *God's* wrath room' - stand aside and let God wreak vengeance.¹²

K. Stendahl, in a very forceful article,¹³ maintains that we must face the fact that, as in much of the Old Testament and Qumran, so in Paul,

10 Cf. II Tim. iv. 14.
11 In the same section of Romans, another clear example of the retributive idea of *deserving* is Rom. i. 32, οἱ τὰ τοιαῦτα πράσσοντες ἄξιοι θανάτου εἰσίν.
12 Cf. 1 Sam. xxvi:18, Sir. xix:17.
13 'Hate, Non-Retaliation, and Love', *H.T.R.* 1, 4 (Oct., 1962), 343 ff.

there is no feeling that the Lord's enemies ought to be spared, but rather a confident expectation of the vindication of the Lord's own against them. The New English Bible hints that the Pentateuchal affirmations are intended to be transcended and replaced by a better way at the point at which Paul goes on to quote Prov. xxv. 21 f., 'If your enemy hungers, feed him', etc. In the Greek, this quotation is introduced merely by ἀλλά. The New English Bible expands the ἀλλά to 'But there is another text'. Stendahl objects[14] that there is no instance to support such a translation, and that the ἀλλά must be either a straight adversative, giving the correct alternative to self-vindication, or else a heightening particle (meaning, I suppose, something like 'No: rather, if your enemy hungers, you must feed him'). I think that Stendahl is probably right grammatically. I only wonder whether the New English Bible may not be right *as a paraphrase*, and whether Paul, by his very introduction of the Proverbs passage and by his application of it, is not giving a new meaning to retaliation. Are we bound to accept Stendahl's paraphrase of the idea in σωρεύσεις:[15] 'If you act in non-retaliation, your good deeds are stored up as a further accusation against your enemy for the day of Wrath to which you should defer all judgment'? May it not be (even if we abandon the New English Bible's rendering of ἀλλά) that Paul is *reinterpreting* vengeance in terms of remorse? And, if so, remorse being capable of leading to penitence, it would no longer be necessary to regard this sort of 'retaliation' as retributive or vindictive. Paul's climactic summary (*v.* 21), μὴ νικῶ ὑπὸ τοῦ κακοῦ, ἀλλὰ νίκα ἐν τῷ ἀγαθῷ τὸ κακόν is suggestive - particularly when the object of conquest is carefully placed in the neuter - τὸ κακόν.

I am bound to say that what looks like a dreadfully vindictive passage seems, after all, to be not far from that paradoxical transvaluation which we have already watched in the Gospel sayings; and I am not persuaded by Stendahl's closing remark,[16] that perhaps even in the Sermon on the Mount the injunction to non-resistance ought similarly to be interpreted as meant to point to the quickest way to vengeance.

(3) But now, thirdly, within the Pauline corpus, we come to II Thess. i. 5-11. The authenticity of this epistle is sometimes questioned, but I have never been able to find persuasive grounds for believing that it is not Pauline. If it is Pauline, it strikes a distinct discord in the Pauline symphony. Within the space of these few verses we have a number of phrases specifically welcoming revenge.

14 *H.T.R.* 1, 4 (1962), 346, n. 9.
15 *H.T.R.* 1, 4 (1962), 348.
16 *H.T.R.* 1, 4 (1962), 355.

The theme is that the Christians are to face their sufferings with a good heart, because these are evidence, not that God is unjust but, on the contrary, that he is just: they are (*v.* 5) ἔνδειγμα τῆς δικαίας κρίσεως τοῦ θεοῦ, and they are going to result in the Christian' being deemed worthy of God's Kingdom (εἰς τὸ καταξιωθῆναι ὑμᾶς τῆς βασιλείας τοῦ θεοῦ); for (*v.* 6) it is only fair (δίκαιον) if God compensates (ἀνταποδοῦναι) with anguish (θλίψις) those who are anguishing them (τοῖς θλίβουσιν ὑμᾶς), and compensates with relief (ἄνεσις) those who are now enduring anguish. For the Lord Jesus will be revealed in (or, accompanied by?) a flame of fire, dealing vengeance (διδόντος ἐκδίκησιν) to those who do not know God or obey the gospel. These (*v.* 9) shall pay the penalty of eternal destruction, excluded from his presence (or destruction which proceeds from before him?), δίκην τίσουσιν ὄλεθρον αἰώνιον ἀπὸ προσώπου τοῦ κυρίου. Short of certain parts of the Apocalypse, this comes as near as anything in the New Testament to the vindictive gloating of a Tertullian. The interesting thing is that in this respect it is unique in the Pauline corpus.

(4) Going outside Paul, we meet, first, in Heb. x. 29, the only New Testament occurrence of τιμωρία, 'penalty', and it is used with a word of deserving: if law was ruthless in the Mosaic dispensation, πόσῳ δοκεῖτε χείρονος ἀξιωθήσεται τιμωρίας . . ., how much worse a penalty will be deserved, do you think, by the apostate from Christianity? There is no vindictiveness here, only dread of apostasy, but the language of deserving and of retribution is plain enough. Three times in the same epistle - and, in the New Testament, only here - occurs the word μισθαποδοσία. It occurs at ii. 2, where it is in the rare sense of penalty. The other two are *in bonam partem* - x. 35, do not cast away your confidence (παρρησία), for it carries a high remuneration; and xi. 26. Moses counting the stigma of the Christ (τὸν ὀνειδισμὸν τοῦ Χριστοῦ) greater riches than all the treasures of Egypt, because his eyes were on the recompense (ἀπέβλεπεν γὰρ εἰς τὴν μισθαποδοσίαν). These last two uses fall easily inside the category of metaphor which we found in the Gospels, and there is no need to interpret them in a mercenary way. The remuneration of παρρησία (boldness and unashamed Christian confession) and of accepting the stigma of being a follower of the Messiah is a fuller realization of the same - it is fellowship with the Christ, not some arbitrary prize.

So far as our concern goes, then, Hebrews yields us one definite phrase of deserving punishment: not a very large result.

(5) II Peter and Jude furnish notorious examples of a retributory justice. Not that in II Pet. ii. 4-9 God is spoken of, as clearly as one

might expect, as bringing retributory punishment on evil. He is said to have brought disaster on the rebellious angels and the antediluvian world and Sodom and Gomorrah, and thus to have judged them (*v.* 6, κατέκρινεν) and made an example of them (*v.* 6, ὑπόδειγμα . . . τεθεικώς). It is not till *v.* 9 that we meet the phrase about keeping the wicked under chastisement until the day of judgement (ἀδίκους . . . εἰς ἡμέραν κρίσεως κολαζομένους τηρεῖν). But the tone of the passage is vindictive, as in that of –

(6) the more condensed phrase in the corresponding passage in Jude 7: πρόκεινται δεῖγμα πυρὸς αἰωνίου δίκην ὑπέχουσαι.

Finally, (7), the Apocalypse contains a number of not only retributive but positively vindictive passages. There is no lack of emphasis on the necessity for Christians to *suffer*, like their Lord and Master; and there is no suggestion in the Apocalypse (a point sometimes forgotten) that Christians ought ever to resist the secular power. They are to suffer passively; and the blood of the martyrs, like the blood of the Lamb, is supremely powerful. But, although the blood of the Lamb has indeed redeemed the Christian community, it is now viewed as powerful, not to redeem the enemies of Christ, but to smash them with a rod of iron; and there is never any sign of doubt that that is what they deserve.

This is too familiar a fact to need illustrating at length. Let me remind you simply of xvi. 5 f., δίκαιος εἶ, ὁ ὢν καὶ ὁ ἦν, ὁ ὅσιος, ὅτι ταῦτα ἔκρινας, ὅτι . . . αἷμα αὐτοῖς δέδωκας πεῖν· ἄξιοί εἰσιν; and xix. 1 f., where there is an exultant shout of 'Alleluia!' in Heaven, because God, in his justice, ἐξεδίκησεν τὸ αἷμα τῶν δούλων αὐτοῦ ἐκ χειρὸς αὐτῆς (that is, the Great Whore). In the light of such passages, I find it almost impossible to believe (much as I should like to) that the blood that flows like a great river out of the winepress of the wrath of God, in xiv. 20 is – by a splendid paradox – meant by the Apocalyptist to be the redemptive blood of the suffering Christ. This has been suggested – but can it be so?

This, I believe, completes my review of the main passages of the sort we are considering. There are undoubtedly scattered phrases here and there which could be added to the list, but I do not believe that they would amount to anything considerable. What conclusions, then, is it legitimate to draw?

One thing, I think, is undeniable, namely, that the New Testament writers as a whole (not least St Paul himself) do their thinking in a framework of ideas in which quantitative justice and retribution are axiomatic. Indeed, for the most part, their framework is that of the Old Testament Law; and if there is any reason to think of St Luke as a Gentile (though this is being questioned by some), it is remarkable that his writing, even more than those of known Jews, shows particularly clearly, as we have seen, the consciousness of a quantitative system.

But, this being so, is it not the more significant that - apparently without realizing it themselves - these writers have so remarkably confined and reduced their expressions of this attitude? The passages we have considered where retribution *in its strict sense* is favoured are comparatively few, and mostly evoked by the stress of persecution and set in a context of apocalyptic. The language of punishment and retribution, also, is strikingly confined. ποινή does not so much as occur in the New Testament; τιμωρία occurs only in Heb. x. 29 (the verb, τιμωρεῖν, being applied only to Paul's persecution of Christians before his conversion - Acts xxii. 5, xxvi. 11); κόλασις - except in I Jo. iv. 18, where it is specifically criticized, comes only once again, in Matt. xxv. 46; κολάζεσθαι (apart from Acts iv. 21, where it describes what the opponents of Christianity wanted to do) comes only in II Pet. ii. 9; and, in any case, it is a neutral word for the infliction of pain, without necessarily carrying retributive notions. It can easily be reformatory. The same applies to ζημία and ζημιοῦσθαι, which denote deprivation, for whatever reason - it could be deterrent (as in a fine) or educative.

Am I, then asking you to believe that the deliberate infliction of suffering has no place in a Christian society? Am I an eccentric, advocating the removal of sanctions from community life? Indeed not! What I am trying to say can, I hope, be gathered up in a few sentences as follows.

(1) First, I am pleading for a clear recognition of distinctions between the various purposes for which suffering may be deliberately inflicted - by God on man, or by man on man.

Ignoring mere cruelty, suffering may be deliberately inflicted with the hope of reforming and educating the offender, or in order to deter from a repetition of the offence. Both these motives, I would say, are perfectly compatible with the Gospel - indeed, required by it. But there is a third motive - that of seeing justice done or causing it to be seen that justice has been done. This motive - distinguishable from the other two - concerns abstract justice; it is essentially retributive and retaliatory; and it is the appropriateness of this motive within a Christian system that I am questioning. The best that can be said for it, I fancy, is (what I quoted L. Hodgson as saying) that it may be the only way of maintaining standards, the only way in which a community can say 'We disapprove of this action'. But I fail to see that that declaration is not already implied by the other two motives. If a community tries to reclaim and reform the offender and to prevent a repetition of the offence, surely that is a clear enough expression of its disapproval.

You may say, the one amounts to the other - so why quibble? I reply, because the satisfaction of abstract justice (although in many cases it may. *look* (and, indeed, feel!) exactly the same and take exactly the same *forms* as the others) is a sub-personal motive; and to allow it into one's scheme of thought does, in the end, distort one's judgement and one's idea both of God and man.

(2) For, secondly, the moment one comes to the level of personal relations - and, most of all (so far as one can conceive them) to the absolute heights of the love of God - mere justice ceases to be relevant. The father of the prodigal son does not say, 'Here comes my son: before I receive him back, I must secure that the family sees justice done'.

(3) Instead - and this is my third point - whereas the suffering involved in a reconciliation is almost infinitely intensified, it is never, when we stand inside the Gospel, *retributive* suffering. Suffering there is in plenty. If a reconciliation could be effected without suffering, it would not be a reconciliation between persons. (The only painless reconciliation I can think of is a mathematical one - as between two columns of figures in an account-book.) A person is, by definition, responsible. If he has committed an offence, he cannot be restored to fellowship until he has accepted the pain of responsibility for his offence and (so far as possible) made reparation. Anything less would be a diminution of his personality. To demand of him less would not be 'grace', it would be insult. But his responsibility is not to some abstract system of justice: it is to God and to his fellow-men. That, and nothing abstract or sub-personal, is the measure of his responsibility. On the side of the injured party - who, ultimately, is God himself - the suffering of forgiveness is boundless. This, too, is the cost involved in the structure of personal relationship, as God has created it.

But, on both sides, the suffering is creative and restorative and healing, and in obedience not to abstract laws of justice but to the demands of the living organism of persons which is most characteristically represented by the Body of Christ. That is why I also query the ultimate appropriateness of a word like 'sacrifice' in its strict sense.

Therefore - to conclude - while I say, with deep conviction, 'I do not deserve God's love', that is not because I have fallen short of some divine code of laws, but because love, by definition, cannot be *deserved* (least of all infinite, divine love). And, accordingly, I am not sure that it is a Christian attitude to say 'I deserve damnation' either. Certainly I may be on my way to damnation as long as I reject God's love, as long as I remain ungrateful and unresponsive; for to be my true self is to respond to God's love, and to fail to respond is to forfeit selfhood. But I doubt if *deserve* or *merit* is the right word on the debit side of the account, any more than it is on the credit side. ἄξιος is doubtfully at home in the Christian vocabulary except in the cry of pure *adoration* – 'Worthy is the Lamb . . .!'. In a word, I am asking whether there is any *ultimate* obligation or moral imperative (however necessary intermediate sanctions may be for the time being) except the obligation to gratitude, which is a personal, not a legal, response. Many other, and secondary, levels of obligation may in fact be needed as scaffolding (so to speak), to build the ultimate structure; a legal code may help, as a temporary crutch, to attain to the level of personal relationship. But the moment we use the secondary as primary and normative and confuse ends with means, we are on the less than Christian track; and this applies as much to the principles and motives behind a so-called penal code as to a preaching of the Gospel in terms of penal substitution.

# 18

## The Theology of Forgiveness

It would be difficult to name an aspect of Christian theology that is wider or more demanding than the theology of forgiveness. To plumb its depths would require not only immense learning and mature thought: it would require also an exceptionally wide pastoral experience. Also, I believe that only he can speak authentically about forgiveness who has himself been greatly forgiven; and, however deeply I may need forgiveness, I do not believe that I have yet begun to understand more than the fringes of the experience. On many counts, then, I am disqualified for anything more than a fragment, at most, of this big task. But I accepted the invitation gratefully because there is a thing that, I hope, I may be able to do - namely, to contribute something towards the definition and clarification of one particular problem in the understanding of forgiveness. It is a problem which happens to be a special concern of mine, and I have more than once before ventured (no doubt rashly) into print about it,[1] and I am not loath to try again to present it. I believe it to be of considerable pastoral and practical importance, though this will not, I fear, be immediately evident. What I am going to say may well sound abstract and academic. But if you will bear with me I hope it will become clear that an understanding of the atonement and of our ministry of reconciliation depends, in some degree at least, upon the clarity with which we grasp the issues in question.

The problem I have in mind may be called that of compensation. Forgiveness is, by definition, free: it is an act of grace or mercy; it is a gift. Yet equally, it is very widely held that an offence requires to be paid for by the offender: repentance is costly. Is there, then, after all, a transaction involved in forgiveness, and is it a matter of barter?

---

1 'Punishment and Retribution: an attempt to delimit their scope in New Testament thought', *Svensk Exegetisk Årsbok* 30 (1965), 21 ff. [pp. 235 ff. above]; 'The Christian Understanding of Forgiveness', *Theology*, 71, 580 (October 1968), 435 ff.

The problem in question thus concerns the propriety of applying quantitative ideas (such as 'cost') to the attempt to analyse the process of forgiveness and reconciliation. And here, as I see it, there are two principles in apparent tension against one another. On the one hand, it is a wholly inadequate - indeed, a stultifying and self-contradictory - notion of forgiveness that sees it as the settling of a credit and debit account, as though the offender paid and the injured party was then satisfied. That may be what happens when an offence is dealt with on the level of legal proceedings, but it is certainly remote from what happens on the level of personal relations when an estrangement is healed. On the other hand, sin seems to be so momentous and its results so objective that it is difficult to describe a breach of personal relationships without having recourse to the notion of a 'quantum' - a measurable amount - of damage, which cannot be ignored, but has to be compensated by an equivalent amount of repair before it can be healed. Both these aspects of the matter concern personal relationship; but in the former case quantitative ideas of debt and payment are manifestly out of place; whereas in the latter case it is difficult to safeguard the objective seriousness of sin without quantitative language. The relation between two persons cannot be described quantitatively, and yet the measure of the offence somehow needs to be taken. I believe that a formula can be found which does justice to both these considerations and to the reality they attempt to describe, but I think that it needs careful definition; and I believe that the attempt to reach such definition does help to deepen understanding and to resolve some problems in the Christian interpretation of atonement. That is why I hope that, ultimately, this will be a great deal more than a merely academic inquiry. It will affect, in the last analysis, the theory and practice both of pastoral care and of legislation.

That a credit-and-debit way of speaking is out of place on the personal level of forgiveness, repentance, and reconciliation is obvious enough. Forgiveness, I repeat, is, by definition, free. Indeed, the first and most difficult lesson that an offender has to learn is that he cannot deserve or earn forgiveness. Forgiveness would not be forgiveness if it were offered as a *quid pro quo*. The offender may make material reparation for any material damage he may have caused; but, if he is to be forgiven by the person he has offended against, he must be humble enough to accept the forgiveness *gratis* and not try to pretend he can earn it. This is exactly what St Paul's doctrine of justification by grace through faith is urging in regard to divine forgiveness. The response is by faith; but the offer is *gratis*, it is sheer generosity, it is grace. By the same token, there is (as far as I can see) no place at all in a Christian understanding of forgiveness for the forgiving person to indulge in retaliation, reprisals, or punishment, as such. The exclusion of punishment and its bracketing with retaliation and reprisals may surprise some of us. But I do exclude it, and rank it side by side with those others, because, ordinarily at least, the word 'punishment' implies some satisfaction of abstract justice, over and above whatever infliction may be necessary for educating the offender or deterring him and others from repeating the offence. And, whereas a 'penalty', in the commonly understood sense, may help to bring home to the offender his responsiblity and to discourage further offences, the demand for satisfaction as such – the infliction of punishment in the name, not of education or deterrence but of retribution or abstract justice – seems to be quite outside the realm of the reconciliation of two persons.

Thus, on the level of the relationship itself between persons, quantitative ideas seem simply not appropriate – indeed, positively false. Forgiveness is not logical and quantitative: it is always a miracle of free grace. Tit for tat is no part of forgiveness and repentance – even if the *lex talionis* was originally a great advance beyond the jungle law of vendetta. On the other hand – and this is an important part of my contention – there appears to be as strict a natural law of cause and effect (still on the level of personal relations) as anywhere else – so strict that it does not seem inappropriate to describe it, albeit metaphorically, in terms of a sort of conservation of energy. It is as ineluctable as Karma or Nemesis. What I mean is that a breach of fellowship by some offence commited by one person against another is comparable to a quite objective – if you like, quantitative – disturbance of the total equilibrium. The destructive energy of sin – of a violation of a personal relationship – is something that cannot be counteracted except by the ouput of an equivalent energy of repair. The impact of the offence sends out ripples which must somehow, somewhere, be accounted for – either bounced back in retaliation, or else absorbed – if the equilibrium is to be restored. Or – to change the metaphor – the ravages of disease have to be countered by the corrective activity of all the leucocytes and lymphocytes and the rest of the militia that the body calls into action until the crisis is over. The process, in other words, is a matter of energy pitted against equivalent energy.

So there is our dilemma. On the one hand there is this doctrine of free, unconditional forgiveness, matched by a penitence which is humble enough to acknowledge that it cannot earn or pay for forgiveness – seemingly a most *un*-quantitative process; but on the other hand is the need for an estimate of the character of sin, so realistic and objective and serious, that it has to resort to analogies of the quantitative type in order to safeguard *quanti ponderis sit peccatum* (to quote the inevitable tag). And I suggest that it is the failure to bring these two considerations together into a single, realistic system that is partly responsible for the fact that different Christian theories of the atonement come into collision with one another. A crude doctrine of a feudal God who demands a penalty to be undergone by Jesus Christ as satisfaction, before he can forgive the sins of mankind, is monstrous and clearly unacceptable. But it is because any alternative may appear to be unrealistic in its estimate of the objective seriousness of sin that suspicion is apt to fall on theories which reject the penal element.

By way of attempting a single system which will do justice to the realities both of the mystery of free grace and of the measurable force and objective 'quantum' that is sin, I suggest a distinction between motives and consequences or between the description of a relationship and the description of the activity of sin; and in the interests of this, a specialized use of the metaphor of cost and expenditure. The point is that sin does have to be 'paid for': that is a true insight. But where we are apt to go wrong in the use of such quantitative terms is in assuming that the payment is bound to be made by the offender (or some representative, acting on his behalf) to the injured one; whereas, in fact, payment has to be made by both of them, the injured party and the offender, to - what shall we say? - God's own system of personal relationship. Forgiveness, real forgiveness, is undoubtedly costly to the forgiver: 'it takes it out of you'. Not that genuine forgiveness can ever be unwillingly offered or can ever have to be dragged out of a man: its essence is that it is an act of spontaneous generosity. The father of a prodigal son, if he is a real father, will run eagerly to meet him and will fling his arms round him. There is nothing quantitative in his motive. But that does not alter the fact that the forgiveness is costly. A generous person is, by definition, one who can feel keenly and who, therefore, can be hurt; and the readiness to forgive is not lightly won: it is part of a character that is subject to great depths of agony. Therefore, into the sheer joy and alacrity of the father's welcome to his son there has gone, and continues to go, any amount of costly pain and suffering and nervous energy, even though this is no conscious part of his intentions. Forgiveness uses you up. It is free, not because it costs nothing, but because the price is willingly, or perhaps even unconsciously, paid by the donor himself.

I hope this is a true account of what happens. If it is, then we are nearer to understanding the quantitative side of the description. As I said, personal relationships are seen to be subject to strict laws of cause and effect such that the impact of sin can be neutralized only by some compensatory action of equivalent weight. And forgiveness and repentance are both costly. Just as the wronged party will be less than his full self as a person if he retaliates and is not willing to pay for his gift of forgiveness, so the offender will be less than his full self if he does not wish to compensate. Notoriously, real repentance 'feels like death'. Repentence cannot take place except by the penitent's stooping low and losing all *amour propre* and giving up all thoughts of deserving forgiveness. And the very repudiation of any attempt to pay turns out (by a strange paradox) to be itself infinitely costly. It involves the painful confession, 'I was wrong. Father, I have sinned: I don't deserve to be your son.' Thus, strangely enough, although forgiveness is a costly gift, purchased by the donor and offered as a gift such as cannot be earned or purchased by the recipient with however costly a satisfaction, yet neither can it be accepted without the cost of the offender's self-esteem. He cannot purchase it for anything, but neither can he receive it as a gift without giving everything of himself. And more: a real forgiveness really received by true repentance means that the offender conceives a burning desire to make reparation and to share the burdens of the one who forgave him. The prodigal son, if he is really penitent, will share with his father in a costly, conciliatory appeal to the scornful elder brother. Though he cannot earn the forgiveness, yet the true penitent does expend all that he has. The original self-concern which, in the process of repentance, is transformed into a concern for the one he has injured, makes the penitent eager to lavish on the one who forgives him all that he has and is.

Thus a process of reconciliation which, by its very nature (being on a fully personal level), is quite beyond a nicely-calculated less or more, may nevertheless be well described (indeed, must be described) in terms of expenditure and cost. But it is not the cost of a debt paid by the debtor to a creditor. Payment does not enter into the motive or the description of the *relationship*. There is an act of free generosity, but it happens to be costly. And cost does enter into the description of the *process*. And there turns out to be a sacrificial output of energy on the other side of the dialogue also. The generosity of forgiveness which is ready to pay the full amount wakes, as it were, an echo from the recipient, and he too gives out all that he has in response. If, in this metaphor of cost or expenditure of energy, there is no transaction between the two parties, neither is there any question of there being a payment to some mythical recipient. This is not a rehabilitation of the crude theory of a ransom paid to the devil. It is not concerned with a decision to pay at all. That is why I said that a specialized use of the metaphor was called for. Rather, it is a physical metaphor of compensation. There is a 'quantum' of energy needed to repair the breach, to restore equilibrium, to heal the disease. If there is payment to anything, it is a payment made by both sides to what I have already alluded to as that system which we believe to be God's own system, by which persons estranged find their full stature as persons reconciled by costly energizing.

Perhaps one might bring the two realms of thought – the non-quantitative and the quantitative – within a single system by saying that, on the personal level, the motive of forgiveness is always to heal and to restore the offender and never to 'take it out of him' by punishment or reprisals or retaliation; and the motive of the true penitent is always to express his love and concern for the one he has injured, not to attempt to make himself worthy (which is impossible); but that, in fact, these two attitudes involve, albeit unconsciously and without any deliberate intention, a process which can only be described as one of balancing, of restoring the equilibrium, of absorbing poison, of neutralizing the disease – use what metaphors you will for the compensation. This would mean that a doctrine of free grace, involving no demand for distributive justice or reparation – indeed, repudiating it – is nevertheless no violation of what we normally call the justice of God, since, when we speak of the justice of God, what we really mean is that it is God's concern that every person should be brought to his full, undiminished stature as a son of God. And such regard for the full stature of personality involves a love which is realistic about the inexorable cost of things; a love which both forgives freely and also is too concerned for the offender's full, responsible personhood to spare him the pain of acknowledging his responsibility and rising to that personhood. It is a love which cuts no corners.

The appropriateness of quantitative language to the process is further illustrated by the very fact that several times already mention has been made of diminishing or enhancing personality. It is a diminution (we may intelligibly say), a reduction of a man's personality if he is not treated as a responsible person. Equally it is a diminution of the injured person's self if he nurses a grudge or demands reprisals or metes out punishment. The persons of both parties will be enhanced and brought to full stature precisely by the non-quantitative attitudes of unconditional, free forgiveness and unlimited repentance. In other words, the non-quantitative motives of personal relations and volition seem nevertheless to be inseparably linked to the quantitative consequences – the waxing and waning of personal stature.

Objectors to my plea for the elimination of punishment (so as to leave only education and deterrence as motives for the infliction of pain on the offender) have sometimes urged that the offender is, as a person, positively owed punishment; indeed, that offenders have been known to ask for punishment, because of an instinctive feeling that they cannot respect themselves again until they have been given what they deserve. In reply I would say that the offender, as a person, can never be owed punishment as such. As a precious, divinely-created person, he is owed only whatever will lift him to his full stature as a person; and, for that end, what is needed is not punishment (which, in ordinary usage at least, means the satisfaction of justice, the assignment of a suitable penalty, the exacting of satisfaction), but rather whatever will bring him to a free acknowledgement of his responsibility and a desire to meet it. This may be achieved by the infliction of pain; or it may be achieved by the refusal to inflict pain. In either case it will be by action aimed at something other than punishment or penalty or retribution or distributive justice, as these words are normally used. As for the offender's longing to recover his self-respect by being allowed to undergo punishment, that (strictly defined) is not the same thing as what I have been calling the desire to make reparation and the urge to give himself. The latter is outward-turned and is the result of true repentance and is a symptom of the humble acceptance of the free gift of pardon. It is essentially other-regarding. The former may be self-regarding, albeit with an enlightened self-regard. It is precisely what St Paul combats in his doctrine of justification by pure grace through faith.

Here I must acknowledge, in parenthesis, that I have been begging a vital question, namely, what is meant by 'personality'. I have been talking of the value of personality as an axiom, and speaking of the diminution of personal stature as axiomatically evil. But I am well aware that personality is a word that can too easily be used as a blank counter in a game without any proper definition. I can only plead that, for the purposes of this discussion, we know what we mean by the ability to be rightly related on the personal level. We can distinguish between autistic behaviour at one end and excessively dependent behaviour at the other. We can recognize, when we see it, a full, integrated personality, combining real independence and initiative with being open and humble towards others and able to live in community. And further, Christians believe that in a sense personality *is* a known entity, since in Jesus Christ the outlines of ideal human personality are revealed.

I turn now, at last and more briefly, to the more strictly theological side of the question. As I said, I am not competent to produce anything approaching a full-scale Christian theology of forgiveness; but I am naturally under an obligation to try to relate to the New Testament the assertions I have been making in more general terms about the structure of reconciliation.

My first point concerns God's initiative. Jesus, by the jealousy and fear of his opponents, was wrongly deprived - so the Christian inter- preter believes - of his good name and of his life. Falsely accused of blasphemy before a Jewish court, and of sedition before Pilate, he was crucified. But (so Christians came to be convinced) the life of God asserted itself through and beyond that death. Subsequent Christian reflexion on the events of Jesus' life and death, and on the extra- ordinary sequel, led to the conclusion that, in a unique sense, this had been God himself, submitting himself to man's ill will, and, by accepting it into himself, asserting his love as more powerful than man's hatred. St Paul saw it, on the titanic scale of the story of mankind collectively, as God's reply, in the ultimate Adam, to the first Adam's transgression. Man's first disobedience - the disobedience of the human race collec- tively - is met and reversed, not by retribution, but by the costly obe- dience of ultimate Man, who, while representing mankind collectively, is equally God himself at work in man:

> ... if the wrongdoing of that one man brought death upon so many, its effect is vastly exceeded by the grace of God and the gift that came to so many by the grace of the one man, Jesus Christ. ... For if by the wrongdoing of that one man death estab- lished its reign, through a single sinner, much more shall those who receive in far greater measure God's grace, and his gift of righteousness, live and reign in the one man, Jesus Christ. ... For as through the disobedience of the one man the many were made sinners, so through the obedience of the one man the many will be made righteous. Rom. v. 15-19 (N.E.B.)

Thus, in Jesus Christ, God himself is seen willingly and eagerly work- ing out the pattern of his will, *in* and *through* the tragic, agonizing, infinitely painful circumstances created by man's self-concern. In other words, here is a realistic reckoning with the damage caused by sin - the breach, the alienation, between man and God; and the New Testament gospel declares that the cost of the repair is borne by God himself in Jesus Christ. So far from wreaking vengeance, God himself 'absorbs' the evil: 'God was in Christ reconciling the world unto himself' (II Cor. v. 19). That the breach has caused concrete damage which must (so to

257

speak) be 'paid for' is also clear enough in the New Testament. The predicament of man cannot be met by a mere cease fire, or by a mere decision, like a 'royal pardon', to ignore the wrong. Sin has got to be taken account of. The idea that an offence is, as it were, a 'quantum' that must be disposed of is certainly at home in the New Testament, for instance, in Rom. v as just quoted. Quantitative metaphors are recognized by the New Testament. And the good news is that the slack is taken up (so to speak) by God himself, in Jesus Christ; or, if I may again resort to that physiological metaphor, the lesion in the body's tissue can be healed only by the output of creative energy. It is a sovereign act of the Creator. New creation is very much a Pauline idea: II Cor. v. 17; Gal. v. 15; Eph. ii. 10; Col. iii. 10.

Now, I have deliberately framed that statement in terms of God's initiative: God throughout is the subject of the verbs. And I do not believe that anyone will deny that this is true to the New Testament. But Jesus – so Christians believe – is man as well as God; and, if this act of repair is indeed God's act and at God's cost, yet it is carried out within man and, in Christ, it is offered up to God as the obedience of man to God, as the dutiful co-operation of a Son with his Father. This is the second point. Though it does not purchase God's forgiveness, it does express the Son's response of eager love (Eph. v. 2). And Christ, as the utterly obedient ultimate Adam, is in this sense the representative of man's costly repentance, as well as of God's costly forgiveness (see, again, Rom. v. 12 ff.). While Christ is (as Christians believe) in perfect harmony with his Father and acts for him towards men, his suffering also gathers and sums up the collective reparation which man must wish to offer to God as soon as man repents. Christ is the representative and 'first fruits' of mankind's response to God's initiative. Thus in Christ, as he is understood on a more than merely individual scale, are effected simultaneously God's free forgiveness and man's costly repentance. As we have seen, the gracious free gift of God, in its very acceptance as a free gift, evokes the ultimate output of energy from responsive man. And in Christ the two sides of this reciprocal movement are already both a reality.

Now, once again, I believe that this account will be recognized as true to the New Testament, or at any rate to Paul; so that the heart of the New Testament gospel concerns a process of reconciliation such as I have been trying to define, a process which is immensely costly and demanding, but which involves no retribution or punishment, as such. But is it not a direct contradiction of this that the New Testament undoubtedly contains also a good deal about retribution? It was a widespread notion in Christianity after the New Testament era that the fall of Jerusalem was divine retribution on the Jews for deicide; and already in the Gospels there are one or two hints that point in that direction - e.g. the retribution on the insulting guests in the Matthaean story of the great feast (Matt. xxii. 7) and the strange coda to the Lucan story of the money in trust (Lk. xix. 27). Moreover, 'wrath' (*orge*) is a familiar New Testament theme, especially in Paul and in the Apocalypse; and, even if Paul's use is so specialized that a front-rank New Testament scholar like C. H. Dodd can argue[2] that it does not mean anger as an emotion against sinners but disaster as a consequence of sin, this still (even if true) does not dispose of the retributive motive from Paul's teaching. Rom. ii. 6-11 is a very explicit passage about retribution, and Rom. i and ii as a whole are full of the theme. *Orge* itself, indeed, is rendered by 'retribution' in the N.E.B. at i. 18, ii. 5, and (perhaps) ii. 8.[3]

As for the Apocalypse, it is, in some places, vindictive in the extreme (e.g. xvi. 5 f.). Similarly, the climax of certain of the Gospel parables sounds retributive (Matt. xiii. 42, 50; xxv. 46; etc.). The language of retaliation, then, and the idea of deserved punishment are not difficult to find in the New Testament.[4]

Formally, this is certainly a contradiction of what I have been saying. And, although I believe that most of the apparent examples of retribution in the parables turn out, on closer inspection, to be picturesque ways of describing the inevitable results of estrangement rather than God's intention to penalize, neverthless there is enough in St Paul and the Apocalypse and a few other places to prove that retribution and punishment formed part of the system of thought accepted by these writers. But that is almost inevitable, seeing that New Testament thought is largely in the framework of Old Testament presuppositions, which give much prominence to the portrayal of God as a God of justice, vindicating his moral law by bringing retribution on the guilty. This was itself a great advance on pagan ideas of venal gods who had no consistency and in whose behaviour justice was no consideration - gods who had, in fact, no moral character at all. It was one of the chief glories of the eighth-century Prophets of Israel that the God whom they preached had a consistent character; and it would have been virtually impossible for New Testament thinking not to have had a correspondingly juridical structure. What is remarkable, however, is the extent to

---

2 E.g. in *The Epistle of Paul to the Romans* (London, 1932), p. 29.
3 And Rom. i. 27 uses the word *antimisthia*, 'recompense'.
4 Details in *Svensk Exegetisk Årsbok* 30 (1965). [Above, pp. 235 ff.].

which these axiomatic preconceptions have been modified by the Christian revelation. There is, as a matter of fact, extraordinarily little about punishment, properly so called, in the New Testament. Words which may be so translated are rare. Thought about wrath too has, at least in Paul, begun to be redirected. The sheer paradox of God's undeserved graciousness is so compelling that Paul's justification by grace through faith cuts away the ground from under the legalism that wrath ultimately implies. God is a God who puts the wicked right; who is content, in Jesus Christ, to suffer at the hands of the ungodly; who exercises his sovereign creative power by suffering, not by causing to suffer; who himself pays for the entail of sin instead of demanding satisfaction from the sinner. All in all, it is wrath and punishment which turn out to be the anomalies, in the full blaze of the New Testament gospel, not the other way round. It would thus appear that the implications of the New Testament gospel are to treat the consquences of sin quantitatively, but not to quantify relationship, which is what I was trying to argue in the first part of my discourse.

Now it is not for me to say what bearing all this may have in detail upon the pastoral ministry - especially the ministry to the sick. Nor have I even brought into view the agonizing problem of human beings who, for environmental or psychological or hereditary reasons, appear virtually to have ceased to come within the category of personality with which I have been exclusively working. I have not made reference to the work of Dr Frank Lake and others on the psychology of forgiveness and penitence, and I have left aside all sorts of other relevant literature, including that notable study *The Ethics of Punishment*, by Sir Walter Moberly.[5] But because I believe that a false evaluation of the problem of compensation, as I have called it, distorts atonement doctrine and the interpretation of absolution and penance, and therefore vitiates our ministry of reconciliation, I venture to hope that even this very limited study of it is not wholly irrelevant to the debate.

5 London, 1968. [See now E. Moberly, *Suffering Innocent and Guilty* (London, 1978); cf. p. 235 above.]

# 19

## Obligation in the Ethic of Paul
### for J. Knox

In *The Ethic of Jesus in the Teaching of the Church* (New York, 1961; London, 1962), Professor John Knox analyses the dilemma facing the Christian when he recognizes at once the inescapability and the impossibility of the demands of Christ. The demands of Christ are self-authenticating; they are such that the honest conscience is bound to accept them. And yet they are unattainable. Therefore the Christian is forced into a tension, a tension which would be unendurable - 'how can we be really obligated to do the impossible?' (p. 15) - were it not for the accompanying forgiveness which is offered - a forgiveness, however, which, because it is real forgiveness and not a mere forgetting or ignoring, involves not the slightest relaxation of the demand.

This characteristic of the ethic of Jesus - namely, the undiminished costliness of repentance - is described with the writer's usual clarity and feeling, and in an entirely convincing manner. Professor Knox has brought back into view an element in the teaching of Jesus which had tended to be forgotten; and I have no intention of making clumsy attempts to improve on it. It is in connexion with the treatment, in the same book, of Paul's standpoint that I venture to offer some further reflexions. In this part of his argument, Professor Knox reiterates a conclusion which he had expressed some ten years earlier in *Chapters in a Life of Paul* (New York, 1950; London, 1954), ch. 9. He accuses Paul (*The Ethic of Jesus*, p. 76)[1] of, unconsciously and unintentionally, relaxing the demand and sowing the seeds of antinomianism by his doctrine of justification. Paul's opponents and his heretical followers did interpret his gospel in an antinomian sense; and Professor Knox suggests that such was, indeed, the logic of his position, though not, of course, his intention - still less, his experience.

The Pauline doctrine of justification, Professor Knox maintains, divides forgiveness into two parts - justice and mercy; and this is a

1 All page references without further designation will henceforth relate to this book.

disaster, because it tends to make us see God's justice as mere justice and his mercy as mere mercy, whereas, in reality, God's justice and mercy are never thus divided. For 'when we say that God *forgives*, we are saying that *this* is the character of *his* justice and of *his* mercy' (*Chapters in a Life of Paul*, p. 148). It is not that there is a shadow of doubt about the depth of Paul's own experience. The 'single act' of God's forgiveness 'has unquestionably taken place within Paul's experience' (*ibid.* p. 150). It is only his interpretation and explanation of it that Professor Knox questions. Paul's interpretation, he holds, 'obscures the fact that love has its own way of dealing with sin - a way which is compatible with the highest demands of truth, but which does not need to make use of the terms or devices of either the law court or the market place. We do not have to be "acquitted" before the Judge in order to be reconciled to the Father' (*ibid.*). In short, Professor Knox expresses surprise and regret that Paul, using the potentially misleading category of justification, did not make more use of the category of *penitence*, which is used with such effect in the teaching of Jesus. Had he done so, he might have safeguarded mercy against being thought of as 'mere mercy'. As it is, he speaks of God justifying the ungodly 'not on the ground of his repentance (what can repentance have to do with justification?), but on the ground of Christ's expiatory act, which one appropriates by faith' (*ibid.* p. 153).

In this complaint, Professor Knox is by no means alone, for Paul's failure to reckon with penitence is a charge frequently levelled against him (see further p. 270, n. 7 below). But it is precisely this charge that the present essay attempts to re-examine; and, to that extent, it is a modest contribution to the larger problem of the relation of Jesus to Paul,[2] as well as a grateful acknowledgement of the stimulating and challenging character of what Professor Knox has written.

Accepting Professor Knox's challenge, and believing that he will treat this attempt to hold dialogue with him as the sincerest token of my regard, I shall put forward the view that Paul's alleged neglect of penitence is only apparent, not real, because the Pauline conception of faith-union with Christ itself presents a profound analysis of penitence, albeit translated into other terms. Thus, the logic of obligation is not surrendered by Paul, for he has as demanding a doctrine of repentance

2 On this, particularly valuable light has been shed by W. G. Kümmel (see the three papers on Jesus and Paul in his collection, *Heilsgeschehen und Geschichte* (Marbaurg, 1965)) and by E. Jüngel, *Paulus und Jesus* (Tübingen, 1964). See also the important survey by V. P. Furnish, 'The Jesus–Paul Debate from Baur to Bultmann', *B.J.R.L.* 47 (1965), 342 ff.

as Jesus had. Indeed, I would go further, and suggest that Paul offers an analysis of penitence where the teaching of Jesus does not, Paul making explicit what, in the teaching of Jesus, is only implicit. Conversely, I would suggest that the teaching of Jesus was as anti-legalistic and - if one may put it so - as 'situational' as Paul's. For Jesus himself, as for Paul, it was the new eschatological situation which was the decisive factor.

But, before I reach my main point, it will be useful to discuss two related matters: first, the legitimacy and value of the term 'legalism' to characterize what Paul is attacking; and, secondly, the relation of 'legalism' to sin.

I

The term 'legalism', although deplored by some scholars, can be a useful tool; and I suggest that, if it can be legitimized, its use may help to clarify something of considerable importance for the present investigation. What Paul means by νόμος is a thorny and endlessly debated problem.[3] But the term 'legalism' conveniently summarizes an important aspect of the subject; for I suggest that, in the tangled thickets of discussion, it is more important to draw a distinction between different uses of law and attitudes to law, than between different conceptions of its nature or contents: and this is usefully done in terms of 'legalism'. In other words, more important than whether law is viewed as a code or as a necessary ground of obligation, is the question whether a man is trying to justify himself by keeping the law, or whether he allows law to be a medium through which God reveals himself. On the basis of this approach, a provisional answer may at once be offered to one vital question. (The answer is a drastically simplified one, and ignores, no doubt, many nuances and subtleties, but perhaps it is adequate as a start.) The short answer to the question 'In what sense, if any, did Paul speak of law as abrogated?' is that Paul saw Christ as the *fulfilment* of law, when law means God's revelation of himself and of his character and purpose, but as the *condemnation* and *termination* of any attempt to use law to justify oneself. And it is this latter use of law which may conveniently be called (for short) 'legalism'. It has been objected that '... the Greek language used by Paul had no word-group to denote

3 Besides the well-known discussions in E. de W. Burton, *Galatians* (I.C.C., Edinburgh, 1921), pp. 443 ff., and G. Kittel, *T.W.N.T.* iv, 1061 ff., see, more recently, the analysis on p. 44 of C. E. B. Cranfield, 'St Paul and the Law', *S.J.T.* 17 (1964), 43 ff.

"legalism", "legalist", and "legalistic" '.[4] But, for that matter, neither has he a distinctive word for any other aspect of law. The many shades of meaning attaching to νόμος have to be deduced from the ways in which the word is used; and it is clear that νόμος is used by Paul in (among others) the two quite distinct connexions which may be called respectively 'revelatory' and 'legalistic'.

Thus – to take only some very obvious examples – νόμος is used in allusion to the revelation of God's requirements and character in the two following passages:

So the law is holy, and the commandment is holy and just and good. (Rom. vii. 12.)
The commandments, 'You shall not commit adultery, You shall not kill, You shall not steal, You shall not covet', and any other commandment, are summed up in this sentence, 'You shall love your neighbour as yourself'. Love does no wrong to a neighbour; therefore love is the fulfilling of the law. (Rom. xiii. 9, 10.)

In the former of these two passages, even the more specifically imperative word, ἐντολή (commandment), is equally recognized as representing something good and permanent.

In sharp contrast to these, there are well-known passages in which law is disparaged. In such a passage as Rom. iii. 20, for example, νόμος is recognized as impotent to save, though able to pass sentence: 'For no human being will be justified in his sight by works of the law, since through the law comes knowledge of sin.' Even more explicit is Gal. iii. 21b, 22a: '. . . for if a law had been given which could make alive, then righteousness would indeed be by the law. But . . .' The same applies to Rom. iii. 28: 'For we hold that a man is justified by faith apart from works of the law.' And, to make it doubly clear that this is not a denial of the validity of νόμος as a statement of God's requirements and character, Paul adds (*v.* 31), in so many words: 'Do we then overthrow the law by this faith? By no means! On the contrary, we uphold the law.'

This contrast between the two contexts in which νόμος is used is perfectly familiar to all students of Paul. The only point I want to make is that it is here that the word 'legalism' comes in useful as 'shorthand' for an idea which is of primary importance in the discussion of obligation in the ethic of Paul. If by legalism we understand the intention to claim God's favour by establishing one's own rightness, then legalism is

4 C. E. B. Cranfield, *S.J.T.* 17 (1964), 55.

a convenient summary of what Paul is alluding to when he speaks of justification by works of the law.

What I am saying, then, is that, for the purposes of this debate, it is not so important to define the law as to define a man's motives in relation to it and his methods of using it; and the vital distinction is not between law *in itself*, whether as a code or as a ground of obligation (p. 96), but between two different attitudes to and uses of law - on the one hand, the recognition of law as a revelation of God's will and purpose, and, on the other hand, the attempt to use it 'legalistically', to establish one's rightness.

Gal. v. 3 is a verse which, perhaps, throws light on this distinction. Here Paul says that anyone who get himself circumcised is under an obligation to keep the whole law. He is apparently referring to Christians who became converts to Judaism and who were circumcised as adults. That is, they had come to the conclusion that trust in Christ was not enough: they must add the safeguard of Judaism. If so, Paul says, then you must accept Judaism as the mechanical system which your decision to make use of the law implies: having adopted the law as a 'safeguard', you must abide by it in a spirit of meticulous literalism. What Paul indicates as, by contrast, desirable is not the abolition of law. What needs to be abolished is the arrogantly human use of the law for the purposes of human 'safety'.

## II

Thus, it is legalism that Paul consistently attacks. Indeed, for him it is a symptom of *the* essential sin, namely, Adam's self-centredness. And this brings me to the second of my two preliminary points - a point concerning the relation of legalism to sin. Paul's contention is not only that, since man is never going to be able to keep the law merely by trying, therefore the intention to claim God's favour by establishing one's justice is *futile*. Worse than that - such an intention is positively *sinful*, because it implies an uncreaturely refusal to accept man's need of God and dependence on him.

Thus, when Paul contrasts grace with law, he is not for a moment setting up some supposed gracious indulgence over against the absolute demands of God, in such a way as to relax these demands. On the contrary, he is declaring that the only realistic step towards meeting God's inexorable demands is to recognize them as frankly unattainable without the power of God; and to recognize, further, that to presume to try to attain them without God's aid is man's essential sin. It is not that grace abolishes law, but that dependence on grace, instead of the attitude of legalism, is the only way to fulfil God's law. There is obligation, but it is to grace, not law.

That this is Paul's meaning is, I think, evident in the contrasting uses of νόμος that have already been referred to. But, given this conclusion, there are other passages which, in their turn, seem to be illuminated and to be given their proper point. For instance, Rom. vi. 14: 'For sin will have no dominion over you, since you are not under law but under grace.' This sounds paradoxical, because one might expect that subjection to law would provide precisely the firm discipline and obligation that would make for the avoidance of sin. In any normal ethical context, it would have made good sense to say: 'sin will have no dominion over you, since you are securely under law.' But instead, Paul inserts his 'not': it is precisely because you are *not* under law that you can escape from the dominion of sin.[5] Are not those commentators right who interpret this in the light of legalism? Professor C. K. Barrett's comment puts this interpretation as clearly as possible:

> Law means the upward striving of human religion and morality, and therefore colours all human activity with sin, for it represents man's attempt to scale God's throne. Those who live under the reign of grace, however, have given full scope to God's freedom, since instead of pressing upward towards God they humbly wait for his descent in love. Ultimately, therefore, justification by faith, which means living under grace, though it is rooted in a region of divine-human relation which lies beyond morals, becomes the one hope of a truly moral life. (*A Commentary on the Epistle to the Romans* (London, 1957), p. 129.)[6]

5 Perhaps the extremely obscure passage, Gal. v. 17 f., is akin to this passage in its logic.

6 Somewhat differently, O. Kuss (*Der Römerbrief*, II (Regensburg, 1959), p. 384), who takes it to mean that one is removed from the domain of a law which could only demand but not succour, and transplanted to a realm of grace which brings God's help and strength. Professor Knox himself, in his commentary in *The Interpreter's Bible*, edd. G. A. Buttrick and others, 9 (New York, 1954), pp. 480 f., stresses the future tense ('will have no dominion') as indicating that Paul recognizes that the release is not yet accomplished in the present age; and, for the meaning of 'you are not under law . . .', asks whether it is that (a) all of the commands of the law are now invalid, no longer binding, for the believer; or (b) the believer, because of the power of the Spirit, now finds himself able to fulfil the law and is therefore not aware of its restrictions and demands; or (c) the believer does not now have to rely upon his obedience to the law for his acceptance with God. Of these, (b) is nearest to the meaning indicated by Barrett, but not quite the same.

On this showing, the very essence of sin is precisely the human attempt to establish autonomy; and it is only by ceasing to be 'under law' in that sense - the sense, namely, of attempting to establish for oneself one's own law-abidingness - that one may begin to gain release from the tyranny of sin. The very paradox of the 'not' seems to point to an interpretation in terms of legalism. And this is borne out by the rest of the chapter; for Rom. vi. 15 ff. urges that release from νόμος (in the sense implied by the context) means *not* antinomianism (*v.* 15), but a firmer obligation than ever: to be released from the self-concern of legalism is to be free to devote oneself as a slave (*vv.* 16 ff.) to 'obedience' (*v.* 16) or to the shaping force of Christian teaching (*v.* 17), or to 'righteousness' (*vv.* 19 f.). It is possible, I think, that Rom. viii. 3 may stand within the same circle of ideas. It says that the law was impotent διὰ τῆς σαρκός. This is generally interpreted in some such sense as (R.S.V.) 'weakened by the flesh'. But may it not rather mean that law, in the nature of the case, can only operate externally, on the physical level? The law is impotent and weak because its scope is limited to a man's material, physical aspects, and does not touch his motives (τὸ . . . ἀδύνατον τοῦ νόμου, ἐν ᾧ ἠσθένει διὰ τῆς σαρκός). It can, at best, only coerce a man's body, not affect his will. In other words, a mere statement of God's will - however excellent in itself - cannot be *applied* to a man except in terms of external restraint or compulsion. When law has made its announcement - its good and holy announcement - it still remains for something less external to put it into effect. But to proceed from law to legalism is precisely to remain on the level of externals.

Thus, it is not that one is released from obligation by ceasing to be under law (p. 103). Rather, it is that only by abandoning the self-centred and self-chosen obligation may one hope to fulfil the genuine obligation. But even if one agrees to all this, Professor Knox's complaint is still not met. He does not question Paul's recognition that Christians are under the obligation to live a life of love nor Paul's own experience of the joyfully accepted 'bondage' to God's love. What he questions is whether Paul's 'understanding of what God has done in Christ and of the corresponding status of the believer provided any *adequate theoretical and theological basis* for the obligation' (p. 97, my italics). For - so Professor Knox maintains - Paul's *theory* really does represent a radical rejection of law. Thus he writes:

> But, it may be asked, is Paul's rejection of the law as binding on the believer so radical as this? Is not the 'law' he rejects simply an external code, a list of thou shalt's and thou shalt not's, in particular the code of Judaism? Whatever may seem to be implied in

267

some of his practical teaching, I feel sure that in his 'theory' of
the Christian life Paul went much further than this. Although undoubtedly he is frequently referring to the Jewish law, one cannot deny the presence – often, if not always – of a more radical,
more inclusive, reference. The Gentiles also are subject to law
(Rom. 2: 15); will they not share, with redeemed Jews, in release
from the burden of its demands? And when Paul speaks of this
release, can he have only an external code in mind? Would he
have said, 'God has freed us from a code of particular rules by
making us subject to a higher, more exacting law – a law which
lays its demands upon the very thoughts of our hearts and calls
for an absolutely unremitting obedience?' Jesus speaks to this
effect, but I do not believe Paul would have done so. Certainly he
does not in fact speak so. It is striking that when, in the seventh
chapter of Romans, he is telling of the difficulties he himself had
under the Jewish law, he mentions particularly only the one commandment of the Decalogue which involves a demand upon the
inner life, 'You shall not covet'. Now many of us would make a
significant distinction between 'rules' and 'principles', and would
say that whereas the law in the external sense of rules is abrogated
in Christ, the principles remain valid and binding. In line with this
distinction we might insist that the Christian is no longer under
any specific command touching outward behaviour, even a command as important as 'Thou shalt not kill'. But would we not
concede that he is still subject to the law against covetousness?
But can we think of Paul as making any such concession? Would
he have allowed continuing validity to the law at the very point
where it had caused him the greatest pain and anxiety? There is
no evidence that Paul differentiated between various elements
within the law – or various kinds of law – as, for example, between
the ceremonial and moral, or the general and the particular. Law,
as such, is no longer valid for the Christian. We are not under law,
but under grace (pp. 98 f.).

Agreed – Paul did not distinguish explicitly between ceremonial and
moral law. But I question whether he disallowed the continuing validity
of 'thou shalt not covet'. What he is affirming is that the law against
coveting could not be achieved by 'law' in the sense of 'legalism'. I do
not think that he is denying that the law, pronouncing the words 'Thou
shalt not covet', continued to be a revelation of God's will. But it was,
Paul saw, disastrous to adopt, as one's way of life, a self-centred, am-

268

bitious determination to establish oneself as a keeper of the law. The moment law is accepted in that light, one is as good as dead.

Thus, Paul did not claim release from the law of coveting, but only from an inability to keep it arising from a fatal and futile determination to establish one's own success. It is necessary, then, I would hold, to interpret Paul as seeing the antithesis to grace, not in law so far as it is the revelation of God's character and demand, nor even in law as obligation, but in law as an arrogantly and arbitrarily chosen target of human ambition and as a system of human achievement, that is, legalism. This brings us back to the matter of essential sin. On p. 28, Professor Knox writes :'We are as natural finite men self-centered – this is neither wrong nor avoidable; it is our nature – but as sinful men we are also, equally inescapably, corrupted by pride. Our self-centeredness passes inevitably into selfishness.' Now, Professor Knox may be using 'self-centred' here in a special way (reflecting, possibly, a Tillichian vocabulary); but I wonder whether this distinction between a self-centredness that is natural and right and a sinful self-centredness, is Pauline. Paul would, I think, identify self-centredness *tout court*, as Adam's primal sin: it is mistrust of God; it is a refusal of creaturely dependence; it is legalism. And is not this essentially in line with the teaching of Jesus – for instance, in the Sermon on the Mount, where the ideal attitude depicted is that of a son in full dependence on his Father? There is no other state that is not sinful.

## III

So far, I have asked for a recognition that it is 'legalism' (as defined), rather than 'law' that Paul opposes to grace; and that this legalism is seen by Paul as a symptom of man's essential sin. It is this, and not law, from which he claims release. But the main point of this inquiry is concerned with the remedy for the ill; for it is here, if anywhere, that the logic of obligation will be found. If the law, as an exhibition of God's Name and Nature, is holy and just and good, but man, in his self-centredness, continually imagines that to have seen it is to be able to achieve it, and, by his very efforts to achieve it, expresses this essential self-centredness and so plunges deeper into sin, who can deliver him? If God's good law is constantly turned, by man's self-centredness, into legalism, who will break the vicious circle?

Now, Christ's answer to man's inability to meet God's demand, the answer so movingly described by Professor Knox in his exposition of the teaching of Jesus, lies, in essence, in penitence, for penitence is a realistic way of meeting failure without lowering the sights. Without for a moment relaxing his absolute requirements, God constantly offers his forgiveness. And forgiveness (as I have already said) means no relaxation of demand, because, infinitely costly to give, it is notoriously costly also to receive: true penitence is itself costly and demanding. It accepts, unabated, the stringency of God's demand. Though it does not earn forgiveness, it is the only way in to forgiveness. True penitence, so far from bringing a relieved sense that 'Allah is merciful' and will not be exacting, means a renewed committal to the ideal. Forgiveness means no relaxation of the stringency of demand, as the extreme painfulness of true penitence shows. Logically, the obligation is perfectly clear.

But, it is precisely in this connexion that a charge is frequently levelled against Paul; and this charge now requires careful examination. Paul has often been accused of paying scant attention to repentance;[7] and Professor Knox repeats the charge (pp. 86, 87):

> Those who find an antinomian tendency in the Christian doctrine of grace, who say, 'Let us then sin that grace may abound', who ask, 'Why should we try to fulfil God's law when we know not only that we cannot succeed, but also that God stands ready graciously to receive us even in our sinfulness?' or who take the even more radical position of saying, 'Christ has destroyed the law', all of these (and, I think, Paul is included here) forget or neglect the great significance of repentance in the Christian doctrine of grace.

A little further on (p. 90), he points out also that Paul, while speaking often of God's love for man, has comparatively little to say about the response of love from man to God.

Now, it is indeed true that μετανοεῖν occurs in the Pauline corpus only at II Cor. xii. 21, and μετάνοια only at Rom. ii. 4, II Cor. vii. 9 (and II Tim. ii. 25); and the statistics for man's loving God are comparable. The same, it may be said in parenthesis, is true of the word 'will': it is usually God's will, not man's. It is true also (pp. 76 ff.) that Paul's 'justification', though sometimes claimed as his equivalent for penitence, is not strictly equivalent. All this is undoubtedly true; and it can be argued that the nearest parallel to justification is, in fact, not penitence but forgiveness. But if 'justification' is not an equivalent for penitence, that is not to say that no equivalent is known to Paul. One

---

7 See, for instance, H. J. Schoeps, *Paul* (English version, London, 1961, of *Paulus* (Tübingen, 1959)), p. 188, and many before him, both Christian and non-Christian.

only needs to ask what penitence and love really mean, to find that Paul is full of them. For what is penitence, and what is love? Penitence, in contrast to mere remorse, is genuine concern for the injured party. Remorse is the sinner's concern for himself, it is his mortification over failure or exposure. Penitence, by contrast, is distress over the wrong done to the other; and its positive side is obedient self-surrender to God – the offering to God of one's will and one's person, for him to use in the repair of the damage done. It is a voluntary entering with God into the pain and distress which one's own sin has caused, and which, in God's hands, can be turned into the creative means of healing and repair. For the teaching of Jesus, Professor Knox makes very compelling use (pp. 80 ff.) of the story of the prodigal son. But that story is not explicit about the meaning of penitence. If we are to be explicit, we must follow the direction of the parable, and ask: What form is the prodigal son's penitence, if it is real, going to take when it is translated into practical terms? The answer, clearly, is that it will mean aligning himself with the father's self-sacrificing, eirenic, forgiving appeal to the elder brother. Instead of resenting and reciprocating his brother's caustic words, he will join his father in patient entreaty. This, I believe, is exactly what is implied by Professor Knox when (p. 75) he says that 'forgiveness in its very nature presupposes the acknowledgment of, and submission to, a moral requirement'. True repentance is going to be shown in the same kind of costly suffering for others as was shown in the initial act of forgiveness: it means responding in kind to the creative effort of reconciliation: 'Forgive us our debts, as we also are forgiving our debtors.'[8] This is what repentance and love mean.

But, if so, all this, I would contend, is precisely what Paul is all the time expressing, although without using μετάνοια or ἀγάπη. It may be true that a doctrine of 'justification', by itself, would divide justice from mercy and remove all logical grounds from obligation. But is this true of Paul's justification *by faith*? And has not Paul, in addition to 'faith', an impressive array of other expressions for the meaning of penitence? For he not only speaks of faith,[9] but also uses terms borrowed from cultus and sacrifice, and the figures of death and burial, and of union with Christ. It is a familiar fact that, for Paul, faith has far-reaching connotations of trust and self-surrender and loyalty. And, even if this were not clear in itself, he reinforces it by such phrases as

8 Cf. J. Jeremias, 'The Lord's Prayer in Modern Research', *Exp. T.* 71 (1960), 141 ff. (p. 146, 'as we herewith forgive our debtors'). [Cf. p. 279 n. 4.]
9 On faith in Paul, as contrasted with Jesus' idea of faith, see M. Buber, *apud* Kümmel, *Heilsgeschehen und Geschichte*, p. 442.

'present your bodies as a living sacrifice . . . that you may prove what is the will of God . . .' (Rom. xii. 1, 2); 'we were buried . . . with him by baptism into death' (Rom. vi. 4); 'I have been crucified with Christ' (Gal. ii. 20). So, too, by his use of the preposition ἐν, he denotes incorporation in Christ and the identification of the will with his. In a word, all that is meant by ὑπακοή, 'obedience' (which, incidentally, is an important word in Romans and II Corinthians), implements in a very realistic way the content of penitence and love. Justification, in Paul's use, is no doubt based on the finished work of Christ, quite independently of man's worth or effort. But justification *by faith* denotes such a response to that finished work as identifies the believer most intimately with the costly work of Christ, involving him inescapably in the cost and pain of repentance. It may be added that, conversely, there are areas of Christian literature where, although actual words for repentance are more prominent, the inner meaning of it is seriously misconstrued, and where the idea of merit is evident. This is well brought out by S. Laeuchli in *The Language of Faith* (New York, 1962; London, 1965), p. 94.

It would appear, then, that, so far from ignoring repentance, Paul offers a profound and realistic analysis of it, even when he does not use the word. And if he is constantly saying that we must become what, in Christ, we already are (as, for instance, in Gal. v. 25, 'if we live by the Spirit' - that is, if we owe our very 'existence', as Christians, to the Spirit -, 'let us also walk by the Spirit' - that is, let our conduct conform to this), is this any more a mark of inconsistency (p. 100) than the constant appeals of Christ himself? The *datum*, both for Jesus and Paul, is always God's initiative in Christ and the individual's initial decision and response in faith and baptism. But the ἐφάπαξ of the *datum* has as constantly to be re-appropriated by repeated 'becomings'.

On p. 63 Professor Knox acknowledges that the teaching of Jesus himself did not show *how* his demands were to be met. But Paul, if I have at all justly represented him, does attempt to analyse how the dominical commands may be met, without abating one jot of them. It is not that he preaches the abrogation of the demands in favour of a reign of gracious relaxation. Rather, he penetrates to the heart of the ethical dilemma by recognizing that the attempt to meet the demands in one's own strength had always been self-frustrating and of the essence of sin; and that the first step towards meeting the demands is to acknowledge one's need and one's inability to do so in one's own strength, and to capitulate, in penitence and love or, in Paul's vocabulary, in the self-surrender of faith and obedience, to God's forgiveness.

Paradoxically, it is the most costly process imaginable, although it cannot start until we have confessed that we can give nothing out of our own resources.

This brings us to a reconsideration of one of the most hotly debated passages in the Pauline epistles – Rom. x. 4: τέλος γὰρ νόμου Χριστὸς εἰς δικαιοσύνην παντὶ τῷ πιστεύοντι. Up to the time of writing, the controversy is still swinging to and fro. E. Bammel argues for τέλος meaning 'termination',[10] C. E. B. Cranfield, for its meaning 'fulfilment'[11] – to quote only two of multitudes of debaters. The decision depends upon whether one takes νόμος in the first or the second of the meanings I have tried to isolate; or, to put it syntactically, on whether one construes εἰς δικαιοσύνην with νόμος or Χριστός. The Revised Standard Version renders it: 'For Christ is the end of the law, that every one who has faith may be justified.' The Jerusalem Bible (*Le Nouveau Testament, traduction nouvelle*, Paris, 1955) renders it: 'car le terme de la Loi, c'est le Christ, pour que soit justifié tout croyant.' The New English Bible (text) has: 'For Christ ends the law and brings righteousness for everyone who has faith', or (margin): 'Christ is the end of the law as a way to righteousness for everyone who has faith.' Cranfield ('Νόμος Χριστοῦ', p. 49) suggests: 'For Christ is the goal of the law, so that righteousness is available to everyone that believeth.' Of these versions, Cranfield's clearly construes εἰς δικαιοσύνην with Χριστός, and the New English Bible margin almost as clearly with νόμος. The New English Bible text's 'brings righteousness' would be compatible with τέλος meaning goal, though 'ends' would be difficult to treat as though it meant 'brings to fulfilment'.

If one takes τέλος as 'termination', and construes νόμος with εἰς δικαιοσύνην to mean 'law used as a means to righteousness', Paul is saying that Christ put an end to legalism. This would, I know, be strictly illogical, because, on Paul's own showing, legalism (as we have called it) had never at any time been valid or other than sinful, so that Christ could not, strictly and correctly, be spoken of as terminating it. But it is intelligible, nevertheless, that Paul should so speak of Christ, in the sense that the Christian era constituted at any rate the final exposure and discrediting of legalism. If, on the other hand, one adopts the alternative and takes τέλος to mean 'purpose' or 'goal', then Paul is saying that Christ, as the way to righteousness, constitutes the goal and fulfilment of that revelation of God's way and character which the law contains.

10 'Νόμος Χριστοῦ', *Studia Evangelica*, 3 (ed. F. L. Cross, *T.U.* 88, Berlin, 1964), pp. 120 ff. Cf. Schoeps, *Paul*, pp. 171 ff.
11 *S.J.T.* 17 (1964), 43 ff.

Either interpretation is compatible with Paul's thought, but I suspect that he mainly intended the former - Christ put an end to legalism (this is borne out by *v.* 3, and, perhaps, by the fact that, in his 'targum' on Deut. xxx. 12 ff., in Rom. x. 6 ff., he seems to substitute Christ for Torah), although (he might have added) legalism, it is true, never was really valid. But Paul is by no means incapable of intending double meanings, and, especially in view of Rom. xiii. 10, '. . . love is the fulfilling of the law', he could simultaneously have meant it in the second. sense - Christ fulfils all that the law stands for.[12] As W. D. Davies has pointed out (*The Setting of the Sermon on the Mount*, Cambridge, 1964, p. 356), Jesus is, for Paul, parallel, not so much with Moses as with the law. If there is a new Moses, it is Paul; the new law is Christ himself.

I have discussed this famous phrase in Rom. x. 4 at some length because the very fact of its ambiguity and of both senses being compatible with Paul's thought illustrates well the double meaning attaching to νόμος in respect of its use rather than of its contents. It is legalism that Paul is forever attacking and renouncing, and that he sees finally and decisively exposed and rejected by Christ; but the Mosaic Law as a revelation of God's will and purpose, so far from being abrogated, is seen as finding its fulfilment and culmination in Christ. Once this is recognized, Jesus and Paul can be seen to be speaking, at least on this matter, with one voice. As E. Jüngel points out (*Paulus und Jesus*, pp. 266, 267), Paul retains the idea of judgement according to works, regarding it as a criterion of responsibility no less than Jesus' teaching on rewards and penalties expresses responsibility. Similarly, Jesus and Paul both show the grace of God meeting responsible but sinful man. It is not the validity of a code that Paul is denying. He is only denying that a code can or should be used for uncreaturely attempts at boasting and autonomy. And the rejection of this use means no relaxation of the code.

But Paul does much more than merely reaffirm what had, all the time, been the right use of the law. He interprets it in a new and distinctively Christian way. He finds in Christ the embodiment and implementation of that relation between God and man which was represented by the law as a revelation of God, and he does, therefore, see Christ as superseding the law - but only in the sense that Christ, by

12 Professor Knox himself, in his commentary (*Interpreter's Bible*, 9, 554), says: '. . . meaning probably that in Christ the law is superseded (cf. 3:21; Gal. 3:25), rather than that the goal of the law is reached, although that too is a perfectly congenial Pauline idea.'

totally and completely obeying the will of God revealed in it, includes and transcends it. To be united with Christ is, therefore, not to by-pass law, but to fulfil it in a supremely costly way. For instance, the death of Christ is seen by Paul as the surrender of Christ's entire body, his whole self, and, thus, as the greater, the all-inclusive 'circumcision'. To be baptized into Christ's death is, therefore, to have surrendered one's whole self with him in death, and thus to obviate the need for circumcision: the greater includes the less. But does this eliminate the logic of obligation? In a striking phrase of R. T. Brooks,[13] we who are forgiven are 'ruled more firmly by the pardon than we ever were by the law'. And, if the acceptance of the pardon is analysed into a total giving of oneself in union with the self-giving of God in Jesus Christ, is not this a sufficiently clear logic of obligation? If the Pauline faith and death with Christ are given their full value, then it would seem to me that the judgement and mercy of God are as inseparable in Paul's logic as in that of the teaching of Jesus.

## IV

In conclusion, then, it would appear that, conversely, the element of obligation in the teaching of Jesus is similar to that in the teaching of Paul and as free from 'law', in any legalistic sense, as Paul's. When Paul attacks legalism, he is attacking precisely what Jesus attacked in the Pharisees of his day. Jesus attacked the Pharisees; Paul attacked the Pharisee he had himself once been. The use of the law in an attempt to establish one's righteousness was condemned by Jesus every bit as much as by Paul, and, indeed, perhaps, by most other Jews except the most rigorous Pharisees.

In neither case is there antinomianism. Neither the ethic of Jesus nor that of Paul was exercised in a vacuum. The great presuppositions and principles of Jewish morality - rectitude, integrity, honesty - were obviously axiomatic for both. But actual moral decisions have to be taken in a situational way, and were evidently so taken by Jesus as much as by Paul. Man was not made for the sabbath, but the sabbath

13 *Person to Person* (London, 1964), p. 66: 'Those who reject the code and those who bewail its rejection are alike in the belief that the only possible pattern of relationship between God and man is that of ruler and ruled, and that the only possible way of operating such a relationship is by the inexorable application of a code of prohibitions and punishments. That we are both condemned and pardoned - and ruled more firmly by the pardon than we ever were by the law - that is the missing insight.'

275

for man; and general rules about the details of ethical practice are as lacking in the traditions of Jesus as in Paul's writings. Both Jesus and Paul did still more than that, for both speak with the voice of the new age. What Jesus brought to the Law of Moses was not only a repudiation of its legalizing and a reaffirmation of its broad and religious sense, but, still more, the new light of the new age in his own Person. E. Jüngel, in *Paulus und Jesus*, p. 269, remarks that the validity of the law was treated by Jesus as self-evident; but that, when one asks how Jesus implemented its validity, the answer is, by treating men as responsible in the light of the nearness of the kingdom and in the light of the new strength of love. In other words, Jesus' approach to the law is eschatological.

What Paul added to the teaching of Jesus, maintaining to the full the eschatological dimension, was not a relaxation of ethical principles but a definition and analysis of the relation between, on the one hand, law (in the good sense) and grace, and, on the other hand, legalism and merit.

W. G. Kümmel, in *Heilsgeschehen und Geschichte*, p. 191, analyses Klausner's misunderstanding of Paul as bound up with a failure to recognize Jesus as the eschatological Bringer of Salvation and as thus bringing about the end of the Old Testament epoch of salvation (cf. Lk. xvi. 16). This is why Klausner has to drive a wedge between Jesus and Paul and represent Paul as the enemy of true Judaism. But in reality, Paul stands on the same side as Jesus. In both Jesus and Paul, love, in an urgently demanding, eschatological embodiment, is the essence of the law.

The conclusion, then, that I would venture to draw in this last section is that Paul shows as much and as little of the logic of moral obligation as Jesus himself; and that the essentially eschatological character of the tension between demand and succour which Paul so firmly grasped is precisely what was presented by the Person of Jesus himself. And the logic of it, it seems to me, is as taut in Paul as in Jesus. Indeed, it is Paul who analysed the meaning of the repentance by which the tension is made endurable.[14] Justification and faith, burial with Christ and incorporation in him, self-surrender, and obedience – all these in Paul's teaching represent an analysis of forgiveness and repentance. He

14 P. G. Verweijs, *Evangelium und neues Gesetz in der ältesten Christenheit bis auf Marcion* (Utrecht, 1960), p. 77, commenting on the essential agreement between Jesus and Paul about the fulfilling of the law, remarks that the distinctiveness of Paul's teaching is in keeping with 'die neue pneumatische Heilszeit'.

thus makes explicit - although perhaps without conscious reference to the teaching of Jesus - something which, in the teaching of Jesus is only implicit.

That is the kind of apologia I would offer for Paul against the charge that the logic of his position is a relaxation of obligation, and that he neglects the elements of forgiveness and penitence. Very likely I have misinterpreted Professor Knox; perhaps I have misconstrued Paul. But I offer these reflexions on Professor Knox's delineation of Paul as a token of my serious concern to wrestle with the implications of what he writes and of the way in which he stimulates a reader; and I know that he will welcome friendly debate on paper in exactly the same spirit in which he has always welcomed and engaged in it, with lively and genial interest, in verbal dialogue.

# 20

'. . . As we forgive . . .': A Note on the Distinction between
Deserts and Capacity in the Understanding of Forgiveness

for D. Daube

In a celebrated essay on the Lord's Prayer,[1] Israel Abrahams contrasted
the limiting clause, 'as we forgive . . .', which follows the petition for
forgiveness, with the unconditional forgiveness of God as it is affirmed
in Jewish liturgy. Incidentally, the two versions of the Lord's Prayer
differ, as is well known, at this very point. If we follow the generally
accepted texts, Matt. vi. 12 has:

> καὶ ἄφες ἡμῖν τὰ ὀφειλήματα ἡμῶν,
> ὡς καὶ ἡμεῖς ἀφήκαμεν τοῖς ὀφειλέταις ἡμῶν,

whereas Lk. xi. 4 has:

> καὶ ἄφες ἡμῖν τὰς ἁμαρτίας ἡμῶν,
> καὶ γὰρ αὐτοὶ ἀφίομεν παντὶ ὀφείλοντι ἡμῖν.

The version in the *Didache* (viii. 2) corresponds, in respect of the tense,
to Luke's version:

> καὶ ἄφες ἡμῖν τὴν ὀφειλὴν ἡμῶν
> ὡς καὶ ἡμεῖς ἀφίεμεν [sic] τοῖς ὀφειλέταις ἡμῶν.

It has been observed that the versions of Luke and the *Didache*, using
the present tense, are less patient than Matthew's of being interpreted
in the sense that God's forgiveness depends on man's initiative, for if
one pressed the perfect tense, ἀφήκαμεν, in the Matthaean version, it
would mean that the worshipper claimed that he had already forgiven
his debtors before he asked God to forgive him, whereas the present
tense in Luke and the *Didache,* ἀφίομεν (ἀφίεμεν), makes the two con-
temporaneous, or might even be interpreted as future in intention. J.
Carmignac[2] argues that, on the contrary, Matthew subtly distinguishes
the *petition* for forgiveness from God's actual *granting* of it, and that
Matthew's perfect tense (representing *nasânu*[3] in the original - Hebrew,

1 Ch. XII of *Studies in Pharisaism and the Gospels*, second ser. (Cambridge,
1924). See especially pp. 95–100.
2 *Recherches sur le 'Notre Père'* (Paris, 1969), pp. 230 ff.   3 *Ibid.*, p. 396.

278

not Aramaic - as Carmignac conceives it) is to be read in relation merely to the petition for forgiveness, not to the offer itself of the divine forgiveness. Then, if so, Luke and the *Didache* represent a failure to recognize this subtlety and an attempt simply to make more room for the divine initiative. But J. Jeremias[4] reconstructs the original (Aramaic, as he believes, not Hebrew) behind both versions as *ušᵉboq lán hobaín kᵉdišᵉbáqnan lᵉhajjabaín*, i.e. 'and forgive us our debts, *as we also herewith forgive* our debtors'.

However, the differences in the versions of this clause are a matter only of degree; for in either case, the petition is a conditioned one. Accordingly, Abrahams, whose two essays on forgiveness[5] should be read side by side with the one on the Lord's Prayer, makes a point of the fact that, in Jewish liturgy, no such condition is expressed. To be sure, outside liturgy, the idea of conditional forgiveness is by no means absent from Jewish writings, as Abrahams recognised. He cited Sir. xxviii. 2 as a well known example:

ἄφες ἀδίκημα τῷ πλησίον σου,
καὶ τότε δεηθέντος σου αἱ ἁμαρτίαι σου λυθήσονται.[6]

And in the essay on Man's Forgiveness[7] he had cited M. Yoma 8. 9 (not even the Day of Atonement atones for wrongs done by man to man: it effects atonement only if a man has appeased his fellow), T.B.K. 10. 18 (the man who brought a sin-offering and remembered at the very altar that he still held the stolen goods, was ordered to stop his sacrifice, make restitution, and then come back to his sacrifice, cf. Matt. v. 23), and Philo, *opif, mund.* 1 and 4 (though of this I cannot see the relevance). Similarly, G. Friedlander[8] cited B. Yoma 23a ('all who are forbearing and forgiving and do not insist on their rights will be forgiven

4 *The Prayers of Jesus* (E.T., London, 1967), pp. 94, 103, or *The Lord's Prayer* (E.T., Philadelphia, 1964), from *Das Vater-Unser im Lichte der neueren Forschung* (Stuttgart, 3rd edn., 1965). The transcription follows *Abba* (Stuttgart, 1966), p. 160. More recently, in *New Testament Theology*, vol. i, *The Proclamation of Jesus* (E.T., London, 1971), p. 196, from *Neutestamentliche Theologie*, I. Teil: *Die Verkündigung Jesu* (Gütersloh, 1971), the form used is . . . *hōbēnan* . . . *lᵉhayyābēnan*.

5 Chh. XIX and XX, 'God's Forgiveness' and 'Man's Forgiveness' of *Studies in Pharisaism and the Gospels*, first ser. (Cambridge, 1917), pp. 139 ff., 150 ff.

6 And see, indeed, the whole passage, *vv.* 1-7, elaborating the theme.

7 *Studies in Pharisaism*, i. 162; cf. S.-B. i. 287 f.

8 *The Jewish Sources of the Sermon on the Mount* (London, 1911; reprint with prolegomenon by S. Zeitlin, New York, 1969), pp. 156 f.

279

their sins'), and compared Taan. 25b[9] and Meg. 28a;[10] also Test. Zeb. 5. 3 ('Have therefore compassion in your hearts, my children, because even as a man doeth to his neighbour, even so also will the Lord do to him', cf. 8. 1, 2), and Test. Jos. 18.2 ('if any man seeketh to do evil unto you, do well unto him, and pray for him and ye shall be redeemed of the Lord from all evil').

But, despite the presence of this element in Jewish thought, Abrahams still believed that it was significant that it had been kept out of the actual liturgy, where the unconditional generosity of God is allowed to stand alone; and he contrasted with this the conditionality of the clause in the Lord's Prayer, and pointed to the difference as a mark of the distinctiveness of that prayer.[11] Incidentally, C. G. Montefiore, in the second edition of his commentary on the Synoptic Gospels, criticized Abrahams for this view, and suggested that the apparently conditional element in Matthew's version need not be taken strictly, and that the sentiment, broadly interpreted, was perfectly in accord with Jewish views.[12] If, however, we are looking for statements about the fully unconditional character of the divine forgiveness, the extreme instances are, as a matter of fact, not in Jewish Liturgy but in certain sayings attributed to Jesus, and in the Pauline epistles. Among the sayings attributed to Jesus, the most obvious example is 'love your ene-

9 '. . . this man was answered . . . because he is ever forbearing and the other is not.' (Cf. T.B.K. 8. 7, 8. 10, etc.).

10 'He who waives his right to retribution is forgiven all his sins.'

11 *Studies in Pharisaism*, ii. 98. Dr W. Horbury of Clare College, Cambridge [now Dean of Corpus Christi College, Cambridge], calls my attention to the fact that, actually, Jewish liturgy does contain at least one 'conditional' phrase, viz. 'repentance and good deeds are a shield against punishment', quoted from Aboth 4. 13 in the Afternoon Service for Sabbath (see W. O. E. Oesterley, *The Jewish Doctrine of Mediation*, London, 1910, p. 107).

12 *The Synoptic Gospels*, ii (London, 1927), pp. 102 f. For an acute discussion of Jewish views on the conditions on which an offence may be condoned, see D. Daube, *Sin, Ignorance and Forgiveness in the Bible* (The Claude Montefiore Lecture, London 1960). But the recognition that there are certain conditions on which an offence may be condoned is not precisely the same thing as the free forgiveness of what is clearly not to be condoned. If the two approximate at all to one another, it is in those interesting cases, discussed by Daube, where what would normally count as deliberate, conscious sin is described as, on a deeper level, unwitting in the sense that all sin is in the last analysis, a failure in *understanding* – in understanding true values: '. . . the sinner deserves forgiveness because his very misdeeds prove him to be a helpless creature . . .' (*Sin, Ignorance and Forgiveness*, p. 27.)

mies'[13] with the supporting sayings appealing to the character of God himself, who is kind to the unthankful and evil (Matt. v. 44-8, Lk. vi. 35 f.). And Paul's allusions to God's free forgiveness are, at times, notoriously so radical and unqualified that he has been accused by Jewish and Christian scholars alike of opening the door, logically at least, to antinomianism,[14] with his 'God who clears the wicked' (. . . τὸν δικαιοῦντα τὸν ἀσεβῆ, Rom. iv. 5).

But is there really a conflict between the conditional terms of the Lord's Prayer and the unconditional terms of Jewish liturgy or - even more extreme - of other sayings attributed to Jesus (such as the ones just adduced) and of Paul's gospel? The key to an answer to this question lies in distinguishing between, on the one hand, earning or meriting forgiveness, and, on the other hand, adopting an attitude which makes forgiveness possible - the distinction, that is, between deserts and capacity. Israel Abrahams more than once formulates the latter idea - that of capacity -, but seems strangely ready to entertain the former also - the idea of deserts. Thus, formulating the latter, he says: '. . . though there is no limitation to God's forgiveness, there must be a limit to man's taking advantage of it';[15] or, again: 'The Gospel exhortations to forgive take it for granted that, though the response must be prompt and complete, it is response rather than initiative that is contemplated'.[14] Yet, elsewhere he allows himself phrases such as these: '. . . religion is disciplinary. It must . . . make forgiveness in some measure dependent on desert'.[17] Or, again (describing the Pharisaic position): '. . . man's duty to *strive* to earn pardon, and his *inability* to attain it without God's gracious gift of it';[18] or (on the very same page as an example of the other type of formulation): '*He* must forgive, but you must try to earn his forgiveness.'[19] But I venture to think that there is

13 A saying criticized by Eschelbacher and C. G. Montefiore, in the latter's *The Synoptic Gospels*, ii (1st edn., 1909), p. 523, for being 'strung so high that it has failed to produce solid and practical results just where its admirers vaunt what it differs from, and is superior to, the ethical codes of the Pentateuch, the Prophets and the Rabbis.' In the second edition (1927), Montefiore omits this and goes so far, instead, as to speak of 'rather foolish modern Jewish criticism about this command' (p. 80).
14 See J. Knox, *The Ethic of Jesus in the Teaching of the Church* (New York, 1961; London, 1962), p. 76; H. J. Schoeps, *Paulus* (Tübingen, 1959), p. 197; *Paul* (E.T., London, 1961), p. 188. [see above, pp. 261 ff.]
15 *Studies in Pharisaism*, i. 145.
16 *Ibid.*, p. 162.     17 *Ibid.*, p. 141.     18 *Ibid.*, p. 147.
19 *Ibid.*, p. 162 - Abrahams' own italics in both these quotations.

a confusion in these phrases. To make forgiveness conditional on repentance is by no means the same as saying that forgiveness has to be (or, indeed, can be) earned by the recipient. Real repentance, as contrasted with a merely self-regarding remorse, is certainly a *sine qua non* of receiving forgiveness – an indispensable condition. However eager the forgiver may be to offer forgiveness, it cannot be received, and reconciliation cannot be achieved, without repentance. But repentance cannot earn the forgiveness or make the recipient worthy of it, for, by definition, forgiveness is always an act of unearned generosity. Repentance alone makes the recipient capable of receiving the forgiveness which is offered, but the offer remains one of free generosity. Even to say that forgiveness, though freely offered, is actually withdrawn again if there are signs of an unforgiving attitude in the potential recipient is not the same as saying that the recipient must or can earn the forgiveness by his forgivingness: it is only an emphatic and almost pictorial way of describing an incapacity to receive the unearned gift of forgiveness. That forgiveness is conditioned by repentance is true, because reconciliation is a personal relationship, and cannot be achieved without responsiveness on both sides of the relationship. But that forgiveness is earned by repentance or deeds of reparation is not true. Therefore, if, on occasion, God's forgiveness is described in absolutely unconditional terms – he is good to the thankless, he clears the guilty – that is no contradiction of the principle that such generosity cannot be had without appropriate response. And conversely, to insist on appropriate response is not to rob the forgiveness of its character as an unmerited free gift.

There is thus a simple but fundamental distinction to be drawn between deserts and capacity; and, in the light of it, some relevant passages in the New Testament may now be examined more closely. And first, it will be as well to dispose at once of one misunderstanding. There is a story in Lk. vii. 36 ff., peculiar (in its details at least) to Luke's Gospel, in which a woman with a bad reputation comes in when Jesus is being entertained to a meal by a Pharisee named Simon, and stands at his feet wetting them with her tears, kissing them, and putting expensive perfume on them. When his host expostulates to himself, Jesus tells him a story. There were two debtors, he says, one of whom was let off a nugatory debt, while the other was let off a huge one. Which of the two, then, will feel the greater love? Why, I suppose, the one who has been spared the greater sum, replies Simon. Now, the principle indicated by this story is obviously that the degrees of love or gratitude evinced by two people will be an indication of the respective degrees of their indebtedness – that is, their 'forgiven-ness'. And the application to the circumstances follows inescapably. Jesus has been shown scant courtesy by his host; but the woman has lavished extravagant signs of gratitude on him. Consequently, she must have been forgiven much. But the pronouncement in *v.* 47 seems, at first sight, to be saying quite the reverse, namely, that her love has earned the forgiveness: 'I tell you, her many sins are forgiven, because she loved much.' If it is indeed the meaning of this phrase that her love is the ground of her being forgiven, then the parable of the two debtors simply does not fit the context, and one has to assume that the Evangelist has unintelligently strung together two incompatible bits of tradition. And this is indeed the assumption adopted by those who interpret the woman's state of forgiven-ness as the result of her love. Thus (to take one example). C. G. Montefiore, wrote:[20]

> The Parable does not fit the story which it is meant to illustrate. It does not substantiate the moral which one is intended to draw from it. For the parable says: The greater the measure of forgiveness, the greater the love which flows from and succeeds it. Much forgiveness causes much love. But what we find in the story [Montefiore means not the parable but the Evangelist's narrative] is the reverse. The greater the love, the greater the forgiveness. Much love justifies much forgiveness.
>
> It would therefore seem [Montefiore continues] as if the parable had a separate origin and occasion, and was inserted here in this story from a mistaken conception of it.

But it would be an astonishingly stupid Evangelist who could be blind to so glaring an inconcinnity, and it is reasonable to look for a more likely interpretation of the facts. Montefiore himself mentions the attempt to save the situation by pressing the perfect tense of the verb ἀφέωνται 'have been forgiven', but calls it very strained. Actually, however, it is worse than strained: it is useless for the purpose in question, for it fails to alter the causal connexion between the forgiveness (in whatever tense) and the love, which is what contradicts the message of the parable. No: the essential question is not the tense of the verb 'to forgive', but upon which verb the ὅτι, the 'because', depends. Why not recognize that the offending ὅτι, the 'because', can depend as easily on the λέγω, the 'I tell you', as on the ἀφέωνται? 'The reason', Jesus is saying, 'why I [am able to] tell you that her many sins are forgiven is

20 *Synoptic Gospels*, ii. (1927), p. 902.

the fact that she is showing so much love.' This makes sense and is completely in line with the parable; and, if it be then objected that the next verse 48, in which Jesus declares the woman forgiven, suggests that, after all, the forgiveness is offered there and then, and is consequent on the exhibition of love, it may be replied that, in view of the consistency of the whole of the rest of the passage, it is not unreasonable to assume that, in this verse, Jesus is simply reassuring the woman by reaffirming a fact which had already been proved a *fait accompli*. The same applies to *v*. 50, where Jesus says to the woman: 'Your faith has saved you; go in peace' (ἡ πίστις σου σέσωκέν σε· πορεύου εἰς εἰρήνην); and, indeed, this phrase serves to confirm that the message of the whole section is not that love has earned forgiveness but that the woman's trusting response has enabled her to receive what was offered as a free gift with no relation to her deserts. It is not her love that has saved her, but her faith – her trustful reponse. The whole incident thus becomes a notable example of the distinction between deserts and capacity; and the justification for discussing it at such length is precisely that misinterpretation (as here defined) makes the pronouncement into a saying about the earning of forgiveness, but the correct interpretation (if the reasoning here justifies such a claim) makes it a striking expression of the conviction that forgiveness cannot be earned but must be responded to. It thus serves as a paradigm for the insight that forgiveness is not conditional on merit.

There are other New Testament passages which bring out more emphatically the positive stress on the fact that forgiveness, though not conditional on merit, is nevertheless conditional – conditional on response to the gift, conditional on the capacity to receive it. Perhaps the most emphatic example, which will serve to represent others, is in Matt. xviii. 21 ff.,[21] the parable of the ungrateful servant. A servant (δοῦλος) has, as a result of his piteous entreaties, been let off a debt of astronomical proportions. (Presumably, to incur such a stupendous debt, he must be conceived of, although called a δοῦλος, as some high-ranking civil 'servant' or official in a colonial empire, unless one simply accepts the size of this debt as a piece of hyperbole, and does not press details realistically.) But as soon as his debt is cancelled, he goes off, finds a fellow servant who owes him a petty sum, and nearly throttles him in a savage attempt to make him pay. On hearing this, the king in whose employ they both work reverses his decision, reaffirms the vast debt, and hands the debtor over to prison and torture till he has paid. And so to the moral of the story: 'that is how my heavenly Father will deal with

21 Cf. Abrahams, *Studies in Pharisaism*, i. 163.

you, unless you each forgive your brother from your hearts' (*v.* 35). This, admittedly, is a vindictive formulation of the principle that without forgivingness no forgiveness may be received; but this is, perhaps, intelligible if it is meant as a piece of popular preaching and is shaped by the analogy of the oriental despot in the story to which it forms the conclusion. And, apart from the vindictive tone, it still says no more than that the free forgiveness could not be had without the debtor's capacity to receive it. There is no hint that he could ever earn or deserve it. Now that he is in prison for debt, the question of forgiveness is no longer in view: as things are, he must wait until he can discharge the debt. And if he does, it will not be any forgiveness that he will have 'earned': he will simply have cleared the debt. There is, perhaps, some danger of the clearing of the debt in this way confusing the issue as to free forgiveness; but the distinction in fact remains. Accepting forgiveness is not the same thing as earning enough money to pay off a debt.

Other conditional sayings in the Gospels are:

> For if you forgive others the wrongs they have done, your heavenly Father will also forgive you; but if you do not forgive others, then the wrongs you have done will not be forgiven by your Father (Matt. vi. 14 f. - a direct comment on the conditional clause in the Lord's Prayer in *v.* 12);
> ... when you stand praying, if you have a grievance against anyone, forgive him, so that your Father in heaven may forgive you the wrongs you have done (Mk xi. 25).

In neither of these sayings is there any reason for seeing any reference to deserving: it is a matter simply of capacity - of making it possible for God's free forgiveness to be accepted. The same applies to Matt. v. 23 f., the passage already alluded to in connexion with T.B.K. 10. 18, cited by Abrahams. It only says that it is no good offering a sacrifice while still at odds with one's neighbour, which need only mean that one is incapable of receiving what God has to bestow on a worshipper until one is reconciled with one's fellow man.

But do the Gospel sayings which have been mentioned, including the clause of the Lord's Prayer, really belong to Jesus himself? One might smooth away the contrast between the conditional and the unconditional sayings of the New Testament by eliminative criticism in one direction or the other. One might urge that the conditional sayings represent authentic traditions of Jesus' own teaching, and that the unconditional type represents a Christian invention; or, conversely, that the conditional sayings are Christian invention, and that the teaching

about God's unconditional forgiveness is the only original part. But
there is little evidence, if any, to suggest a consistent assigning of either
stream (details apart) exclusively to one stage or the other; and the
most plausible conclusion is that Jesus himself, from time to time,
uttered both kinds of saying – just as, for that matter, Paul is perfectly
capable not only of presenting the free unconditionality of God's forgiveness in extreme terms, but also of pressing the importance of response, even to the extent of what, by itself, might look like 'justification by works'.[22] So Jesus could claim, at one time, that the disreputable
woman's tears of love did not earn forgiveness but proved that she had
already been forgiven, thereby underlining the gospel of God's generosity to the undeserving; but, in another context, he could tell a story of
an ungrateful debtor who forfeited his remission by being harsh on a
fellow man. Both are true to the essentials of reconciliation between
God and men, which depends both on a sovereign divine initiative in
making a free offer and on a human responsiveness in transferring concern from oneself to others; but neither says anything about deserving
forgiveness. The only thing that is totally alien to the Christian position
is the idea that forgiveness needs to be, or even can be, earned or meri-
ted. This is undeniably an idea which crept disastrously into Christianity after the New Testament era, and which seems not to be absent
from Jewish thought either, at certain periods. But the Jewish and
Christian faiths would be at one, I suspect, today at least, in repudiating
this idea. At any rate, this short note attempting to clarify the distinction between merit and capacity is offered with affection as well as
admiration to one who, I believe, would share this sentiment.

22 E.g. Rom. ii. 6 f.

# 21

## The Sacrifice of the People of God

I am proposing, in this paper, to discuss the place of giving, in contrast to receiving, in Christian life and worship generally; and only within this very general field, to discuss the place and function of sacrifice - and within this, in turn, of Eucharistic sacrifice. I have reached this decision with considerable hesitation, knowing my incompetence in so vast a question; but nevertheless with some conviction, partly because discussion with other contributors has suggested this division of functions, but partly also because it seems to me that a great deal of discussion on the more strictly liturgical level is confused by reason of an unrecognized confusion at the more fundamental level of the subject I have named. For instance - to take only one recent example - I am on almost every page perplexed by Max Thurian's suggestive and deeply devout work on the Eucharistic Memorial,[1] because (as it seems to me) he does not first squarely face the most basic implications of the ideas with which he is associating *anamnēsis, mnēmosunon,* and the rest.

At the risk, then, of doing something stupid and unconstructive, I want to pose some radical questions, such as whether (despite the witness of the New Testament itself) the words 'sacrifice', 'intercession', and 'pleading' have any *logical* place at all within the language of Christian atonement-doctrine; and, as I say, to look at these questions in the light of an even more general consideration of the place of giving, as contrasted with receiving, in the Christian understanding of God and man. Is there (to pose the problem in terms of hymnody) any real compatibility between, on the one hand,

> 'Nothing in my hand I bring,
> Simply to thy cross I cling' (Toplady)

---

1 *L'Eucharistie. Mémorial du Seigneur, Sacrifice d'action de grâce et d'intercession* (Neuchâtel/Paris, 1959), translated as *The Eucharistic Memorial,* Part I, *The Old Testament* (London, 1960), Part II, *The New Testament* (London, 1961).

and, on the other, William Bright's noble paraphrase and adaptation of the *Unde et memores*,

> 'And now, O Father, mindful of thy love
> That bought us, once for all, on Calvary's Tree,
> And having with us him that pleads above,
> We here present, we here spread forth to thee
> That only offering perfect in thine eyes,
> The one true, pure, immortal Sacrifice'?

Of course we can see without further discussion that Bright is saying that we wholly depend, for our access to God, upon the cross; and that therein he is at one with Toplady. But he goes further, in the verse I have quoted, and describes that dependence on Christ in terms of an appeal to him as a heavenly Advocate, and of a presenting before God of Christ's offering and sacrifice; and it is precisely these terms that I ask you to consider.

I find myself compelled, at the risk of tedium, to try to clarify my own ideas by a most elementary series of statements, as follows.

First, the Christian gospel rests, we know, on God's initiative and his own self-giving: 'scarcely for a righteous man will one die: . . . but God commendeth his love toward us, in that, . . . Christ died . . .'; he 'spared not his own Son, but delivered him up for us all . . .'; 'God was in Christ, reconciling the world unto himself'; 'herein is love, not that we loved God, but that he loved us, and sent his Son . . .'. This gospel, so good that it perennially seems too good to be true and is perennially in danger of being contaminated with human merit-seeking, turned pagan ideas of worship inside out. Without overstating the case, it is possible to say that it has literally transposed object and subject in the use of the verb *hilaskesthai*. I am well aware that this is still contested;[2] and, in supporting it, I am myself prepared to recognize that, in their zeal over this paradoxical phenomenon, some of its proponents have overstated their case. For instance, one is bound, I think, to recognize that the idea of propitiating God is by no means absent from the Old Testament, and that a misleading picture is gained if one concentrates only on the uses of the root *hilask-* in the Septuagint and *kpr* in the Hebrew, and overlooks such phrases as 'a sweet smelling savour', and so forth. But making all allowance, and still exercising great care not to overplay

---

2 See, e.g. L. Morris, *The Apostolic Preaching of the Cross* (London, 1955), who, however, gives his case away (as it seems to me) when he finds himself compelled to admit that 'God has reconciled himself' (p. 220)!

this hand, we are still able to assert that (with negligible exceptions which will be noted) in no single instance of the use of this root in the New Testament is its translation by 'propitiate' or 'propitiation' inevitable, while in most of its occurrences it is impossible: God is so clearly recognized as the initiator of the movement that he is virtually the subject, instead of the object, of the action; and, this being so, the one translation that cannot possibly be adequate is 'propitiate', and we are compelled to find, instead, a word appropriate to God as subject and sin as object. Here are the occurrences:

Rom. iii. 25: *hon proetheto ho theos hilastērion,*
N.E.B. 'For God designed him to be the means of expiating sin'.

Heb. ii. 17: *eis hilaskesthai tas hamartias tou laou,*
N.E.B. 'to expiate the sins of the people'.

I John ii. 1b, 2: *paraklēton echomen pros ton patera, Iēsoun Christon dikaion: kai autos hilasmos estin peri tōn hamartiōn hēmōn.*
N.E.B. '... we have one to plead our cause with the Father, Jesus Christ and he is just. He is himself the remedy for the defilement of our sins ...'

I John iv. 10: *... kai apesteilen ton huion autou hilasmon peri tōn harmartiōn hēmōn.*
N.E.B. '... in sending his Son as the remedy for the defilement of our sins'.

It will be observed that in I Jo. ii. 2 the word is very closely associated with Christ's advocacy before the Father, and that, for this reason, the idea of propitiation might seem appropriate here; but such an interpretation is stultified by the second occurrence in I John, for one can hardly speak of the one whom God himself 'sends' as designed to make God propitious.

What I described as the negligible exceptions within the New Testament are the following, which, I think, scarcely need further comment:

Matt. xvi. 22: *hileōs soi, kurie (halilah).*
Lk. xviii. 13: *hilasthēti moi hamartōlō.*
Heb. viii. 12: *hileōs esomai tais adikiais autōn*
(= Jer. xxxi. 34, *'eslah la'awônam).*
Heb. ix. 5: *to hilastērion (kapporeth).*

Now, it is open to anyone to say that the N.E.B. has gratuitously altered the metaphor when, in I John, it translates *hilasmos* as 'remedy for defilement'; but, on the ground I have stated, it is difficult, at any rate, to defend the A.V. 'propitiation'.

In Eph. v. 2, admittedly, we find the full Levitical phrase, *eis osmēn euōdias* 'for a pleasing [or soothing] fragrance', and that, in relation to the self-offering of Christ to God: and in Heb. ix. 14 again Christ is spoken of as offering himself to God, though without the propitiatory phrase used in Ephesians. But the rarity of these phrases (to which we must, however, return later), and the transformation of the use of *hilas-kesthai* are enough, for the present, to bear out my first point – the gospel of God's initiative in compassing man's reconciliation, in vivid contrast to the pagan's efforts to bribe God and persuade him to be propitious.[3]

Secondly, then, as a deduction from this stress on God's initiative, we must affirm that there are certain ideas of movement from the manward side to the Godward, certain attitudes towards God, that are flatly ruled out on the basis of this Gospel of the free, undeserved initiative of God in forgiveness. It is utterly unthinkable that sacrifice viewed as 'bribery' should any longer be contemplated. With the notion of propitiation there disappears also the crude notion of buying off the deity's wrath by sacrifice. Equally (must we not agree?) all notion of *pleading* with a reluctant God is rendered impossible, as are all ideas of *reminding* God about what Christ has done. Emphatically the Johannine Christ says (Jo. xvi. 26b) '. . . I do not say that I shall pray the Father for you, for the Father loves you himself . . .' On this simple, basic conviction, the notion of pleading with a reluctant God is denied. And I would add, myself, that I do not believe that the linguistic evidence supports the contention that *eis tēn emēn anamnēsin* means 'to bring *before God* my memorial'.[4] Indeed, so clear is it that the very essence of the Christian gospel is that God gives and man receives, that I am tempted, in the interests of safeguarding against any dilution of this astounding gospel of unmerited grace, to avoid altogether the use of cultic terms like sacrifice, oblation, offering, and to have recourse, instead, to metaphors of cost and expenditure on the part of God, of creative energy, of costly

3 G. Aulén, *Eucharist and Sacrifice* (E.T. Edinburgh, 1958 from the Swedish of 1956), p. 144, says: 'This biblical view of sacrifice overturns common conceptions of sacrifice in religion . . . in the sacrifice of Christ everything is different. Here God's own love goes the way of sacrifice . . .'

4 *Pace* Max Thurian, *L'Eucharistie*, J. Jeremias, *The Eucharistic Words of Jesus* (E.T. London, 1955, of *Die Abendmahlsworte Jesu*, Göttingen, [2]1949), pp. 159 ff.

renewal. These would help to remind us *quanti ponderis sit peccatum*, without at the same time suggesting that it is God who exacts the cost, when instead (astonishing as it is) it is he who pays it. And, as a matter of fact, this kind of idea is actually to be found in Ephesians, where (despite that emphatically cultic phrase which has been noted) there is much emphasis on the wealth and riches of God's grace and his boundless resources and overwhelming power (i. 19 to ii. 10).

Yet - and this brings me to my third point - the matter is, of course, not so simple by a long way. What I have been referring to is clearly *charis*, the undeserved graciousness of God - God's gracious action, undertaken without regard to our deserts. It is *agapē*, God's own spontaneous love. But graciousness, by definition, cannot 'pauperize' the recipient; and *agapē* can never be 'a charity' in the odious sense of a benefit condescendingly conferred upon a passive beneficiary. Of its very nature, this action of God is one in which he shows respect for human personality, preserves the freedom and the responsibility with which he has himself endowed us, and, in a word, treats us as persons. Despite the utter dependence of the creature upon the Creator, it remains mysteriously and paradoxically true that, in the Creator's gracious approach to his creatures, he respects in them his own image - he treats us as responsible persons. And therefore the divine initiative, the unmerited grace, never relieves us of the responsibility for response; the illimitable riches of God's 'grace' and generosity cannot be accepted without the most costly response of which we are capable. For the pearl of great price - beyond price - we do have to give all. The prodigal son was welcomed back by his father freely and for no merit of his own. But he can have been truly reconciled only if (which we are not told in the story) he was ready to align himself with his father in a conciliatory attitude to the resentful elder brother. Though we cannot *earn* forgiveness, however much we are prepared to give, yet neither can we receive it without giving all, *in the very process of receiving it.* That, surely, is a law of personal relationship, a condition not based on quantitative justice but simply built into the structure of personality and relationship, so that we pray 'Forgive us our debts, as we herewith forgive our debtors'.[5] Relationship means (as it were) closing the circuit, so that there is a circular flow of intercourse.

Fourthly, then, must we not, by analogy, also postulate something corresponding to this even where there is no sin in the situation -

5 Cf. J. Jeremias, 'The Lord's Prayer in Modern Research', *Exp.T.* 71, 5 (Feb. 1960), 146.

indeed, even within the Deity itself? Does not the incarnation, and religious experience in other realms also, point to some such reciprocity (in a mysterious and indefinable form, no doubt) between the 'Persons' of the Godhead? The Father–Son terms are only an analogy, but it is the best analogy we can find. Must we not postulate a movement of adoration and obedience from Son to Father within the Godhead, as well as a movement of (shall we say?) injunction and mission from Father to Son? To make God a single, undifferentiated energy of *giving*, altogether to rule out *receiving*, is, in the last analysis, to make him a unitarian God.[6] The nature of *agapē*, as it is understood in the light of the incarnation, seems to be inevitably reciprocal. And it is at this point, I suppose, that that Johannine sentence a fragment of which I quoted just now must be given back in full; Jo. xvi. 26 f.: 'When that day comes *you will make your request in my name*, and I do not say that I shall pray to the Father for you, for the Father loves you himself, *because you have loved me and believed that I came from God.*' While the idea of God as someone who needs to be persuaded is repudiated, the idea of prayer in Christ's name is maintained, with reference to the mediating function of the incarnation. Is it not in the light of this that the use of the word intercession has to be interpreted? We have Christ as an Advocate, says I Jo. ii. 1; the Holy Spirit, and Christ, intercede for us, says Rom. viii. 26, 34; Christ intercedes for us, repeats the Epistle to the Hebrews; he is mediator between God and man, says I Tim. ii. 5.

C. K. Barrett's comment on Jo. xvi. 26 is worth quoting at this point:

There is no division between the Persons of the Godhead. Any thought of a merciful Son over against a just or wrathful Father is excluded; indeed, *ou legō* ['I do not say'] may suggest the combating of some such view as this. It would not however be true to say that John contradicts Rom. 8. 34 [and] Heb. 7. 25, which speak of the heavenly intercession (*entugchanein*) of the Son, since these deal not with petitionary prayer but with *the status of the Christian before God, a status which rests entirely upon the eternal consequences of the priestly work of Christ.* Cf. I John 2. 1. (My italics.)

Rather similarly Westcott had said: 'The modern conception of Christ

6 Aulén, *Eucharist and Sacrifice*, p. 145, writes (following the sentence quoted above): 'This view does not mean that we eliminate what we have said before, that Christ acts on behalf of humanity, and that God accepts his sacrifice.'

pleading in heaven His Passion, "offering His Blood", on behalf of men has no foundation in the Epistle [to the Hebrews]. His glorified humanity is the eternal pledge of the absolute efficacy of His accomplished work. He pleads, as older writers truly expressed the thought, by His Presence on the Father's Throne'. (*Hebrews* (1889), p. 230.)

All this, as it seems to me, underlines the position I have been feeling after – that, although room must be found for a movement (as it were) from man to God, sacrifice is a less appropriate word for what is implied in the Christian gospel of the incarnation than intercession; and that even intercession has to be interpreted, not in terms of one who begs some favour of a reluctant potentate on behalf of a condemned person, but in terms of something that has been accomplished, an act of repair that has been achieved, an absorption of the poison (as it were), as a result of which God (precisely because it is God's own work in man) is able to enter into fellowship with man.[7]

At this point, let us turn to another centre of controversy – the question of the finality of the sacrifice of Christ. It is a striking fact that the Epistle to the Hebrews, which is often regarded as providing the chief scriptural support for the idea of the continual presentation of the sacrifice, contains also some of the most emphatic statements of its once-for-all character: vii. 27, 'He has no need to offer sacrifices daily, as the high priests do, first for his own sins and then for those of the people; for this he did once and for all (*ephapax*) when he offered up himself'; ix. 12, '. . . he has entered the sanctuary once and for all (*ephapax*) . . .'; ix. 26, 28, '. . . he has appeared once and for all (*hapax*) at the climax of history to abolish sin by the sacrifice of himself . . . Christ was offered once (*hapax*) to bear the burden of men's sins' (marg. [better], 'to remove men's sins'). These emphatic statements need to be remembered, side by side with the familiar statements about

7 Some of my friends, while agreeing with me in excluding the word propitiation from the Christian vocabulary, are convinced that the word 'sacrifice' is highly desirable, holding that it signifies both God's self-giving to man and man's adoration offered to God; and they maintain that when sacrifice is viewed as bribery and propitiation, this is a warped view or (to use a metaphor adopted in a letter by Mr [now Canon] de Satgé) an astigmatic one, needing the corrective lens which is Christ. Again, if as has been suggested, the New Testament turned the word *hilaskesthai* upside down, it was only because it had first been turned topsy-turvy by sin. That may be so: we shall recur to this topic before the end of this paper. But I still maintain, for the present, that these words had, at least, been widely misunderstood, and that to this day they carry, for the most part, the wrong associations.

the continuance of the work of Christ: vii. 25, '. . . he is always living to plead on their behalf'; ix. 24, '. . . Christ has entered . . . heaven itself, to appear now before God on our behalf'; and the real meaning of the writer appears to be, not that Christ is perpetually offering, but that the single offering, made *ephapax*, is perpetually effective: the phrase quoted from ix. 12, 'he has entered the sanctuary once and for all', continues, 'and secured an eternal deliverance'. Thus the frequent use of that adjective 'eternal', *aiōnios*, in this epistle seems to indicate not a sacrifice eternally being offered – indeed, not even quite an eternally efficacious sacrifice, but rather one which, in contrast to the repeated and only symbolic sacrifices of the Jews, is 'absolute' or 'final' and belongs to the New Age. The famous phrase in ix. 14, *to haima tou Christou, hos dia pneumatos aiōniou heauton prosēnegken amōmon tō Theō*, is rendered in the N.E.B. '. . . the blood of Christ; he offered himself without blemish to God, a spiritual and eternal sacrifice'. It is questionable how far the Levitical analogies ought to be pressed; but the ritual of the Day of Atonement, which is expressly among the writer's analogies, does (so far as it goes) confirm that the thought is of the extended effects of a sacrifice which itself is already in the past. It is, to repeat Barrett's phrase, a matter of 'the eternal consequences of the priestly work of Christ'.[8]

The Evangelical concern against bringing into the Eucharist the idea of offering a sacrifice springs, I take it, partly from the sense that it is going beyond Scripture to make the Epistle to the Hebrews say more than I have just indicated: but, still more, no doubt, from a sense of the danger of suggesting that man can in any sense 'offer' anything relevant to his salvation. Man's salvation, it would be said, is wholly dependent on God's divine initiative; it is achieved 'once for all on Calvary's tree', and to suggest that it requires any further sacrifice is to cut from beneath the believer his chief ground of assurance and to attribute to humanly initiated action an unwarranted validity for salvation. But the reason why so many (including myself) are disatisfied with so simple an exclusiveness lies, I think, somewhere in the considerations I have tried to formulate – the recognition that a reconciliation is necessarily a reciprocal activity. God reconciles the world by his generous expenditure of creative energy and love; *in Christ* this actually

8 Cf. Aulén, *Eucharist and Sacrifice*, p. 150: 'No matter how closely the New Testament combines the cross and resurrection, the resurrection is something else than the sacrifice on the cross'; p. 152: '. . . this sacrifice made once for all is eternally valid'. His full statement, pp. 152 f., too long to quote here, is important.

takes the form of human obedience - obedience, in the human setting *sub Pontio Pilato*, to the nature and person of God; and human obedience can be described as offered up to God, as a sacrifice of adoration. If Christ is the New Adam, if we might say (coining a sentence complementary to that of II Cor. v. 19) that man was in Christ, being reconciled to God, then there must be a real sense in which the obedience of Christ includes and encloses and draws into itself the derivative obedience of man.

And this goes on continually: 'This is my way of helping to complete, in my poor human flesh, the full tale of Christ's afflictions still to be endured, for the sake of his body which is the church' (Col. i. 24, N.E.B.). This means that every human act of obedience, whether it is the cup of cold water or the blood-donation outside Church, or the coin in the plate and the presentation of the bread and wine in Church, is an offering[9] of adoration to God in union with the sacrifice of Christ. Indeed, in the New Testament, sacrificial and other cultic terms are used as much for the response of Christians to God's initiative as for Christ's offering (Rom. xii. 1; xv. 16; II Cor. ii. 15; Phil. ii. 17; Heb. xiii. 15; I Pet. ii. 5; Rev. viii. 4). And the oblation of the bread and wine, to be taken and consecrated and sacramentally used, is a focus of that uniting of our thankful and adoring obedience with Christ's, and could rightly be associated more closely with whatever is regarded as the consecration itself.

All this I wholeheartedly recognize and welcome. And if 'sacrifice' is a spontaneous and inevitable term for the costly offering of Christian adoration, thanksgiving, and obedience, then perhaps it must be retained (as it undeniably is in the New Testament) - but let it be rid of all evil connotations of bribery or propitiation.[10] If 'pleading the merits of

9 But I would question whether the words of institution (even in their fullest form) can be taken as actually enjoining the *offering*, as (e.g.) A. H. Couratin says in *Ways of Worship: the Report of a Theological Commission of Faith and Order* (edd. P. Edwall, E. Hayman, W. D. Maxwell, London, 1951), p. 192. He goes on to say (p. 193) that the purpose of this dominically appointed thankoffering is to enable the People of God to gain admittance to the heavenly worship. If the 'offering' of bread and wine is a symbol of our obedience (as he allows, p. 194), then no doubt this is true. But is this just what is meant? Later he speaks of the Heavenly Altar (*not* an idea belonging to the Epistle to the Hebrews), where the Passion is the *Lord's* Sacrifice which *we* offer in heavenly places.

10 When F. D. Maurice (*The Doctrine of Sacrifice* (Cambridge, 1854), pp. 117 f., 179, quoted by J. Burnaby, *Christian Words and Christian Meanings*, London, 1955, p. 106) spoke of sacrifice as 'implied in the very nature and being of God', so that it is 'impossible to imagine a blessed world in which

Christ' means reminding *ourselves* that in Christ man has obeyed and is obeying God, and that we who are in Christ may appropriate the resulting communion between God and man, well and good: but is it not almost impossible to rid the phrase of a suggestion of pleading with God to accept the price that Christ offers? Again, if Christ's intercession is a dramatic figure intended to affirm the status of renewed mankind in fellowship with God, once more, well and good: but it seems to me to be important, when using such phrases, to remind ourselves that this is (if I may put it so) rather for *our* reassurance than for *God's* information; and it is for the same reason that I deplore the current fashion in interpreting *anamnēsis* and *mnēmosunon* – especially as I believe it to be bad exegesis, in any case. I am not here denying that these words signify more than bare mental recollection (*nuda commemoratio*). I believe that they mean something infinitely more 'dynamic' than that: to 'remember' Christ in this context (and, with the incarnation, to remember and give thanks for all God's work in creation) is to be united with him as really present.[11] But that does not (does it?) involve also 'presenting Christ to God' or 'reminding God of Christ': rather, it is a being presented to God in Christ, and a being 'reminded' of God in him – and so an act of obedience.

It is at this point that a matter of prime importance, of which hitherto I have said nothing, forces itself upon us – the doctrine of the Holy Spirit. According to St Paul, it is the Spirit of God's Son (Gal. iv. 6), the Spirit that causes us to be adopted as sons (Rom. viii. 15), that utters in us the same 'Abba!' of filial adoration and obedience which Jesus himself, according to Mark (Mk xiv. 36), uttered in the garden of

it does not exist', he must, I suppose, have meant something like this. So G. Every (*Basic Liturgy*, London, 1961, p. 8) writes of sacrifice that its 'primary meaning is the hallowing, consecration, or making sacred of persons, places, or holy objects to serve as symbolic means of communication . . .' And when 'sacrifice' means a costly present, a symbol of love and gratitude, no doubt it is wholly compatible with a Christian view. But there is a distinction between 'sacrifice' and 'consecration'; and when 'sacrifice' is used in connexion with the 'repair' of a broken relationship (and how often in the New Testament can it, in fact, be divorced from such a context?), then I question whether this very metaphor, 'repair' or 'remedy', or at most the word 'offering', is not more apposite than the clearly cultic terms. Perhaps one point which arises out of this whole discussion may be that more attention ought to be paid, in Eucharistic doctrine, to the question, How does *sin* affect adoration?

11 If one is in any doubt whether St Paul thought of the Eucharist 'dynamically', one only has to remember I Cor. x. 16 and xi. 27–34, which show beyond all doubt that for him it meant a relationship (terrifyingly for worse if not for better) with the living and present Lord.

Gethsemane. It is, in other words, the Spirit who makes possible the costly response, in man, to what God in Christ has done and is doing: it is the Holy Spirit, through Jesus Christ, who, as it were, 'closes the circuit', sending back from us the filial obedience which represents the due response of man to God. It is the Spirit who gives meaning to our inarticulate yearnings after fellowship with God. Indeed, just as we have seen 'intercession' attributed to Christ, so, in the same chapter of Romans, intercession is the work of the Holy Spirit also (Rom. viii. 26, 34). The Spirit is the Spirit of God the Father achieving in man the attitude belonging to his Son.

Rightly, then, the Spirit is invoked in the epiclesis upon the worshippers, to enable them to respond with adoration and self-giving to the gracious gift of God. I do not believe it to be in keeping with New Testament teaching - or, indeed, with any Christian evaluation of personality - to invoke the Spirit on inanimate matter, such as the elements.[12] But when the elements are consecrated - set aside for a sacred purpose - it is fitting to invoke the Spirit on the persons participating.[13] Epiclesis and consecration should go together, just as man's acceptance of God's gift and man's response with all that he can give belong together.

Thus, we have found ourselves led, by reflecting on the nature of the Christian's receiving and giving, to a fully trinitarian conception of God. And I want, dogmatically, for the sake of provoking discussion, to formulate my conclusion thus: Whatever in liturgy obscures the Father's undeserved grace or hints that man can compass his own salvation must be rejected. Whatever in liturgy obscures the completeness and 'once-for-allness' of the Father's gift must be rejected. Whatever in liturgy suggests a distinction in character between Father and Son - as that a merciful Son pleads with a reluctant Father - must be rejected. But what God in Christ has done must be implemented by man in Christ; and every act of human obedience - theological, liturgical, ethical - is found to be united with Christ's obedience by the Holy Spirit. The offering (or sacrifice, if we must have it so) of the People of God is man's obedience united by the Holy Spirit with Christ, in whom God was, on Calvary, reconciling the world to himself: it is man's response, by the Holy Spirit, in Christ, to God's unalterable gift.

12 The *prosphora . . . hēgiasmenē en pneumati hagiō* in Rom. xv. 16 is nothing other than the Gentile converts.

13 In all this I am assuming that there is no need to discuss here the literalist objection that Christians by definition already possess (or are possessed by) the Spirit. If one took that line, one would never pray for anything more than once.

# Index of biblical and other references

## OLD TESTAMENT

# Index of biblical and other references

## NEW TESTAMENT

## APOCRYPHA AND PSEUDEPIGRAPHA

## THE QUMRAN TEXTS

# Index of biblical and other references

## RABBINIC TEXTS

## APOSTOLIC FATHERS

# Index of biblical and other references

## OTHER CHURCH WRITERS

## NAG HAMMADI TEXTS

## OTHER GREEK PSEUDEPIGRAPHA

# Index of biblical and other references

## OTHER SOURCES

320

# Index of authors

321

# Index of authors

Burkitt, F. C. 82 n. 19, 84 n. 27
Burnaby, J. 295 n. 10
Burton, E. de W. 155, 157 n. 18,
   263 n. 3
Buttrick, G. A. 31 n. 53, 266 n. 6

Cadbury, H. J. 123
Caird, G. B. 99, 185, 187, 188,
   194 n. 28
Campbell, J. Y. 83 n. 26
Campenhausen, H. von 180 n. 44
Cantanzaro, C. J. 214 n. 29
Carcopino, J. 168 n. 10
Carmignac, J. 278, 279
Carrington, P. 50, 134 n. 1
Cassien, S. B.    96 n. 7
Cerfaux, L. 185
Chadwick, H. 143 n. 9, 168 n. 10
Chase, F. H. 171, 172
Chaytor, H. J. 40 n. 8
Christ, F. 13 n. 30
Clark, N. 222 n. 1
Collange, J.-F. 200 n. *
Colpe, C. 80 n. 13, 82 n. 18
Conzelmann, H. 8 n. 13 (on p. 9)
Couratin, A. H. 295 n. 9
Cranfield, C. E. B. 13 n. 29, 263
   n. 3, 264 n. 4, 273
Cross, F. L. 13 n. 29, 133, 135,
   136, 137, 138, 139 140, 145,
   273 n. 10
Cullmann, O. xii, 13 n. 30, 104 n.
   24, 165, 170 n. 20, 185 n. 7,
   197, 218 n. 38, 222 n. 1, 227

Dahl, M. E. 188 n. 13, 206
Dahl, N. A. 8 n. 10, 27 n. 43, 46
   n. 17, 185 n. 7
Dalman, G. 28
Daly, R. J. ix, ix n. 1
Daniélou, J. 166 n. 4, 168 n. 10,
   169 n. 15, 170 n. 18
Daube, D. 158, 159, 241 n. 9,
   278, 280 n. 11

Davies, J. G. 57 n. 13, 62 n. 25
Davies, W. D. 67 n. 1, 205, 210,
   274
Debrunner, A. 157 n. 19, 232 n.
   21
de Halleux, A. xii
Deissmann, A. 117 n. 9, 224
de Lacey, D. R. 84 n. 27
Delling, G. 8 n. 10, 10 n. 15, 23
   n. 40, 30, 204 n. 4
de Satgé, J. 293 n. 7
Descamps, A. xii, 29
de Wette, W. M. L. 40 n. 9
Dibelius, M. 222 n. 5
Didier, M. 76 n. 3
Dix, C. 60 n. 20
Dobschütz, E. von 189, 194 n.
   28, 198 n. 34
Dodd, C. H. 6 n. 6, 22, 71, 75 n.
   2, 80 n. 14, 81 n. 17, 90, 95,
   98, 102 nn. 19, 20, 21, 169 n.
   13, 186, 187 n. 12, 237, 259
Duncan, G. S. 116 n. 6
Dunn, J. D. G. 227, 228 n. 5

Easton, B. S. 118
Ebeling, G. 37 n. 3
Edgar, S. L. 90 n. 49
Edwall, P. 295 n. 9
Eissfeldt, O. 205
Ellis, E. E. 10, 169 n. 16, 195 n.
   29 (on p. 196), 200 n. 1, 218
   n. 39 (on p. 219)
Eltester, W. 46 n. 17
Emerton, J. A. 80 n. 13
Enselin, M. S. 59 n. 18
Eschelbacher, 281 n. 13
Every, G. 293 n. 7, 295 n. 10 (on
   p. 296)

Falconer, R. 120, 121
Farmer, W. R. xii, 40 n. 10, 160
   n. 5, 227 n. 3

322

# Index of authors

324

# Index of authors

# Index of authors